BEHIND THE CURTAIN

BOOKS BY

JOHN GUNTHER

•

BEHIND THE CURTAIN

DEATH BE NOT PROUD

INSIDE U. S. A.

INSIDE LATIN AMERICA

INSIDE ASIA

INSIDE EUROPE

D DAY

THE TROUBLED MIDNIGHT

THE HIGH COST OF HITLER

•

BEHIND THE CURTAIN

BY

JOHN GUNTHER

HARPER & BROTHERS PUBLISHERS
NEW YORK

BEHIND THE CURTAIN

PRINTED IN THE UNITED STATES OF AMERICA BY
KINGSPORT PRESS, INC., KINGSPORT, TENNESSEE

For *JANE*

Acknowledgments

This book is partly based on material that appeared recently in *Look* and the New York *Herald Tribune*. But it is not in any sense a compilation of articles; the whole has been handled afresh from a new and different point of view, remodeled, recast, and greatly enlarged. The present manuscript runs to something like triple the length of what was printed in *Look* and the *Herald Tribune* together, and I have worked over every word of the original material. But I want to thank warmly the editors of *Look* and the *Herald Tribune* for having given hospitality to what I wrote for them, and for permission to use some passages. In particular let me express my cordial appreciation to Gardner Cowles, editor and publisher of *Look,* who helped substantially to make the whole work possible.

J.G.

NEW YORK *April 5, 1949*

Table of Contents

BEHIND THE CURTAIN

CHAPTER 1
INTRODUCTION—ITALY AS BREAKWATER

SOMETHING like one hundred million people live today in the thick bolt of territory lodged between the Soviet Union and the countries of western Europe. This book is in the nature of a brief report on what we—my wife and I—saw recently in this broad and complex region. Also we visited other European areas, where the impact of Soviet policy is likewise formidable, and we saw how the United States has risen to be the principal antagonist to Communist expansion almost everywhere. Europe today is a vastly different thing from Europe before the war, and the chief reason for this is the sharp extension of the American frontier, in response to Russian forwardness.

We went to Italy first; the Apennines were our breakwater. Then came flights to Greece and Turkey and back, followed by an interlude in Trieste. We were lucky enough to get visas to four Iron Curtain countries, and so visited Yugoslavia, Hungary, Czechoslovakia and Poland. We spent some time in Vienna, stopped at Frankfurt briefly, and flew with the air lift in and out of Berlin. Then Paris, Antwerp, Amsterdam, London and home.

We were refused visas by the Soviet Union, and hence could not visit Moscow, but for long weeks we traveled in Russian-saturated territories. I have been almost tempted to call this book Inside Outside Russia.

Years ago in London I asked Mr. Churchill, one of the few men alive who held supremely great office in both world wars, how the two wars differed. His reply was that World War I was a war merely of nations, whereas World War II was one of peoples, ideologies, and continents. This year I asked Count Carlo Sforza, the Italian Foreign Minister, who played a substantial role in the affairs of Europe after each war, how these two postwar periods differed. His answer was that, after 1918, the Soviet Union was convulsed by civil war and hence could play no great role in western European affairs, and that the United States was likewise isolated for domestic reasons. But now, after World War II, both Russia and the United States are direct and major actors in the European scene. Indeed the face of Europe has irremediably changed. The world has become a two-power world, and it is in Europe that the two powers meet most sharply, with Moscow pulling one way, Washington the other.

Before proceeding to the variegated new sphere of the Soviet satellites it may be wise to pause by way of introduction in Italy, where so many of the problems we shall face later stand out in preliminary relief. And before proceeding at all I should like to point out how extremely fluid Europe is at this moment, how difficult it is to be categorical about any fact or issue, how the elusive sands of history shift very fast these days, and how almost all generalizations must necessarily be crude and tentative. There is a nice old Polish proverb: "If is a king."

Mobile Virgin

By all odds the chief problem of Italy is poverty, and a major contribution to this problem is the birth rate; the dominant actors on the Italian stage today are the Catholic Church, the Communist party, the United States of America, and fecundity. A scene comes vividly to my mind:

We were driving from Assisi down the golden powdery plain of Umbria, and we paused at dusk before a church. It was an ugly church, modern, built in the Renaissance manner, with a glaring white façade, by name the Basilica of Santa Maria Degli Angeli. I was not particularly interested in the church itself. What did interest me—and several other people staring up the steep façade—was an eighteen-foot-high statue of the Virgin on the roof.

On the evening of February 10, 1948, this Virgin moved. It was seen by onlookers to move as if it were bowing slightly. Word spread through the superstitious peasantry of the countryside like a marshfire; thousands came to see the miracle. And every once in a while, usually at dusk, the Virgin was duly seen to move.

Now when we peered and strained our eyes upward we could not detect any movement in this great statue, which must weigh several tons. But it was easy to appreciate how the perspective of the Virgin high up there on the roof could produce an optical illusion. The striking thing was the congregation of the faithful who waited patiently hour after hour, hoping that the miracle would occur again.

The whole area—I do not mean any irreverence by this—has taken on the aspect of a county fair. Hawkers sold sandwiches; concessionnaires rented out chairs and dark glasses; children scampered on the grass; a long series of booths did a flourishing business selling images of the Virgin. Italy is a country where a miracle is taken very, very seriously. Our chauffeur said sadly when we departed, "Too bad—this is the third time I have come to watch, but not yet have I seen her budge!"

Note that the Virgin "moved" just as the Italian election campaign of last year got under way. The Communists are alert and powerful in this part of Italy. In Assisi itself (which has a Communist mayor—Assisi of all places!) we saw hammers and sickles scrawled in red on every other wall of the steep twisting streets leading to St. Francis's own basilica. And the Communists were very angry at the miracle. They said that it was an electioneering trick worked out by the anti-Communists. They even said that the government has installed an electrical device within the statue, so that it would tip slightly on an impulse sent by radio all the way from the United States!

Certainly the miracle had some local political effect. The collection boxes in the church were filled with torn-up Communist party cards—so at least we heard—in the first days when the Virgin was particularly mobile.

I tell this small story because it illustrates well the essential conflict of modern Italy, the conflict of basic loyalties so piercingly alive in the hearts of so many Italians. Belief in miracles, belief in Marx—this is the taut gamut. In no other country is the tension more sharply drawn, more nakedly acute. And let us keep in mind that at least two of the satellites the Soviets rule, Hungary and Poland, are profoundly Catholic.

Near Umbertide we stayed a few days in a thirteenth-century castle. Our host, a most delightful and intelligent young man, derives from a family founded in A.D. 1050; he can count his ancestors back for literally twenty-three generations, and the atmosphere of his establishment is positively crystalline with the tradition of aristocracy. He showed us the church in his fortress-castle. It is empty Sunday mornings. He showed us the school he maintains. The children of his own peasants chant "Long live Stalin!"

Politically Italy is fairly stable as of the moment. The Communists made their great bid for power in April 1948, and failed; the government of Alcide De Gasperi (called "the Priest") has its haunches firmly in the saddle. But no one can know how long it will last. It faces problems of great persistence, depth and magnitude.

Above all, consider poverty and the birth rate. Italy, the population of which is only 45 million, produces a surplus of approximately 400,000 births over deaths a year. This means, each year, that Italy has to support the equivalent of a whole new city the size of Albany or Houston. The country, most experts say, is only capable of supporting about 32 million people at minimum standards; but it has to take care of 13 million more than this, with an annual increase of population of 400,000 to boot. The blunt demographic result is an intolerable mass poverty.

This is not to say that rich Italians don't exist. They do exist. Indeed, a visitor's first impression in Rome is apt to be of the acute and painful chasm between a tiny minority of rich and a huge majority of poor. I have seen shoeless children pick sodden cigarette butts out of a gutter—not to smoke but in order to get a bit of tobacco which they dry and sell—outside shops where luxury silks were priced at $40 and $50 a yard.

When I saw Mr. De Gasperi he said with a wry grin that he would gladly surrender all American aid under the Marshall plan if he could export 400,000 of his own countrymen every year. Of course, he didn't mean this literally; he could not survive without the Marshall plan; what he was trying to do was give pictorial emphasis to the point of Italy's mounting and crushing overpopulation.

Birth control is an extremely ticklish subject; oddly enough it is one on which Catholics and some Italian Communists more or less agree. The Church opposes birth control for reasons known to everybody; many Communists oppose it for other reasons too: (1) from a long range nationalist point of view the Communists, just like Mussolini, want Italy to have as big a population as possible; (2) the more overcrowded and poor Italy is, the more fertile a field it is for Communism.

An enormous problem in Italy is the necessity of land reform. There are something like 5 million landless peasants; in other words, more than 10 percent of the total population, a stupendous proportion. One percent of the population owns roughly 50 percent of the total arable land; 7 percent owns 69 percent.[1] Mr. De Gasperi, a decent and humane though limited man, has promised to wrestle with the staggering social and economic implications of all this; so far, and it is the chief blur on his record, he has not done so, largely because circumstances have forced him more and more into the arms of the right wing of his coalition. Landowners—and the Church is a tremendous landowner in Italy—don't like to give up land.

Italy: Catholics and Communists

I asked almost everybody I met in Italy a simple question, "How can an Italian be a Catholic and a Communist at the same time?" Because, obviously, a great many Italians are both. Italy is overwhelmingly Catholic—99.6 percent. But the Italian Communist party is the largest in the world outside Russia, with 2,250,000 enrolled members, and it got roughly 30 percent of the vote in the 1948 elections. How reconcile such startling percentages?

Answers to this question are subtle and various, and to outline them all would be far beyond the province of this foreword. The Catholics say that, manifestly, no "good" Catholic can possibly be a Communist; the word good, in quotes, is the escape clause. The Communists on their side say that many Italians, particularly the men, while remaining within the fold of the Church, do not consider their religious convictions to

[1] Barrett McGurn in the New York *Herald Tribune*, March 9, 1949.

be interfered with by party membership. Most Italian men take their church-going very casually.

In fact the Vatican maintains perfectly correct relations with individual Communists, and so far as I know no prominent Italian Communist has ever been excommunicated. Officials of the Vatican gave refuge to Communist leaders during the Nazi occupation, and when Palmiro Togliatti, the top Italian Communist, was shot last summer, important churchmen were among the first to send him messages deploring the attempted assassination.

Nevertheless, the great fixed antipathetical poles of modern Italy are and will of absolute necessity remain the Church and the Communist party, and the future of the country will be largely decided by the struggle between them.

Has Communism been permanently checked in Italy? The De Gasperi government, assisted heavily by the Church—never before has the Church played such a direct role in the politics of modern Italy—beat back the Communists last spring. Is this setback permanent? Nobody I met in Italy thought so—not a single person. Why? Because, in the words of one cabinet minister, "The great ally of Communism is misery—and Italy is so miserably poor."

It is not permissible to quote the Pope, with whom we had a long private audience. It is, I hope, permissible to venture the guess that, in the Supreme Pontiff's mind, the connection between unemployment and Communism is very intimate. And Italy has something like 1,900,000 industrial unemployed.

A member of the Italian government said to me, "If unemployment rises by another million, it will mean handing Italy over to Togliatti on a platter."

The Communists lost the national elections, but they remain a strong and adhesive political power almost everywhere in the peninsula on a local level.

I mentioned that even a town as cloistered as Assisi has a Communist mayor. So—to pick at random—has a village so seemingly remote from politics as Positano, near the Bay of Naples. A list of important towns with Communist mayors is staggering: Mantua, Venice, Parma, Piacenza, Ravenna, Grosseto, Siena, Foggia, Florence, Taranto, Leghorn, Spezia, Savona, Pisa, Genoa. And the left wing Socialists allied to the Communists have the mayoralty and local administration in Brindisi, Arezzo, Belluno, Perugia and Udine.[2]

"History," Mussolini once wrote if I remember correctly, "has this generation by the throat."

Can Italy, by itself, save itself from Communism? No. This is where we in the United States come in. It may not be what our own American caprices would prefer, but the fact is that Italy would almost certainly go under without American aid, and as things stand at present only the United States can save Italy from Communism.

Since 1943 United States financial assistance to Italy has amounted, roughly, to $1,900,000,000 (almost the cost of the atomic bomb), of which $1,200,000,000 was given scot-free. Included in these sums were such items as $376 million contributed through Allied Military Government, $134 million from the Foreign Economic Administration, $375 million from UNRRA, and $131 million from the Export-Import Bank. In addition, Italy was scheduled to get no less than a cool $703 million in the first year of the Marshall plan, and in 1949 it asked for $601 million more, of which $555 million is promised.

These are vast sums. They will not be enough.

For the true gist of the matter is that Italy cannot be saved by gifts of bread and cash alone. For one thing, the statisticians say that, even after four years of Marshall plan aid, the national income of the individual Italian will be raised by only 3 percent. Barrett McGurn has reported in the New York *Herald Tribune* the unbelievable statistic that 3,500,000 Italians are without roofs over their heads. The European Recovery Program can make spaghetti white instead of gray; it can give coal to factories and penicillin to sick children; it cannot, alone, rebuild an entire national economy. Besides, the time will eventually come when the United States will almost certainly have to stop contributing aid on so massive a scale. Bread alone is not the full answer, necessary as it may be for a time. Money

[2] Also the tiny independent republic of San Marino in the Apennines has a Communist administration. This is in fact the only Communist "government" in Europe west of the Iron Curtain. New York *Times*, February 28, 1949.

alone is not the answer. The full answer should be in the realm of Italian self-reliance, social reform, education, self-sacrifice, financial reform, and ideas.

It seems to me that the great difference between France and Italy is that whereas Communism could only come to France at the price of civil war, it could be put over on the Italian people overnight, practically to the tune of a lullaby. This is because the rank and file of the Italian people—including Italian Communists themselves—have no idea what Communism really means. They talk of its promises; they do not realize what it could portend. The peasants think of themselves as "Communists"; they have utterly no notion of what collectivization of the land might entail. Here the Church has in a way defeated itself, because the system of education it enjoins militates against the free play of thought which should be the best defense against Communism, equally for a person, a community, or a nation.

Most members of the Italian ruling class we talked to gave the impression of being defeatist, of living on borrowed time and knowing it, of being fully aware that their numbers were almost up.

What Italy needs, in addition to material assistance from the United States, which is imperative but which by its very nature ought to be temporary (else it will corrupt both giver and givee), is to put its own house in order. What Italy needs is fresh air in old corners, a program for the better distribution of wealth, a tax system that works, redistribution of land, and above all, social reform. Italy is doomed—a goner—if it does not liberalize and reform, reform, reform.

I saw a campaign poster near Ravenna left over from the last election, a blue oak leaf with the slogan, NOT FOR RUSSIA, NOT FOR AMERICA, BUT FOR OURSELVES—FOR ITALY! If I were an Italian I'd feel the same.

Remnants of Fascism and the Monarchy

How much monarchist sentiment survives in Italy now that the country is a republic? What strength, if any, have the

Fascists today, and what do people think of Mussolini? Any visitor who knew Italy well before the war will be prompted to ask these questions.

So far as overt political strength or influence is concerned, the monarchists are as dead as Cheops. They ran directly as a monarchist party in the April elections, and barely got 3 percent of the vote.

A wise and well-informed American observer explained this to me in this way: "The monarchists killed themselves off by failing utterly to realize the temper of the times. In 1946, before the referendum that made Italy a republic, they tried to warn the voters with the slogan, 'A vote for the republic is a jump in the dark.' But the people jumped, and Italy is by no means dark. Then they said, 'Monarchy is the only real bulwark against Communism.' But the republic came into being, and the Communists are still out of power. Finally they said, 'The coming of the republic will mean the end of the Church.' But the republic came—and the Church is certainly still here!"

The prestige of the present President of the republic, Luigi Einaudi, is considerable, and he decisively influenced a good many people when he said, in effect, "For many years I was a loyal supporter of the monarchy. But now I devote myself with equal loyalty to the new republic."

Mr. Einaudi is, incidentally, a personage about whom pleasant stories may be heard. He is a frail old gentleman, seventy-four, with no great love for pomp or ceremony. He was hurt in a streetcar accident once, and has a limp. One of his close associates told him, just before he was to review a detachment of troops, a task for which he had no relish, "You must stand up and conduct yourself in a truly presidential manner!" Mr. Einaudi's comment when the baleful experience was over was, "What an adventure for a retired professor to have to go through!" Far cry from the strut and bombast of the Fascists![3]

In the languid upper crust of what remains of "Society," in the navy, and in some geographical areas, a vestigial yearning

[3] Einaudi has several sons. One is a professor of political science at Cornell; another lives in Milan, and is the head of a publishing house distinguished for books very much on the left wing.

for the monarchy may still exist. Rural Piedmont is mildly monarchistic, and so are Sicily and the vicinity of Naples, which is a world all its own. "When I travel below Naples," one Italian told us, "I feel that I am in an entirely different country."

As able and vigorous as anybody in modern Italy is Randolfo Pacciardi, a leader of the Republican party and Minister of National Defense. Several times, both in the United States and Rome, Mr. Pacciardi has shared his wisdom and discernment with me. Once he was known as a red-hot radical. Today he is an uncompromising anti-Communist and one of the stalwarts of the De Gasperi regime. Once the Department of State thought very ill indeed of Mr. Pacciardi; today the American Embassy in Rome knows him as an efficient ally. Pacciardi fought with the Loyalists in Spain; he was, indeed, head of the Garibaldi Battalion in the Spanish Civil War. Today his office in the defense ministry is sprinkled with officers whom he himself defeated at Guadalajara and who are loyal members of his staff —a striking illustration of the way times—and Italy—have changed.

The Vatican, it is often said, runs De Gasperi and the Italian government. Yet Pacciardi, a typical anticlerical of the Italian historical tradition, against whose outlook and philosophy the Church threw its whole weight in Spain, is a key member of the De Gasperi coalition.

Fascism as an overt political movement is as dead in today's Italy as the monarchy. The actual party is, of course, abolished, and in theory it is a criminal offense to praise or practice what it stood for. The "epuration" process, i.e., cleansing the Fascists out of the body politic, is more or less concluded; this purification was much milder than that in Germany, and only about two thousand Italian Fascists are still in jail. The Italian policy was to make as broad an amnesty as possible. Even the Communists approved this when the republic came in. Partly this was a political trade involving the Lateran treaty. Several prominent Fascists—even men like Federzoni, who were members of the Grand Fascist Council—have returned to Italy, but nobody pays much attention.

Count Sforza, the veteran Foreign Minister, said to me one

morning in Mussolini's old office in the Palazzo Chigi, "Don't forget that we are people with a long history, who know how to be at ease with disaster!"

A Neo-Fascist party exists, known as the M.S.I. (Movimento Sociale Italiano), but it failed miserably in the last elections, getting only 1.9 percent of the vote. Its members held a rally in Rome recently, and because they knew they could not possibly fill the Piazza di Spagna or some similar sizable spot, they chose instead the narrow steps of the Piazza Mignanelli nearby. But even these steps were half empty. Outside Rome the Neo-Fascists are strongest in the Bari region and the Adriatic heel—those parts of the country which, because of remoteness and the feudal system gripping them, knew least of what Fascism was while it was going on.

The M.S.I. group came into being two years ago, and its major tenet is to oppose equally both Communism and the U.S.A. It calls the American military operation that liberated Italy an "invasion"; it considers men like Pacciardi and Sforza to be traitors because they were pro-American; it takes the line that an Italian should be judged not on the basis of which side he fought on but on whether he fought at all—which is an interesting enough incidental sidelight on the national character.

What do people think of Mussolini? This is a complicated question. The big industrialists do not miss him much, because the present government, which they help to run, interferes with them less than he did; nor does the aristocracy, the Church or the working class. I should say that the one group that, by and large, does feel a certain nostalgia about the Duce is the bourgeoisie; members of the small middle class liked the parades and fanfare of Fascism, they ate better, they were strongly nationalist, and they were duly protected—at a price!—against strikes.

A good average Italian comment might be this: "Mussolini? Granted he was wicked. But many men are wicked. After all he was an Italian, a true Italian. He made us respected, and he made us feared. Why, even the British feared us! Civil liberties? Italians don't care much about civil liberties. He made people stop stealing and obey the laws. Of course his own gang did a lot of stealing and they did break the law. Even so, he might have gone down into history as a commendable enough Italian if he hadn't gone crazy, got jealous of Hitler, and started the war in Ethiopia. But, my friend, we are talking about the past. Who cares? Have a drink and I will tell you about the wonderful new movies we are making."

Person of De Gasperi

This is an interesting man. Alcide De Gasperi, Prime Minister of six consecutive Italian governments since December 1945 is puzzling to observe. He is pale, slim, about five feet eight, with sloping shoulders and an explosively cocked eye. He gives the impression on the one hand of being frail, an ascetic, almost too delicate to withstand the burden of such onerous office; on the other of an impatient sharp vitality. His blue eyes snap and shine; his lean and mobile lips jut out; his vigorously sensitive hands indicate a man both passionately devout and intellectually contemptuous of inferiors. Savonarola might well have looked like this.

De Gasperi is in his sixty-eighth year, but his mannerisms and indeed his appearance are those of a man much younger, even though he works a murderously hard fourteen or fifteen hours a day. I would have guessed him to be in his early fifties. His step is alert, his laughter sharp, and his hair only a medium gray.

Signor De Gasperi's office is in the Viminale Palace, traditionally the headquarters of Italian Ministers of the Interior. Inevitably, visiting him, you think of Mussolini before the war. What a contrast! De Gasperi works in a room smaller than the anteroom adjoining it, whereas Mussolini famously surrounded himself with acres of shining space. Moreover, his behavior is informal in the extreme. He wore a brown tweed jacket and gray slacks when I saw him. Three or four times as we talked, the telephone on his desk rang; he picked it up and answered it himself, apparently without knowing who the caller was and without any intermediation by secretaries. There is very little pomp or solemnity to De Gasperi, even though, as the phrase goes, he is more papal than the Pope.

De Gasperi has, or hopes to have, a good deal to say about the hundreds of millions of dollars the United States is sending to Italy this year through what the Italians call "Il Marshall." His own salary is $56 per month.

Whenever I visit a country and ask about the leading political personality and talk to him, I try to focus on two questions: What are the real sources of power behind this man? What does he believe in most?

One cannot be in Italy twenty minutes without becoming aware that the forces behind De Gasperi are two: First, the Vatican. Second, the United States. (There are other forces as well, it might be argued; for instance, the big landowners, the banking and financier class, and in particular the industrialists in the north. But they do not count on the same scale as do the Catholic Church and the U.S.A.)

Certainly the Church entered into the last campaign with a directness that shocked many good Italians—and Catholics. But it would be something of an overstatement to say that De Gasperi is a tool of the Pope's or takes orders from the Vatican. There is no question that he has strong Vatican support; he is in constant touch with Vatican officials, and his ideas and those of the Vatican are closely parallel. But nothing so simple as giving or taking direct instructions happens customarily in a country as sophisticated as Italy. As a matter of fact, De Gasperi told me that he has seen the Pope only once since he first took office three years ago; this was a ceremonial visit which lasted only ten minutes, and he was accompanied by the then President of the republic, De Nicola.

As to the United States, the matter may be summed up and dismissed in a sentence. Without active American support and aid, De Gasperi could not survive a month.

Life Story and Characteristics

Of course De Gasperi is as Italian as Michelangelo or macaroni. But the plain fact of the matter is that, when he was born, in 1881, his birthplace, Trento, was not part of Italy; this mountainous region is in the Tyrol and it belonged to Austria-Hungary. Though largely populated by Italians, it did not become Italian in fact till the end of World War I. Thus De Gasperi was born an Austrian, a subject of the old Emperor Franz Josef; he grew up speaking German as well as Italian, and he went perforce to churches and schools with Austrian, not Italian, priests and masters. Vienna was his polestar, as well as Rome.

This—and also the fact that he is a mountaineer—has contributed a good deal to his character. Of course he is Italian. Yet, having been brought up outside Italy, he can see it with a certain detachment and perspective; unlike most Italians, he is realistic rather than emotional about his own country. And the circumstance that he grew up on a frontier, under alien domination, probably intensified his patriotism. He has always (like Hitler whom he in no other way resembles) had the implacable nationalism of the frontiersman, the erstwhile exile.

De Gasperi was a student, an intellectual, and a politician, from the beginning. He took his degree at the University of Vienna; his thesis was an abstruse treatment of the influence of Italian drama on German drama in the eighteenth century. He returned to Trento, entered political life, and in 1911 became a deputy in the old Austrian parliament; he remained a deputy through the whole of World War I, sitting in the parliament of the country of which he was legally a citizen, but which was fighting the country really his. Equivocal? Yes.

Trento and the South Tyrol became part of Italy after the war, and De Gasperi plunged into Italian politics in 1921 as a member of the Partito Popolare, a moderate Catholic party, then headed by the well-known priest, Don Luigi Sturzo. For some years, when Mussolini came to power, De Gasperi tried to perform the difficult juggling act of keeping the party alive and at the same time being guardedly anti-Fascist. The Duce outlawed the Partito Popolare in 1926 and De Gasperi went underground in a manner of speaking. He was arrested several times, but politely. When World War II began and Mussolini put real pressure on the anti-Fascists,

De Gasperi fled into Vatican City, which gladly gave him refuge. He was a Vatican librarian until the armistice.

Then in September 1943, the Allies fished around for various people to run Italy and put it on its feet during the difficult transition from military to civilian government. De Gasperi was an obvious choice. He had strong Vatican support; he had an anti-Fascist record; he was leader of a party representing what were presumably the most liberal Catholic elements; and he had had a good deal of concrete political experience. So it was natural that he should become a member of the Committee of National Liberation, then minister without portfolio and Foreign Minister several times, and finally Prime Minister.

But a point should be made: Shrewd and experienced as he is, De Gasperi became Prime Minister much more out of negative than positive reasons. What really lifted him to power was not himself, but lack of anybody else. Fascism had blotted out a whole generation; its bile had to be regurgitated. Scarcely anybody survived capable of leading this reborn nation, except men almost neolithically old, like the former Prime Ministers Nitti and Orlando. De Gasperi was pretty old, but not quite so old as these. Also, he was a good choice because, though not by any stretch of the imagination a left winger, he was not of the ultra-extreme right either. He was moderate and progressive enough, it seemed, to be a kind of bridge between the two great camps in Italy of that period—the Communists and Socialists on one side, the Monarchists and Neo-Fascists on the other.

In various cabinet reshuffles too complicated to go into here, he has been renamed Prime Minister five times. Renamed? Actually Italy was in such a state of confused flux during most of this period, when the wounds of war were first being healed and the transition from monarchy to republic accomplished, that De Gasperi, in a sense, named himself, though not without some violent tussles.

One great and cardinal event was that, in the early summer of 1947, he chucked the Communists out of his cabinet. Look back: it may be a shock now to recall that the De Gasperi regime was a coalition with the Communists for a considerable time; Togliatti himself was his Minister of Justice, and in fact De Gasperi might never have reached office in the first place except by virtue of a deal with Togliatti. But the Communists were noisy and obstructive in the processes of government, and tension between De Gasperi and Togliatti inevitably coiled up. Imagine Stalin and the Pope at the same council table.

De Gasperi got rid of the Communists finally by the simple expedient of resigning office when he was reasonably certain nobody else could form a government. He took a long chance but his guess was right, and after several other politicians tried to form cabinets and failed, he was called back, and got a narrow vote of confidence. The Communists screamed bloody murder, but they had been outmaneuvered, and they have been out of the Italian government ever since. But let us keep in mind that they are the second strongest party in the country and have (together with the left-wing Socialists) 183 seats in a chamber of 574.

De Gasperi's life is two things—his job and the Church—and there is rather little to write about him personally. Rome does not boil with anecdotes about the Prime Minister. I did hear one little story, however, indicative of his somewhat bleak sense of humor. He turned to one of his associates, a Republican notable for anticlericalism, and grinned at him with, "Well, I haven't seen much of you in church lately."

He is married, and has four daughters; one is a nun, and another, who recently gave him his first grandson, is married to a butcher in Milan. He still lives in a modest apartment in a building near the Vatican which he rented as a refugee. He has no hobbies; with situations as difficult as De Gasperi's, very few statesmen have time for hobbies. For relaxation, he likes to climb in the Tyrol near his birthplace; but now, he told me, he feels a bit too old for serious mountaineering.

He takes every aspect of his job with extreme conscientiousness; for instance he will study a visitor's background before receiving him, in order to be well informed. He even sent out for a copy of *Inside Europe* before our interview! He loves good talk, and rather fancies himself as a linguist; conversation with him can turn into a vivid but appalling hodgepodge. He is sharp and voluble and the words spill out in mixed profusion, as if he were forgetting what language he is speaking; he will say things like "*Das ist* a very serious problem, *n'est-ce pas*?" His German is excellent, naturally, his English fairly fluent, and his French fair, provided he keeps it separated from the others.

De Gasperi has, most people think, grown a great deal in the past few years. He has broadened out and gained confidence. The office of Prime Minister in a country like Italy will either educate a man, or break him. One point of interest is that it is much harder for him to rule now than before, if only because the Communists *are* excluded. When they were part of his government he could always plead interference by them or the necessity to placate them as an excuse if things went wrong. Now he is on his own. Before he cleaned out the Communists, he could always say, "That was not *my* fault," or "My partners forbade my doing this." But today he has no Communists to hide behind, if I may phrase it so.

CHAPTER 2
ORIENT EXPRESS

WE ARRIVED in Trieste from Venice on one of the quick little scooter trains the Italians are so proud of, and left two or three days later on the Orient Express for Belgrade, having tried in the interval to digest something of Trieste's atmosphere and consequence. This city is the southern hinge of the Iron Curtain, and it presents some highly abstruse manifestations and characteristics.

Any Triestino over, say, the age of thirty-five, has lived a remarkably varied existence from the point of view of nationality. He was born a subject of the old Austro-Hungarian monarchy if he saw the light of day before 1918. He then became an Italian for a little over twenty years. But his native city was occupied by the Germans toward the end of World War II, and then formally annexed by Germany, so he was under German sovereignty for a time. In 1945 he was taken over by the Yugoslavs for an angry interlude, and then rescued by New Zealanders. Now, if he lives in the British-American zone of the newly constituted Free Territory of Trieste, he is ruled, in the last analysis, by the Security Council of the United Nations; if he lives in the Yugoslav zone he has become to all practical intent a Yugoslav—even though ethnically he has been an Italian all along.

Buried upside down in seventy feet of clear water just outside Trieste's magnificent harbor is the carcass of the Italian battleship *Cavour*. It was sunk by the British at the Battle of Taranto; raised, repaired, and brought to Trieste by the Italians; sunk again by United States bombers (who had the habit of dropping any leftover bombs on Trieste on their way back from missions in Rumania); now it is to be raised again by joint Anglo-American endeavor.

Walking or driving around Trieste today you encounter many other contradictions. Along the quai the day we arrived the American cruiser *Huntington* was smartly moored. Sipping coffee in the baroque square nearby we saw that the architecture was purest Viennese, and then we ate *fettuccini* and *fritto misto*. We lived in a hotel run by Allied Military Government that had been partly destroyed by Allied military action. We lunched in a castle that once belonged to Habsburg retainers as the guest of a British general. This general, T. S. Airey, and a first-class officer he is, derives his authority as supreme boss of Trieste from a peace treaty that disarms a former enemy, Italy, to which we now want to give Trieste back, although a disarmed Italy could not possibly defend it in case of war. We saw G.I.'s (there are five thousand American troops in this isolated Adriatic outpost), British technical advisers, Yugoslav sentries, Slovene peasants, and the sun-helmeted police of Venezia Giulia, the adjacent Italian province, in their bright orange khaki uniforms.

Road Block No. 8 is in the middle of a greasy winding hill where the piney hills, made of a barren rock called Karst, climb upward toward Yugoslavia. We drove there in a drowsy rain and paused to inspect what is called a *fojba*—one of the deep hidden natural caverns in which this region abounds. Here the bodies of Italian and German troops were tossed when Yugoslav Partisans got through with them. Passion runs hot—and cold—in this part of the world. We tiptoed close and looked two hundred feet down. As many as a hundred bodies have been excavated by U.S. engineers and A.M.G. civilians from a single cavern. It is not pleasant work. Road Block 8 is one of sixteen in all, half of which are maintained by the Americans, half by the British. Our guide told us that this was once the high road straight from Paris to Constantinople, the road by which Napoleon hoped to traverse Europe and conquer all that was beyond. I do not know if he would have been stopped by what stopped us.

The frontier here, between the F.T.T. (Free Territory of Trieste) and Yugoslavia is marked with crude red splotches of paint on the rocks and trees, and follows the road in zigzag fashion. A pole hangs across, painted white and red. Two orange-clad Venezia Giulia policemen stood by a rough guardhouse, a hundred yards forward of a small detachment of American troops. Then ahead we could see the Yugoslav sentries with their own pole beside a hut with a torn and patched iron roof. There are no obstructions on our side of the frontier, except the pole; the Yugoslavs have, however, dotted their approach with concrete slabs and dragon teeth. We try to concentrate all big vehicular traffic on this road, the better to control it. Our policy is to let out almost anybody who wants to get out, but to be very careful about anybody coming in. The Yugoslavs, on the contrary, let anybody come in, but nobody out except for good official reasons.

A peasant lady, carrying a scythe and with her shoes in her hands (a familiar enough Balkan trait—to save wear on leather when it is sloppy underfoot), tramped up the crown of the road and started to cross the frontier, and we watched with interest. Our guards asked her to show her papers, and examined them closely; then ceremoniously our pole was lifted. The Yugoslav guards did not stop her for papers or other examination nor did they bother to lift their pole; she squeezed under, and passed out of sight behind the dripping trees.

All this paraphernalia of suspicion and precaution may seem foolishly farfetched. But early this year a British armored car patrol (I cite an official report) "inadvertently crossed the boundary by a few hundred yards at an unmarked spot and was arrested. Sixteen days elapsed before the personnel and equipment of the patrol were returned."

Trieste, in its present form, came into precarious being on September 15, 1947, when the Italian peace treaty entered into force. Its status is the result of a compromise reached between rival Italian and Yugoslav claims after bitter and prolonged negotiations.[1] The metropolitan area of Trieste is 85 percent Italian, but its hinterland is almost as solidly Yugoslav; the city is on the sea, but its lifeblood comes from the hills behind; it squats on the coast, but faces backward. Much of the trade that customarily flowed down into the Italian city from the Slovene hills—after all Trieste was a major port for the whole Austro-Hungarian empire—has been cut off, and so the famous old city has dried up. Result today: one out of every three employable Triestinos is unemployed.

[1] Incidentally the Yugoslavs spell Trieste "TRST."

In theory Trieste is under the protection of the U.N., but this has never been fully operative, because the Security Council has been unable to agree so far on the appointment of a civilian governor as projected by the peace treaty. So authority comes down to General Airey from the Combined Chiefs of Staff—or from what is left of this body—in Washington. Meantime the division of the F.T.T. into two zones, British-American and Yugoslav, which was intended to be transitory, perforce continues and will probably have to continue indefinitely. There are two confrontations in Trieste between the Allies and the Yugoslavs: (1) between the British-American zone and Yugoslavia proper, as described above; (2) between the two rival zones within the territory itself. The Yugoslav zone has to all intents and purposes been transmuted into part of Yugoslavia. This is hard luck for the Italians stranded there; but no frontier can ever be drawn in this region—any more than you could draw a frontier through a macédoine or fruit salad—without leaving some luckless folk on the wrong side of the border. The Yugoslavs have completely communized their zone, and the line between the two is so sharp today that it is extremely doubtful if they can ever be welded together again, as was planned by the peace treaty. The Yugoslavs blame us for delay in appointing a governor and setting up a constitutional legislative authority; they say that, if we did, we would be under the legal obligation to withdraw our troops, which is indeed the case, and that we do not do so because we want a pretext for keeping armed force on the strategically interesting Yugoslav frontier. The real reason why we are so reluctant to withdraw is, of course, the fear that the Yugoslavs would march in and take over and communize the rest of the territory, including metropolitan Trieste itself, which is 85 percent Italian and which would be a great diplomatic prize for Tito.[2]

During the Italian election campaign the United States, Britain, and France proposed jointly the return of Trieste to

[2] Recently the Russians suggested the appointment of a Swiss engineer and diplomat, Colonel Hermann Flueckiger, as governor, hoping thus to straighten out the quarrel over the governorship. Previously this gentleman had been suggested for the job by the British. But no agreement was reached. New York *Times*, February 18, 1949.

Italy. Of course—it is easy enough to say this now—it should never have been amputated from Italy in the first place. But Italy, let us recall, was an enemy in World War II, and Tito's Yugoslavia was a fighting ally—how short the memory is apt to be!—and Yugoslavia had to be rewarded at Italy's expense. Now to have proposed the return of Trieste to Italy during the hottest days of the Italian election was an item in political warfare, designed as an astute political maneuver to strengthen De Gasperi's hand against the Communists, who always behaved like good nationalist Italians on this issue and were themselves clamoring to get Trieste back.[3] It is now our permanent policy to advocate the eventual return of Trieste to Italy. Tito on his side would, I think, accept division on a zonal basis as a solution; that is, he would agree to give the British-U.S. zone to Italy in return for the right to keep his. But the state of Italian public opinion on this issue is so acute that no Italian government could agree to such a division without being turned out of office. What about the Triestinos themselves? Mostly, even though poor, they seem to be enjoying the status quo. The Triestinos are a very special breed; most other Italians think of them as a sort of different species, roughly in the way that non-Texan Americans think of Texans.

In actual fact what might be described as a steady "Italianization" of our part of Trieste is proceeding. Inevitably, just as the Yugoslav zone is becoming indistinguishable from Yugoslavia, our zone is becoming more and more Italian. And Italy, it should be remembered, hard pressed as it is financially, pays Trieste's bills.

The American military units in Trieste bear the handsome name TRUST (Trieste U.S. Troops); they are not stationed in municipal Trieste (which is British), but in the northern sectors of the zone. Could this vestigial force, no matter how well equipped, brave, and smartly trained, withstand a sudden overt Yugoslav assault, which would leave it with its back to the sea and faced with overwhelming superiority of numbers?

[3] The Communists, it might be thought, were put in a pretty quandary by this stratagem. But Togliatti's reply was clever. He cried: "Shame!"—and denounced the Americans for attempting to play politics and perpetrate a cheap, vulgar, and insincere maneuver at the expense of people's "freedom."

Of course, since the Cominform split between Yugoslavia and the Kremlin, such an attack is unlikely in the extreme. Tito is no fool. He is having too much trouble elsewhere. But there is always the danger of some crazy frontier incident; a smoldering colonel full of *slivovitz* and propaganda could, conceivably, cause a mess of trouble. Most experts I met thought that the best to be hoped for is that Trieste would become a sort of Bataan. The area is very vulnerable indeed. For one thing it is dependent on the Yugoslav hinterland itself for its entire water supply and electric power. (But it would be awkward for the Yugoslavs to have to cut off the power, which is gridded into their own Istrian network.)

Perhaps it is inevitable given the circumstances of an explosive situation that plays havoc with local nerves, but something profoundly startled us in Trieste, namely the aggressive militancy of some of our own officers on the spot. I do not mean merely the contemptuous way that almost all Americans (and British) talk of the Yugoslavs as "Tugs," as if they were loutish interlopers from a subhuman stratum of society; I mean the active hope seemingly held by some of our military that there *would* be trouble, that the trouble *would* eventuate in war, and that we could then let loose our atomic bomb once and for all on the Bolsheviks and all their kind. Later we found something of this same belligerence in other American military quarters; in fact the only times we thought that war was imminent anywhere in Europe was when we traveled in American domains. In the satellites themselves there is plenty of fear of war, but absolutely no talk of starting one. But in Trieste, as in Germany later, we could not help feeling that all the irritants and exasperations to which the local American population is undoubtedly exposed had produced a preoccupation with aggressive war much at variance with normal American standards of conscience and behavior. Most American officers would, of course, deny hotly that they advocate a preventive war against the Soviet Union, but they have what might be called the "Of course we don't want war *but*" attitude, which is itself a kind of invitation to catastrophe. In any case some Americans in Trieste seem to be spoiling for a fight. Luckily most of these are juniors and underlings. The responsible commanders are of an altogether different frame of mind.

Communist Imbroglio in Trieste

The sensational and mysterious rupture between Marshal Tito and the Cominform, about which we shall write much in this book, had explosive minor repercussions in Trieste, and the episode is worth brief mention because it tells a good deal about contemporary patterns of Communist behavior.

To an orthodox Marxist, the extreme political end in view is eventual communization of the world, under the exclusive and explicit direction of Moscow. If, for this end, it is necessary to sacrifice a community, a party, even a whole country, the sacrifice must be made, and should even be welcomed by those sacrificed. The sole directive discretion is that of Moscow. This is the major point to keep clenched in mind.

Immediately after the war the Communist party in Venezia Giulia was in theory subject to the commands of the Communist party of Italy itself, as was right and proper, under Togliatti, who in turn was under Moscow. Then control of this region moved to Belgrade (again under Moscow of course) as the result of a secret agreement made by Tito and Togliatti. For a time the party line was that Trieste should eventually become the seventh of the federated Yugoslav republics. Came the disruption between Tito and the Kremlin. As a result the Trieste Communist party split up, with one wing, mostly Slovene, remaining loyal to Tito and thus sharing his excommunication; the other, mostly Italian, stuck to the Cominform. This of course is exactly what the Kremlin hates to see happen; it imperils the myth of indissoluble Latin-Slav "brotherhood" and of the essential unity of the working class no matter what nationalities are involved.

So a well-knit and well-disciplined Communist party broke up as a result of nationalist pressures. This in turn produced other fractures and fissions. For instance the Italianates promptly began to shout for the return of Trieste to Italy, and thus they became, in effect, allies of De Gasperi, the British, and the Americans; the odd position was reached whereby an old-line Communist leader named Vadali, the leader of the Italianates, was denounced by the Slovenes as an Anglo-Saxon "spy," although we think of him as the official agent of the Cominform!

One detail in background is that Trieste was a subordinate reason for the quarrel between Tito and the Cominform. Togliatti begged the Kremlin to urge Tito to be less "nationalist" about Trieste, i.e. less active about urging its incorporation into Yugoslavia, in order to strengthen his (Togliatti's) hand in Italy. Togliatti said to Moscow in effect, "Tell Tito to be quiet about Trieste, because Yugoslav agitation strengthens Italian national spirit here which I am trying to fight. He may lose Trieste, but I can give you all Italy instead, a much richer prize!"

Another note is provided by some antics in the world of journalism. There are two Communist newspapers in Trieste, *Il Lavoratore* in Italian, the official organ of the local party, and the *Primorski Dnevnik* in Slovene. Both are printed in the same building on the same presses.[4] The Italian paper sided with the Cominform, and the Slovene with Tito, but they still continued to be printed by the same staff—to the tune of occasional fistfights between the linotypers—and both were financed by Belgrade (at least as of the time we were there) even though *Il Lavoratore* had become Tito's bitter enemy. For a while each printed attacks on the other in a special column in the other's language! The plant these journals occupy shows how comparatively affluent a small Communist group can be in this part of Europe. It cost $600,000, which is a big sum for Trieste; it is so modern that there are sun lamps in the composing room.

Journey to Belgrade

As I say, we left Trieste for Belgrade on the Orient Express. I knew this train well before the war; it was, and is, one of the

[4] There are no newspapers at all in the Yugoslav zone incidentally, except one feeble weekly.

most celebrated trains in the world. Its various sections covered half of Europe; it was like a blue steel worm assembled and then cut apart, crawling over the swell of the continent in segments and then rejoining; it set out from Calais, Paris or Amsterdam and ended up in Bucharest, Istanbul or Athens, a neat blue worm again.

Perhaps it was innocent of me, that warm summer night, to expect to see once more the long line of sleek blue sleepers waiting in the Trieste station.

What we did see was exactly one blue car—and it was hooked onto what seemed to be partly a freight train, partly a series of dilapidated cars made of laths. We got aboard, and discovered that we were the only passengers in the entire sleeper. The next car, too, a Paris-Belgrade coach, was as empty as a gutted trash can. The train crept out of the dark station, and I felt almost as if it were a ghost train, somehow stealing back into a lost past, a train of shadows like one in a movie by Alfred Hitchcock.

Empty? By morning it had become the most inordinately crowded train I have ever been in, except for the single sleeper.

We tried to force our way through half a dozen coaches to the dining car; we had to push and crawl and struggle, inch by inch, through masses of people jammed together in the aisles like raisins in a pack. Gypsies; barefooted old men; soldiers in greasy uniforms; peasant women literally in rags—these were our companions. Breakfast, when we got there, was a chunk of dark bread tossed on a grimy bare table, and the waiter's hands were not, to put it mildly, clean.

All over eastern Europe the trains are insufferably crowded, and the reason is quite simple. Most traffic by road has disappeared, on account of shortage of gasoline, and very little new rolling stock has been built since the war. Also one must take into account the frightful devastation caused by the war itself.

We did not attempt to squeeze into the dining car again. It was simpler not to eat. Once or twice, when we stopped at village stations, hawkers came up to the windows but they had nothing to offer except a few shriveled, pock-marked apples.[5]

[5] But the Zagreb and Belgrade newspapers were on sale. The regime pays more attention to intellectual hunger than physical.

Later friends told us that the crush to get to the diner on the Orient Express was a conventional experience. "Did you push or sprint?" they asked. Some brave souls wait for the train to stop and then dash alongside to climb aboard again six or seven cars away, but this is a risky business because in this part of the world no signal is customarily given when a train is about to start.

I watched the worn and stolid faces of our fellow passengers. They stared at us, but were never rude. I suppose what impressed us most was the shocking state of their clothes. We knew that any woman wearing a skirt must have bought it before the war—it was so short. Many people were barefoot, or had rags wrapped round their feet. The uniforms of the soldiers were of an indescribably cheap, coarse, and shabby texture. Few people carried suitcases: all their possessions, it seemed, were piled into the aisles in nets or paper parcels. Some too—a Balkan touch—had flowers in baskets, and wriggling in the nets were chickens.

At one station I made to get off, but the conductor had to pull me back and shut the door quickly, because mobs of people tried to surge on the train. There was a primitive wildness about this scene, a sense of churning passion that could explode into the most violent incident. Wildness, yes—that is the proper word to use.

Out of the windows gray rain obscured the fertile and lovely country. Other trains passed us and we saw U.S. ARMY painted on one locomotive tender, and the symbol UNRRA on some freight cars. Occasionally flat cars came by bearing modern artillery and a unit of what seemed to be a hospital train. Once in a while we saw old guns and the wreckages of tanks still out in the fields.

Particularly I was struck by the children. They looked wolfish with hunger and prematurely aged by the tragedy of the war they had somehow managed to live through. The young girls looked like men; except for their coarse heavy braids they could not have been told from men—all of them seemed to have enormously developed leg muscles—and the boys, with their pinched and bony faces, looked like men too, men who had suffered the most bitter anguish.

Yet at the same time—this paradox we will confront time and time again—one could detect a vitality in the atmosphere, a feeling of push and energy, almost an exhilaration.

The friendly conductor (a Bulgarian, it happened) in the familiar brown *wagon-lit* uniform told us when to expect the customs. A young Yugoslav bounced into our compartment, gave only the quickest and most cursory glance at our faces to see that they matched our passport photographs, spelled our names completely wrong in the money declaration we filled out, and never looked at or opened any of our eight bags. The conductor said, "*Les Yugoslavs sont très gentils aux étrangers.*"

We got to Belgrade that night at about 9:20, after twenty-one hours. This trip was a sharp experience. It made us ashamed that we in the United States had such plenty, while these peasants were manifestly all but starving, that we had so much of the world's wealth, and they so little. And I felt that the Yugoslav regime could be excused much, no matter what, if only it could or would better the living standard of these brave people.

CHAPTER 3
CHINKS IN THE CURTAIN, PLUS CERTAIN OBSERVATIONS AT LARGE

ONE great misconception about the Iron Curtain is that it is solid, opaque, and made of iron. Actually it is full of chinks. We entered by way of one obvious chink, the Orient Express, and there are many others. Certainly the satellite states are isolated enough, and it is Moscow policy to make them more isolated all the time, but some rays of light do get through, and it is my conviction that in time—provided war does not come—the satellites will want more and more contact with the West.

Anyway, just for the record as of the time we traveled, you could still buy a railway ticket from Paris all the way to Istanbul through three satellite countries (of course it would be prudent to have your visas in good order), and you can still fly from Prague, say, or even Warsaw, to any European capital. Conversely Hungarian and Czech athletes distinguished themselves in London at the recent Olympic games, and Yugoslavia did well at Wimbledon. You can still cash an American Express check in Belgrade or Zagreb, buy the Paris edition of the New York *Herald Tribune* on the streets of Budapest, and telephone Chicago from Prague. And you will see the American flag outside the United States Information Service libraries and also British flags and information centers in each capital.

Travel is absolutely cut off between Yugoslavia and Greece. This border is hermetically sealed so far as official relations between the two countries are concerned and no traveler will get through unless he happens to be my friend Homer Bigart, but this is the only case in the whole area where communications aren't fairly normal, provided you have the proper documents.

Never once, incidentally, did we have our own papers tampered with, nor were we ever followed so far as we know. Never once did we have to show a passport, except for routine examination at the frontier or when registering at a hotel, nor did we ever have to produce any special passes or permissions of any kind. What is even more striking, customs inspection at the various borders was casual in the extreme. Never did we have to open a bag or suitcase except in Czechoslovakia, where the inspection was quite perfunctory.[1]

Also in this field I have to report that officials of at least two satellite governments told us almost imploringly that they would like to have more American visitors, that they would refuse nobody a visa, that they hoped not merely for a revival of trade but of tourist traffic, and that they would like to see instituted a systematic exchange of such categories of folk as students, teachers and technical experts of all kinds. This offer should, of course, be taken with several shovelfuls of salt. Most officials in this part of the world are definitely suspicious of United States policy, even if they are friendly to individual Americans, and if Americans came in large numbers they would be carefully watched.

Then again the conference last summer of so-called intellectuals at Wroclaw, Poland, which was pretty much of a failure even from the Communist point of view, showed how crude and inflexible is the Russian attitude toward any intellectual exchange and how impossible it is for Westerners and Easterners to get together on any productive cultural basis so long as the Russians and their satellites use the lie—not merely the distortions of propaganda but the lie direct—as a direct instrument of policy.

But to return to chinks and apertures. Recently the British announced a $520 million trade agreement with Poland, by which Britain becomes Poland's best customer. If that is not an aperture, I do not know what one is.

[1] I do not think this could have been out of any special consideration for me as a newspaperman. For whenever our names were written down at frontiers, as on the train to Belgrade, they were horribly misspelled and garbled. Nobody in the lower echelons ever had the faintest idea who we were.

Some Preliminary Generalizations

1. A tendency exists to think that the satellite states form a solid block, homogeneous in structure and uniform in spirit and behavior. Actually this is not at all the case; indeed it was striking to discover how remarkably they differ. While the satellites are all Communist dictatorships and while there are other important and suggestive common denominators, as I shall point out, there are wide and radical distinctions too.

Yugoslavia is obviously a special case since the celebrated break with Moscow. Yet in some respects it is more like Russia than any of the others; for instance it is the best integrated and the only one which follows the Soviet Union tit for tat in federal structure. And it should not be forgotten—as we shall see—that although Tito and Stalin are bitter enemies as of the moment, most Yugoslavs decidedly think of themselves as still being very good Communists emphatically in the Russian sphere.

Poland is probably the country the Russians are least sure of; though it is so close geographically, it shows a very special individual spark and creative will. Czechoslovakia is the most abject and broken of the puppets, politically and otherwise. Hungary, in many respects, is the best off. The country most under the Russian thumb is Rumania; it is the one most cut off from the world outside and the hardest to get into; it is in the position of a mouse under the elephant's foot that doesn't even dare squeak. Bulgaria is probably the most "advanced" of all in matters of social and economic reform, and also the most dictatorially run.

The fact that these countries still maintain their own special characteristics and have their own national problems is an important consideration for the future. Will international communism succeed in removing or softening the violent nationalist tensions that have distinguished—and disgraced—this part of the world for so long? Suppose eastern Germany should become another satellite. Would that mean that the old inborn, bone-based fear of Germany by fellow satellites like Poland and Czechoslovakia will disappear?

I asked almost everybody I met in Hungary if Magyar nationalism were dead. What I was driving at was whether Hungarians could envisage a future in which all their own most precious national instincts would or could be merged into an international structure. The main answer I got was that Hungarian Communists have no objection to a man loving his own country. But, they stressed, nationalism is being used by reactionaries as a secret or potential rallying-point against the government; therefore, it has to be guarded against and talked down.

Poland is a very particular case, since it lies exposed without good natural frontiers between the two giants—Germany and Russia. It has the Red army not on one of its borders, but on both. What will happen to Poland if Germany, as I have just suggested, ever does become Sovietized? Can the Poles hold their own opposite Moscow if Russia wants to make a better arrangement with Berlin? Or worse, suppose at some future date there should be another Russo-German war, with Poland once more the battlefield in between. The answer of Polish Communists to these questions is that under international socialism the old national hatreds and exasperations will disappear. These Poles feel that a Communist Germany, Poland and Russia would all stand side by side together, co-operating with full amity under similar and mutually friendly regimes. But—I wonder.

2. All the Iron Curtain countries (except possibly Bulgaria) strenuously deny that they are dictatorships, and call themselves "people's democracies" or "people's republics." At first I thought this was only the most transparent kind of double talk. The Soviet Union has never bothered to disguise itself in this manner. Why should the puppets?

The answers would appear to be several. First, incredible as the fact may seem, the satellite leaders, in a perverted, self-deluded, almost-crazy way, do genuinely consider that they *are* "democratic." Second, they seek to pay some lip service to the democratic ideas of the West as a means of encouraging support from their own people. In other words, totalitarian as the whole region clearly is, the power of democracy in the rest of the world is still such that the men who run these countries continue to find it necessary to speak of it admiringly.

Then there is a third consideration. Some years ago the locution *demokratiia osobogo tipa,* "democracies of a special type," began to appear in Marxist literature, and the term "people's democracy" arose to denote a special form of transition government which was socialist in theory but not completely so in fact, a government in which some capitalist elements—like private ownership of small business and of land—were permitted to survive. Technically, if we adjust ourselves to the Soviet idiom, a people's democracy is a socialist state in which "a private sector" of economy still exists.

Finally, the Russian definition of the very word democracy differs sharply from ours. To a good Communist in eastern Europe "democracy" means a system under which the state guarantees the people economic "freedom" rather than political, and where civil liberties and free expression of political opinion do not rank in importance with the security of the masses as a whole against war, Fascism, and other dangers. This may seem to us a highly naïve and misleading contradiction in terms or misuse of words. But the Soviets think that our criterion of democracy is just as distorted and disingenuous as we think theirs.

But in plain fact every satellite is a totalitarian state, no more, no less, though dedicated in theory to the people's good. How overtly dictatorial is each? Conditions vary. Yugoslavia is certainly an out-and-out police state, and so are Rumania and Bulgaria. Czechoslovakia is rapidly becoming one. There is no actual terror in Hungary comparable to the terror under the Nazis; even the harshest Hungarian critic of the regime will concede that life under the Gestapo was much worse. Nor is there any overt terror in Poland. Things are done much more subtly—by intimidation, economic pressure, favoritism in jobs and housing and so on. The terror is, so to speak, cold, not hot. In the long run it amounts to the same thing.

Of course real freedom of the press and of assembly have disappeared everywhere. These are almost always the first things to go. But in none of the countries we visited is there any censorship of foreign correspondents, though a correspondent may be expelled if he consistently irritates the regime. Our mail was, so far as we know, only opened in one country, Hungary—and in Vienna where, although the American, British, and French armies are present, an overt Russian censorship of mail is permitted to exist.

Freedom of worship? This is a highly complicated issue. The Mindszenty trial in Hungary, followed by inflamed attacks on the Protestant Church in Hungary and Bulgaria, shows amply the fierce and fixed enmity of Communists to almost all religious forms. There has been a considerable acceleration to this process in the past year. For instance, four expert and impartial observers for the New York *Herald Tribune,* who roamed all over eastern Europe, testified as recently as the summer of 1947, "Everywhere we found freedom of worship. Even in Yugoslavia . . . churches were open and crowded. In Poland and Hungary religious instruction by priests is still compulsory in state schools. Nowhere has there been an official attempt to prevent people worshipping as they please."

I do not think that these *Herald Tribune* reporters[2] would make quite such a blanket statement today. Yet the Communists on their side would insist that the practice of religious offices is still perfectly free, and that no priest or pastor will get into any trouble whatsoever unless he crosses the borderline, which is admittedly shadowy, into political affairs. And it is certainly a fact that the churches are open—and crowded—everywhere. People do still worship. But also the fact remains that religion is by far the greatest competitor Communists have to fear, because it sets up a rival authority, that of God. In the long run, if they are honest, most Communists would admit that their eventual "ideal" is to get rid of religion or modify it to suit their own aims and ends.

To return to general considerations of totalitarianism, the adhesive eye of the Communist bureaucracy is not always so all seeing as one would assume. There are chinks in the curtain; there are also chinks in every interior façade. Even in Czechoslovakia the pattern of espionage isn't quite all that it's supposed to be. For instance in Prague we spent some hours in the company of James A. Farley; we accompanied him on a visit

[2] Walter Kerr, Ned Russell, William Attwood, and Russell Hill.

to Lidice and were fellow guests at a luncheon honoring the Archbishop of Prague. But high Czechoslovak authorities we met subsequently had no knowledge at all that Farley was in the city. They could hardly believe it when I happened to mention that this distinguished American, so antipathetic to Communism, was a visitor in their capital and was going about quite freely—as a guest of the United States ambassador!

3. It should never be forgotten that none of these states, except Czechoslovakia, ever had much experience of democracy in our sense of the term. Their parliamentary regimes, if they had them, were colossally inefficient and corrupt; several countries were feudal oligarchies dominated by Fascist reactionaries or royal dictatorships. Hungary and Bulgaria were German allies, and Rumania had outright Fascism. We shall return to this point again. One cannot judge the present status of a country without some perspective on its previous institutions. A basic reason for the success, if it may be termed such, of the Communist and para-Communist regimes is a fierce and sullen resentment by the great mass of the people at the way they were formerly milked and exploited by a selfish, greedy, and medieval feudalism. They were willing to welcome almost anything as a relief from what they had. A peasant who was a serf and who wallowed in mud like his owner's pigs, and who now despite intense privation may be tilling his own small plot of land, in circumstances where his children go to school and where he has at least the promise of decent roads and electric light, may be pardoned if he pays more attention to the propaganda of Moscow than of reactionary refugees in New York. Or, if you prefer, put it this way. The communization of eastern Europe is a penalty the people bear for the grievous sins and avarice of the regimes that went before.

4. Nor should anybody ever forget what the war cost these people. The tornado of destruction and horror let loose and practiced by the Germans is a living burn and insult to millions, and it would be the height of recklessness if we in the United States should ever become committed in time of peace to building up a German army as a threat against these countries. Unanimously, unforgivingly, eternally, eastern Europe

hates the Germans. Just look at what the Germans did to Warsaw alone. That was a matter of millions of people. Look what they did to the shinbone of my friend the Countess P., by medical experiments in a concentration camp. That was a matter of one person. If any single thing could unite practically the whole east of the continent against us even more than it is at present united, it would be an active pro-German policy on the part of the United States.

Here another point arises, namely that one paramount reason the Communists reached power in this group of countries is the extremely vital role they played in the resistance movements against the Germans during the war. In *every* satellite state, the Communists were the earliest and most effective fighters against the Nazi invaders and oppressors; it was the Communists, as a rule, who initiated and led military and political action; it was they who were hounded most mercilessly by the Fascists, and expunged like eyes gouged out of a socket when they were caught; it was they who imparted discipline and organization to the scattered patriotic forces. So, when freedom came, it was quite natural that they should demand to rule what they, plus the Red army, had been largely responsible for liberating.

5. Russian influence is tremendous, of course, in all the countries we saw—even Yugoslavia. This does not mean, however, that Russians are much in evidence, or that a local cabinet minister has to pick up a phone and call Moscow to make a decision. As a matter of fact, we never once saw a single Russian anywhere. Russian garrisons, called "communication troops," exist in Hungary and Poland. But they are carefully segregated and kept out of sight.

Soviet ambassadors and ministers in the various capitals are not, it would seem, running each country from behind the scenes, though they may claim a privileged position—much as, say, an American ambassador to a Central American state has a privileged position. For a Soviet diplomat to appear to be too powerful would be embarrassing, because the pretense is carefully maintained of the complete independence of each country. In fact, just as they deny that they are dictatorships, the satellites deny that they are satellites. What does happen in the great majority of cases is that the local official has no need to communicate with the official Russians since the party line is clear anyway, and the local man knows it as well as the Russian does.

There are no actual present-time Russian citizens in any important government post in any satellite state, so far as I know. On the other hand, practically the entire ruling caste behind the Iron Curtain was Russian trained. And most of the elite go to Moscow often, where all decisions of major policy are laid down.

The Russians themselves deny incidentally that the Iron Curtain exists at all. This is of course laughable. Try to get in or out of Russia. The barrier is double—not only to keep our world out, but to keep their world in. The best discussion of this I have seen recently is in an article by the British historian Edward Crankshaw.[3] As he says aptly, "Stalin is seeking to isolate the consciousness of the Soviet people from the living consciousness of humanity as a whole. . . . There is your real Iron Curtain—the conditioning [of the Russian] into unquestioning and more or less painless acceptance of an intolerable state of affairs."

Devolving from all this are difficult questions in human values. An orthodox Marxist would say that the power and pressure of the great Communist Idea, that of an egalitarian economy destined in time to be operated by the people for the people's good, with the disappearance of the state as such as an ultimate goal, is bound eventually to enhance such values. But they are certainly not enhanced at the moment. In fact most human values as we define them are being liquidated steadily. Consider—just to name one point—how the free intellect has been dispossessed. Another point is that nobody has much of a private life—which is indeed a lamentable hallmark of most dictatorships. Wise Communists recognize that the cost of their system is the sacrifice (they say "temporary" sacrifice) of human values; hence, it has become a minor tenet of the faithful to encourage love for the family and so on, as an effort to counteract other antisocial tendencies implicit in the system as a whole.

[3] *New York Times* Magazine, December 5, 1948.

Minor note in the aesthetic field—the badge of the veteran Communist these days is stainless steel teeth. We saw them almost everywhere. The reason is that few people had adequate dental care in prison or during the resistance years, and their teeth decayed. Then gold was scarce and stainless steel turned out to be a useful substitute. As a matter of fact a steel tooth is no more unsightly than one of gold. This phenomenon in the realm of dentistry is reminiscent, like so much else behind the Curtain, of Moscow many years ago. If a man lost up to seven teeth it was considered merely a matter of aesthetics and he had to bear the cost of dentistry himself; if the loss were greater than seven, the state paid the bills on the ground that health had become involved.

6. The Kremlin fight against Tito is—as of the moment—an all-out affair. Russia must at all costs keep the other satellites from similarly becoming "contaminated" and going native. On the other hand, many Yugoslavs themselves would probably like to be forgiven and taken back into the fold.

7. None of the puppet states is equipped for a war, is capable of fighting a serious war, or wants war. If they should be driven into a war by Moscow, it will mean their own ruin, and they know it.

8. The basic attitude of these countries to the United States is compounded of respect for our power, ignorance and fear. Of course a major constituent of foreign policy everywhere in this part of the world is and always has been fear. Many satellite leaders genuinely think that the United States is going to attack them, and perhaps attack them soon. They consider the Marshall plan to have been an "aggressive" move against their security and they justify all their countermeasures as a "consolidation" against this so-called aggression. They are apt to say angrily, "You cannot kill ideas by dollars," and to play down or conceal the fact that at least two satellites wanted badly to share in the European Recovery Program, but were refused permission to do so by the Russians.

In this connection it seems notable to me that we were always treated so well, despite the fact that the great mass of eastern Europeans are systematically fed the silliest kind of propaganda about the United States. Americans are portrayed by and large as being exclusively of two categories: (1) sinister imperialists grasping for world domination; (2) ignorant and depraved dollar-chasers starving the workers and lynching Negroes. So one may fairly reach the conclusion that the propaganda either doesn't convince everybody or that the rank and file of people do not apply it personally.

Everywhere we went, if there was any talk at all about the United States, people asked us about Henry Wallace, pronounced Volis. Naturally most Communists thought he would get a very much bigger vote in November 1948 than he got. I even heard it said before the election that if Wallace got more than 10 percent, the Russians would intensify their diplomatic and political offensive against the United States, on the ground that the fifth column in America would soon be in a position to strike. If, on the contrary, Wallace got much less than 10 percent, the Kremlin was prepared to make an about-face and try to ameliorate the tension between the Soviets and America. This prophecy has indeed been borne out by events. To revert to "Volis" personally—the satellite attitude was one of anguished hope, not so much from the point of view that he shared Communist views, but out of fear that the United States might at any moment go to war and attack Europe, and that Wallace stood for peace, and might prevent this. Never forget—it is an absolutely major motif throughout eastern Europe—that the Communists are frightened sick that America will let loose and attack.

9. On the domestic side, the satellite governments all follow a definite pattern. The Communists are a minority—a distinct minority—in each country, and hence the technique is to rule by coalition. The nature of these coalitions varies. At present the tendency is to form "workers' parties" on a broad basis including the Social Democrats and other left-wing elements and then establish what may be called a "Fatherland Front" or "Independence Front." It may surprise Americans to know that many prominent ministers, even today, are not Communists. The Prime Minister of Poland is not a Communist; neither are the Prime Ministers of Rumania or Hungary. Even

in Yugoslavia no fewer than eight ministers out of twenty-six are non-Communists. But the steady trend is toward a more and more overt and inexorable assumption of power by Communists under a screen of wide mergings and popular fronts. It is important, however, to keep in mind (much as you may dislike to hear it) that in almost every country non-Communists of the highest talent and experience play along freely with the Communists, and take part in their administrations.

10. Jews play a very prominent role in several governments. Here we tread delicate ground. The three "Muscovites" who run Hungary are Jews, the men who dominate Poland are Jews, the secretary general of the Communist party in Czechoslovakia is a Jew, Ana Pauker of Rumania is a Jewess. This brings up the grave point that Jews, as a race and a nation, may be unjustly assessed blame—by the ignorant—for the nature of these regimes. Also if there should ever be a reaction and a new white terror in this part of the world, there might well be a recrudescence of organized anti-Semitism of the most dangerous and vicious type. A tendency is already manifest to lump Jews and Communists together and to assume that, because an occasional important Communist is a Jew, all Jews are Communists. Let us spike this lie once and for all. The Jewish people were practically wiped out by the Germans in these countries. More than 3 *million* Polish Jews alone were tortured, massacred and murdered. Of 600,000 Hungarian Jews before the war, only about 20 percent survive today; of 280,000 Jews in Czechoslovakia, not more than 10,000 remain. The great bulk of the survivors, it is hardly necessary to point out, are not Communists, never have been Communists, and never will be Communists. So anti-Semitic propaganda in this whole direction should be discounted, guarded against, and scotched when it appears.

Then too consider another factor which should clinch the point that Jews in the large are not to be held responsible for what we of the West do not like about these countries. It is that several satellite governments themselves have anti-Semitic tendencies.

11. Every Iron Curtain country has a plan, either a two-,

three-, four-, five-, or even six-year plan. The pattern of nationalization and industrialization is roughly the same in each. Most enterprises employing more than one hundred people have been nationalized. Of course all mineral wealth, utilities, and the like have become the property of the state. The land, however, has not been collectivized to any extent as yet. Land reforms have broken up the big estates—very few estates still exist in eastern Europe bigger than say a hundred acres—but a land reform is quite a different thing from collectivization. But Moscow is pushing for collectivization and it may come in several countries soon.

Small businesses are as a rule not interfered with. But a wide net of government restrictions and controls makes it difficult in the extreme for the small businessman to do anything—for instance in the realm of wages, prices and the like—that the government doesn't favor. In fact he is a helpless prisoner. Sooner or later the bourgeoisie will disappear.

12. The most trenchant and overriding impression the visitor will get in any of these countries is of poverty. Socialism may work out to equality of income and a higher living standard for the people in time, but this certainly hasn't happened yet. Here, to an extent, the fault is that of Moscow, not of the satellites themselves. The Stalin line is to keep class struggle the dominant motif in each country, which means destruction of the previous economy. Also the satellites are systematically drained of exports by Moscow. Perhaps, as I heard it said, the Russians for the sake of their own prestige cannot allow any Stalinoid state to have a higher standard of living than that of the Soviet Union itself; hence they are deliberately impoverished. Another point is industrialization. To industrialize an agrarian state under pressure during a short interval inevitably means drastic impoverishment at least for a time.

Here then is a preliminary glimpse of what the Communists call the new world. It contains much more than we think. We may not like it, but we will have to deal with it.

CHAPTER 4
YUGOSLAVIA, THE HOW AND WHY

YUGOSLAVIA, the brawniest and most stubborn of the Balkan states, a lusty country containing 15,320,000 Serbs, Croats, Macedonians, Bosnians, Slovenes, Montenegrins, and other commingled folk, is ruled by Marshal Tito and a small clique. Its uniqueness—as of the moment of writing—is that it is flanked not by one Iron Curtain, but by two. Marshal Tito is probably the most isolated political phenomenon on earth. Since June 28, 1948, when his government was formally cast out of the Soviet orbit, the Yugoslavs have had to hew out their own path, and a thorny and difficult path it may well prove to be.

We shall go into the reasons for this formidable quarrel between Tito and the Cominform and its ramifications and results in Chapter 6 below. The details are as complexly fascinating—even bewildering—as, say, a verbatim report of one of the great Russian treason trials before the war. Certainly the mere fact of the rupture is the most important and pregnant development in Russian relations with the rest of the world since the Hitler-Stalin pact of 1939. But by way of introduction there is something else to say, which is that Yugoslavia is still very much a Communist state despite the quarrel, its government follows the Soviet model more closely than does that of any other satellite as I have already mentioned in the preceding chapter, and its temper and spirit are much closer to Moscow than to us. Cominform split or no, the Yugoslav leaders still consider themselves to be Communists—in fact, better Communists than the Kremlin Communists themselves.

I asked one official if, in the event of war, Yugoslavia would fight against the United States. "Certainly," was the reply.[1] I asked why. "Ah, because we are *real* Communists!"

This contradiction, I warn the reader, will haunt the pages

[1] Events may very well prove him to be wrong.

following. Belgrade has split off from Moscow and a great quarrel rages. But by far the easiest way to describe Belgrade is to say that it is a Moscow in miniature. Poverty and drabness; the disappearance of gentility; lack of all elegance and grace; a severely moral atmosphere; long queues everywhere; terrible shortages in consumer goods; emphasis on industrialization; wildly inflated prices; intense xenophobia and suspicion of foreigners; inaccessibility of most officials and a heavy pall of bureaucratic secrecy—these are characteristics common to both capitals.

But also one gets the same sense of brutal forthrightness that Moscow gives, a sense of power and change, of a world being utterly reborn for good or ill, pulled out by the roots, everything topsy-turvy, with a transvaluation of all values, everything being tried for good or ill in a radically different way.

Here I must mention a second contradiction that will also mark these pages, not merely in reference to Yugoslavia but to the other satellites. Poverty? Suspiciousness? Brutality? Yes! But there are compelling factors on the other side. It is incontestable that Yugoslavia is a police state, afflicted by some savage miseries human and political. But on the other hand any visitor is almost bound to feel a strong impression of confidence, *élan,* and above all patriotism and vitality, as well as of duress. The government certainly represses the bulk of the people—in theory for their own future well-being—but Tito himself is far from being unpopular. The mass of people are made to bear the most appalling hardships, and any overt expression of discontent would be ruthlessly stamped out; yet a great many Yugoslavs continue to think of Tito as an authentic national hero.

Journalism is not, we well know, an exact science. I can only attempt to report scrupulously what I saw, while freely conceding that there was much that I didn't see. But even restricting myself to the barest kind of factual report, almost every sentence needs qualification. The Iron Curtain countries, we will find, are full of paradox. It would be a brave soul who would be dogmatic about Yugoslavia. Innumerable shades of gray lie between the black and white. Privation, disgruntlement, hatred, hope, discipline, fear, faith—all these qualities are intermingled.

Finally, let us mention Yugoslav stamina and durability. This has nothing to do with Communism; it has to do with the national character. One feels that nothing is going to stop or thwart these people. They are tough as leather, with a terrific capacity to take punishment.

First Impressions of Belgrade

Brusqueness and animation—you feel this first of all. The sidewalks are choked with people walking swiftly; passers-by bump and stumble. I heard one explanation for the crowdedness of the chief streets that may or may not be true—many people feel freer in the open than at home; outdoors and on the move, they are comparatively safe. But I saw little evidence of tension or fright in anybody's demeanor. The rush hours are early in the morning and early afternoon, because the government—to help lessen the burden on local transportation—has set office hours from 7 A.M. to 2 P.M.; hence the employee has to make the trip from home to office only twice, instead of four times which is the general custom in this area of Europe, where everybody likes to eat lunch at home. Most office workers and government functionaries get a second breakfast in their offices late in the morning. After 2 or 3 P.M. they are free for the most part. Then at dusk comes another great rush on the streets; people, having lunched and taken a siesta, go out to stroll and visit the coffeehouses or merely stand around on street corners. I was ready to risk one generalization after I had been out in the streets an hour: Belgrade is the city where every living human being carries a briefcase. Or perhaps I just happened to see streets more than normally full of men and women who looked like engineers, professors, and government employees. Anyway the Balkans were always famous for the number of bureaucrats they produced.

The sidewalks are jammed; in striking contrast, the actual streets—which are clean and well kept up—are almost empty. I stood one morning at the intersection of the two chief boulevards; down each I could see a half a mile, and not one automobile was in sight. Automobiles are, indeed, very scarce in Yugoslavia; practically nobody has a private car, except high officials of the government and members of the diplomatic corps. But there are neatly uniformed traffic cops at the half-dozen leading intersections. The automobiles that do exist operate their own traffic system. Coming to a corner, the driver honks once to indicate that he is going straight ahead, twice for a left turn, and three times for right. Noisy? No—because the cars are so few.

Even bicycles are seldom seen. For one thing they are an expensive luxury; for another the roads are so bad, even close to the big towns, that there would be small point to owning one. Having arrived from Italy, where bicycles and motorbikes are practically as numerous as bambini, I was particularly struck by this lack of bicycle traffic; then I noticed another contrast to things Italian. Never once did I see anybody pick a cigarette butt off a street in Belgrade (which happens all the time in Italy), and never once did I see a beggar in Yugoslavia.

Some of the streets have been renamed; there is of course a Marshal Tito Street, also a Marshal Tito Boulevard; Gladstone Street has become Pushkin Street, and so on. But there remain at least three streets named for Americans and British—Franklin D. Roosevelt, George Washington, and Charlie Chaplin.

Queues form everywhere. Belgrade, like London, has glass-encased public telephone booths out in the streets; I never saw one without two or three people waiting their turn. I went into Putnik, the official travel agency, to cash a check one day; instantly I backed out again, stunned. Each of several queues to the ticket counter was fifty people long. Travel space is an extremely scarce commodity in Yugoslavia today—as I should have known from our trip in.

We watched peasants down from the hills, wrapped in rags and patches; mountaineers wearing their curved-up slippers which look like little canoes; old women barefoot—all so poor as to make the heart sick. And they watched us. Never did we encounter any discourtesy or unfriendliness. My wife is a very pretty girl, who, even though we had been traveling hard for several months, still managed to look quite chic. The New Look doesn't exist in Yugoslavia, and we could scarcely move without people staring at her with bewildered curiosity. Nobody in Belgrade, it seemed, had ever seen anything quite like it. Her toenails happened to be painted bright red, and she wore open-toed sandals on our first walk through the town. She did not make this mistake again, because so many of the citizenry congregated to follow her and inspect her feet.

Even lipstick is virtually unknown in this part of Yugoslavia. True representatives of the people's democracies do not use bourgeois cosmetics!

The streets become utterly quiet early in the evening, and it gave us an eerie feeling to look out of our hotel window at midnight. A squad of workers was washing the streets down; these are cleaned every night, even if there has been a cloudburst. Also the bright street lamps (in this part of town anyway) are kept on all night, which gives a startling incandescence to the shiny wet scrubbed pavements, with not a soul in sight.

Speaking of the hotel, it was quite clean and comfortable. In fifteen or twenty cities all over Europe, it was the only one (except Claridge's in London) where we found a cake of soap waiting in the bathroom. It even had toilet paper!—firm little scalloped doilies of a strange tough paper. The bath had a recessed shower in pink tile; the desk was big enough to hold all my papers; the furniture was Austrian—modern in blondish glossy wood. But we discovered that this hotel had recently housed several of the delegations to the Danubian Conference just concluded; the Yugoslavs wanted everything to be up to Western standards of spit and polish, and so they had cleaned it up from stem to stern. Possibly we were using a cake of soap left there by Madame Ana Pauker. . . . That soap haunts me now, come to think of it. Certainly there was none available in any shop.

The comparative luxury of the hotel made the poverty around us even more conspicuous. One afternoon I came back to our room unexpectedly. There, carefully placed next to the mop and slop pail the servant had been using, was a soggy crust of dark bread left over from our breakfast, which she was carefully preserving to take home.

The telephone operator, we found, was expert in all languages, and much better at the transliteration of difficult foreign names like Gunther than the switchboard girls in Rome or Venice. Everybody on the staff spoke at least one Western language; we felt quite at home with everybody, and the atmosphere was cozy and secure. Then at lunch we met a friend who mentioned casually, "Oh, by the way, two of the servants at your hotel were arrested this morning, did you know? One was that phone girl who speaks English so well. How do I happen to know already? My dear fellow, news does get around in this place! Why were they arrested? Goodness gracious, somebody didn't like the color of their hair!"

I knew Belgrade reasonably well before the war, and am fairly callous to the inconveniences of Balkan travel. But my wife, though she has been in western Europe often, had never been east of the Adriatic before. We walked down to the nearest coffeehouse one morning. She was almost blinded by shock. She literally could not believe the squalor that she saw. I had not been too much struck by Belgrade's poverty (Belgrade has always been a city full of poor), nor by Balkan down-to-earthness, greasy tables, or dirty fingernails. But this was worse even than the breakfast on the train, and I saw it the more sharply through my wife's incredulous eyes. Here were crudenesses and filth almost beyond belief.

Then a day or so later an American friend took us out to Avala, a restaurant in the hills nearby, maintained by the state itself as a kind of black market haven for foreign diplomats and the like. I blinked. I gulped. It reminded me of Moscow in the days when the Russians, for a short interval, set up a few cafés and restaurants as a deliberate means of draining off foreign exchange from tourists. I saw bottles of Scotch whisky at a well-stocked bar; the tables were cozily set on a terrace with white napery and flashing silver; the waiters were well trained and polite; we had caviar flown in (or so I imagine) from the Black Sea and coffee, actual coffee; the bill for five was about $60.

The scarcest thing in Belgrade is meat. We always scurried to get to the restaurants early, before the first customers ate what meat there might be, if any. I have a great fondness for a Serbian meat sausage known as *cerbabcici* (spelling approximate); I explored several places I had known before the war but I never found any; when I mentioned this lost delicacy to Serb friends, they shook their heads sadly and said that, alas, *cerbabcici* was no more.

Our hostess at a dinner party told us that she had got up at 5 A.M. to scour the markets to get a roast for that evening. Yet Yugoslavia is a peasant country, normally swarming with livestock; moreover the Serbs, like all the Slavs, are great meat eaters. Deductions: (1) the peasants are withholding their produce; (2) the government is seizing meat for export.

But to return to other more concrete impressions. Very early the morning after our arrival we were awakened by a tremendous racket outside the hotel. We leaned out, and saw battalions of young people marching. Often later we ran into these parades. They are of the Voluntary Labor groups who give up several hours a week, mostly on Sunday or late in the afternoons, to work on government construction projects. They sing as they march, without any musical instruments or bands; I watched their faces, which were alert, almost rapt, though hardened by suffering; I looked at their clothes, which were appalling. The leader of each detachment, who bears a big flag aloft, wears a blue shirt; his followers wear what they have. In my whole life, I have never seen anything so ragged and pitiably unkempt. Most of the marchers were in their teens or early twenties; the girls wore trousers mostly, with their hair either cropped short or heavily braided. They were just as full of snap and vigor as the men. Everybody marched with fervor, in fact. And why not? These are the youthful Communist élite.

How voluntary is this "voluntary" labor? Nobody, I was told, would be overtly punished if he refused to take part; but very few people, even non-Communists, could possibly dare to resist the social pressures (from office, schoolroom, trade union, and so on) that virtually force them to participate. In fact, it is not merely the young who do voluntary labor. No age group is exempt, and later we saw middle-aged men and old women hard at work with pick and shovel. One project is "New Belgrade," the federal capital (we inspected the foundations) going up on the swampy banks of the Danube; another is the "Road of Brotherhood and Unity" being constructed to link Belgrade with Zagreb, the capital of Croatia. Incredibly, no such direct road exists; which is almost as if there were no road between Chicago and New York. Also, it is being built by the bare hands of workers—no machines! Almost all the Yugoslav projects bear politically suggestive names; for instance a new bridge at Bogojevo is the "Bridge of Fraternity and Unity." The Communists go in heavily for semantic jargon. The war is never called "World War II"; it is "The National Liberation Struggle."

One story we heard casts further light on "voluntary labor." A Western diplomat—an actual ambassador in fact—found a card in the mail one day, a routine card that reached his home by error (even the best of bureaucracies slip up sometimes) asking why he had not reported for his "voluntary" labor assignment the month before!

Most interesting were the shops—and prices. Again we noted the Moscow touch. The emphasis is all on modern technology and vocational crafts. In the window of the Belgrade equivalent of Bonwit Teller's or Fortnum and Mason you will see brass plumbing fixtures, electric cables, a hose bibb, a doctor's anesthesia outfit, and choice assorted nuts and bolts.

A few antique shops survive; one had the usual miscellany of old violins, pieces of Persian rug, harmonicas, and bits of porcelain. But the place of honor went to some second-hand spectacles and a slide rule. This, again, is just what one would have seen in Moscow ten years ago.

Consumer goods were scarce, shoddy, and expensive. The foodshops were practically bare; we could find no wine, and even the national drink, *slivovitz,* is hard to get. I never saw anything more bleak than a candy shop, with children outside staring hungrily at windows naked except for a few hideous-looking lollypops. You can buy a dynamo, but to get a pair of shoes is a real problem. We saw practically no foreign goods, though one German dentifrice (Odol) was available, one empty store still showed the Cyrillic characters for Singer Sewing

Machine, and, wonder of wonders, we saw some Elizabeth Arden skin lotion. No lipstick or face powder; just skin lotion. All over Europe, even in the most remote towns, one American company that seems to have penetrated every barrier is Elizabeth Arden. We spent an hour in a shop resembling an American chain store. A radio loud speaker played music. The cheapest kind of man's shirt was 900 dinars ($18.00); women's lingerie in preposterously shrieking colors was quadruple what it would have been in New York. The cheapest cotton stockings were 33 dinars (66¢), a pair of pajamas 1485 ($29.70), a toilet seat (we saw these everywhere in shop windows) 167 ($3.34), and a cornplaster 1 (2¢). Here are some other prices:

Child's toy mandolin	37 dinars *or* $	.74
Spool of thread	4.50	.09
One mink skin	7000	140.00
Pipe	26.50	.53
Man's overcoat	4465	89.30
Girl's beret	140	2.80
Can of sardines	57	1.14
Tin funnel	48	.96
Notebook	2.50	.05
Child's teddybear	304	6.08
Imitation leather purse	3100	62.00
Postcard of Molotov with a sunny smile	2	.04

But now in all fairness it is necessary to point out that these are what might be called open market prices; anybody who has a ration card, or who belongs to a trade union or a co-operative, would get most articles much cheaper. Wages are paid partly in cash, partly in a scrip which entitles people to buy at special rates. Another factor is the black market. We lived with strict legality in Yugoslavia; hence, we paid the official rate for dinars, fifty to a dollar. But in Trieste or Zurich we could have got 350 or even 400 dinars to the dollar. The Yugoslav government is well aware of this. In fact one big and fashionable shop exists in the Albania building (the only skyscraper in Belgrade) on the Terazije, with the prices deliberately set at a black market level, on the assumption that the foreigner will certainly be using cheap black market dinars even though this is strictly against the law. For instance an embroidered tablecloth, beautifully handworked by peasants, was on sale for 7,500 dinars, or $150 at the legal rate. But the supposition is that the purchaser will have got his 7,500 dinars for $50 or even less. Similarly a child's smock was priced at the equivalent of $40 in legal dinars—high if you obey the law, cheap if you don't.

I mentioned the postcard of Mr. Molotov. Surprisingly enough, considering the Cominform split, pictures of Lenin and even Stalin are conspicuous on many streets. This is in sharp contrast, odd as it may seem, to the situation in such "loyal" Communist states as Hungary and Poland, where portraits of the Russian leaders are hardly ever seen. Also red flags and stars are everywhere.

I looked at signs in the office buildings. Trade is largely a matter of state monopolies, all cabalistically named, like "Jugodrvo," which handles wood and wood products, "Jugolek," (drugs and medical supplies), "Jugoslovenska Knjiga" (books, music, gramophone records, periodicals), and "Jugometal" (minerals and quarry products). This again is like Moscow. But I do not think I would have found in Moscow (I am not quite sure) the state insurance company with its big advertisements, LIFE INSURANCE MEANS SAVING.

One thing quite impressive was that within two hundred yards of our hotel we counted no fewer than thirteen bookshops. The intellectual hunger of these people—cut off during the dictatorship and the war from any printed matter of consequence—is voracious. In one window were, of all things, books by two friends whom we had seen in Capri a few months before, Frederic Prokosch and the Dutch novelist Fabricius. Certainly not Communist authors! Most of the books fell into two groups: standard Marxist-Leninist works, and technical and vocational literature of all kinds. Then there were sprinklings of European classics in translation (sets of Tolstoy, Balzac, Dante, also Dickens) and a few scattered translations of American authors like Upton Sinclair, John Dos Passos, Jack London, and Mark Twain.

We prowled around in the handsome state bookshop in the Albania building. Magazines in English were the *Lancet, Min-*

ing Journal, *Gas Journal*, and *Building Industries*—nothing else, except a few British left-wing publications like the *Labour Monthly*. The *Rudé Právo* (the official Czech Communist paper) and the Moscow *Pravda* were the only foreign newspapers on sale, and I heard that the *Pravda* was on thin ice. The books available in English were an odd miscellany: Beveridge's *Full Employment*, T. S. Eliot's *Murder in the Cathedral*, the *History of Everyday Things in England*, John Rothenstein's *Life and Death of Condor* (how that got there I shall never know), a volume of Sir Thomas Browne, *Diagnosis of Smallpox*, *England Under Queen Anne* by Trevelyan, the *Oxford Companion to Music*, and a fat textbook on pharmacognosy. The only American book in English (technical books aside) I saw here was Dreiser's *American Tragedy*. The only modern English writer with a substantial shelf of translations was Virginia Woolf. I got into conversation with one of the salesmen. He said that, of course, it was practically impossible to import new books or even periodicals because of the restrictions of foreign exchange. He was pessimistic but not without a sense of humor. "What we have is mostly nothing."[2] But this is nothing to be surprised at. Very few Yugoslavs read English, and it is in fact remarkable that even these few books exist. What is really important is the immense mass of general literature being made available to the people in their own tongue.

Quite near this bookshop is a movie; I looked at the posters, and they seemed familiar though I could not decipher the Serbo-Croat script. Then I guessed—*Great Expectations!* The only other Western movies playing were, so far as we could find out, *The Seventh Veil* with James Mason, and Charlie Chaplin's *Great Dictator*. But half a dozen houses were showing Russian films.

On our first walk we had a shock, and a very pleasant one. Halfway up the main street (I rubbed my eyes) were two large American flags, waving defiantly. Here is the American Reading Room, run by the United States Information Service, with

[2] There was, Cominform rift or no, a tremendous amount of Russian ideological literature available, in French, Russian, and Serbo-Croat. Last year Yugoslav publishers issued 1,637,000 copies of books by Marx and Lenin.

well-stocked shelves of American photographs, books, magazines and trade papers. This library has had hard sledding in Belgrade. Partly this was our fault. A former American ambassador waged what was practically a one-man war against the Tito regime, and in retaliation the Yugoslavs shut the library down. Now it is open again, though under some restrictions, and doing a superb job in its proper field—the dissemination of authentic news about the United States. About a thousand Yugoslavs make use of its facilities daily. I asked if they could do so without risk. Answers varied. But this considerable number of citizens of Belgrade is apparently willing to take whatever risk there is. Of course if anybody goes to the library conspicuously day after day and is arrested as a result, the reason given is not that he was reading American books, but that no good Yugoslav should be able to give so much time to the decadent and degenerate literature of the bourgeois West when there is so much "voluntary" labor waiting to be done.

I asked our American friends when we arrived if we would be followed by spies or police. The answer was that nobody would pay the slightest attention to us, because every available agent was too busy shadowing the Russians, Czechs, and so on, with no time or energy to spare for mere Americans. Once or twice I carefully left papers in a calculated disarray; only someone fairly skillful could have gone through them without leaving some trace. I never found evidence that anything was touched at all.

Nevertheless there is great fear of foreigners. The authorities take great care, as in Moscow, to keep at a minimum any contacts between outsiders and the local citizenry. We went to one Western dinner to which a Yugoslav official had been invited; our host and hostess waited with palpitating interest to see if he would dare show up. (He did.) But he had been obliged to ask permission of his superiors first.[3] One evening we had dinner in a restaurant (no meat, no wine, omelettes and cheese only,

[3] This Yugoslav gave me a nice preliminary insight on what some Communists think of the United States. He said that he admired Americans but that he deplored our habit of measuring everything in terms of money. "If a girl is pretty enough, you call her a million dollar baby!"

price for five about $20), and noticed a pretty girl at a nearby table. She was an interpreter in the foreign office, and she would have been a pleasant addition to our party. But we could not ask her to sit down because she had not yet been "cleared" by the authorities for "free contact" with foreign journalists.

A foreign embassy, which may need a lawyer for such a routine business as checking a lease or a doctor for somebody's stomach-ache, will have considerable difficulty getting proper professional attention, because most Yugoslav doctors and lawyers are afraid to be seen with foreigners. Lawyers are now "assigned" by the government to each embassy. A foreign business house in Yugoslavia needs interpreters of course; these have to be segregated and put to work in different quarters, if possible, in order to keep them from falling under suspicion and getting into trouble. The cook at one legation noticed one cold night that the Yugoslav sentry in his box outside was shivering, and she brought him a cup of coffee. He was promptly accused of "fraternization" and taken off duty the next day. At another legation another guard was transferred because he played with the foreigner's dog.

Family Lunch and Mr. Z.

Let nobody think that Yugoslav Communists eat babies for breakfast. Somehow the silly illusion persists among Americans that Bolsheviks wear shaggy beards, have manners as rude as their eyeglasses are thick, and harangue the casual visitor as if he were at a revival meeting. It is indeed true that many Communists are contemptuous of what they call bourgeois ethics, and that they consider themselves entitled to use any weapon whatever in their dealings with the Western world, which (so they rationalize) does not have the sense to realize that it is doomed, and hence makes necessary the continuation of laborious class conflict. I think that many Communists are genuinely sad that, as they put it, they are forced to sacrifice ethical values in order to gain what they consider to be their inevitable historical ends. Be this as it may be, many Communists we met were persons of considerable cultivation, discriminating intellectual equipment, and deep devotion to a cause they consider literally sacred. Also their table manners are perfectly good, they love their families, they dress neatly, and they are chockful of such bourgeois virtues as humility, obedience, self-respect, and diligence.

Someone whom I shall call Mr. Z. telephoned us one day and asked us to lunch. Mr. Z. is one of the most influential Communists in Yugoslavia. This was the first time in a good many years I had been asked to an intimate social occasion in the home of a responsible Communist official. So my curiosity was keen. A small villa with a lovingly tended garden; four or five simply decorated rooms including a good workmanlike library; a wife whom Mr. Z. obviously adored, and who adored him; a very pretty child; an apèritif and then a modest lunch with free talk, badinage, and laughter ("Ha, ha! So how do you find our Iron Curtain!" was the remark with which our host greeted my wife); then coffee and cigarettes and the luxury of a fresh peach for dessert in the sunny garden—all this made the scene, and so far as physical atmosphere was concerned, we might have been in the home of a $6,000-a-year engineer in Saskatchewan, a hard-working young architect in Queens, or an associate professor of economics at a university in the middle west.

I began to see what a new world I was in when I asked a question or two about education and the struggle being waged against illiteracy.

We take so much for granted in the United States! It had never occurred to me that in the Balkans (whether or not under Communism) literacy was so closely interlocked with two problems seemingly far afield—housing and electricity. Why? Because, Mr. Z. told us, obviously a peasant returning home from hard work in the fields all day couldn't devote himself to adult education at night if his dwelling had no light. Nor can a workman in the town easily study his ABC's if he has to share a room with seven others. Actually in Yugoslavia boys who were taught to read while in the Partisan army have now begun to forget their hard-learned literacy because of these circumstances. So when one mutters a catchword like "education" it is well to remember that it is a fighting word in this area and means the confrontation of a whole intermixed web of political and economic difficulties, not just the limitations of books and teachers.

When we broke up after lunch I got another glimpse that this was not, after all, Saskatchewan or the campus of Ohio State. "What a pity!" our host exclaimed, "what a pity it is that the world is divided into two hostile spheres! You on your side, with all the wealth and material resources! We on ours, with all the brains and wisdom!"

He was perfectly serious. It should never be forgotten that Communist leaders behind the Curtain believe in their mode of life and philosophy and political behavior just as fervently as we do in ours—if not more.

Later I called on Mr. Z. at his office. It was after hours. The doorman looked surprised when I came in, and dashed with quick courtesy to run the elevator himself. There is a great friendliness and informality about Balkan folk, once you break through the protective crust. (I found, incidentally, that the secretaries of big Communist personalities, particularly the girls who answered the phone, were almost always aloof and distrustful at first; only when they were absolutely sure that the boss was also friendly would they be friendly too.) Mr. Z. and I talked alone at considerable length. He was, and is, a person of superior and cool, not hot, intelligence. Until this moment I had always assumed that the locution "People's Democracy" was used by Communists with cynical tongue in cheek. But Mr. Z. really *believed* that Yugoslavia *was* really a democracy. We went over this over and over, arguing it from every side; it was beyond my power to disconvince him, and beyond his to disconvince me. He talked among other things about Cromwell and Robespierre—they were authoritarian, but were they not good democrats also? I was forced to face the question of what it was that *made* a man so intelligent *believe* in some things that were (I thought) demonstrably untrue. A major part of the secret of the success of Communism resides in this paradox. The Communists profess to be devotees of reason, but in fact they are mainly moved by obedience to faith.

We talked at length about war. Like almost all the satellite chieftains I met, he did not think war was likely unless America attacked. But I put forward the following hypothesis which had once been suggested to me by a famous publicist in the United States: "You Communists got Russia by reason of World War I, and much of Europe and Asia by World War II. Realistically, why should you not actively hope for World War III, on the presumption that the rest of the world will then fall to your arms?"

Mr. Z. laughed. His confidence was sublime: "We do not need a war, because we will win anyway, by the sheer power of our ideas!"

Then he paused a moment and exclaimed: "How can you doubt it? Our movement was created eighty years ago by two men in, of all places, the British Museum. And now we have one-third of the earth! You ask us to risk all that by stupid, unnecessary war?"

Talk like this can be frightening. Before the summer was over I met half a dozen Mr. Z.'s. Do not mistake it: these men are fanatics; they are incorruptible except in terms of power; their strongest ally is the ineptness and selfishness of capitalist democracy; they are confident, durable, skilled, and very dangerous. And we have a duty to try to learn from them.

Finally I asked Mr. Z. a question on a personal level, "How did you yourself happen to become a Communist?"

The answer came with a chuckle of delight, and it surprised me: "Woodrow Wilson!"

Mr. Z. explained—I must foreshorten some of the pictorial details—that his father was a passionate Serb patriot; the family lived in Istria and young Mr. Z. grew up during the First World War nourished on a flaming chauvinism and hatred of the Austro-Hungarian oppressors. One day his father came home and surreptitiously showed the boy a photograph of a gaunt man with pince-nez, Woodrow Wilson. Wilson had just announced the Fourteen Points; he was promising self-determination to all the peoples of the corrupt old empire. Came the armistice. And, as Wilson promised, freedom—freedom!—followed it. Young Mr. Z. dashed with happy excitement down the streets; he literally sobbed with exploding joy. Freedom lasted exactly nine days—at which time the Italians took the area over! So Mr. Z. was a slave once more. He determined then and there never to be a slave again. He finished school and fled abroad. I interrupted to say that all this was a familiar enough pattern to me—that his story was duplicated a hundred times in my experience, the conventional story of a Balkan political exile moved by nationalist pride. Where, I asked, did Marx come in? "Ah!" Mr. Z. explained, "That is just the point!" He read a couple of years in the libraries. And Marx taught him that the only solution to the evils and excesses of competitive nationalism was international socialism. So he became a Socialist, a Communist, a conspirator, an agitator, and eventually one of Tito's own Partisans—all out of a germ (so he says) originating with an American gentleman who was first president of an eastern seaboard university and then of the United States.

But Mr. Z., I make bold to point out, has not yet quite escaped from nationalism. Marx taught him much, but not enough. Because nationalism is the root basis of the quarrel now going on between Tito, Mr. Z.'s master, and the Kremlin.

Yugoslavia, Its Girth, Problems, and Politics

Yugoslavia, once called the Kingdom of Serbs, Croats and Slovenes, known officially today as the Federal People's Republic of Yugoslavia (FPRY), may connote to many Americans a vague Balkan something-or-other of no particular beam and bulk. But as all of us should know this country is one of the most powerful in Europe. Next to the Red army itself, that of the Yugoslavs is probably the strongest on the continent. Roughly 10 percent of the troops are women, incidentally. Also Yugoslavia is much bigger and more substantial than most people realize; it stretches from the plains of Hungary almost to the Aegean, and from the Alpine gateway of Austria along the eastern shore of the Adriatic to the frontiers of Greece.[4] This geography has, too, great strategic implications.

Ever since it was created in 1919 the basic problems of this husky country have been two: political consolidation and how to sell its grain; it is 65 percent agricultural, and even today

[4] I have paraphrased a few sentences here and below from *Inside Europe*.

(no matter what strides industrialization may have made) 54 percent of its exports are agrarian. Almost from the beginning it was torn by angry domestic quarrels. The chief of these was the permanent and apparently insoluble rift between the Serbs, Balkan folk centering on Belgrade, and the dissident Croats in the north. The Serbs use the old Russian script and are Greek Orthodox in religion, with a strong substratum of Turkish culture; they are basically pan-Slav, and have intermittently had strong ties to Moscow. The Croats are gentler folk, representing a much more European type of culture, who lived for centuries in the orbit of Vienna; they are Roman Catholic for the most part (as are the neighboring Slovenes), and they use the Latin alphabet; they have usually had strong pro-German leanings. The Croats number roughly one-third of the total population.

Then—at least in passing—one should mention other main subdivisions of the old kingdom, which are now the constituent republics of Tito's realm: Montenegro, populated by isolated and primitive mountain folk; Bosnia, where Turkish and Moslem influences still survive strongly, and Macedonia, an ethnological crazy-patch famously overlapping into Bulgaria and Greece.

Before World War II the Serb-Croat quarrel was probably the fiercest intrastate dispute in Europe. It was the complete failure of Serb-Croat relations under a parliamentary regime that forced the late King Alexander to install his ill-fated dictatorship. It is difficult to appreciate nowadays the intensity of passion that attended this epoch. The Serbs called the Croats lazy troublemakers. The Croats called the Serbs "Mexicans" and "bandits." The Croats said they would prefer even the old Austro-Hungarian monarchy to the dragooning tyranny of Alexander. The Serbs scoffingly quoted the old proverb that if there were only three Croats left alive, there would be four Croat political parties, and that the Croats had done everything for independence for a thousand years—except fight for it.

It is Tito's chief claim to lasting accomplishment that he has, to a large extent, ameliorated this tragic quarrel, and so consolidated this young country into greater unity, most observers agree, than it has ever had before.

Yugoslavia has one considerable uniqueness among the satellites; it is the only one that liberated itself during World War II. It is quite true that the Russian armies entered Yugoslavia at the end, and were welcomed as "liberators," but their active role was minor. The Yugoslavs did the job themselves. They created their own resistance to the Axis, fought their own campaigns against Germans, Italians, Hungarians, and Bulgarians—brilliantly successful guerrilla campaigns which at one time tied up as many as twenty-eight enemy divisions—and came out the winner. Not only did the pro-Ally Yugoslavs have the foreign Axis forces to fight and overcome; they had to fight a civil war on the side, against the Ustashi, Croat separatists and terrorists. Also, as everybody knows, bitter fratricidal fighting took place between the first great leader of the resistance, General Draja Mikhailovic, who led the Chetniks, and Tito's Partisans. Possibly Tito could not have won except for American and British aid. Churchill backed him from early 1943. Ironic as it may seem today, Tito was, in a way, a creation of Winston Churchill's. For a time the British Prime Minister, enraptured by the Partisans, even got into the habit of calling Yugoslavia "Titoland."[5]

Tito set up his National Committee of Liberation as a provisional government in November 1943, Belgrade was liberated, and the last Germans were scoured out of the country. A period of consolidation followed. Then the Tito forces held what purported to be a national election in November 1945, and in the Balkan manner won with 88.7 percent of the total vote. A Balkan rule (all question of Communism apart) is that the party that makes the elections, wins them. The new national assembly then convened and named Tito Prime Minister. I foreshorten here a story that would take many pages to tell adequately. The

[5] For an opposite interpretation of most of these events see *The War We Lost*, by Constantin Fotitch, for many years the distinguished Yugoslav ambassador to Washington, and now a political exile who was sentenced in absentia by Tito's courts to twenty years' hard labor. But Dr. Fotitch agrees on the subject of Churchill's influence. Indeed he views Mr. Churchill as the decisive "villain" of the story.

monarchy was abolished, and the new republic came into being. It has ruled Yugoslavia ever since—for all of three-and-one-half crowded years.

Tito may have been a "creation" of the British (and Americans); this does not mean that the Anglo-Americans approved of what he did on reaching power. For instance consider this passage from *These Eventful Years,* a publication of the Encyclopaedia Britannica:

> At the time of the recognition of Marshal Tito's government, U.S. Acting Secretary of State Dean Acheson made public instructions ... declaring that in view of conditions existing in Yugoslavia, it could not be said that the guarantees of personal freedom and of liberties of speech, press, and assembly, promised in the Tito-Subašic agreement and underlying the Yalta declaration, had been honored. Nor did the elections of November 11, 1945, provide, in the opinion of the U.S. government, an opportunity for a free choice of people's representatives. Under these circumstances the U.S. government warned that the establishment of diplomatic relations with the regime in Yugoslavia "should not be interpreted as implying approval of the policies of the regime, its methods of assuming control, or its failure to implement the guarantees of personal freedom promised its people."

Turn now to the present day. Yugoslavia—the Cominform fissure quite aside—is a unique specimen. The governments of Poland, Hungary, and even Rumania are—as of the moment of writing anyway—coalitions. Many Yugoslav ministers are not Communists as I pointed out in Chapter 3 (indeed the head of state himself is not a Communist), but the government is not a coalition between *parties.* Yugoslavia is the only Iron Curtain country in which left-wing Socialist groups are not incorporated in the government.[6] What does this matter? We shall see.

In structure, as we know, the pattern of Yugoslav rule very closely resembles that of the Soviet Union, whereas the other satellites, in general, still follow the political conventions of Western states. The six Yugoslav constituent republics (Serbia, Croatia, Slovenia, Montenegro, Bosnia-Herzegovina, and Mace-

[6] Cf. *Political Trends in Eastern Europe* by Andrew Gyorgy, *Foreign Policy Reports,* November 15, 1948.

donia) are in theory autonomous as to certain powers and privileges, just as are the Ukraine and Byelorussia in the USSR. It is not unlikely that on some future date the Yugoslavs may ask representation for several of these "republics" in the United Nations. Several of the Yugoslav ministers are exclusively federal and their authority extends over the whole country—national defense, foreign affairs, posts and telegraphs, federal trade, electricity (*sic*) and economy, and shipping. But each of the six republics, as well as the country as a whole, maintains its own Minister of Finance, Interior, Justice, Agriculture, Labor, and so on. To explain further: Yugoslavia has only one National Defense Minister, but it has seven Ministers of Finance, one for the federal union as an entity, and one for each constituent republic. Cumbersome? Yes, but it seems to be an effective compromise between the centralization that good government demands, and the decentralization and autonomy that Croatia and the other regions have always asked.

The supreme organ of the FPRY is, in theory, the People's Assembly, which is split into a council of nationalities and a federal council. The directorate of this assembly, known as the "Presidium," is the chief executive of the government. From it stem the various ministries on both the federal and local levels, the supreme court, the public prosecutor, and such organisms apparently inevitable to socialist economy as the Federal Planning Commission and a Federal Control Commission. Now completely dominating this whole complex arrangement is the Communist party. This, just like the C.P.'s in Russia and the other satellites, is run by a small Politburo at the top chosen from a Central Committee. The Yugoslav Communist party itself numbers about 480,000 members. Moscow says that this is too many; it considers the Yugoslav C.P. to have been vastly "inflated." The Yugoslavs say it is not big enough, but that this is because the qualifications for membership are so strict.

Behind the actual party is something else—another Yugoslav uniqueness—the People's Front. This, which numbers about 7 million, is *not* a "Popular" Front, i.e., a working agreement between several different active parties, but instead a kind of amalgam of the remnants of the old parties and such organizations as the People's Youth, the United Trade Unions, and the anti-Fascist Woman's Front. The People's Front is a very effective device in that it combines in a single instrument the spearhead quality of the Communist minority and a very wide and spreading membership in the community at large. "It provides both mass and point in the same body," as I heard it put. In fact one of the major Russian complaints against Yugoslavia was that this People's Front was "an uninstructed mob" and had swallowed up the C.P. to a point where the C.P. was in danger of losing its identity.

Here is a description of the People's Front from Marshal Tito himself:

> Our People's Front actually represents the political foundation of the new people's authority in Yugoslavia. It was created from below, from the masses, from the most progressive elements, regardless of party adherence. With the attack on Yugoslavia, all the bourgeois parties disintegrated, supported capitulation, or openly went over to the side of the Fascist aggressors, and the masses were left without leaders. Only the Communist party preserved its organizational form. In the most difficult moment, it was the only party capable of putting itself at the head of the masses of the people and leading them in the fight. During the war the People's Front took on an even stronger form of organization,[7] because at that time it was not only a question of fighting against reaction and Fascism, but also a question of an armed fight against the occupier of the country.
>
> Our People's Front, which numbers about seven million persons in our country, is still not sufficiently known to some reactionaries abroad, who spread the ridiculous rumors that Yugoslavia, in the event of provocation, will fall apart, and that then something new will happen there, and I don't know what else. They are, however, very much mistaken.

The chief ambition of the Yugoslav government is the successful accomplishment of the Five Year Plan (again the terminology is verbatim from Moscow), which began in 1946 and which terminates in 1951. Of course this may merge into other future plans. The Yugoslavs will adduce some fairly hearty sta-

[7] That is, it vastly enlarged itself by taking in non-Communists. (J.G.)

tistics to show that it is succeeding in its intention to industrialize the country. But there are labyrinthine difficulties. To industrialize you have to have heavy machinery; but to buy this you have to have customers for your grain and raw materials. The Russians, to punish Tito, have cut off most of their trade with Yugoslavia (although late in 1948, despite the break, a Yugoslav trade mission was negotiating in Moscow), and this trade was of prime importance; not less than 63 percent of Yugoslav exports customarily went to Russia. If you can't sell you can't buy—especially if the hostile West will not give credits. The only alternative is to grit your teeth and squeeze out of your own people every last drop of sustenance, in order to import essential machinery, even if this means starving them. Which is exactly what is happening.

Meantime the process of nationalization of most forms of enterprise goes on steadily; the Yugoslavs have been more thorough about this than the other satellites. Small shopkeepers and artisans are still free, more or less, to pick up what business they can get; but everything in any way substantial has been taken over by the state. Substantial? A decree in April 1948 went right down to the level of nationalizing hospitals, hotels, and movies. Also all ships and barges with a capacity of fifty tons or more were nationalized; so were all tugboats of more than fifty horsepower and all passenger steamers carrying more than fifty passengers (the magic number seems to be fifty); so were all warehouses and power plants of any size, health centers, and even wine cellars with a capacity of more than thirty tons. "The last vestiges of capitalism are gone," the chief of the Planning Commission announced when this decree was passed. "The state apparatus has developed sufficiently to take over all industry."[8]

A touchy point with the Yugoslavs is foreign exploitation. Before World War II according to documents recently issued, foreign capital controlled 77.55 percent of the Yugoslav metal industries, 81.69 percent of machine industries, 78.48 percent of chemicals, 55.5 percent of coal, 60.3 percent of electrical energy, 71.6 percent of sugar, and a flat 100 percent of bauxite. The report points out that at a time (1938) when the daily wage

[8] Homer Bigart in the New York *Herald Tribune*, April 29, 1948.

of a Yugoslav worker was $1.30 a day, the foreign owners of one mining property (the Bor copper mines controlled by French interests) earned 250 percent on their invested capital. Over a longer period the earnings were more than 2,000 percent.[9] Similarly foreign owners of the match monopoly made enormous profits, which were of course drained out of the country. Details like these make modern Yugoslavs foam at the mouth. They have much the same attitude about "colonial" exploitation that the Chinese have, or the Argentines, or what good Americans would have if vast percentages of the wealth of the United States were sucked out of the country at preposterous rates by alien entrepreneurs who gave nothing in return.

The land—which is the heart of Yugoslavia—is something different. All properties bigger than thirty-five hectares (ninety acres) were broken up and distributed to the peasants; the Yugoslav land reform is far more effective than that of Hungary, though the latter has been more widely advertised. But to main line Communists land reform is only an intermediate step, a temporary redistribution; their ultimate object is the actual collectivization of land, i.e., its nationalization by the state and operation through co-operatives. This Tito has been extremely guarded about. He knows how intensely close to the earth his peasantry is, and that the peasants number at least 70 percent of his total population; he knows that a forcible attempt to collectivize agriculture on top of the violently stringent difficulties caused by the industrial aspects of the Five Year Plan might provoke a storm which even he could not survive. So Tito's program subsequent to the land reform has been very cautious though there are intermittent campaigns (merciless campaigns, too) against the so-called kulaks, "rich" peasants, who have their livestock seized and taxes raised. This was one of the minor reasons behind the Cominform split. Moscow thought that the Yugoslavs were "coddling" their farmers, and that Tito should collectivize forthwith. But he refused.

We visited several farms in the Voyvodina and near Zagreb and talked to various peasants. Many of these, as in the USSR, resist to the uttermost turning in their grain to the government

[9] M. S. Handler in the *New York Times*, December 5, 1948.

collectors. Ninety-five percent of the produce of one farm we saw had been taken, half paid for in cash, half in government scrip; yet the owner of this property had spent two months at forced (not "voluntary") labor near the Albanian frontier, as punishment for not having produced "enough." This peasant was by no means poor. We had a spectacularly good lunch with him. What he complained about most were the frightful shortages in things like soap, chocolate, coffee, sugar, clothing. He gratefully accepted some American cigarettes from us, and then hid them; he said he'd get into trouble if they were found. This was a very worthy peasant. Maybe he didn't understand the brutally worked-out logistics of Communist economy: the harder industrialization is pressed in an agricultural country, the greater will be the shortages in consumer goods. That, in theory, all this sacrifice was for the health, wealth, and betterment of the nation as a whole, *in the future*, was not a philosophical concept that appealed to him. We asked him about Tito. "Fine clothes," he muttered, "and look at our rags!" Then: "We were told that what was his was ours, and ours his, but what has happened is that now he has his, and he has ours too." Perhaps I should add that almost all European peasants, if rich enough, are rock-bottom and standpat conservatives. I asked this old man which of the many rulers of Yugoslavia he had lived under he liked most. He answered: "Emperor Franz Josef!"

Later we saw other peasants at other farms and talked to them; at one a little girl kept staring at a comb in my wife's hair. It was an inexpensive comb that you could buy anywhere in New York for a dollar. The little girl touched it, took it in her hand, fondled it, and caressed it as if it were the most beautiful thing she had ever seen, as if she had never seen anything like it in her life before (as indeed she probably hadn't), as if it were made of solid gold.

But it is time now to turn to Marshal Tito himself, and inspect something of the personality of this extraordinary man who has wrought such a revolution in his native land.

CHAPTER 5
TITO

DR. ALEŠ BEBLER, the Deputy Foreign Minister of Yugoslavia and a very able and attractive person, called up one morning and said that Marshal Tito would receive us—in Zagreb—the next day. This caused a considerable flurry, because Belgrade isn't the easiest city in the world to get around in (taxis hardly exist) and a lot of arrangements had to be made. There were exit visas to obtain since we planned to go to Hungary after visiting Zagreb; moreover, these visas had to name the specific town where we would cross the frontier. Then somebody's secretary telephoned to say (apologetically) that we must understand that Yugoslavia wasn't like the United States, and that special permission had to be given even for the railway trip from Belgrade to Zagreb. Then this was countermanded on the ground that the permission for the exit visas covered it. I hustled to the travel bureau to get the rail tickets and found that, by special dispensation, the Ministry of Communications had reserved us a place on the night sleeper. Otherwise we could not have got on. We went to the station, picked up the precious tickets which had to be called for in person, packed, did some shopping for food on the train into Hungary, said good-by to our newspaper friends, retrieved our passports with the corrected visas, went to a dinner party, and were finally deposited by our host on the train.

This was a very different thing from the Orient Express. We rode in a brand new Yugoslav car, well made and well kept up, built like the prewar German sleepers and much roomier and more comfortable than French-style *wagon-lits.* I took a last look at Belgrade as we pulled out. It was striking, in this bare and primitive capital, so dingy in so many respects, to see that flower boxes bright with summer blossoms hung from the dirty rafters of the station. One more paradox!

A youthful official met us the next morning in Zagreb, and our talk with Tito duly took place. But first let me give some background.

Tito, Human Being and Statesman

There has been immense publicity about Tito; actually, comparatively little authentic is known about him, and long passages in his career are still soaked in mystery. It is an odd point: no official biography of him exists. Tito today is seven things: (1) the only Marshal of the Yugoslav army and Commander-in-Chief; (2) Minister of National Defense with control of the army, navy, air force, and police; (3) secretary general of the Yugoslav Communist party and member of the Presidium; (4) chairman of the Central Committee of the Communist party, its leading body; (5) head of the Yugoslav Politburo, the organ by which it runs the country; (6) chief of the People's Front; (7) Prime Minister of the federal government of Yugoslavia.[1]

All this sounds sharp and concrete enough, but even about Tito's very name there is mystery. His actual name—probably—was and is Josip Broz, though variants are sometimes used, like Brozevic. I have a pamphlet before me, issued by a Yugoslav group in New York in 1944, in which he signs himself "J. B. Tito." Officially nowadays his signature is J. Broz-Tito, Marshal of Yugoslavia; more familiarly he is addressed as "Comrade Marshal." Like almost all Communist conspirators, he used several names in his underground days; one was "Valter," and this still crops up occasionally. There are several theories, all fanciful, about his choice of "Tito" as cognomen: (a) He named himself out of admiration for the Roman Emperor Titus, of which Tito is the Serbo-Croat form; (b) Ditto, but the Titus involved is St. Titus, an early Balkan missionary; (c) The initials stand for *Tajna Internacionalna Terroristicka Organizacija* (Secret International Terrorist Organization); (d) The sound "Tito" is fairly close to that of the Yugoslav words

[1] Here the terminology differs from the Moscow pattern. In the Russian republics the Prime Minister is always known as "Chairman of the council of people's commissars." Tito prefers the plain "Prime Minister," or, in French, "president du conseil."

"you" and "do"; the legend has arisen that Tito gave orders, "You do this!" and his followers got into the habit of calling him by a similar locution. Actually Tito picked the name himself in his underground revolutionary days simply because he liked it; it stuck, and it is impossible to think of him today as anything else. Many Yugoslav institutions have been named for him in the Russian manner; for instance the Montenegrin town Podgoritza is now known as Titograd.

The leading sources of Marshal Tito's power are I should say the following. He is a practical man, not an intellectual, which appeals to the people. He has courage, and Serbs like bravery. Also he is proud, stubborn, and patient, three qualities that cardinally reflect the national character. People say, "This Tito of ours is a real *Yugoslav*; he shows how superior we are to the Bulgars and Hungarians and Albanians." Then again he appears to be an excellent judge of human nature; he has picked his assistants ably, and he arouses intense devotion in his subordinates. Above and beyond all this is the basic historical fact that it was he who mainly built up the Partisan organization, who directed it through the most bitter years, and who liberated his country in large measure himself. Yugoslavia, be it repeated, is the only country in the Soviet orbit where the government was not handpicked and installed by Moscow.[2]

Tito's ambivalence about Russia is another source of power, curiously enough. For he is an ardent "practical" Communist—which gives him a close hold on the youth of the country, the devout, and also the party mechanism. But also many Yugoslavs, since the quarrel with Russia, see him as their best defense against undue Soviet pressure and forcible collectivization

[2] Soviet orbit? Let me go into this puzzling business once more, since the reader may still be confused by this double-edged attitude of Yugoslavia to the rest of the world. I have said that although the split between Moscow and Belgrade is yawningly wide and so far unbridged, the Yugoslavs still consider themselves in the Russian sphere. This may sound like a violent paradox. As a matter of fact, it is a violent paradox. All I can say is that it is also true. Moscow may consider Yugoslavia heretical and unreliable. But Yugoslavia, even though cast out—and even though yielding not a whit to Russian pressure—still thinks of itself as an ally of the Soviet Union and a full sympathizer with basic Communist aims. For instance, despite the split the Yugoslavs still co-operate closely with the USSR at U.N. meetings and in other international fields. Also, a point not to be minimized, it is just conceivable that the rift may be healed in time.

of the peasantry. Nor do they forget that in the Partisan days he energetically protected private property (he would never permit indiscriminate looting), and—more striking—he never interfered with people's religious beliefs.

The political basis of Tito's support is, first and foremost, the party organization. Second, military folk who admire him as a soldier. Of course the rank and file of the military have no choice—as of the moment—but to support Tito. Third, many citizens who think that, following the Cominform split, the West may be persuaded to help Yugoslavia. Fourth, many non-Serbs, who like him because he ended the old Serb hegemony. Fifth, citizens at large who hated the confusions, corruptions, and exploitations of the old regime, and welcomed any new strong hand with a broom.

Then atop this are personal qualities. This stout creature is not a lout. Tito is no great intellectual; but this does not mean that he is not intelligent. He plays good chess. He knows six or seven languages well, including Russian, Bulgarian, Czech, and an obscure Asiatic tongue he picked up when he was a prisoner of war in Turkestan. His German is excellent; he speaks it with a good rough Vienna accent. Some Serbs say, incidentally, that he speaks his own language, Serbo-Croat, with a strong Russian intonation. He reads French and Italian, and, as we shall see, his knowledge of English is far from imperfect. Tito writes little. Profundities in ideology have never interested him particularly. But I have seen several of his early pamphlets, which are direct and forceful but which were possibly written for him, and he is credited with being the author of one book, *Borba za Osobodjenje Jugoslavije, 1941-45*, "The Struggle for the Liberation of Yugoslavia."

Most dictators are monsters—either distorted ascetics, frustrated egomaniacs, or men with pathologically bitter resentments against society. But Tito appears to be a calm, friendly, and fairly normal person. He likes to eat and drink copiously. He likes people. He likes to swim and take long walks in the hills carrying a staff. Another quality is his very considerable personal charm, about which people "warned" us in Belgrade. They said, "Look out—don't be taken in!" Women in particular are strongly attracted to him, and he likes them; at a party, he is courtly and gallant, and he exerts a great hypnotic appeal on women when he speaks in public. Also he is one of the very few dictators with a lively sense of humor; one of his most interesting mannerisms is a running chuckle while he talks.

His first wife was, it is believed, Russian. She died many years ago. A twenty-three-year-old son survives, who fought in the Red army during World War II, under the name Zarko Popovic, and lost an arm. Tito was married again, to a Slovene woman, but a good deal of mystery still attends this marriage. By her he is supposed to have had a second son, about whom little is known. For some years a close associate was a lady named Olga Nincic, a good-looking young woman who was his secretary and interpreter; she fought with him during the Partisan wars, and was, of all things, the daughter of a former Foreign Minister of the country, Momcilo Nincic, a servant of the monarchy who was one of his bitterest opponents.[3]

Tito, who is very closely guarded, lives in Belgrade in undisclosed whereabouts. For official entertaining he uses the so-called "white" palace in Dedinje (an outlying residential section of Belgrade) which was the home of the former regent Paul; in summer he goes as a rule to Bled, an enchanting lakeside town in the Julian Alps, where he lives in the former royal villa. Also he has quarters in Zagreb—or, for that matter, anywhere he wants to have them. Driving out from Belgrade one day we passed another of his houses, on a farm on the Novy Sad road. It was once a tile factory. A short round watch tower now commands the site.

The four main centers of opposition to Tito, on the domestic side, are, first, the old Serbs, who despise him as a Croat interloper; second, the "rich" peasants, if any still exist; third, the Catholic Church in Slovenia and Croatia; and fourth, members of secret reactionary groups. These last exist in all the Balkan and Central European countries. They are the only Europeans we met who actively want a war, because they know that they

[3] Cf. "Tito" by Stoyan Pribichevich, *Life*, February 14, 1944. This is the best and most authoritative as well as colorful account of Tito I know. Also see articles by Mr. Pribichevich in *PM* printed in the summer of 1944.

are finished unless the United States of America sends an army in to rescue them. It may shock Americans to hear it, but an upper crust of surviving oligarchy in this part of the world would, if it could, foment any kind of internal trouble, in the hope that this might in turn produce American intervention. Their only hope is war. And they want the United States to fight it.

In one country—not Yugoslavia—a shrewd American ambassador told me that he had just had a painful discussion with a leading representative of the *ancien régime,* a churchman. The ambassador was bitterly anti-Communist. But also he was a good and responsible American who had some conception of the realities of our foreign policy. The eminent dignitary (for whom he had great personal admiration and affection) said, "But of course it is only a question of time. All we have to do is hold out. In the end you will of course make war and rescue us." The ambassador replied that, indeed, war might eventually come, but that the dignitary ought to keep in mind that, if the United States did fight, it would be because of very large pressures and major self-interest on the part of America, not as a reckless adventure for the sake of Scarlet Pimpernels and unhappy aristocratic lame ducks and refugees.

Tito on his side has talked plenty of nonsense about America. His behavior when American pilots were shot down over Yugoslavia in 1946 was shameful. But the persistent campaign of his domestic enemies to embroil the United States in Yugoslav affairs has been an irritation. Perhaps the Marshal hates America so deeply that, like most Communists, he can make no sense on the subject any more. Here is a brief transcript from an interview he gave recently to a delegation of Communist youths from China, Malaya, and New Zealand:

"What, in the opinion of the Comrade Marshal, are the prospects for the success of the American and English reactionaries who are making various attempts to destroy the democratic [*sic*] countries?"

"I cannot evaluate them equally. I must say that the main danger threatens from the American imperialists, from the American trusts and financial magnates. But by this I do not mean to say that the English imperialists are any better. The latter are only less powerful, and therefore the American ones are more dangerous. As for their success . . . I don't believe in it. I don't believe in a large scale war because the peoples do not want war. Great conflicts can only occur when people are more or less prepared to wage a war. The war which the imperialists wish to instigate would, however, be imperialistic on the one side, and liberating on the other. This would not be a general world liberation war of all the united nations against the Fascist peril, as was the case with the last war. No, in this war, the masses of the people in those countries where the imperialists would be the aggressors, would not be interested in the war because they would not be in danger from anyone. For them, this war would be an intolerable burden and shame. The peoples of these countries, therefore, would not fight as they fought in the recent war, in which they themselves were in danger. They would realize that the war was being waged for the fulfillment of the aims of a narrow clique, and the desire for war would not exist among them. And without the will of the people not a single war has been won so far, regardless of the atomic bomb.

"Therefore, let us sum up. On the one hand it would be aggression against the freedom and independence of other peoples on the part of the imperialists. In this aggression, the peoples of the countries concerned would participate, not voluntarily, but against their will, and therefore the result of the war would be problematic. On the other hand, it would be a war of liberation, a life and death struggle of the peoples who do not wish to lose their independence or their liberty. The imperialists also know this very well, and they are therefore using all possible means to deceive the people in their own countries, hiding themselves behind a screen of democracy, and libeling the democracy of the new type, in accordance with the old proverb: 'The real thief is the one who cries thief!' In this way they want to incite the masses of the people in their countries, and to create a war atmosphere among them."

This is well worth careful reading as a good example of present-day Communist thought and logic.

Finally, the Russians are of course out to get Tito. But he is very ably guarded; he learned the technique of taking precautions in a thoroughly efficient school, that of Moscow itself. When he makes a public appearance, the streets are cut off to traffic and houses are searched along his route; his movements are never made public and only a few intimates know where he is at any given moment; I even heard that all his food is tasted. Even so, some people think that the Russians will eventually succeed in getting rid of him. I even heard well-informed people (but not Yugoslavs) make wagers in a café that he would be dead within a year.

Career of the Stout Marshal

No one knows exactly where or when Tito was born or of what parents. He came of peasant stock, and in this part of Europe nobody bothers much about birth certificates. Apparently his father was a Croat, his mother a Slovene or possibly a Czech. They are never spoken of. He was brought up as a Catholic. An "official" birthplace has now been bestowed on Tito; it is in the wild region near Zagreb called Zagorije and known colloquially as "Behind the Mountain." Certainly he springs from somewhere in the Zagreb area. The date of his birth is usually given as sometime in May 1892.

Tito, then known as Josip Broz of course, got a job as a metal worker, which was apparently his father's trade. Also he went to school in Vienna for a time. In 1914 or 1915 he was drafted into the Austro-Hungarian army; he was made prisoner by the Russians in the Galician campaign of 1915—or perhaps he simply crossed over to their side—and then, like many other personalities we shall meet in these pages, spent several years in Russia as a prisoner of war. Came the Russian Revolution. Perhaps Tito was already a Communist at this period. At any rate the vast upheaval of 1917 freed him, and he fought in the Russian civil wars. Apparently he did not return to Yugoslavia till about 1923, when he resumed his old trade of metal worker. He worked in Zagreb and the industrial town of Kraljevica and became secretary of the metal workers' union. In 1924 he was arrested as a Communist conspirator and agitator, and was sentenced to five years in prison (practically all the Iron Curtain luminaries are political jailbirds), which he spent in the famous Mitrovica jail; here he met and commingled with most of the people who are still his close associates. He was released in 1929. Then till 1934 there is scarcely any trace or record of him; what he did in these years is still a mystery.

But I met one Austrian Communist who told me he had known Tito well in Vienna, and also it appears that he lived in Paris for an interval. Tito was a personage of some consequence by this time, and undoubtedly he was an agent of the Comintern. He must have returned to Yugoslavia, secretly and at great risk, several times. He denies having actually fought in the Spanish Civil War, but he seemingly worked for the Loyalists in France as a recruiting officer. By 1937 he was prominent enough to become secretary general of the outlawed Yugoslav Communist party and a member of its secret Politburo. But he was still Broz and still utterly unknown to the world at large. One must try to keep in mind what the life of underground Communists was during this period. They lived in a surreptitious world of stealth, conspiracy, continual harassment by the police of a dozen countries, privation, and dedication. Underneath the calm external surface of Europe, they had an interlocked and explosive secret life all their own.

Came World War II. When the Germans attacked Yugoslavia in 1941 Tito was in Zagreb using the name Tomanek. He was smuggled, the story goes, by Czech engineers—not out of the country—but farther in, so that he managed to get to Belgrade and help organize the first Partisan resistance there. The rest of Tito's story, including the tragic quarrel with Mikhailovic, is too well known to need repetition here. Of course there is no doubt that he took advantage of the patriotic war to further his own Communist ends. One story is that his real identity was first disclosed to his followers at a famous secret conclave at Bihacs late in 1942; the guerrilla from the mountains, Tito, was found to be none other than the old revolutionist Josip Broz. In November 1943, the title of Marshal was conferred on him, as president of the National Liberation Movement. In 1944, when his Partisans had liberated more than half the country, he met Churchill and other Allied leaders for a conference in Italy; the reason Churchill was so impressed by him was, of course, predominantly military. Tito, not Mikhailovic, was the man who was really delivering; Churchill would have made a deal with Satan himself, if Satan were killing enough Germans and driving them out of Yugoslavia. Then came abstruse and labored negotiations between Tito and the Yugoslav leaders outside, culminating in a secret agreement with Ivan Subašic, who was Prime Minister of the government in exile in London, for a regime of national unity after the war. Tito has been in the saddle ever since.

Of course very little indeed was known about any of this at the time. Operations in Yugoslavia were necessarily cloaked by the most steely censorship. Nobody—not even Allied leaders—was allowed to know much about what was happening in the dark Yugoslav byways, in order to avoid giving anything at all away to the Germans. The Nazis, be it remembered, had offered 100,000 gold reichmarks for Tito's capture, and they had flooded the country with posters bearing what they thought was his photograph. But nobody was sure of his identity. His name first began to be printed in American and British newspaper stories late in 1943, and these make fascinating reading now. One of the best was by Cyrus L. Sulzberger in the *New York Times* of December 5, 1943; it was written in Cairo, and contained this passage:

> Anybody who states with flat positiveness who Tito is, is talking through his hat. Not even the Allied liaison officers now stationed with him have that knowledge. The secret of Tito's identity is one of the best kept of this war, and there are reasons for this. Use of an anonymous fighting name is a common practice in the Partisan army. . . . This method avoids the enemy's learning the exact identity of the leaders of the patriots and making reprisals against their families. . . . Furthermore . . . it unquestionably has a certain romantic appeal.

Then Mr. Sulzberger goes on to say that "there would seem to be little doubt that Tito himself is a Communist," that he was born near Zagreb in 1892, and that his real name was probably Josip Brozovitch or Broz. Smart guessing, Mr. Sulzberger!

Two of the legends about Tito that I heard in Belgrade years later appear in this article. One is that there have been several Titos—that different people operated under the same name. I am inclined to dismiss this as unlikely, because the main line of Tito's personality and works (part of which can now be confirmed by captured police records and the like) is so consistent. But it would not have been beyond the realm of the collective

Partisan imagination to have given successive leaders the same name, Tito, in order to confuse the enemy. (Tito himself, according to another story, succeeded to the name when a previous secretary general of the party was tortured to death by the Serb police before the war.) People may die; the name is permanent and immortal; this seems to be the theory. The second legend is in a comedy vein, and it is to the effect that Tito (the Tito of early Partisan days anyway) was in reality a woman. A British officer in Yugoslavia, none other than Evelyn Waugh, is supposed to have asked Tito facetiously if this were true. Tito, a lusty type, is reputed to have answered, "Well, if you *were* one, I could quickly prove that I am not."

Tito's sense of humor, though perhaps crude, is quite advanced. Last summer Randolph Churchill, son of Winston, tried vainly to get a visa to visit Yugoslavia. He finally appealed by telegram direct to Tito, ending with the words "Don't you know who I am?" The story goes—probably it isn't true—that Tito telegraphed back, "Certainly, you are Vic Oliver's ex-brother-in-law."

The terrific heroism and romance of Partisan days have left a strong impact on all those who shared them. Read books like *Guns For Tito,* by an American major, Louis Huot, who partook in a mission to Tito's secret headquarters. Even retrospective articles written today by eye-witnesses who hate Tito's politics are warm with personal admiration; apparently nobody who ever fought closely with this doughty chieftain will ever forget him. And most of his wartime comrades and associates never seem to think of him as a Communist at all, but as an undivided Yugoslav and nationalist.

Impressions of Our Talk

As I say, we were met at the Zagreb station by a young and courteous official. He carted us off in a modest car to a nearby hotel (Zagreb itself I shall describe later) and said that he would telephone in an hour or so, after we had breakfast, to tell us the exact time of our appointment with the Marshal. I noticed that this young man's use of Western languages was extremely limited. In fact he was the only person I have ever met in my life who accomplished the feat of using monosyllables of three different languages in a three-word sentence; he pointed to a street and said, *"Très* big *weg."* (Very big road.) When he announced that he himself would take us in to Tito I asked as tactfully as possible if he could bring along someone else as interpreter.

He picked us up as arranged, and there in the car was someone who looked like a longshoreman out of a job for years—wearing a coarse cap and sweater, without a necktie, unshaved and dilapidated. I asked politely, "You speak English?" and he replied, "Please, you are very welcome." So far as I ever learned this was his total command of English. The nervous official who met us must have assumed that he *had* to find, on the shortest notice, someone who knew at least a word of English, and had simply picked up this worthy citizen—who had perhaps once been in America—off the streets. It was all rather disarming, alarming, and engaging.

Our official explained as we drove along that we would be allowed to give our "impression" of the Marshal but that we could not quote him directly. This was not the kind of interview I had hoped for and maybe if we had argued about it with Tito himself later—we argued plenty about other things—the stricture might have been modified. But I didn't want to abuse the hospitality we were being shown.

We were whisked through a park until we found ourselves before a villa in a garden on the outskirts of Zagreb. A soldier not very conspicuously armed opened a gate in a wooden lath fence, and passed us through a second gate without formality. Here, at the doorstep of the villa, we were met by someone who—apparently without the knowledge of the official who met us—had already been given the job of being interpreter for the occasion. He was a Belgrade newspaperman. So our official disappeared like a streak of lightning, and with him the longshoreman picked up on the street, whom we never saw again.

There was considerable difficulty in getting this Belgrade newspaperman to state precisely what we could and could not print. I had the feeling later that Tito would not have minded having his remarks quoted. But I will abide by the stipulation first set, and give only my "impression" of what went on. I do this also because another official present made a somewhat nasty statement to the effect that all American journalists were wont to promise that an interview was off the record, and then always broke the promise.

A very large dog—an Alsatian crossbreed—leaped out as we climbed to the front door. This is Tito's famous Tiger, an animal with a great Partisan history. Tito captured him from an S.S. colonel during the war.

We were led briskly through a couple of rooms furnished in a somewhat heavy Middle European manner and there was the Marshal himself coming across a third room to greet us. He led us out on a terrace after shaking hands. There he asked my wife and me to sit with him in comfortable chairs at a small table. I was fascinated to observe that the interpreter—and also a secretary whom we were never able to identify—were made to sit on straight chairs about eight or ten feet away. This made conversation somewhat laborious. It isn't easy to have an informal chat with a dictator when you have to talk through people who are kept off at such a respectful distance. Both the interpreter and secretary held pads of paper on their knees. They wrote very little down however.

Conversation was difficult for another reason too; there were language troubles. Tito speaks good German but my own German is not too fluent and my wife knows none. The interpreter's English—though a bit more copious than that of the man off the street—was about on a par with my German. Then we found that Tito himself knew English quite well. He appeared to understand almost everything—once he interrupted to say that he hadn't quite got the last word in a sentence of my wife's, and the word was a fairly difficult one, "fathom." Another time, he corrected the interpreter by pointing out that the correct English for a word he himself had used in Serbo-Croat was not "epoch" but "episode," which shows that his knowledge of English is, indeed, quite sensitive. But he was loath to speak it. My wife spoke French, and I did some translating from German into English. The interpreter was useful only when Tito broke into Serbo-Croat, which he did when he was expressing himself at length on a serious political point.

But the first thing that the Marshal said, after we sat down amiably, was that there could be no talk of politics at all. This was a blow indeed. We prepared ourselves for a nice half-hour of discussion of the birds, the beasts, and the flowers; a terrible floundering moment came in which nobody said anything at all in any language. Then somehow—I swear I do not know how—I asked some sort of question that must have at least approached the political field; it interested him and we were off. From then on we were in politics and nothing but politics up to our necks with no holds barred.

Something may have aided this. A servant arrived with a tray of drinks. We had *slivovitz,* white wine in very large gold goblets, and Turkish coffee. It was still only about eleven in the morning, and alcohol at this hour is notorious for what it will do to improve conversation. Tito, however, drank nothing but a sip of wine. My wife and I had a *slivovitz* or two. The secretary and interpreter were offered nothing. Tito, by the way, smoked cigarettes steadily, using a very small holder in the shape of a pipe. This is one of his most famous mannerisms.

The Marshal looked well. He gave the appearance of being calm, relaxed, and solid. He has no nervous gestures of any kind. The Soviet press has been portraying him as a cowering wreck, which he certainly is not.

He is a heavy-set man, rather short, very handsome, and possessed of much of the charm we had been told about. His eyes are small, somewhat cold, and very blue; his hair, once blond, is graying. He has good-looking teeth, and he laughed a great deal—a laugh good-humored, tolerant of the questions we were asking, not at all guarded or ironical, and sometimes—yes—bored. He wore a white suit with a dark red polka-dot tie, with a single medal in the lapel. He has often been accused of flamboyance in dress and manner and there has been much talk of a huge diamond ring he always wears. Indeed he wore it, but it did not seem to us very big or unnaturally conspicuous.

The range of talk covered everything from the United States

presidential campaign to whether or not Mr. Dewey was an isolationist; from trade relations between Yugoslavia and the Soviet satellites to the work Tito has done to ameliorate the old frictions between Serbs and Croats; from the Marshall plan to whether America ever interfered in the domestic politics of foreign countries; from the role of the new "People's Democracies" in European economy to whether or not Communism and capitalism could eventually survive together in the same small world.

Also we, on our side, tried to tell him something about the United States—about the kind of nation the United States is, what it believes in, what it likes, what it doesn't like, how it responds to incidents, how it is both extremely powerful and extremely sensitive, how it is puzzled by Russian ignorance and bad behavior, how it is in Europe for a long time to come. And Marshal Tito listened with what appeared to be attentive curiosity and interest. Another point is that just before we left, after an hour, I asked if, looking back at everything in the large, he thought that Marx had ever made any mistakes. He chuckled, but did not answer.

In summary I would say the following. Marshal Tito and his closest associates seem to believe: (1) There will be no war. (2) If there is a war, it will be the United States that starts it. (3) If there is a war, Russia will win it. (4) One reason for this is that aggressors usually lose wars. (5) Despite the Cominform split Yugoslavia would prefer to fight on Russia's side rather than ours. (6) The Marshall plan is distasteful to Yugoslavia because of its "political" motivation. (7) If the peace can be held countries like Yugoslavia may well turn out to be bridges between East and West. (8) Yugoslavia hopes to continue to have good relations with the other satellites in spite of the Moscow quarrel. (9) Good relations are possible between the United States and Yugoslavia on the basis of improved trade relations if the United States doesn't attempt any political interference in Yugoslav affairs.

These are, in fulfillment of my promise, impressions only. But I have full authority to give them now, and they are accurate.

CHAPTER 6

THE COMINFORM RUPTURE

IT IS time now to tell the detailed and documented story of the rupture. This became public on June 28, 1948, but we know now, by the published correspondence, that friction began to develop much earlier, and had reached ignition point by March. Tito's first letter to Molotov is dated March 20. But hardly a dozen people in the world knew that this letter had been sent.

So far as the general public is concerned the first intimation that something very odd was happening was the announcement on May 8 that two important ministers, Andrija Hebrang (Light Industry) and Sreten Zujovic (Finance) had been dismissed from their posts. The charge was "deviationism," but nobody knew quite how or in what direction the deviation had taken place. It is always so in a Communist state: policy is made in secret by a tight clique at the top, and nobody as a rule knows which side anybody is on; moreover, the most exiguously narrow dialectical points, so subtle as to be almost beyond the comprehension of an outsider, may determine the issue one way or another. At any rate there was guarded speculation about Hebrang and Zujovic—especially after they were arrested and committed for trial—but nobody linked the case to the USSR; the general impression was that it was a domestic party crisis, strictly a Yugoslav affair.

Then on May 25, Tito's official birthday, some bright spirits in Belgrade noted that Stalin had sent him no congratulations, though the year before the papers had been full of them. Still, this might have been an accident. Next rumors spread that the Cominform meeting scheduled to take place in June was not going to be held in Belgrade, as planned, but in Prague, and that the deliberations would be secret.[1] Then the Manchester

[1] Belgrade was at that time the headquarters of the Cominform. (Nowadays it meets in Bucharest.) "Cominform" is an abbreviation of Communist Information Bureau. This was set up in 1947 by the Communist parties of the chief European countries, under Moscow supervision, as a kind of extension of the old Comintern or Communist International, which was dissolved in 1943.

Guardian correspondent in Budapest got a clear scoop by reporting on June 26 that a crisis was impending between Yugoslavia and the Soviet Union; nobody, however, paid much attention to this story, because it was so speculative. On June 28, finally, the Cominform resolution excommunicating Yugoslavia came out. It was printed in a Prague newspaper, the official party organ *Rudé Právo*; the Yugoslavs had not attended the Cominform meeting which was, indeed, called for the purpose of casting them out; but this was not publicly known at the time. Probably the first notification the Yugoslavs themselves had was this release to the *Rudé Právo*. The Yugoslavs answered, via Radio Belgrade, on the night of June 30, and the whole world suddenly became privy to this unprecedented family quarrel—to the spectacle, moreover, of a satellite refusing to kowtow to its master, and defying Kremlin infallibility.

But for some time dense mystery attended most details. Then, about July 25, clandestine pamphlets began to appear on the streets of Belgrade, which had been printed in the Serbo-Croat language on the presses of the newspaper "Pravda" *in Moscow*. The Yugoslav police did their best to prevent the circulation of these, but plenty were distributed; they gave the Soviet side of the case, and were in effect an appeal to the Yugoslavs over the head of their own leaders. A fortnight later the Belgrade government released a pamphlet of its own, which was at first made available only to party members; later it was put on sale in the official bookshops, while, of course, the Russian pamphlet continued to be suppressed.

The letters read like the angry recriminations of a man and wife long and happily married who are plunged suddenly into an acrimonious divorce. Indeed a principal theme is infidelity. And money is a subordinate exacerbating irritant, as in most divorces. The Yugoslavs are the defendants and, as we shall see from the letters, their tone is hurt, horrified, and at the same time respectful—even deferential—as if hoping that the plaintiff will have mercy and call off the suit.

The Russian letters are so appallingly brutal, dogmatic, and unreasoning, that one is completely at a loss at first to explain why Moscow should ever have taken the lead in releasing them. They are by far the most revealing evidences of Communist psychology since testimony in the great purge trials of the 1930's. But the temper they show—an almost insane arrogance plus misinformation and ignorance positively stupefying—precisely explains why they *were* released. Moscow was so ill-informed and superconfident as to assume that, once the whole affair became public, the Yugoslav people would rise, throw Tito out, and lumber over to their side.[2] Once again let us hit the relevant point hard—an immensely important factor in many of the troubles afflicting the world today is Russian ignorance.

Out of Their Own Mouths

Here are some passages from the letters. I obtained translations of the original pamphlets when I was in Belgrade; subsequently they have been published by the Royal Institute of International Affairs.[3]

The first letter (Tito to Molotov) of date March 20 refers to the fact, of course secret at the time, that the government of the USSR had withdrawn from Yugoslavia its military and civilian experts who had been stationed there. Tito's tone is of respectful protest. He complains at the peremptory methods of the Russians:

> Of course the government of the USSR can, when it wishes, recall its military experts, but we have been dismayed by the reason which the government advances for this decision. [The reason was, as given by the Russians, Yugoslav "lack of hospitality and confidence."] We are amazed, we cannot understand, and we are deeply hurt . . .

The letter continues with reference to a complaint that Soviet agents had been unable to get information from minor Yugoslav officials:

[2] In fact some Belgrade Communist organizations did, it is believed, appeal to Stalin direct before people knew of the substance of the letters, which shows that Stalin was in on the business from the beginning.

[3] *The Soviet-Yugoslav Dispute. Text of the Published Correspondence.* London, 1948.

Your people were told long ago that the official representatives of the Soviet Government could obtain all important and necessary information direct from the *leaders* of our country. This decision was issued on our part because all the civil servants in our Ministries gave information to *anyone*,[4] whether it was necessary or not. This meant that they gave various people State economic secrets which could, and in some cases did, fall into the hands of our common enemies. Whenever the Soviet Ambassador, Comrade Lavrentiev, asked me personally for necessary information, I gave it to him without any reservation, and this was also done by our other responsible leaders. We would be very much surprised if the Soviet Government were not in agreement with this attitude of ours from a State [*sic*] standpoint.

Then the conclusion:

It is our desire that the USSR openly inform us what the trouble is, that it point out everything which it feels is inconsistent with good relations between our two countries.

Once again, accept the expression of my respect.

President of the Ministerial Council

J. B. Tito

The Soviet reply, addressed to "Comrade Tito and other members of the Central Committee of Communist Party of Yugoslavia," of date March 27, and signed with rude impersonality, "CC of the CPSU" (Central Committee of the Communist Party of the Soviet Union), begins with the blunt statement:

We regard your answer as incorrect and therefore completely unsatisfactory. . . . As is known, our military advisers were sent to Yugoslavia upon the repeated request of the Yugoslav Government and far fewer advisers were sent than had been requested. It is therefore obvious that the Soviet Government had no desire to force its advisers on Yugoslavia.

This is as clear evidence as ever needs to be produced—if anybody ever doubted it—of an interesting phenomenon. The Soviet extension of power in central and eastern Europe is not merely the result of Soviet pressure, but of direct and forth-

[4] Italics mine.

right invitation. The undiscriminating have talked ceaselessly through the years of Soviet aggression (and indeed the Soviets have been aggressive enough) without ever taking into account the corollary manifestation, namely that vast numbers of people on the earth's surface do genuinely admire the Soviet Union and look to it for leadership. It would be foolish to minimize the importance of this in underdeveloped and ill-educated sectors of the world; we should always, for our own good, keep in mind not only the outward push of Moscow, but the eagerness of some other peoples to receive the push. It does not pay to be ignorant. Moscow pushes out; but it also attracts. There is a double magnetism working.

But to resume. The Russians now descend to argument *ad hominem*:

> In the light of these facts we can understand the well-known and insulting statement made by Djilas[5] about the Soviet army, at a session of the CC of the CPY, namely that the Soviet officers were, from a moral standpoint, inferior to the officers of the British army. As is known, this anti-Soviet statement by Djilas met with no opposition from the other members of the CC of the CPY.

Of this we shall hear later. Then comes a sentence, "The Yugoslav military leaders began to abuse the Soviet military leaders and to discredit the Soviet army," and next the striking statement, "Yugoslav security organs controlled and supervised the Soviet representatives in Yugoslavia." So—spy was checking spy.

The Russians continue:

> One might well mention that we have come across a similar practice of secret supervision over Soviet representatives in bourgeois States, although not in all of them.

What bourgeois states?

Next:

> In your letter you express the desire to be informed of the other facts which led to Soviet dissatisfaction and to the straining of rela-

[5] Milovan Djilas, head of the agitation and propaganda department of the Yugoslav Communist party. "CPY" means Communist Party of Yugoslavia, and "CC" is of course Central Committee.

tions between the USSR and Yugoslavia. Such facts actually exist. . . . We consider it necessary to inform you of them.

(a) We know that there are anti-Soviet rumors circulating among the leading comrades in Yugoslavia, for instance that 'the CPSU is degenerate,' 'great-power chauvinism is rampant in the USSR,' 'the USSR is trying to dominate Yugoslavia economically' and 'the Cominform is a means of controlling the other parties by the CPSU,' etc. These anti-Soviet allegations are usually camouflaged by left phrases, such as 'socialism in the Soviet Union has ceased to be revolutionary' and that Yugoslavia alone is the exponent of 'revolutionary socialism.' It was naturally laughable to hear such statements about the CPSU from such questionable Marxists as Djilas, Kidric, Rankovic and others.[6] However, the fact remains that such rumors have been circulating for a long time among many high-ranking Yugoslav officials, that they are still circulating, and that they are naturally creating an anti-Soviet atmosphere which is endangering relations between the CPSU and the CPY.

We readily admit that every Communist Party, among them the Yugoslav, has the right to criticize the CPSU, even as the CPSU has the right to criticize any other Communist Party. But Marxism demands that criticism be above-board and not underhand and slanderous, thus depriving those criticized of the opportunity to reply to the criticism. However, the criticism by the Yugoslav officials is neither open nor honest; it is both underhand and dishonest and of a hypocritical nature, because, while discrediting the CPSU behind its back, publicly they pharisaically praise it to the skies. This criticism is transformed into slander, into an attempt to discredit the CPSU and to blacken the Soviet system.

We do not doubt that the Yugoslav Party masses would disown this anti-Soviet criticism as alien and hostile if they knew about it. We think this is the reason why the Yugoslav officials make these criticisms in secret, behind the backs of the masses.

Again, one might mention that, when he decided to declare war on the CPSU, Trotsky also started with accusations of the CPSU as degenerate, as suffering from the limitations inherent in the narrow nationalism of great powers. Naturally he camouflaged all this with left slogans about world revolution. However, it is well known that Trotsky himself became degenerate, and when he was exposed,

[6] Kidric is head of the Yugoslav Five Year Plan; Rankovic is a Vice Prime Minister.

crossed over into the camp of the sworn enemies of the CPSU and the Soviet Union. We think that the political career of Trotsky is quite instructive.

(b) We are disturbed by the present condition of the CPY. . . . Decisions of the Party organs are never published in the press, neither are the reports of Party assemblies.

Democracy [*sic*] is not evident within the CPY itself. . . . Criticism and self-criticism within the Party does not exist or barely exists. It is characteristic that the Personnel Secretary of the Party is also the Minister of State Security. In other words, the Party cadres are under the supervision of the Minister of State Security. According to the theory of Marxism, the *Party* should control all the State organs in the country, including the Ministry of State Security, while in Yugoslavia we have just the opposite: the Ministry of State Security actually controlling the Party. This probably explains the fact that the initiative of the Party masses in Yugoslavia is not on the required level.

The spirit of the policy of class struggle is not felt in the CPY. The increase in the capitalist elements in the villages and cities is in full swing, and the leadership of the Party is taking no measures to check these capitalist elements. The CPY is being hoodwinked by the degenerate and opportunist theory of the peaceful absorption of capitalist elements by a socialist system, borrowed from Bernstein, Vollmar and Bukharin.

Never, in recent literature, has clearer light been thrown on basic Russian thought.

Next comes the flat charge that a man named Vladimir Velebit, who was at that time assistant Foreign Minister, was an "English spy." A suggestive sentence is, "It is possible that the Yugoslav government intends to use Velebit precisely as an English spy. As is known, bourgeois governments think it permissible to have spies of great imperialist states on their staffs with a view to insuring their good will, and would even agree to placing their peoples under the tutelage of these states for this purpose. We consider this practice as entirely impermissible for Marxists." Finally the statement is made that so long as Velebit remains at his post the Soviet government, unwilling "to place its correspondence with the Yugoslav government under the censorship of an English spy, will refuse to carry on correspondence with the Yugoslavs through official channels."

Belgrade Makes Reply

The next letter is dated April 13, 1948, and is addressed not only to Molotov but to Stalin as well, and is signed by Kardelj as well as Tito. Kardelj is Tito's Foreign Minister. It begins:

In answering your letter of 27 March 1948, we must first of all emphasize that we were terribly surprised by its tone and contents. We feel that the reason for [this] . . . is insufficient knowledge of the situation here. . . . We cannot understand why the representatives of the USSR, up to today, have not insisted on confirming such information with responsible people in our country, that is, on verifying such information from the CC of the CPY or from the Government.

Then a significant and eloquent sentence:

No matter how much each of us loves the land of Socialism, the USSR, he can, in no case, love his own country less, which also is developing socialism—in this concrete case the Federated People's Republic of Yugoslavia, for which so many thousands of its most progressive people fell.

The Yugoslavs then make what would indeed seem to be a justifiable observation:

It particularly surprises us that none of this was mentioned when Kardelj, Djilas, and Bakaric[7] were in Moscow as delegates of our Party and Government. As can be seen from your letter, your Government had the information in question, and similar information, prior to the arrival of our delegation in Moscow. . . . What happened was that the Government of the USSR, by its decision to withdraw military experts without any official notification, confronted us with a *fait accompli*.

The letter proceeds to rebut the main Soviet charges, denying that Yugoslav officials had ever "blackened the Soviet system," denying that the Communist party was "semilegal" (as the Russians had preposterously alleged), denying any lack of "democracy" in the CPY, and asking how "it is possible to believe that people who spent six, eight, ten, and more years in prison—

[7] Vladimir Bakaric, Croat Prime Minister.

among other things because of their work in popularizing the USSR—" could be traitors. Almost naïvely the Yugoslavs ask, "Why . . . dispute facts which are undeniable and have been known for a long time?" It is all, they say, "terrible and insulting," even the Moscow charge (which almost certainly had some ground) that the Yugoslav secret police "followed" Soviet "specialists" in Yugoslavia.

Then a suggestive statement: "Love for the USSR did not come of itself. It was stubbornly inculcated into the masses of the party and the people in general by the present leaders of the new Yugoslavia." Plaintively the letter points out that a history of the Russian Communist party was printed four times illegally in Yugoslavia during the war and republished in all the national languages after the war in an edition of 250,000 copies, and that 125,000 copies of Stalin's book on Lenin were distributed. While hurt and angry, the Yugoslavs always try to stress their basic loyalty. They go on to say that national and international exigencies compelled them to develop socialism in their country in *a somewhat different form* from that attained in the Soviet Union, but they repeat (while at the same time protesting bitterly at the Soviet practice of recruiting intelligence agents among Yugoslavs) that their country "is going toward socialism and is the most faithful ally of the USSR," that Yugoslavia is "a most faithful friend and ally prepared to share good and evil with the USSR in case of severe trial," and, once more, that Yugoslavia "will be a most faithful ally" in the future, if need be and if "struggle" (i.e., war) should come.

About Djilas the Yugoslav letter says that he never made the statement attributed to him in such a form (that Soviet officers were from a moral standpoint "inferior" to British officers) and that Tito explained this to Stalin "orally and in writing in 1945." The mind rocks at this. A casual remark by a Yugoslav Partisan fighter, made in 1941 or thereabouts, has to be denied and repudiated by Tito himself in 1945, and is still the subject of angry recrimination three years later. How this episode demonstrates some Kremlin attributes!—sensitiveness, unforgivingness, suspicion, and autocracy!

This is the dignified statement the Yugoslavs (still earnestly hoping to be forgiven) make on Velebit. It should be pointed out that Velebit was once Tito's ambassador to London, and his associations there may have prompted the Russian charges.

As to Velebit and why he still remains in the Ministry of Foreign Affairs. The matter stands thus. Kardelj and Djilas once told Molotov that we are not all clear about Velebit; we never had any proof then and we have none today. The matter is still under investigation and we would not care to remove and destroy a man on the basis of suspicion.

What induces us not to be too hasty with Velebit, is, first, that he has been a Party member since 1939 and before that he did great services for the Party. In 1940 Tito gave him the confidential task of renting a villa in Zagreb in his name in which to place the radio station of the Comintern. . . . Velebit was at the same time a courier. All this continued some time under the occupation and of course represented a danger to his life. Upon the decision of the Party, Velebit joined the Partisans in 1942 and conducted himself well. We are now investigating his entire past. If the Soviet Government has something concrete about him we beg it to give us the facts. However, regardless of this we cannot immediately remove him from his position in the Ministry.[8]

Finally, the Yugoslavs suggest humbly that Moscow send a commission to Belgrade to study the whole matter on the spot.

Russian Counterreply and Conclusion

The Russians waited three weeks, and finally sent an answer on May 4. It starts out by calling the Yugoslav document "exaggeratedly ambitious," "bourgeois," devoid of honest intent, groundless in fact, "childish," and "merely laughable." Then the whole matter is recast under formal subheads like "Regarding the Anti-Soviet Statement by Comrade Djilas" and "On the Incorrect Political Line of the Yugoslav Politburo in Regard to Class Struggle in Yugoslavia," in words lecturing the aberrant Yugoslavs like schoolboys. One section (the letter is 10,000 words long, and I would like to quote from it copiously, but space forbids) is entitled, "On the Arrogance of the Yugoslav Leaders

[8] Some time later Velebit was indeed removed—by being pushed upstairs into a higher post.

and Their Incorrect Attitude toward Their Mistakes." It concludes by refusing to send a mission to Belgrade as requested, bluntly charging that "the CPY, which will not admit or correct its errors, is crudely destroying the principal directive of Lenin," and announcing that the entire business will be put before the Cominform. As before, the signature is merely the rude and impersonal "CC of the CPSU."

Several tidbits from this long letter have special interest. For one thing the Russians demand to know why the United States ambassador in Belgrade is permitted to act as if "he owned the place" (he certainly doesn't) and why "his intelligence agents, whose number is increasing," are permitted to move about so freely.

The Yugoslavs had made previous reference to Trieste, complaining that the Soviet Union had not given them support on this issue. Reply: "Because of the exhaustion of other means, the Soviet Union had only one other method left of giving Trieste to Yugoslavia—to start war with the Anglo-Americans . . . Yugoslav comrades fail to realize that after such a serious war, the USSR *could not enter into another war*" [italics mine].

Finally, the Russians go to considerable venomous length to disparage the role of Tito's Partisans in liberating Yugoslavia. This leads them to a grandiloquent analysis of the nature of guerrilla warfare, which is presented as an invention of the Russians themselves in the war against Napoleon—a conclusion that fits nicely into the new Soviet mythology whereby the inventors of penicillin, the electric light, and atomic energy are all nationalist Russians.

The Yugoslav answer to this last assault is brief:

We received your letter of 4 May 1948. It would be superfluous to write of the depressing impression created on us by this letter . . . It has convinced us that all our explanations are in vain.

Then:

It is impossible for us to agree to have this matter decided now by the Cominform. Even before we were informed, the nine Parties received your first letter and took their stand in resolutions. The contents of your letter did not remain an internal matter for individual Parties but were carried outside the permissible circle, and the results are that today, in some countries such as Czechoslovakia and Hungary, not only our Party but our country as a whole is being insulted, as was the case with our parliamentary delegation in Prague.

The results of all this have been very serious for our country.

But the letter, signed by Tito and Kardelj, concludes, "We will resolutely construct socialism and remain loyal to the Soviet Union, loyal to the doctrines of Marx, Engels, Lenin, and Stalin."

To this the Russian answer is also brief:

". . . The Yugoslav leaders have gone a step further in aggravating their crude mistakes of principle . . . Italian and French comrades did not oppose the rights of other parties to criticize their mistakes. They have on the contrary received blows of Bolshevik criticism and benefited from them. . . . The Yugoslavs are asking for a privileged position. . . . Comrades Tito and Kardelj assure us with words they will show us with deeds that they will remain true to the Soviet Union. . . . After what has happened, we have no reason to believe these assurances. . . . By refusing to attend the Cominform meeting, they admitted their guilt and cut themselves off from the united socialist peoples' front."

And:

Comrades Tito and Kardelj complain that they have got into a difficult position and that the consequences of this are very serious for Yugoslavia. This of course is true, but the blame for this lies exclusively with Comrades Tito and Kardelj and with other members of the Politbureau of the CPY, who have put their own prestige and ambition above the interests of the Yugoslav people, and instead of admitting and correcting their mistakes, in the interests of the people, have stubbornly denied their mistakes, which are *fatal* for the Yugoslav people."

Other documents follow, but they do no more than reiterate what has been said. On June 20 the Yugoslavs addressed themselves to the Cominform conference, once more pleading their case; the Cominform replied on June 28 with its decree of excommunication. Tito was put beyond the pale.

Aftermath

Belgrade took the shock of all this calmly. There was no disorder, and experienced observers could see no sign that any new measures of public security were in force. Tito carried with him the party apparatus and the People's Front, and any known opponents must have been quietly submerged. There was no hint whatever of the one thing that could have displaced him, armed insurrection. Nevertheless an episode like this has its effects, if only by leaving an emptiness, or scar. Yugoslav Communists feel that they are living in a kind of vacuum.

The only overt episode to follow was the affair of General Arsa Yovanovic in August. This general was formerly Tito's close friend and indeed for some years his chief of staff; you may see photographs of the two amiably playing chess in old copies of *Life*. Yovanovic was sent by Tito to Moscow in 1946, and on his return to Belgrade he was not reappointed chief of staff, but made head of the military school. In mid-August he and several other officers applied for permission to visit the inaccessible river country near the Rumanian border to shoot wild boar. The hunting licenses were duly given. Yovanovic then attempted to cross the frontier into Rumania, and was intercepted and shot in the attempt. One of his companions did get across. The story is that, had the plot succeeded, Yovanovic was to set up a kind of Yugoslav government-in-exile under Ana Pauker's thumb, on Rumanian soil.

What the episode really proves is that there could have been very little serious opposition to Tito in the upper ranks of the Yugoslav army, because, if such opposition had in fact existed, Yovanovic would not have felt it necessary to flee. Also it is evidence of Tito's watchfulness and ruthlessness. The Russians on their side proclaimed Yovanovic a hero. (Very few other "heroes," it might be noted, have attempted to escape from Yugoslavia; there is a steady leakage of prominent people out of Czechoslovakia and Hungary, but from Yugoslavia almost none.) Russian and Cominform pronunciamentos about this affair are in the usual idiom: "Glory to Yovanovic! Greetings to Zujovic, Hebrang, and all the victims of the terror unleashed by Tito, Kardelj, Rankovic, and Djilas!"

The ferocity of the Soviet press campaign against Tito has mounted steadily, and is shared fully by the other satellites. He is denounced nowadays in terms worse than Moscow ever used for Goering or Hitler. But harsh words don't break bones. What counts is the Soviet economic boycott, which has been merciless. And the other puppet states, on Moscow orders of course, have joined this attempt to crush Tito by economic means. For instance the Czechoslovaks went so far as to withdraw their tourists from Dalmatia, which for generations was their traditional favorite spot for summer holidays. So far Hungary has been the chief platform for Cominform measures against Tito of all kinds.

But Moscow suffered too, if only because the unity of the satellite ring was shattered and the Kremlin lost massive and irretrievable prestige. One wonders again and again how the Russians could have made such a blunder, and having made it, persisted in their course. They forced their own hand, I heard it said, by prematurely disclosing details of the quarrel to the other CP's. Then they couldn't back out. But the basic reason for their behavior, as the Yugoslavs themselves point out, remains conceit, ignorance, and bad nerves. And the net result is of incalculable importance—that the international front of world Communism has for the first time been broken.

I would not say, however real and serious it is today, that the break is irrevocable on an extremely long-time basis. I do not think that the Yugoslavs can easily back down now, but strange and unforeseen things happen often in the Marxist ethos. Then too—in time to come—Moscow might conceivably have to change its own tune. Remember the Hitler-Stalin pact. The recent shakeup in the Kremlin Politburo may conceivably presage a change of policy in regard to Tito.

Prominent Yugoslavs, when they talk about the break, do so with considerable detachment. They say that the particular and specific items referred to in the correspondence were nothing but contributory irritants. The sole fundamental issue, as a member of the Yugoslav government expressed it to me, was simply whether or not Belgrade had to dot every Russian "i" and cross every Russian "t" on command. The Yugoslav conception was different. It was that a group of independent socialist republics, some big, some small, could develop freely together as friendly and co-operating equals. The Moscow conception was that everything had to be under the spreading iron thumb of Moscow.

Tito rebelled against this; therefore Tito had to be destroyed. It was not so much a question of nationalism as of simple authority and obedience. The Soviet allegation of faulty party "democracy" was simply an attempt to get more latitude for their own sympathizers in Yugoslavia to undermine Tito. (Here I am paraphrasing the words of a wise observer in Belgrade.)[9] The charge of "anti-Soviet bias" was a device whereby the Russians hoped to obtain an easier atmosphere for agents to work in. The derogation of the Partisans was an attempt to diminish Tito's military and political prestige. The charge of neglect of the class struggle was a deliberate ruse to set Tito off on a witless adventure against his own peasants. And so on.

"We resented it that we were not trusted. It was as simple as all that," one Yugoslav told me. "Our belief was that a free socialist state should be permitted to grow up according to its own inherent instincts." This conception, the Yugoslavs cogently add, might well help rather than hinder future Socialist aims, in that Communist revolutions in France, Italy, and so on will be much more likely to come about if each country is (a) given some trust and free rein; (b) allowed to build out of its own specific national institutions.

Was the Break on the Level?

Yes. Some folk, particularly those who think that if it doesn't rain in Kansas or if the aurora borealis changes color it is the result of a deep-seated and nefarious Communist plot, assert that the Stalin-Tito break is bogus. I cannot agree. Travel behind the Curtain half an inch, and you will get from every side

[9] I dislike attribution to anonymous sources just as much as the reader presumably does, but sometimes it is necessary.

evidence of the sharp and conclusive reality of this conflict. Let me repeat that it may possibly be patched up in time, if there are more big changes in Moscow and the Kremlin reverses itself, or if Tito himself is liquidated. But as of the moment, the break is absolutely genuine.

Surely a careful reading of the full correspondence, or even of the brief extracts given above, is enough to disprove the "phony" theory. The suggestion that the entire affair was a plot, designed to pull wool over the eyes of the West, has been dismissed as impossible by every Balkan expert. The theory that the whole thing was contrived out of the full cloth simply will not hold water, if I may mix a metaphor. What would the motive be? Then again the Yugoslavs would not have made the correspondence public in such a manner if it had been deliberately falsified. Moreover, as far as the Russians are concerned, let it be remembered that Moscow Communists believe in two things above all: discipline and prestige. The Kremlin would never have risked the very serious infractions of the former and very serious damage to the latter that the split was bound to produce, unless impelled by the most urgent of imperatives.

The Two Thugs Theory

It was Mr. Bevin, the British Foreign Minister, who once brusquely dismissed the Stalin-Tito fissure as "a quarrel between two thugs," with nothing to choose between them. Mr. Bevin, who has put a blunt foot in his mouth many times, never made a more grotesque or painfully short-sighted error—an error showing both lack of grasp and of intellectual fastidiousness. Stalin a thug? Perhaps. Tito a thug? Perhaps. But still there is a great deal to choose between them. The question of "thugs" has no relevance. A sensitively astute diplomat, which Mr. Bevin is not, should be able to play on this situation as on a piano. The trouble with the British Foreign Secretary is not merely that his fingers are all thumbs. He is like a blind bull not in a china shop but let loose in a labyrinth he cannot find his way about in, even by smell.

The breaking off of an important satellite from Moscow, in

this era of expanding international Communism, is an event of supreme interest. Merely to weigh the long-range philosophical involvements, to judge what leverage these may bear on political developments tomorrow—for instance in places so remote as China—might well require months of careful study. What we have here is the first sign of breakup in the Soviet empire. We have demonstration of bad brains in Moscow, and the blunt revelation that a basic division exists, within Communist ranks, between ideas of international and national sovereignty. Again consider what stupendous importance it will have for us if the new China (to say nothing of other regions in Asia) is Titoist, not Stalinist. Quarrel between two thugs? Hardly!

Here I touch on what is in fact a subordinate theme of this book. The satellite states are not so important for what they are, but for what they may become. That a country as great as Poland, for example, or Yugoslavia, should be a Kremlin convict is both morally and politically detestable. Now Yugoslavia has escaped at least for the time being. Moreover the old era in eastern Europe is gone forever; it is as dead as the Ptolemies, for the simple reason that people, once they are educated, are never going back to feudalism or jalopy democracy. It is almost too painfully obvious; clocks can be stopped, but they cannot be made to run backward. The days of orthodox *laissez faire* capitalism in eastern Europe, and indeed probably in all of Europe, are done with. To one degree or another, the future Europe will be socialist. Most of it of course is socialist already. And the best hope for eastern Europe, it would seem, is the eventual emergence of independent socialist states, free of Moscow, but also free of any other dominations. Whether this will come in my time or yours is not for me to say. But it is coming. Nothing can stop it. Hence the arrival of Yugoslavia into tentative freedom from Russia is so deserving of scrupulous attention.

The Yugoslavs, provided they do not trespass on others, have it seems to me the right to have any kind of government they themselves freely choose. So long as a state is nothing more or less than a puppet of Moscow's, it must expect the same treatment that Moscow gets. But once it becomes independent, no matter with what great or small degree of socialism, and again provided it does no poaching on neighboring preserves, we are being blind not to help.

That the Soviet Union makes frightful blunders and aggressions and commits stupidities almost more than the human intelligence can bear, should not excuse or mitigate the stupidities we make ourselves.

What Should United States Policy Be?

To keep the split from being healed. Of course! But to encourage Tito overtly would defeat its own end; we need to play this game with considerable adroitness and finesse, two attributes which, alas, do not often distinguish American foreign policy. Our overtures to him, if any, have to be managed with great polish, or we will push him back into the arms of his own extremists. Conversely Tito has to be very cautious in his dealing with the United States, because if he should seem to be courting the West too warmly, this will alienate his own fanatic following.[10] But don't think he doesn't want American trade and plenty of it!

Surely a provisional solution might be found in the realm of credits. The Yugoslavs desperately need business with the West, in order to make up shortages caused by the Soviet blockade. They may denounce the Marshall plan, but in their heart of hearts they would love to partake of its advantages. Loopholes might well be chipped out whereby the Yugoslavs could be given advantage of commercial aid without their losing face. This is both a technical matter and one of diplomacy. Good brains could work it out.

Yugoslavia, it goes without saying—but why not say it?—could be an extraordinarily powerful and useful ally in the event of war. The admitted basis of *all* American policy in Europe today is to oppose, check, and neutralize the Communist

[10] In Washington I discovered what difficult subtleties may obtain in this field. For instance the best propaganda approach was judged to be general emphasis on Communist duplicity and arrogance. But at the same time it was considered wise not to attempt any flat overture to Tito or attack on the Soviet Union—not merely because this might cause a backfire in Tito's left wing—but because the Yugoslavs are a proud people who would think it "opportunistic and naïve" of us to try to bribe them.

offensive. In Yugoslavia we would seem to have a situation made to our hand. If what we are aiming at is, in effect, strategic control of Europe, to neglect Yugoslavia which has broken off politically from Soviet domination would be lunatic.

Some Other Conclusions and Results

1. Surely the danger, remote anyway, that Russia will make war in the foreseeable future is reduced considerably, since from the Kremlin point of view the great Yugoslav flank stretching from the Danube to the Adriatic can no longer be counted on as secure. This sector is vital to Soviet strategy, and the fact that the Russians think it disloyal weakens their over-all position and consequently should be a severe deterrent to aggressiveness.

2. On the other hand, Russian loss of prestige over the Tito affair has served to make the Kremlin stiffer in its diplomatic opposition to the Western powers. The Russians feel a deep necessity to regain their prestige, especially in the eyes of their own partners. This is one explanation of the Soviet blockade of Berlin. So what Tito did in remote Belgrade has already had drastic effects on American policy in Washington.

3. Very important stirrings and fermentations are already apparent in most of the other satellites, below the surface. A dramatic shakeup has occurred in the Bulgarian Politburo, and there have been widespread purges of "rightist," "nationalist," "deviationist," and "Titoist" elements in Czechoslovakia, Hungary, and in particular Poland.

4. The split has brought some surcease to the people of Yugoslavia itself—for instance when we were in Belgrade the bread ration was suddenly raised—though the concessions have been meager. For at all costs Tito must maintain the loyalty of his own administration.

5. Tito himself has risen in stature. His prestige in the country is probably higher than it has ever been. He is closer to the people and he has learned a great deal. Certainly this is one of the most interesting characters of modern times.

CHAPTER 7
MEN AROUND TITO

THE Russians, with Tito's defection sticking in their throats, have four alternatives. Punish Tito they must; otherwise there may be other serious defections. This recalcitrant Yugoslav must be brought to heel. He is more than a mere Henry the Eighth. Excommunication is not punishment enough for heresy so heinous.

The first alternative would be to make war on Tito, which is an obvious impossibility. Second, threaten him with economic sanctions directly or through the other border states. This is what is happening now, but the procedure is not without risk, because the greater the pressure on Tito, the greater the possibility that he may line up overtly with the West. Third, instigate a counterrevolution against him. Fourth, bump him off.

But it isn't going to be easy to foment insurrection in Yugoslavia or assassinate Tito. Also, the men close to him are, so far as one can judge, almost fanatically loyal; even if he were removed, they themselves would carry on. This, aside from their intrinsic interest, is what gives them such importance. Of course quarrels and jealousies might easily develop; Communism is always full of schisms. Just the same, three men at least are so close to the Marshal at the moment, and their careers and functions are so intimately notched together, that Yugoslavia might well be called an actual quadrumvirate. Tito is of course the chieftain. The others are Kardelj, Rankovic and Djilas.

Several common denominators exist among these three. They are almost completely unknown outside Yugoslavia, but they exert substantial power. They are all comparatively young, they were buffed and hammered in the hard school of Tito's own Partisans, they suffered long terms in jail, they were trained politically in Moscow, and they are both intellectuals and soldiers. The dominant characteristic of each is a fanatic belief in militant revolutionary Communism. And, of course, as we have just seen, they are closely bound together by being the chief "culprits" in the Cominform attack.

Eduard Kardelj, in his early forties, is a Slovene by origin. Merely to list his jobs takes a paragraph. He is Vice-Prime Minister, chairman of the control commission of the Federated People's Republic of Yugoslavia, and Foreign Minister. It is he who represents Yugoslavia at most U.N. meetings and other international conferences, assisted by his able deputy, Dr. Aleš Bebler.

Kardelj is a member, it goes without saying, of both the Central Committee of the Yugoslavia Communist party and of the Politburo, its supreme organ. He is a member of the executive committee of the Yugoslav People's Front, a vice president of the Yugoslav Federation of Veterans, a deputy in the Council of Nationalists, and vice president of the Slovene Liberation Front. Considering the break between Moscow and Belgrade, it is interesting to recall that he was one of the two Yugoslav representatives at the Warsaw Conference in 1947 that set up the Cominform. Also he is one of the comparatively few foreigners whom Moscow has ever decorated with the Order of Lenin.

Kardelj wears pince-nez and rather resembles Molotov in manner, though he is much younger. He has a high, dry voice, and is neat, colorless and intellectual. He likes detail, and is the outstanding theoretician in the party; when it is necessary to formulate policy, Kardelj is the man who does it, and his speeches are sometimes three or four hours long. He has been called the "outstanding Partisan intellectual," the "chief political architect of the new Yugoslavia," and "the very probable successor to Tito," if Tito should ever be removed.

His history follows a familiar pattern of revolutionary conspiracy. He was a schoolteacher by profession and then a writer of distinction (under the pen name Sperens), an ardent Slovene nationalist and a Communist from his earliest days.[1] He was arrested several times, and in all has spent about five years in jail. His toes are said to have been broken under torture by the Serbian police, and he still walks with a limp.

[1] His chief book is a history of Slovenia, *Razvoj Slovenskega Narodnega Vprasanja.*

Released from jail in 1933, he fled to Moscow, where he was trained for two years by the old Comintern. Also from 1934 to 1936 he was "Professor of the History of the Comintern and of Slovene Social Problems"—so it is on the record—at Sverdlovsk University; then chief of the "Special Revolutionary School for the Balkans" at Odessa. The Kremlin really trains its men! Then he returned secretly to Yugoslavia in 1935, and became the leading Communist agent in Slovenia. He was fiercely anti-German, and fought actively with the Partisans. His resistance nickname was Edo. In 1943 he was the Slovene delegate to the National Liberation Committee which Tito organized; in 1944 he went to Moscow again, met Stalin there, and helped make the new federal Yugoslavia a reality. Ever since he has been Tito's No. 1 collaborator.

Lieutenant General Milovan Djilas, a Montenegrin who was born in 1911 or 1912, is a picturesque youthful character. The wrath of the Kremlin descended on him, as we know, because of his "tactless" strictures about the character of Russian officers. He is a mountaineer who perfectly looks the role he plays, Minister without Portfolio in charge of Agitation (*sic*) and Propaganda. Also he is chief of party affairs and is Tito's personal deputy.[2] At an important meeting the Marshal often sits back to let him do the talking. For instance it is reported that at one Kremlin conference Djilas and Zhdanov did all the hard negotiation while Tito and Stalin in the same room sat smilingly silent.

Djilas was once called "the eye of the Soviet Union in Yugoslavia." Not only, with Kardelj, did he lead the Yugoslavia delegation to the meeting that founded the Cominform, but he was its first permanent secretary. He has, of course, been cast out by Moscow now, but for many years he was a devoted Kremlin follower.

Djilas got a degree in law as a young man, became a Communist, and went through the usual routine of arrest and imprisonment. In 1936 he escaped to Spain, and fought there in the civil war. He organized an uprising in Montenegro in 1941 —against the Germans and Italians—and by 1943 had become

[2] See Gyorgy, *op. cit.*

a member of the supreme command of the National Liberation army, under Tito. Since 1945 he has been a member of the Presidium of the Yugoslav National Assembly, a member of both Politburo and Central Committee of the party, secretary of the party organization in Montenegro, and editor of *Borba*, the official party newspaper.

Djilas is strong, crude, temperamental and ambitious. Because he is supposed to lack organizational ability he is a Minister without Portfolio. Supposedly he is the chief ghost writer of Tito's speeches, and he has even been called the Marshal's "brain." He has the reputation of being ferociously anti-British and anti-American. His wife, a well-known Communist intellectual in her own right, by name Mitra Mitrovic, is Minister of Education for Serbia.

The third of these quadrumvirs, and probably the most interesting of the lot, is General Aleksander Rankovic, Vice-Premier and Minister of the Interior, through whom Tito controls the machinery of administration and the secret police. Rankovic was born in 1909 in Serbia of a poor peasant family; both his wife and mother were killed by the Germans during the Nazi occupation. He is a pale, cold, youthful-looking man, relentless, energetic, and extremely able.

Formerly the Yugoslav secret police was known by the initials OZNA;[3] it was reputedly both as sinister and as efficient as any similar organization on the continent. Recently (just as OGPU in Moscow gave way to MVD), the OZNA became known as UDB instead, which represents the initials for Office of State Security. The populace, even when they were too frightened to mention the name aloud, as well as the authorities, found this unpronounceable; hence an "a" was added to the word, which is now written UDBa or even UDB(a).

Rankovic began life as a tailor's apprentice, promptly joined the Communist party, and at the age of twenty was arrested. He spent six years in the same jail that housed Tito; another prison mate was the venerable Communist leader Pijade, who taught him much. In 1939 he went to Moscow, and in 1941 returned to Yugoslavia to join the fight against the Germans. His Parti-

[3] Standing for Department for Defense of the People.

san *nom de guerre* was Marko. He was leader in a plot to sabotage the Belgrade radio station during the Nazi occupation; he was caught, wounded trying to escape, and imprisoned in a hospital. From this, he was dramatically rescued by a Partisan detachment, and the Germans never caught him again. He joined Tito, and became a chief architect of the National Liberation.

Since 1945 Rankovic has been a member of the general staff of the Yugoslav army, and commanding officer of the national militia. He is, of course, a member of the Politburo, and for a time he, and not Tito, is supposed to have been the secretary general (i.e. supreme boss) of the party itself. In 1946 he became Minister of Interior, with control of the secret police, and in 1948 Vice-Premier.

Tito has chosen these subchieftains well from several points of view. He himself is a Croat, and these three represent other main divisions of the old kingdom, Slovenia, Montenegro and Serbia itself. And one of the three is an expert on foreign relations and what might be called theology, another on propaganda and the third on the vital matter of security.

. . . *And Some More*

Dr. Ivan Ribar deserves mention. In theory he outranks Tito himself, since he is chairman of the Presidium of the National Assembly, or head of state. Strikingly enough he is not a Communist. Dr. Ribar, in fact, when he was a member of parliament under the monarchy many years ago, was once leader of a movement to outlaw the party! Ribar is about sixty-five. As far back as 1918 he was president of the old Chamber of Deputies; he was its first President in fact. He is a big good-looking man, a Croat, and a lawyer by profession. He became close to Tito from 1941 on. They were both patriots, the Communist marplot from the mountains and the respectable bourgeois professional man, and they joined forces to lead one wing of the resistance. Ribar was for a time Tito's actual superior in the National Liberation Movement. Both were furiously anti-Mikhailovic, in part doubtless because Mikhailovic was a Serb. In early accounts of Tito, like the one by C. L. Sulzberger alluded to in Chapter 5, Ribar is spoken of as the Marshal's right-hand man and closest associate. His importance nowadays is largely titular, and his prestige nebulous. Probably Tito gave him the post he holds as a sop to convention and a device to set the dictatorship behind a convenient "parliamentary" frame.

Much sterner—and more romantic—stuff is the remarkable old hunchback, Moša Pijade. He is a Serb of Jewish origin, probably born in 1888 or perhaps earlier and a leading Communist theoretician from the beginning. He joined the party in his teens. Pijade is at present vice-president of the Presidium of the FPRY, and of course a member of the Central Committee and the Politburo. But his importance, emotionally and intellectually, far outweighs his functional rank. He is Tito's paternal mentor. The two met in the Mitrovica jail, along with Rankovic, Popovic, and so many others, and spent many months if not years as constant companions. Whatever ideological structure Tito may have, he got from this shrewd old man. Pijade—the blunt fact may not communicate much emotion, but rotate it in your mind—spent a total of sixteen *years* in prison. Sixteen years is 192 months or 832 weeks or 5,840 days which is a lot of time. Unquenchable, he made the best use of it he could. He translated the whole canon of Marx into Serbian, and then amused himself by learning, from books, seven or eight languages including Chinese of which he is now said to be a famous scholar. He is also an amateur artist of distinction. He has little direct power, but wide influence. Pijade has a remarkable face; very old, very gentle; gray sweeping mustaches fall under a high nose and steel-rimmed glasses; he looks the way your father might look if your father kept a pawnshop on Second Avenue.

Immediately after the Cominform rupture the Yugoslav Communist party held a congress, its first in a good many years. Until this time, the exact composition of the Politburo was secret, though everybody knew who most of its members were. The list at present includes Tito, Kardelj, Djilas, Rankovic, and Pijade of course. The other four are Franc Leskovsek, a Slovene who is Minister of Heavy Industry and who has been a party member since 1926; Ivan Gosnjak, a youthful Croatian (born 1909) who is assistant Minister of National Defense; Blagoje Neskovic, Prime Minister of the Serbian government and a doctor of medicine by profession; and Boris Kidric, the chairman of the planning commission and author of the Five Year Plan. Kidric is a Slovene, born in 1912. I heard him described as "the ablest man in Yugoslavia."

Finally one should mention General Koča Popovic, the army chief of staff, Tito's chief military man, a cellmate from the prison days, and his best soldier among the Partisans.

CHAPTER 8
FROM ZAGREB TO BUDAPEST

OF COURSE Zagreb, the capital of Croatia, once known as Agram, looks better off than Belgrade. It always did. I saw it for the first time many years ago. What a contrast, then as now, between its stately and gracious streets and baroque towers and the bustling, raw-lipped Serbian city! Of course Zagreb, like most things dedicated to grace, carried within it certain elements of decay. That is one reason why the Serbs hated it so. Today the people of Zagreb are still better dressed than anywhere else in the country; the shops have more consumer goods, though these are still crude and scant; the big-windowed clean cafés and modern-looking stores give brightness and variety to the atmosphere; the old cathedral still carries the Croatian coat of arms in red and white tile on the gray slate roof.[1]

In the comfortable hotel I thought we must be in Vienna: lace curtains, flowers, a big puff on the bed, plumbing that worked, and a veritable breakfast. The restaurant had heavy meaty soups and a goulash smoldering with cream and paprika. The clientele was smart. I noticed something in the bar, a new, clean and well-printed paper folder advertising the drinks available—orange blossom cocktail, hot rum toddy, champagne cocktail, silver fizz. It might have been the Waldorf. But of course none of these drinks existed! Perhaps they had been obtainable before the war; no one had bothered to print the list differently. All we could get was *slivovitz,* and not very good *slivovitz* at that. Then I saw that just one change had been written in on this menu; the word vodka was crossed out, and *raki* (the con-

[1] A crazy forgotten note in history is that the Italians resurrected the Croatian monarchy (which had been extinct since A.D. 1089) during the period of their occupation, and even elevated the Duke of Spoleto to the "throne" under the name King Aimone I, in 1941. He never actually sat, however. *These Eventful Years,* IV, p. 785.

ventional drink of Serbia) put in instead. Good Yugoslavs don't drink anything that sounds Russian!

But walking down the spacious streets we counted the movies showing that night. There were ten in all, three French, one English, and six Russian. Once more—Yugoslavia is not an easy country to generalize about.

Almost everybody, it seems, speaks some kind of English in Zagreb—like the first "interpreter" we had for Tito. Many Croatians worked for years in Ohio and Pennsylvania—miners and metalworkers mostly—and then returned and are stranded here. We called at the American Consulate. The consul was out and we asked the doorkeeper in bad French and German when he would return. The doorkeeper replied in perfect Clevelandese—"That guy, yep, he come back soon maybe."

I will not forget (an experience to be duplicated later in Budapest) that two of the last people we saw in Yugoslavia—servants both—shook hands clingingly as we left, with a sort of despairing but stoic hopelessness, begging us to tell people in America something of their plight.

But a few hours before departure I dropped in at the local bank. Here an elderly lady who spoke every language perfectly it seemed, whose clothes and manner showed obviously that she was a survivor of the *ancien régime*, and who could not conceivably have been a Communist, kept telling me how magnificent Yugoslavia was, what a shame it was that we could not stay longer, how glorious were Dubrovnik and Korčula in the summer sunshine, how fortunate indeed we were to have had this brief glimpse of her wonderful country, and how we must, must, must stay longer, or come back soon again!

Our official guide took us for a tour of the town and its environs, and we saw: (a) stout middle-aged housewives and businessmen in street clothes wielding hammer and shovel at their "voluntary" labor (two hours a week) on the Zagreb-Belgrade road; (b) an impressive enough new factory and its housing project; (c) an Alpine hostelry high up a good road corkscrewing to a mountaintop, once a luxury hotel for the rich, now a week-end home for workers, and indistinguishable from similar homes that I have seen in Russia for a concentrated type of spiritual dreariness; (d) a nearby village.

Here the thing that interested us most was the local *Dom Kultura,* Culture House, a room in a threadbare barn. Chess games; newspaper photographs of Tito pinned to a bulletin board; a pile of Marxist tracts mixed with picture magazines; school books; a pitiably thin library for adult education. Years ago I saw this sort of thing in Russia, too, many times. I felt a double emotion, first how commendable—splendid even—the community effort was; second how hopelessly inadequate were the facilities, and how great the obstacles, not merely in the matter of physical equipment—it is no easy task to educate a whole nation!—but in the sense that education which does not produce a free mind is not education. Then, at dusk, we wandered down the dusty corrugated road with blond cows placidly grazing in the fields alongside, and came to the village church. I looked at it, and expressed surprise to our guide that, far from being interfered with (it was a Roman Catholic church), it seemed to be the heart of the village. The guide was dumbfounded at our question. He exclaimed, "But we would never dream of doing anything to interfere with the religion of our people!"

Our travel schedule was complex. To get on to Hungary we had to take a local train, a *Personenzug,* northward out of Zagreb and catch the eastbound Trieste-Budapest express at an obscure intersection named Zidani Most. We left Zagreb at 3 A.M.; and the only chic woman I ever saw in Yugoslavia was the conductor on this train. But she gave us a bad moment—in no language we could understand—by insisting that our tickets were all wrong, and that we should transfer to the express at quite a different point. But we stuck to our original itinerary, though with considerable nervousness. If we were aboard the incorrect train our exit visas (which expired on that date and which were only valid at a certain point) would be no good. We peered out of the windows as the morning gradually became light and watched the stations one by one so as not to miss Zidani Most. Finally we got there. We pulled our bags onto the platform. No porters, of course. There were several hours to wait. We had breakfast in the station restaurant, after trying to find out on what track our new train, if any, would be coming. Breakfast was cognac, hunks of good dark bread, and tea. The train crews and attendants were helpful and polite, and the other passengers impassive. After an hour the restaurant had no more to drink. Rationing is strict. We walked around in the town and looked at the profile of sea-green hills jutting out from the drowsy mist, most of them with a church on top. Croatia will always be to me the land where white churches sit on the very top of the dark green hills.

This Zidani Most is a very poor town. Dozens of windows were boarded up with cardboard, American cardboard too, from UNRRA stocks. Glass is still very scarce in Yugoslavia. One window in the postoffice was marked BEEF IN GRAVY.

The Trieste express came in on time, and we hauled and yanked our suitcases aboard. Our car was Hungarian and it was the dirtiest car I have ever been in. After a while my wife pulled out of our duffel bag an embroidered Venetian tablecloth we had bought a few weeks before, and with hairpins stuck it to the seat, because otherwise it was impossible to sit down. At least we could wash the tablecloth when we got back home. Also the window mechanism was broken and we had to hold up the glass with a belt from my wife's dress.

We lurched slowly hour after hour through the border country between Croatia and Slovenia, along the watershed of the Drava River, until we reached the frontier at Kotoriba. Here came my first concrete experience as to how cardinally the satellites do differ. There were kiosks on the Hungarian side of the frontier selling—who could believe it?—such impossibly rare articles as bobby pins and toothpaste! Then I could not believe my eyes and ears when the train got going again and a tall man in a neat gray uniform snapped to attention outside our compartment and barked in amiable German, in the idiom I have heard on a thousand European trains, "First or second serving for dinner, lady and gentleman!" There next to our car had miraculously appeared a wagon-restaurant, which served as good a meal as I have ever had on a European train, which is to say a much better one than is usually served on trains in the United States.

The customs examination was striking too. The Yugoslav official, a tall boy in an unkempt uniform, pored over our passports page by page. He had never in his life—though a frontier official—seen an American passport before! Which is an interesting enough illustration of how isolated the Iron Curtain countries are.[2] He even thought that we were "officials," as he put it, because the passports had been issued in Washington, D.C. "Ah, ah, Voshinkton!" he kept muttering.

On the Hungarian side everybody showed the courtesy of a grand seigneur. Nobody bothered to open any of our bags, but the *valuta* or finance control was fairly strict. This is the case almost everywhere in Europe these days; you go through the same procedure even in countries like England. The stiffest examination I had was not behind the Curtain at all, but in Holland. Most currencies are soft, and severe precautions are taken against smugglers trafficking in gold, other valuables, or the local moneys. So you have to fill out a form itemizing every kind of cash and credit you may be carrying; in theory, you submit this every time you go to a bank, and then it is approved and surrendered when you leave the country. Always we dutifully filled out these forms, but nobody ever paid the slightest attention to them in Yugoslavia, Hungary, Poland, or even Czechoslovakia, so far as we could see. But to resume. The Hungarian currency officer, speaking German, helped us list our belongings; he duly noted cash, checks, and letter of credit on the proper certificate, and then asked to see my wife's jewelry. She had very little: a gold ornament, which he weighed carefully jogging it in his palm, a bracelet containing some tiny diamonds, and a small emerald. He counted and listed each diamond, one by one! Then he asked us what the emerald was. He had never seen one before, and we got completely bogged down, because I could not remember the German word for this stone. Finally he smiled and sighed, wrote down something, and let us pass, asking us to realize that all this nuisance was in the nature of a favor to us, which indeed it was, to keep us from having trouble on leaving Hungary. Because—again in theory—anybody carrying jewels

[2] But this is the fault of Washington as well as Belgrade, since almost all American passports forbid travel to Yugoslavia.

out of these countries has to have proof that he or she brought them in.

We puffed and rolled smoothly across the southwestern furl of Hungary, watched the people at the stations, looked at jaw-breaking names like Balatonszentgyörgy, stopped at places like Lake Balaton with its scribbled Alpine backdrop, and finally after seventeen hours got to Budapest and were met by a swarm of small taxis bearing down on us like happy ants.

But before treating with Hungary and Budapest I should like now to make a detour. We pause briefly to inspect some other Iron Curtain countries and then examine what might be called the two American satellites, Greece and Turkey.

CHAPTER 9
OTHER LEADERS, OTHER SATELLITES

THE leading personality in Bulgaria[1] is the celebrated Georgi Dimitrov, who was the central figure in the Reichstag fire trial of 1933. The Nazis burned the Reichstag themselves and then blamed the fire on the Communists and arrested Dimitrov among others, who at that time was a refugee in Berlin. His gallantry during the trial that followed, his impudence, the quality of the searching questions he asked in his broken Balkan German, the way he made Goering himself turn publicly red in the neck with impotent rage, and the way he gained an acquittal by the naked power of his wits, won the startled admiration of the world. Nobody knew much about him then; nobody knew what secret eminence he had already reached in the covert hole-in-corner life of the Marxist underground. I watched him day after day both in Leipzig and Berlin. Then the next summer Louis Fischer, the well-known journalist, took me out to see him in a sanitarium near Moscow where he was recovering from the ordeal of the trial. I did not find him particularly interesting, and I can recall very little that we talked about. I thought that he was sick and finished. Certainly I could not have been more wrong.

Dimitrov promptly became secretary general of the Comintern (Third or Communist International) and was officially enshrined as a hero. He could not go back to his native Bulgaria, where Communism was outlawed and from which he had been forced to flee years before, and the Soviets duly made him a Russian citizen. Of course, spiritually, he had never been anything else. That is a point to reiterate about most of the leading international Communists. They are all Muscovites in spirit, even if they were born in Paraguay or Arkansas; no matter how

[1] We did not visit Bulgaria, Rumania, or Albania. I don't like to write about places I did not see with my own eyes, but each of these three states should have at least a brief word.

fond they may be of their own countries, their primary allegiance is to world revolution. Interestingly enough another old-line Communist, by name Vassile Kolarov, also a Bulgarian, who is now Dimitrov's Foreign Minister, was also at one time secretary general of the Comintern. Kolarov is of the ilk of Manuilisky (Ukraine) and Rákosi (Hungary). These veterans all grew up together.

The Comintern was dissolved in 1943 when temporarily and for their own good reasons the Soviets dropped international revolutionary tactics, and Dimitrov slipped back into the Moscow shadows. But I have no doubt he was kept busy. During World War II in fact he was one of Stalin's closest advisers on international questions, and he was naturally the Kremlin's chief expert on anything to do with Bulgaria, just as Ana Pauker superintended Rumanian affairs and so on. The Russians had, and have, bureaus and experts for every country. Bulgaria was liberated by the Red army in September 1944, and Dimitrov returned to his native land. He resumed his original Bulgarian citizenship, took his place as leader of the Bulgarian Communist party, and in November 1946 was named Prime Minister. He has held this post and been the master of Bulgaria ever since.

Dimitrov and Tito have had very close relations. Even if they seldom met before the war, they have probably known everything there was to know about each other as fellow conspirators for twenty years. As far back as 1944 an agreement was made for an eventual merger of Yugoslavia and Bulgaria; Tito was to have been Prime Minister of the combined federal government, with Nikola Petkov, leader of the Bulgarian Agrarian party, about whom more anon, as Deputy Prime Minister. The plan fell through, because the big powers—the United States, Britain, and Russia alike—united to oppose it. Then in 1947 Tito and Dimitrov met in Bled, and signed a secret protocol for the fusion of the two countries into a new state, the Union of South Slav Peoples Republics, to which Albania was to have been invited to join later. Thus the old dream of a genuine Balkan federation, which might have terminated the angry territorial bickerings and frontier jostlings of this area, appeared to be about to achieve reality. But this time Moscow abruptly countermanded it. The Russians apparently feared that the formation of such a Balkan bloc might give too much local power to its leaders. Dimitrov had been the prime mover in this business. Moscow rebuked him. The *Pravda* sharply informed him that it was the business of the satellites "to strengthen their own popular democracies" rather than go in for grandiose ideas of federation. Dimitrov recanted and apologized. He said that he had been misled and was guilty of the offense of "overenthusiasm." In other words, brought to book by Moscow, he did what Tito subsequently did not do—he gave in. And the Kremlin promptly pardoned him as a repentant sinner.[2]

Now, of course, since Tito has been evicted from the Cominform, relations between Bulgaria and Yugoslavia are strained and bitter. In fact they have never been worse. One interesting point is that Bulgaria, which has always been more eager for a settlement than her bigger and more powerful sister, pretended for a while that the Tito schism was simply a party matter which did not reach the "governmental" level; in other words, that even if Tito were an ideological outcast the two countries might still get together politically. But events quickly outpaced this hope. The nugget of dispute between the two countries is, and has been since Turkish times, Macedonia. Both Bulgars and Yugoslavs accuse each other of hungry designs on each other's part of this sorely torn and divided province. The best solution would be what Tito and Dimitrov themselves had hoped for and agreed on—an autonomous Macedonia incorporating areas on both sides of the frontier within a federation. But since the Cominform split fulfillment of this is patently impossible, and anyway the Kremlin would have none of it.

On two counts—remote as it may seem to the average reader—this is of considerable interest. First, the Macedonian question is dangerous. It has been a contributory cause to more than one unpleasant war. Second, it brings up the fundamental question which I alluded to briefly in Chapter 3 above, namely whether or not consolidation of the Communist system will tend to diminish the fierce nationalisms for which Eastern and Central Europe are so notorious. In theory it might be assumed that,

[2] *Life,* March 1, 1948. A city has recently been named for him, Dimitrovgrad.

since the various consociate nations are brethren under the Moscow banner, the Kremlin would do its best to iron out any territorial and minority disputes remaining between them. But it has not altogether worked out this way. It is indeed possible that the Russians are not averse actually to maintaining trouble spots among the satellites, because this gives them opportunity, if necessary, to play one off against another. For instance Transylvania could be useful as a plum dangled between Rumania and Hungary. Can Communism, if it wants to, abolish or at least ameliorate the nationalist jealousies, tensions, and rivalries based on false pride, that disfigure Europe? All the Communists I met insist of course that it can, and moreover that except for Macedonia and a minor business between Hungary and Czechoslovakia, these tensions have already been largely liquidated. The future of a large part of the world may depend on the final answer to this question.

Dimitrov is supposed to be a very sick man now—though he was capable of making a speech six hours long at a party congress in December 1948. (All Communist theoreticians seem to measure their dialectical strength by hours. The notion that any eastern European Prime Minister could present his case in less than four or five solid hours is almost unthinkable.) One story is that he suffers from pernicious anemia. His pallor is very marked at any rate. It has even been suggested that he uses rouge on occasion to modify the deathly whiteness of his cheeks.

Bulgaria is a tough and stubborn little country. It is largely agrarian, very poor (the rector of the state university gets $68 a month and a locomotive driver about $15), accursed by governments that put it on the wrong (i.e., losing) side in every war, and populated by the hardest-grained people in the Balkans—honest, frugal, full of pith. They have mostly had a strong pro-Russian and pan-Slav slant, and at least a third of the people are probably genuine Communists. Not less than 87 percent of the country's trade is with the Soviet Union, and this blunt economic factor is, it goes without saying, an important item in stitching it (the same thing is true of other satellites) to Russia.

Suppose Moscow should threaten to cut off this trade; obviously Bulgaria would be at her big neighbor's complete mercy.

The liberation of Bulgaria by the Red army had peculiarities. Bulgaria was, of course, an Axis ally in World War II and the Bulgars invaded both Yugoslavia and Greece and made a thoroughly unpleasant occupation of Macedonia. But they never, despite Nazi pressure, declared war on the USSR. In 1944 the tides changed and the Sofia government began to flirt with the Western Allies. The Russian answer, to force the issue, was to declare war on Bulgaria! The Bulgars dropped their alliance with Germany—doubtless as a gesture of propitiation to the Kremlin—and, three days after Russia declared war on them, they declared war on Hitler, which sounds—and is—confusing. Russian troops then occupied the country, they were cordially welcomed by most Bulgars, and an honestly democratic Bulgarian government was established.

The subsequent pattern of Bulgarian development includes virtually every common denominator we shall find in the other Russian consorts. Item by item the list is instructive. (1) The former regime, in the case of Bulgaria a monarchy, was liquidated, and a People's Republic set up; (2) This was first administered by a broad coalition embracing all the leftist parties, which in Bulgaria has the name Fatherland Front and which grew out of the resistance movement against the Germans; (3) The minority Communist party established itself in an excellent strategic position because, in Bulgaria as elsewhere, it had been more effective in the resistance than any other group; (4) An election was held and the Communists got an absolute majority, almost 60 percent; (5) The coalition began to break up under Communist pressure, and Dimitrov set out to transform the Fatherland Front into an exclusive agency of the Communists; (6) Also the Communist party enlarged itself by absorbing into its ranks the Social Democrats and other left-wing parties and renamed itself the Bulgarian Workers Party; (7) All opposition was ruthlessly ground out; (8) People's Courts were set up under a new judiciary; (9) A Two Year Plan for industrialization (1947-48) was put in motion, to be followed by a Five Year Plan which, it is anticipated, will effect a practically complete nationalization of the state's economy; (10) Political power became concentrated in the Politburo of the party, to wit Dimitrov, to wit Moscow.[3]

The worst blight on the Bulgarian record, and probably the most outrageous single event that has occurred in any of the satellite states to date, was the judicial murder in August 1947 of Nikola Petkov, the leader of the Agrarian party and a famous figure in Bulgarian politics for many years, who had been (he was an extreme left winger but not a Communist) Deputy Prime Minister in the first Fatherland Front government. He was arrested with twenty-three other Agrarian leaders, charged with conspiracy, tried by a people's court, sentenced to death, and promptly hanged. Dimitrov hated him; they had been intense political rivals for a quarter of a century. That Petkov was guilty of enmity to the Dimitrov regime is of course undeniable; that he was guilty of actual treason or conspiracy to overthrow the government was, by Western standards of justice, never proved. The plain fact is that, like many others who have dared to oppose the Communists when they were consolidating their power or momentarily fearful of losing it, he was peremptorily railroaded to death; then the whole case was window-dressed with the usual "confessions" and other paraphernalia of propaganda. But Petkov was only the beginning. *World Today*, a publication of the Royal Institute of International Affairs, printed the following in September, 1948:

> After Petkov's execution the mopping-up operations for the final destruction of all non-Communist political forces were quick to follow. By the summer of 1948 not a single Bulgarian democratic leader remained at liberty. Some were tried for "economic sabotage" and "reactionary propaganda" and were given prison sentences. Others were arrested and interned without any trial. Those in prison include the Agrarian leaders Dimitar Gichev, Hristo Stoyanov, Kosta Muraviev, and Nedelko Atanassov—all former Ministers. Professor Venelin Ganev, chairman of the Regency Council (i.e., Head of State) of the first Fatherland Front government, the Radical leader Professor Petko Stoyanov, a former Fatherland Front minister of finance, the leaders of the Democratic Party, including

[3] In Bulgaria too, just as in Yugoslavia, the State Department protested that much of the above was in flagrant violation of Yalta, but to no avail.

the 87-year-old former prime minister Nikola Mushanov, and many other prominent politicians, professors, and journalists are all interned. Some two months ago they were joined by all the Social Democrat Parliamentary Deputies, headed by their General-Secretary Kosta Lulchev who last January dared to criticize in the Assembly the new State Budget, and was promptly threatened "with the fate of Petkov" by Georgi Dimitrov himself.

The procedure of Soviet trials and the methods of extracting confessions are well known. The following is the most revelatory document I have read recently in this connection. Its authenticity is beyond dispute; it was read openly in a session of the Bulgarian parliament, and never contested. I reprint it from a pamphlet published recently, called *Dimitrov Wastes No Bullets*.[4] A man named Koev, an Agrarian party deputy and former under-secretary of finance, a close friend of Petkov's, and a pronounced left winger who for years had been as close to the Communists as a finger to a thumb, was arrested on the charge of complicity in the Petkov "plot." Here is his own description of what happened to him, as read out in the Bulgarian parliament by Petkov himself (while Petkov was still free) because Koev was too weak from his experiences to be present in the assembly:

> I shall first describe to you how the interrogation at the Militia Prison was carried out, so that you may have an idea of how "confessions" are produced, and of how Communist charges are built up. You reach a state of utter physical and moral collapse. You become completely indifferent towards your own life and fate, and you long only for an end, any end, which will bring reprieve from suffering. But the complete collapse comes only at the moment when you realize that you are defenceless, that there is no law and no authority to protect you, and that you are in the hands of your interrogators forever. This is actually what they try to make you believe right from the very beginning.
>
> The procedure is different from the one we have known so far. . . . They first explain your guilt and then they ask confessions to prove it. The methods to obtain the confessions are mainly three: physiological—hunger, thirst, and lack of sleep; physical—torture;

[4] By Michael Padev, London, 1948.

psychological—hints that your family have been arrested, will be tortured, etc.

But let me tell you exactly what happened to me. For two days after my arrest I was confined to a small dark cell and given no food whatever. On the third day I was taken to the office of the chief of the department of State Security. . . . They told me that I had been found guilty of an act of sabotage—the burning of Russian cotton stocks at the port of Burgas, in 1945, and that I had also taken part in the organization of a planned *coup d'etat* against the government by Generals Velchev and Stanchev. . . . Then they read confessions written by several officers giving details of their own guilt as well as of my own "participation" in the conspiracy.

Immediately after that I was sent back to my cell and was not bothered with any interrogations for twenty-one days. I was left to "ripen." The first method used to achieve this was hunger—I was given only a little bread and water every day. On the twenty-second day, a Saturday, at eight o'clock in the morning, I was taken up to the fourth floor for the second interrogation. It lasted without a break until eleven o'clock of the following Thursday morning. The interrogation went on, day and night, for twenty-four hours round the clock, without a stop, the interrogators themselves being changed every three hours. During all this time I was left standing, without any sleep, without any bread and, what is worse, without any water. I was handcuffed and I was not allowed to lean either on the wall or on the table. Every three hours the new interrogators asked the same identical questions, so that in the end I knew every question by heart. After the first twenty-four hours I did not feel any hunger. The lack of sleep makes your head feel hollow, and then it starts making funny noises. The interrogators insist that you repeat the same dates, the same names, the same hours, etc. On the fifth day I collapsed and was taken back to my cell, where I immediately fell asleep and slept for twelve hours.

Waking up I thought the interrogation was over, but the same night, at eleven o'clock, they took me upstairs again into a bigger room. The Inspector who was in charge of my interrogation said my obstinacy had obliged him to change his methods to something really tough. At his orders I was put on the floor. My hands were tied behind my back, and I was gagged. Then, for about two hours, I was beaten on the feet with a thick rubber whip. During the beating the Inspector asked the same questions. The interrogations and the beatings were repeated four nights in succession. During the last night, besides many inspectors and militiamen, the Chief of the Sofia Militia was also present. I was then thrown back into my cell, and I was not disturbed until 4th November, at half-past ten in the evening, when I was set free. After ninety days under arrest I was not asked any more questions, nor have I been given notice of any official charge against me.

(*Signed*) PETER KOEV

Sofia, 29th November, 1946, National Assembly.

In three respects the Dimitrov dictatorship in Bulgaria is more forthright than that of any other satellite. First, it admits that it *is* a dictatorship, which is unusual. In his December speech to the party congress, Dimitrov openly used the phrase "dictatorship of the proletariat" to describe his regime; next day, this was qualified by the statement that this dictatorship was of course a "majority" dictatorship.[5] And indeed, the Communists are probably the biggest force in the country numerically. Second, Dimitrov is more explicit than most of his colleagues in avowing complete obeisance to the Soviet Union. A recent communiqué (again I quote *World Today*) states flatly that the Bulgarian government recognizes "as unquestionable truth the fact that the Soviet Union and the Soviet Bolshevik party have the leading and predominant part in the fight against fascism and in the international front of peace, democracy, and socialism. . . . All party members are to study and to apply in all fields of life the experience of the Soviet Bolshevik party, and to observe . . . the wise advice and instructions of the great teacher and leader of all the workers and all working classes in the world, Josef Vissarionovich Stalin." All party members and the whole Bulgarian nation are to educate themselves into "unquestioning and unflinching loyalty to the solid and unbreakable front between Bulgaria and the Soviet Union." Third, the Bulgars go furthest of all the puppet states in economic sanctions against the population. For instance a decree of July 21, 1948, announced that all people "not employed in a way useful to the community" will be deprived of food rations.

The following interchange occurred in the Bulgarian parlia-

[5] Gaston Coblentz in the New York *Herald Tribune*, December 25, 1948.

ment before Petkov was hanged. Dimitrov had accused Petkov's Agrarians of harboring foreign agents.

Petkov: "I will not allow you to go on talking like that. Let me remind you that I have never been a citizen of a foreign country, nor have I ever been in foreign service . . ."
Dimitrov: "I was a citizen of the great Soviet Russia . . . This is an honor and a privilege!"
Petkov: "You became a Bulgarian subject two days before the elections. This was officially announced from Moscow."
Dimitrov: "I'll teach you a lesson soon."

Dimitrov has, however, had troubles with Moscow in his time. Several members of his Politburo were recently accused of making "individual theoretical formulations," and the party leadership was once rebuked by Moscow for "boastfulness, lack of modesty, megalomania, and a tendency to luxurious living." In December 1948 Dimitrov confessed that Bulgaria "had lagged behind and was guilty of some deviations from Marxism and Leninism from 1944 to 1946." But, he proceeded, these errors were now a thing of the past.[6] And anyway, as happened after his "mistake" about the Balkan federation, he was forgiven.

Rumania presents some signal oddities. For instance the Prime Minister, Dr. Petru Groza, is not a Communist, and none of the three people who really run the country are, in the strict sense, native Rumanians. These three are the fabulous Ana Pauker, the Foreign Minister, who is of Bessarabian Jewish extraction;[7] Emil Bodnaras, the War Minister, a Ukrainian; and an old-line Communist named Vasile Luca, the Minister of Finance, who was born in Hungary. Another prominent figure is the secretary general of the party, Gheorge Gheorghiv-dej, but he recently got into trouble for alleged Titoism.

The most dominant and interesting of these (although there are tall tales to be told of Groza, had we the space) is of course Pauker. This lady is the effective boss of Rumania, and beyond

[6] These quotations are from *World Today,* Coblentz, *op. cit.* and the Dimitrov pamphlet.
[7] Kindly recall section No. 11 in Chapter 3 above.

this is a personage very high indeed in the Soviet sphere itself; it would be difficult to deny a recent statement to the effect that she is the most powerful woman alive in the world today. Madame Pauker is about fifty-five; her aged father and a brother, orthodox Jews of the most austere and dedicated type, live in Palestine; she is a widow, whose husband, an engineer by profession, was shot in Russia for Trotskyist conspiracy (the legend that Ana herself gave him away to the Stalinist police is apparently groundless); she has three children whom she is fond of and with whom her relationship is happy; in Bucharest she lives fashionably in the house that once belonged to Madame Lupescu, ex-King Carol's mistress for many years and then his wife; she is an extremely alert woman, decisive, doctrinaire, blindly loyal to the Soviet Union, not without charm, and one who, like so many Communist leaders, gained bitter seasoning from interminable years in jail served for no other reason except that she was a Communist.

Madame Pauker can be vindictive on occasion. Once she paid a state visit to a neighboring country, and a newspaper wrote (not dreaming that this would be an offense) a character sketch saying that she came of "bourgeois" Jewish stock. She complained personally to the Prime Minister, and demanded that the man who wrote the story be punished on the ground that it was a needless irrelevance to discuss a person's background. What she meant of course was that any background was "irrelevant" if it did not fit into a Marxist pattern.

One anecdote, doubtless apocryphal, is well known. She was walking down the streets of Bucharest one day carrying a heavy black umbrella, although the sun was shining. "Why, Madame Pauker, do you carry such a heavy umbrella on such a lovely day?" an acquaintance asked her. She replied, "Ha! You have not seen the weather report. In Moscow it is raining."

By what road did Madame Pauker reach her present status? The story could not be more conventional. The highway to power in a Communist community is polished smooth with precedent. She studied to be a doctor as a young girl in Bucharest, and then earned a living by teaching Hebrew. Thus her basic approach was—and is—that of an intellectual. Never was she a starving worker herself. She joined the Rumanian labor movement out of conviction, became an active agitator, lived the usual arcane life of a Communist conspirator, performed various missions for the underground all over Europe, gained the close friendship of men like Thorez in France, and in 1933 was arrested in Bucharest and sentenced to ten years in jail. In 1941 she was released and went to Moscow, as a result of a trade over political prisoners between the Rumanian and Soviet governments. She returned to Bucharest in 1944 when Rumanian resistance against Russia collapsed (Rumania was Hitler's ally during most of the war), after having played a substantial role in Moscow directing Russian propaganda to Rumania. She became (temporarily) a Soviet citizen and was in fact an actual officer in the Red army. Her special talents are supposed to have been first discovered by Vishinsky.

By the time of her return to Bucharest she was a key figure. Rumania, like Bulgaria, was ruled by a coalition government. It still is, in fact. She helped to "invent" Groza, the Prime Minister who was leader of the "Plowman's Front"; she saw to it that the venerable democrat and leader of the National Peasant's party, Juliu Maniu, was salted away in prison with a life term at the age of seventy-five; finally, in November 1947, she became Foreign Minister. Young Michael, son of Carol, was still King of Rumania on this date, and Madame Pauker is probably the only Communist cabinet minister in existence who ever swore formal allegiance to a monarch. But Michael did not last very long. A great deal of fascinating play and counterplay of intrigue and the kind of corrupt fireworks for which Rumania is celebrated took place during this evolution. The upshot is what counts—that Ana Pauker became the most powerful personage in the country.[8]

I do not include here more than incidental mention of the present political structure of Rumania or the insidious process of consolidation by which the Communists gained control. The story is, *mutatis mutandis,* precisely the same as that of Bul-

[8] More robust detail of Madame Pauker's remarkable career may be found in a comprehensive article about her in *Life* by Hal Lehrman. See also *Time,* September 20, 1948.

garia. The Communist party is called "the Marxist-Leninist United Workers' Party"; it is part of a wider structure known as the "National Democratic Front"; it confirmed itself in power by "elections" held under Communist duress, which gave the party an overwhelming vote—93 percent; all opposition has been extirpated, although marionettes like Groza are allowed to have important office (in fact no fewer than nine out of nineteen cabinet ministers are non-Communist); the secret police hold the essence of power; protests at large from the United States have had no effect; dependence on the Soviet Union morally, politically, economically, becomes day by day more absolute.

Rumania, however, is different from Bulgaria in one significant respect; it is very rich. For generations this fertile country has been the big loot of the Balkans. It spills out grain, petroleum, minerals, agricultural produce, in what should be almost limitless profusion; its traditional curse is that greedy landlords and politicians dishonest and venal almost beyond belief have always sucked it dry, leaving nothing but a rind for the peasants and workers in the towns. Seldom have I seen such a contrast between rich and poor as in prewar Bucharest. We should remember carefully that in the past twenty years Rumania has had at least half a dozen different dictatorships, ranging from exercises in Graustarkian extravaganza to outright Fascism of a type worse than in any country in the world except Germany itself. Nor should it be forgotten that the overriding hallmark of the former ruling class could be expressed in a single word, Corruption.[9] So Communism had a particularly soft and ready field in Rumania. There comes a time when even Zenda must get down to facts and figures. Feudalism; laws which made trade unionism a crime; royal scandals; no tradition of decency in the public administration; a debauched judiciary; political apathy by the educated; fantastic displays of overt luxury by a fat crust of rich—all this existed and it played straight into Ana Pauker's accomplished hand.

On taking office she went through Rumanian officialdom like

[9] A famous joke says that mania means madness, kleptomania means madness to steal, and Rumania means madness to steal applied to an entire nation.

a menad with a vacuum cleaner. Never was a cleanup more thorough—or more thoroughly deserved. The country pulled in its waistline with a snap, and out of what had been chaos, a faint aroma of order began to rise. What it will be like under full Communism nobody can know.

Albania (Shqiperia) is a kind of chip off the Balkan block. It is the smallest country in Europe next to Luxembourg, with a total population roughly that of Baltimore; it is wretchedly poor, unsmilingly backward, and a kind of political outhouse. Its heritage, like that of Rumania, is of a tyrannical oligarchy and lack of education; also of blood feuds, exploitation in turn by Italians and Yugoslavs, no middle class, and never enough to eat. So the Communists once again found fields mellow to their iron sickle.

The big man of Albania is Colonel General Enver Hoxha, who came to power on November 29, 1944; the Albanian counterpart of the mechanism that exists in all the Communist jackdaw states is called the "National Liberation Front." Tit for tat, developments follow the usual pattern—abolition of the monarchy, creation of a party-controlled apparatus suitably disguised, and "free" elections. The job was made easier in Albania, such a primitive and off-the-main-stream country, because there was no Albanian government-in-exile, the land had been run over and terrorized by the Germans after years of colonial exploitation by Italy, and no effective political body existed except the Communists, who were an important element in the resistance.

This General Hoxha is quite a personage. He is a strikingly handsome and stalwart young man; he was educated not only in Albania but in France and Belgium. A French editor converted him to Communism. He returned to Albania, and became a professor. "He was expelled from the French Lycée for refusal to join the Albanian Fascist party . . . and he opened a retail tobacco store which became a Communist cell and resistance center." (I am quoting a recent document issued by the U. S. Senate Committee on Foreign Affairs.) Hoxha then carved out a career roughly analogous to that of Tito; he organized the

"National Liberation Movement," became secretary general of the outlawed Communist party, worked in the cloak-and-dagger underground, and emerged as commander in chief of the Albanian army, while he was still only thirty-four or thirty-five. At present he is not only boss both of army and party, but Prime Minister, Foreign Minister, and Minister of War.

Hoxha was helped into power by both Tito and the Greek EAM.[10] When the Tito-Kremlin brabble occurred Hoxha ardently took the Cominform side; this made the Yugoslavs particularly angry because Albania had, in blunt fact, become a sub-satellite of their own. Belgrade regarded it as a colony, nothing more or less. Then the Albanians, a stout wild folk, took quick advantage of Tito's troubles to expel the Yugoslav missions from the country, break off trade relations, arrest native "Titoists," stop exports of oil, and denounce the Yugoslav-Albanian customs union—all of this, no doubt, on Moscow orders. As a result today the bitterly annoyed Yugoslavs look down on the Albanians as barbarian heretics, exactly as the Russians look down on them. It is the same story once removed.

Albania may be a primitive little country, but under Hoxha it passed some remarkably modern legislation. Before 1939 about one-third of all the land was held by two hundred large proprietors; Albania has now gone further than any neighbor in passing a land reform which amounts to virtual nationalization. All mines and oil deposits have likewise been nationalized on the ground that they "are the common wealth of the people," and so have industry and banking.

[10] Cf. Gyorgy, *op. cit.*, and *Economic Trends in Eastern Europe,* Foreign Policy Reports, April 15, 1948, by Vera Micheles Dean. Much of the background of this chapter comes from these. Also see *Newsweek,* July 12, 1948.

CHAPTER 10

THE AMERICAN WAR IN GREECE

LET nobody write about Greece lightly. Here is one of the most tragic and painful situations in the world. What is going on in Greece today is real war, though the fighting is desultory and the casualties comparatively light—what is worse, civil war, the most ravaging of all kinds of war. Moreover this is not merely a Greek war but an American war; it is the Americans who make it possible to fight it. Athens is almost like an Anglo-American (mostly American) armed citadel, and neither the Greek army nor government could survive ten days without aid—concrete military aid—from the United States. Not one American citizen in a thousand has any conception of the extent of the American commitment in Greece, the immensity of the American contribution, and the stubborn and perhaps insoluble dilemma into which we—the United States—have plunged ourselves.

It will perhaps be a shock to the reader to learn that Greece is, as of the moment, just as completely an American puppet as Bulgaria, say, is a Russian puppet. I am not making any moral judgment between the two. All I am doing, as a reporter, is pointing out the unpleasant fact. Actually one could go further, because in curt reality the American support of Greece goes much deeper than support from Moscow to any of the Russian semistates. For one thing it is United States money that keeps Greece alive. It is the American taxpayer who, month by month, is pouring millions into Greece, which is something one cannot say about the Russian taxpayer in regard to Poland, for instance. For another thing American officers actually on the spot in Greece are in virtual command of the Greek army. For another, final authority over high policy rests just as much, if not more, in the hands of the American Congress in Washington as in the Greek parliament in Athens.

In subordinate fields American activity in Greece does not

exceed, but parallels, Russian activity in the Moscow satellites. For instance we in Greece, like the Russians in their sphere, play a decisive role in the general trend of economic affairs and, more important, we play politics to such an extent (just as the Russians do) that no Greek cabinet could possibly remain in office without our approval. One may proceed into still other labyrinths. Political prisoners are, we know, arrested, imprisoned, and shot in the Russian-dominated areas. These are mostly Rightists. But in Greece political prisoners are also arrested, imprisoned, and shot, the difference being that they are Leftists. Civil liberties have disappeared in Czechoslovakia and so on. They have not quite disappeared in Greece, but they have suffered gravely.

Of course there are differences too. Greece is not a dictatorship, which the Russian satellites are. And American measures in Greece, which are defensive and which have sprung out of the exigencies of the moment in a manner almost impromptu, have an altogether dissimilar motivation from most Russian measures. Our "occupation" was imposed by necessity. Above all, the immense majority of the Greek people welcome heartily our intervention, which is certainly not the case as regards the Soviet Union in Hungary or Rumania.

In any case Greece is the country where the cold war is hot. Communist guerrillas, disguised as fighters for the "Provisional Greek Democratic Government," are on one side; the Athens government, supported by the United States, is on the other. But the guerrillas do not get anywhere near so much concrete help from the USSR as the Greek government gets from us—not remotely. The war has gone on for more than two years now, with no sign of peace in sight. Time and time again it has seemed that the government has gained a decisive victory; but the guerrillas always crop out again, not much weaker than before. A point to be kept in mind vividly is that General "Markos" Vafiades, the first guerrilla chieftain, had roughly eight thousand troops when the war started; today, though the losses in killed and captured have been considerable, they number something over twenty thousand.

Extent of the Fighting

We called on the transportation officer of AMAG (American Mission for Aid to Greece), a young U.S. army sergeant, hoping to take a motor trip from Athens to Delphi, which in peacetime would be roughly analogous to a journey from New York to Pittsburgh. He showed us the map and shook his head. The road is safe—that is, not likely to attack by "bandits"—for about one-third its length, say as far as the Greek equivalent of Philadelphia. "Safe" sections are marked in white on the military map, and territory out of bounds in black. Small fingers and pools of white indicate the main road to Corinth, a few other main roads, and the area around Athens. Practically everything else is black. (Even the narrow gauge train to Corinth customarily has two flat cars preceding the locomotive, as a precaution against mines.) The realization that the guerrillas control so much territory so close to Athens, or at least can deny it to the government or the casual traveler, is sobering, especially in view of the fact that the government has no fewer than 250,000 soldiers in the field.

Communications between Athens and Salonika, the two main cities of Greece, are cut off, except by air and the laboriously roundabout sea voyage. In England, this would be like having no road or railway between London and Liverpool. Travel in much of the Peloponnesus is risky, if not impossible; sporadic raids and outbursts may occur almost everywhere. Of course almost all the north is guerrilla territory. I have before me a recent communiqué of the Greek military authorities. It reports action (most of this minor, it is true) in western Thrace, eastern Macedonia, central Macedonia, western Macedonia, Epirus, Thessaly, Roumeli, Peloponnesus, and Crete—which is almost as if, in and around the United States, insurrectionary activity was reported on the same day in Texas, Montana, the deep south, Iowa, the Bronx, Minnesota, and an island in the Caribbean.

The chief guerrilla strength is near the Albanian and Yugoslav borders, where the major military campaign is now going on. But it would be a great mistake to think of this war in terms of solid fronts or stable, established positions. The "bandits" are like a marshfire; they creep underground, and then gush forth miles away. As Anne O'Hare McCormick wrote recently in the *New York Times,* "Greece is a preview of the frontless, almost faceless war of tomorrow . . . of spectral forces that slip back and forth across the borders." It was in this northern sphere that an offensive conducted by the government, under the guidance of the American Lieutenant General James A. Van Fleet, won a substantial victory last August, when Markos was squeezed out of his base in the Grammos mountains. It was hoped that future operations would be secondary after this—mere affairs for the Greek gendarmerie. But the guerrillas, though poor, uniformed in rags, miserably equipped, almost devoid of supplies, hopelessly short of medicines and the like, and facing political difficulties as we shall see, are still there, still fighting, and still resisting every effort to mop them up.

It is difficult in the extreme to assess accurately to what extent the guerrillas are supplied from abroad, or even to what degree they are actual Communists. The Greeks have had *Andarte* (bandit) troubles for generations, and nobody can easily draw the line between Communists, blood-feudists, simple brigands, and people who just hate the government enough to shoot. An armed leftist movement exists in Greece; also an armed rightist movement. Villages have been ravaged; hapless refugees pour out everywhere; there have been violent and brutal excesses by both sides. It is all but impossible, after many years of internecine bloodshed, to tell where political warfare ends and private vendetta begins.

As a rule the government seeks to deny that the war is a genuine civil war, and dismisses the whole thing as banditry. At the same time it claims that it could easily win if the Partisans were not supported by Communists outside. Homer Bigart of the New York *Herald Tribune,* the only newspaperman of consequence who has ever visited the front on the rebel side, doubts extremely if much help comes from Yugoslavia nowadays, if any at all. The Yugoslavs are too afraid of international complications.[1] From Albania some arms did probably trickle in for a time, but not now. On the other hand a commission set up by the UN is certain that Markos did receive substantial help. Apparently the Yugoslavs (before the Tito-Kremlin rift) sold their stocks of old captured German and Italian equipment to Albania—while they themselves were being rearmed by the USSR—and the Albanians in turn passed this on to Markos.

But the massive and concrete fact of American participation in this war cannot be doubted at all. We are in Greece up to our necks, and until the war is won, we have to stay there, unless there should be a complete changeabout of policy in Washington.

Fifty-one percent of AMAG's total expenditure was military as of the time we were there, and the Grand Bretagne Hotel, the most distinguished Athens hostelry, was packed solid with American officers. Next door, the King George Hotel was completely taken over by the Americans, including stalwart middle westerners who so far compromised with Greek habits as to be willing to have dinner at 6:30 P.M. instead of six—the customary Greek dining hour being 9 P.M. A stone's throw away a huge building covering a whole block is given over exclusively to AMAG and its subsidiary bureaus. The streets and roads are hung thickly with American military signs—I haven't seen so much military terminology since the invasion of Sicily—and you encounter jawbreaking neologisms like JUSMAPG (Joint U.S. Military and Planning Group, Greece). American trucks, half-tracks, command cars, jeeps, crowd their way through the noisy Athens traffic, and you see everything from full colonels fresh from Washington covered with dust and sweat—the temperature may run to 103 degrees—to such homely sights as a flaxen-haired American youngster being led out of the PX by his mother, with a United States lollypop in his mouth and carrying a box of Kleenex.

Some 340 American officers are in Greece, under General Van Fleet. These are much more than the personnel of a mere train-

[1] An incidental point is that neither Yugoslavia, Bulgaria, nor Albania has ever given recognition to the "Free Greece" guerrilla "government." See Bigart, "Are We Losing Out in Greece?", *Saturday Evening Post,* January 1, 1949.

ing mission; they work in close harness with the general staff itself; if a Greek officer—even the highest—displeases them, out he goes. In the field American officers are attached to Greek units on active service; they are called "advisers" in that they do not give or take formal orders and do not carry arms, but their "advice" is certainly listened to respectfully by the Greeks nominally in charge. Other American officers and civilians, as we shall see, are industriously active in every sphere of Greek economy, administration, and civil life.

While we were in Athens William H. Draper, Jr., then Under Secretary of the Army, and Lieutenant General Albert C. Wedemeyer, who has been called the American army's best officer, arrived in Greece to inspect the unsatisfactory position in person. Accompanied by Dwight Griswold, then the chief of the American mission (he was once governor of Nebraska and is a very able citizen) and George McGhee, the co-ordinator of Greek and Turkish aid in Washington, they visited the front, and had long and painful conferences with Greek officials. This series of meetings was in plain fact a council of war. The results were unsatisfactory for the most part. The United States has shipped into Greece munitions and supplies worth several hundred million dollars, but the Greeks—since the war was not going well and since they wanted an excuse for their comparatively poor showing—asked for much more. In particular they wanted bombing planes. Our reply was—quite aside from the point that this would be too direct an international gesture—that bombing planes are of no particular use when the targets are always fugitive, that it would take a year or more to train bombing crews and build runways, and that, in any case, the Greeks could win with what they had, if they really put their noses to the job.

Of course the chief trouble is morale. Greeks don't like to kill fellow Greeks. So there is little esprit to the fighting from the government side, which has to be the aggressor.

One Greek cabinet minister said to me imploringly, "Just *lend* us two or three hundred bombers for a month! We'll give them back!" This remark touches a height, or depth, of unreality seldom encountered. Another Greek, a military man, went so far as to say that the war could not be won unless the United States sent in an actual expeditionary force. It isn't easy for the Americans in Athens, most of whom are genuinely devoted to the Greek cause, to explain that this, under the present state of American public opinion, is an impossibility.

Some months after the Draper-Wedemeyer visit General Marshall himself flew to Athens to see what could be done. The answer was in effect "Not much more than what we're doing."

Markos-Tito

Now turn to the enemy side. It has difficulties aplenty too. In February 1949, the rebel "Free Greece" radio announced suddenly that General Markos had resigned his command, and had also given up his post as president of the provisional "democratic" government. The excuse given was of ill-health, and indeed Markos was severely wounded in the Grammos campaign last summer. But rumors immediately spread that, in reality, he was expelled from the posts he held for so long as a result of internal Communist dissension.

Here of course we have another direct result of the Tito-Cominform squabble. Whether or not Tito and Markos had ever been really close is difficult to say. But Markos looked to Yugoslavia for help, and obviously the Cominform thought of him as being linked to Tito. As a result Dimitrov in Bulgaria, representing the orthodox party line, put pressure on Markos while tension within the Greek CP itself reached a breaking point; one wing accused Markos, in the familiar pattern, of being a "deviationist." Then Communists outside Greece announced smugly that "deviationists took the mistaken view that aid from abroad was necessary in creating a revolutionary army."[2] This would seem to indicate that, rather than allow Markos to be helped by its mortal enemy Tito, the Cominform was willing to sacrifice the Greek war itself. Rather than support a friend of Yugoslavia, the Communists preferred to see their own side lose in Greece. Markos himself is believed to

[2] United Press dispatch to the New York *Herald Tribune*, February 9, 1949, and a Belgrade dispatch, April 1949.

have fled to Belgrade, and the Yugoslav government now officially accuses the Cominform of "sacrificing the Greek Communist movement." The larger Communist conception has reverted to that of an "autonomous" Macedonia. If this were ever set up, presumably the Cominform could use it as a permanent source of aggression against Tito. "The Cominform is trying to turn Greek Communists into an instrument for fomenting separatism in Yugoslavia" instead of helping them with their own "revolutionary struggle" against the Athens government. Meantime, actual "military" preparations against Tito are frequently reported from Albania.

Markos appears to have two successors. On the political side the leadership has gone to the veteran Nicholas Zachariades, who for many years was secretary general of the Greek CP and who is one of the old-line Comintern functionaries like Dimitrov and Luca in Rumania. The new military leader is Ioannis Ioannides, a Bulgarian-born Communist with a long record of agitation, conspiracy, and resistance against the Germans.

Background and Shifting Scenes in Greece

How did all this come about?—in particular, how did it happen that the American commitment in Greece became so grave? This book has, as I hope the reader will understand, no place for a detailed history of Greek politics—to make an elementary outline of which would take a hundred pages—or the origins and evolution of the Truman Doctrine. I confine myself to the bare bone of essential facts.

Politically modern Greece has been sharply divided between republicans, led for many years by the great Cretan leader Venizelos and whose political party was called the Liberal, and the royalists, who are known commonly as Populists. Various shufflings among German-descended kings and princelings who precariously held the throne after the First World War need not concern us. King George II was deposed by a plebiscite in 1923, and Greece became a republic until 1935, when another plebiscite, which most authorities agree was almost giddily fraudulent, brought him back. George was promptly forced by internal convulsions to give the real power to a Fascist dictator named Metaxas, who instituted an overt totalitarian regime. In October 1940, Italy declared war on Greece, and in April 1941 the Germans overran the country. King George fled to Cairo after valiant fighting and then in London became head of the Greek government-in-exile. Greece was liberated after three years of brutal and destructive occupation by Germans, Bulgars, and Italians, and by the end of 1944 a Greek government was again functioning on Greek soil under Allied military help, mostly British. In 1946 still another plebiscite brought King George back to the throne. He died in 1947, and was succeeded by his brother, the present ruler, King Paul I.

Now during the Nazi occupation Greek resistance formed spontaneously and became powerful. This is the heart of the present story. Guerrilla bands took shape in the mountains, and harassed the Germans. The British helped them. Then, almost exactly as in Yugoslavia, where Tito and Mikhailovic struggled fratricidally for ultimate power, two wings rose in the Greek resistance; soon these two were not only fighting the Germans, but each other. By 1943 a bitter civil war was raging. The situation was different from that in Yugoslavia (except that the left wingers were the stronger in both countries), because whereas the British dropped Mikhailovic in Yugoslavia, they continued to the end to support the Right in Greece. The left-wing faction in Greece was called the EAM (*Ethnikon Apeletherotikon Metopon,* National Liberation Front); it was dominated by a Communist spearhead known as the ELAS (*Ellenikos Laikos Apeletheretikos Stratos,* Greek Popular Liberation Army). The Rightist army, deriving its strength mostly from royalist sympathizers and remnants of the Metaxas regime, was called the EDES (*Ellenikos Dimokratikos Ethnikos Stratos,* Greek Democratic National Army).

The most inflamed political and military events developed out of this situation—naturally. For instance during the war a serious mutiny of the Greek army in the Middle East took place against the government-in-exile and its royalist supporters. Eventually, by terms of what is called the Caserta Agreement, both guerrilla armies in Greece promised to call off further fighting, and to join forces under provisional British authority. Also the EAM agreed to support the government-in-exile and its leaders duly entered the cabinet when this was finally established in Athens, after liberation. But in December 1944, a painful and anguishing crisis came and the left-wing EAM ministers resigned office. They were protesting against a demobilization order which, they said, weakened them drastically to the favor of the extreme rightist EDES. Violent fighting, led by Communists, broke out on the streets of Athens; British troops intervened on the direct orders of Mr. Churchill and bloodshed resulted; finally, early in 1945, a kind of uneasy peace (the Varkiza Agreement) was patched up.

We step to the present day. The guerrillas now fighting in the north are nothing more nor less than the rebellious offshoot of the EAM and ELAS. Markos simply carried on what he called, and calls, the national "liberation" movement, under Communist control. The Rightists have persisted too in maintaining a paramilitary force, though the old EDES is liquidated. Terrorist gangs—some Americans in Athens told me that their excesses were just as cruel as those of the Communist guerrillas—are centered in a secret organization known by the Greek letter X; their members are called "Chites" and they have played havoc in some sections of the country—"preventive" havoc, their adherents say.

Now let us turn to the involvement of the United States in this story. On February 24, 1947, the British announced suddenly to the American government that it would be obliged, for reasons of economy, to terminate all the financial assistance it had been giving Greece (and Turkey) since the end of the war, and that its garrison in Greece (ten thousand troops) would have to be withdrawn. The suddenness and unexpectedness of this announcement, plus the fact that it had a time limit, caused panic in Washington. Some wise old heads suggested a wait and see policy—that we should do nothing precipitate until we saw whether or not the British did, in fact, quit Greece. As a matter of fact, though their commitments are much reduced, the British still have a considerable force in Athens, two years after this. But Washington acted with violently nervous dispatch. "In a series of hurriedly convened secret conferences with Republican and Democratic leaders of Congress," writes one authority,[3] "President Truman and representatives of the State Department concluded that Britain's withdrawal from Greece spelled the sudden collapse of British power in the eastern Mediterranean and created a vacuum which Russia would quickly fill if the United States failed to act." Thus what came to be known as the Truman Doctrine was promulgated—"that totalitarian regimes imposed on free peoples undermine the foundations of international peace and hence the security of the United States," and that it was the duty and intention of the United States to offset these threats by economic support and military aid. At this time, be it noted, the Markos troops were indeed conducting their insurrection, but they had not yet set up their "government," and there is no record of any specific intervention or act of overt hostility by Soviet Russia itself. Implementation of the Truman policy got under way, Congress voted $300 million for direct Greek aid, and the American Mission was duly organized. Its membership began to assemble in Athens, and we have been the major factor in Greece ever since.

AMAG, Now Part of ECA

After something over a year AMAG was absorbed into the general mechanism of the European Recovery Program. Partly this merger was stimulated by jealousies over stature and quarrelings between the mission itself and the American embassy in Athens, representing the State Department. Now the whole of American operations in Greece, including the military, are centralized under the direction of the new American ambassador, Henry F. Grady. To appreciate the extent of the rehabilitation we have performed we must consider what the economic and human situation was after the war. Few nations have ever suffered worse than Greece, as witness some appalling figures. The Germans burned 1,700 villages, and shot 21,000 persons. The Bulgarians shot 40,000. Some 155,000 buildings were totally

[3] Winifred N. Hadsel, *American Policy Toward Greece,* Foreign Policy Reports, September 1, 1947.

destroyed, including 6,406 schools, and 55 percent of all the country's roads were rendered useless. Ninety-three percent of all rolling stock was lost, 76 percent of the railway trackage, and half the merchant marine. Greek economy was prostrate.

AMAG stepped in, and briskly got to work. In this great field of rehabilitation the American effort has been admirable. Priorities had to be mainly military at first, in that road construction and the like was so interlocked with the military situation. "I think it is remarkable," said Mr. Griswold in a radio report on June 21, 1948, "that this vast and intricate program of rebuilding Greece is being carried out at the very time that organized bands are doing their utmost to destroy it." Among some concrete achievements: A good road was built to Corinth, along a route where you can still see the gutted remains of locomotives the Germans destroyed; some 2,500 kilometers of other roads are being rebuilt; nine airfields are being reconditioned; fifteen major railroad bridges have been rebuilt and fifty other bridges put back in service; thirty-seven highway bridges and culverts were constructed; the ports of Piraeus and Salonika were cleaned up and put into shape and use; above all, the Corinth Canal has been opened to traffic again—a tremendous job, since the Germans had destroyed it with their customary thoroughness and ferocity.

But this is only the top of the picture. Hardly a day passes without the arrival of some American ship, carrying precious raw materials. By mid-1948 we had shipped into Greece 580,000 tons of nonmilitary supplies, worth $38 million. The AMAG organization (exclusive of military) numbered 629, from lawyers and clerks to specialists in everything from boiler machinery to textile design, since a main objective is to stimulate the revival of Greek industry. Then AMAG brought DDT in by the ton, and five thousand villages were sprayed. It did manful work in public health, mostly in connection with the 700,000 miserable refugees (one-tenth of the total population!) whom the war displaced. It instituted a complete program of agricultural rehabilitation; for instance mission funds procured 40,000 tons of fertilizer, 700 tractors, 1,000 pieces of other farm machinery, thousands of tons of seed, and two artificial insemination stations. AMAG went into bathing beaches, engineering schemes, housing—providing 14 billion drachmas for emergency shelter—water development, and irrigation.

The total American contribution to Greece in dollar terms is the very large sum of $785 million so far. This includes the U.S. contribution to UNRRA as well as the $300 million voted for direct military aid. The Greeks have asked for $198,100,000 more in 1949, and will probably get $170 million.

As a result of all this we have a stranglehold on the entire Greek economy. Take one instance: the Americans control absolutely the allocation of Greek foreign exchange; nothing may be bought from abroad without permission. We have put our foot down firmly on the import of luxury goods, for the rare Greeks that might be able to afford them—there are very few luxurious motorcars in Athens. Even the Greek cement manufacturer or textile merchant is under our control, inasmuch as the cement manufacturer cannot import fuel oil or the textile merchant raw wool without American consent. We touch everything from a tiny ceramics factory to the banks. The national budget itself is under strict U.S. supervision, and our personnel has extraterritorial immunity; in effect the American officials in Athens are laws unto themselves. Finally, a most important point, we control wages and prices, and it is an embarrassing source of dispute that although prices have rocketed sky-high, wages are still low. But generally there is a substantial tendency to improvement.

Athens Snapshot

Athens is under martial law, as is most of the rest of Greece, and everybody has to be off the streets by curfew time. One odd point is that dancing is forbidden, on the ground that such pleasantry is improper while the country is at war. A few dance orchestras do continue to play in the night clubs, but the floors are empty.[4] Another curiosity is that the radio shuts down from

[4] We heard that some "bootleg" dancing exists. That is, a night club may maintain a secret room to which the music is piped and where guests sneak out to dance.

3 till 5:30 P.M. in summer. This is not caused by the war, however, but by the tradition of the siesta. Practically all sensible Greeks sleep during the biting, blazing heat of afternoon.

War and its inevitable concomitant, inflation, is apt to give a fillip to any economy, and so Greece, despite the war and its basic poverty, doesn't look quite so dismal as one might expect. The Greeks, no matter what hardships they go through, have an almost sublime vivacity. Ten thousand of them sit every night in Constitution Square, and the noise of the talk, plus the clang of streetcars, the whine of trucks, the shrieks of taxis, rises up like a kind of surf, hitting you full in the face. This square, covering six or eight acres, and solid with coffee tables owned by a dozen different concessionaries, must be the biggest coffee-drinking establishment in the world. Of the thousands of Greeks sitting and sipping and arguing, every one is two things: (a) an individualist, and (b) a politician.

The war is rigorous, but everybody likes his little joke. One bar in the Grand Bretagne is nicknamed the "Monarcho-Fascist" bar; this is the name Markos taunted the Greek government with. I have even heard Greeks, with a twinkle in their eyes, say that the correct nickname should be the "Corrupt Monarcho-Fascist Bar," the word "Corrupt" being strongly underlined.

One experience I shall not forget came at luncheon at the home of Mr. Tsaldaris, the Deputy Prime Minister. Madame Tsaldaris, our hostess, pulled a huge blue poster from a closet and showed it to us with a mixture of pride, amusement, and detached irritation. It is eight feet by three, and it denounces her husband as an executioner, murderer of freedom, and butcher of human beings. French Communists made it for use in a mass meeting. For a time the family kept it on a wall.

One thing everybody talks about, including especially the Americans, is the drachma. The currency is now stable, but it sells at what seems a fantastic figure, ten thousand to the dollar. The illegal rate is about 13,800. This means that you virtually need a suitcase to carry pocket money in. When we left Athens our hotel bill was several million drachmae. To count it out and pay it over the counter, bill by bill, took a solid half an hour.

Then too, everybody talks about the celebrated gold sovereigns which play a large role in the national economy. During the war, British parachutists dropped 1,735,000 sovereigns into Greece to help the resistance; then the Germans, to counteract this, distributed about 1,200,000 more. The Greeks, having suffered at least one disastrous inflation and fearing another, sought after the war to convert their paper drachmae into these gold sovereigns, and even today the basic index of the drachma's value is how much gold it will buy at the money changer's around the corner. Incidental fantastic result: the sovereign is worth more today in Athens than the actual gold it contains. One odd item in the financial field that we encountered was a sudden strike in the national bank. For a couple of days nobody could get any cash at all.

The pinch is stringent in Greece, but plenty of money exists in some quarters; for instance one Athens newspaper paid the record sum of $50,000 for the Greek newspaper rights alone to the Churchill memoirs. On the other hand, think of wages. The average clerk's salary is 11,000 drachmae a day, or about a dollar. A textile worker may get 60¢ per day. Greece is an extremely expensive country so far as food and consumer goods are concerned, and getting more expensive all the time; people simply cannot live on such sums. This, more than any propaganda by the guerrillas, is what drives people to the Communists.

Consider such a minor item as street repair and paving. Driving in from the airport, you see that the main boulevard is slickly paved—and every side street, without exception, is a channel of dirt, broken rubble and parched sewage. But let us remember in excuse that a war is going on.[5]

Another item is the warning notice in the hotels about saving water. Private homes in Greece get water twice weekly for three

[5] One item interesting for its evidence of security-mindedness in Greece is that entrants to the country must fill out a paper telling in specific detail where they have slept *each* of the preceding fourteen nights. It happened that in the customs shed—where, it should be emphasized, Americans are treated with the most scrupulous courtesy and where the general level of efficiency is very high—I stood next to a lady who had flown to Athens, in quick hops, all the way from California. It took her quite some time to think back and list every night's stop since her journey started.

hours—no more, no less. In the hotel we got it at stertorous unpredictable intervals. This, however, it is only fair to add, has nothing to do with the war except that the war has slowed down or precluded the possibility of building public works like improvement of the water supply. Greece is a very arid country, and Athens has always been very short of water.

One small point that struck me was the change in name of three of the chief streets. Stadium Street (anybody who has ever visited Athens will remember it) is now Churchill Street; Panepistimiou is now Venizelos—even though Greece is today a monarchy—and Academy is Franklin D. Roosevelt. Churchill got the biggest.

Decem Graeces Ondecem Imperatores

At the top of the Greek political heap is of course King Paul, a large bluff man with a hearty sense of humor and much good will. He and the Queen were good enough to receive us one afternoon, and we liked them both extremely; the Queen, Fredericka, is a strikingly pretty young woman of considerable wit and intellectual force. Many people think that it is she, not he, who makes the important decisions; she is even nicknamed "Fredericka the Great." Our talk with them was one of the pleasantest and most stimulating we had anywhere in Europe. Paul is very popular, and he bids fair to make a much better king than his brother, who lost much usefulness through the enemies he made in the bitter partisanships of Greek politics before the war. Both Paul and Fredericka exert their monarchical function with the utmost simplicity as well as dignity, and the familiar Athens remark that "they are the best democrats in the country" is not far from the truth.

The Greeks are, as everybody knows, inveterate and terrific politicians. The government is a shaky coalition with a slim majority, reconstructed after a prolonged crisis in January 1949. Immediately after a vote of confidence in February the parliament was recessed until June, which means that the government rules virtually by decree. The Prime Minister (as of the time this book goes to press) is the venerable Themistocles Sophoulis, a liberal; the Deputy Prime Minister, Foreign Minister, and effective head of the government, is the Populist leader Tsaldaris. The Populists considerably outnumber the Liberals in the chamber. Why, then, should Tsaldaris take second place to Sophoulis? I asked Tsaldaris this, and his answer was to the effect that there are circumstances when it is wise to take "advice" from allies. The plain fact of the matter is that American diplomatic intervention forced the appointment of Sophoulis, rather than Tsaldaris, as Prime Minister, when this combination first took office after agonizing negotiations in September 1947.

The State Department has been severely criticized for having "imposed" this government on the Greek people, but actually it does not deserve this criticism fully, and in fact it was being a liberalizing rather than a reactionary force in so doing; it felt that a straight Tsaldaris government would never go down the throats of the Greek people, and hence insisted that Sophoulis be Prime Minister.

The most serious charge that can be brought against the government is not that it is too strong, but too weak. Its underpinning is feeble in the extreme, and it has obviously failed in what should be its chief mission, the bringing of peace and unity to the Greek people. It has not effectively built up the forces of democracy. In theory, it represents 85 percent of the electorate, but the fact remains that it has been unable to effect concord, even by the exercise of force. Maybe it is the best government that Greece, with America and Britain behind it, can find—but this is not to say that it is very good.

In a way the paragraphs above, though truthful, are misleading, because they give nothing of the intense individualism of Greek politics, their astonishing volatility, good humor, and sheer abandon. Surely it is worth mention that, in the lobby of the Grand Bretagne, you may at almost any moment see three former Prime Ministers beckoning amiably at each other, that the four most effervescent members of the government are nicknamed The Four Horsemen of the Acropolis, that by tradition every cabinet minister must devote at least three or four hours a week to receiving, in person, *any*body who calls, that the newspapers spit and foam with long-memoried criticism of almost everybody, and that most politicians assume as a matter of course that they may well be exiles in Switzerland within a year.

The present government derives its mandate from elections held on March 31, 1946. This was the first chamber to be elected since the Metaxas dictatorship—in other words, for ten years—and its first job was revision of the constitution of—1911![6] The election was superintended by foreign observers, including Americans in particular, and so far as the actual polling was concerned it was fair and honestly conducted. But of course everybody had, as it were, been "conditioned" in advance; most people voted as they thought the British and Americans wanted them to vote. The Communists—called the KKE in Greece—did not vote at all. They abstained on the ground that the elections were being held under circumstances of Anglo-American pressure. What percentage of the vote would they have got? Most people in Athens guess something between 10 and 20 percent. Of course the real reason they refused to participate was that they knew they would lose. This was a serious tactical error—just as their behavior in December 1944, when they had not anticipated that the British would use force, was an error—because, if they had participated, it would have been difficult in the extreme to exclude them from a coalition government.

Many observers insist that the Greek government should be "broadened." But by what, and in what direction? By including the extreme right of General Zervas, the former leader of the ultrareactionary EDES? Hardly! Yet there is no doubt that popular resentment against the Communists has produced what might be called "a flight to the Right."

The King is out of politics—maybe. Royalism as such is no longer an active issue. But if the war goes on indefinitely and the political situation further deteriorates as a result, Paul might easily become a whipping boy; everybody except dyed-in-the-wool royalists might unite to blame him—quite unjustly—for what is going on. It is interesting in this connection that the new commander-in-chief of the Athens forces, General Alexander Papagos, is very close indeed to the King. If Papagos does well, the King is safe. If not—what might not happen?

6 "Ten Eventful Years," *Encyclopaedia Britannica,* Vol. II, p. 51.

Finally, as to matters of civil liberties. No public meetings can be held without police permission, which is a natural enough stricture in a country at civil war. On the other hand there is no censorship or wanton interference with personal liberty of the great bulk of the population. The Athens papers are violently outspoken; they even publish diatribes against Americans like Van Fleet. The Communist paper, the *Rizospastis,* has of course been suppressed, but it still appears occasionally as a clandestine leaflet passed from hand to hand.

There are at least four different police forces at the disposal of the authorities, and they watch closely for subversive activity of any kind: the regular police, the military police under the Second Bureau of the army, the general security service, and a fourth group known as "special" security police. Anybody who commits an offense described as "disturbing to the public mind" is liable to civil arrest. Only by the threat of prison are the authorities able to impose discipline. One minor case I encountered was of a Greek who neglected to vote in the 1946 plebiscite. A couple of years later he applied for a routine pass to go from one city to another; this was held up and he was interrogated for a day, simply because he had not voted, which was regarded as an offense since the government had great interest in getting the vote out.[7] There are many hundreds of Greeks—schoolteachers, minor civil servants, and the like—who are out of jobs mostly for political reasons, dating back to the regime preceding the present government. They became known as radicals, got fired, and have been unemployed ever since.

Greece had three collaborationist Prime Ministers (under the Germans), General Tsolakoglou, John Rhassis, and Professor Logothetopoulos. The first two were arrested and died in prison; Logothetopoulos escaped from the country and was tried and sentenced to death *in absentia*; he is believed to be living somewhere in the American zone in Germany. Altogether the Greeks arrested something like 20,000 quislings and collaborationists. Many, however, were never punished. If you want to embarrass

[7] His excuse was that—alone among Greeks of this generation!—he was not interested in politics and just forgot to go to the polls.

a good Greek official, ask him exactly how many collaborationists were tried, how many convicted, and of those convicted how many had their sentences suspended.

Driving out of Athens one day we passed an island half a mile off shore, Macronissos or Long Island. Here approximately fifteen thousand young men have been confined under highly peculiar circumstances. They are all draftees who refused to serve in the armed forces; i.e., they would not participate in a civil war against fellow Greeks. Now Greece is a small country, with a small army; that fifteen *thousand* young men should prefer to be imprisoned here rather than fight seems striking. There is even a joke that, when the draft call impends, young men will contrive to find a copy of the suppressed Communist paper, stick it in a pocket conspicuously, and thus invite arrest in order to avoid induction. The Macronissos internees are tolerably well treated; we talked to Americans who had visited them. The government seeks to "reclaim" them, and if they give proper evidence of reform, they may be released and sent to the front to fight. Our guide when we happened to pass this island gave us an illuminating, if accidental, insight on how Greeks of the extreme right feel about these boys and the situation they represent. "If only," he exclaimed, "we could be more hard boiled and could arrest sixty or seventy thousand boys, instead of merely fifteen, then all this left-wing sympathy among the youth would cease to be a problem!"

In a different category are the Aegean islands like Ikaria (where the mythological Icarus plunged to his death) which hold the "serious" prisoners. Most of these are Communists, though the government denies that any arrests are "political"; the pretext is made that all are "common" criminals. Once as many as eighteen thousand prisoners were contained on these islands; now the number is believed to be about six thousand.

An ugly matter is that of executions. Hardly a week passes without shootings of persons who have been adjudged guilty of specific crimes. There are two kinds of death sentence in Greece. First, about 1,900 people were sentenced to death by the ordinary courts for offenses predating the outbreak of civil war; some of these have been in jail, awaiting execution, for three or even four years. The reason for delay (probably many will never be shot) is partly that the cases have been held up by the elaborate Greek legal procedure, partly a disinclination by the government to arouse opinion by going through with the executions after such a long interval. Second, there are the court martial cases since the war; of the death sentences imposed by these many have indeed been carried out. Those convicted were for the most part not actual guerrillas, but Communist sympathizers caught distributing tracts, collecting funds, or otherwise indulging in overt antigovernment activity. Also some committed serious crimes like murder. The court-martial regulations are severe; anybody doing anything which can be interpreted as aiming at "the overthrow or undermining of the political or social regime of the country" may be tried by military court. According to figures given me by the press department of the Greek government, the total of death sentences imposed since 1945 is 2,961; actual executions number about 750. Of these about 140 took place all at once in the spring of 1948, directly after the murder by Communists of Christos Lados, the Minister of Justice. The government denies, however, that there was any retaliation involved. No one takes this denial seriously. Protests came to Greece from all over the world —even protests on a governmental level, as from Denmark and Great Britain—at this sudden wave of mass executions, and the Greek authorities had to resort to some fancy semantics in reply. I have before me a handout which says, in explanation of the fact that more reprieves were not given, "It should be stressed that a fundamental principle of our democratic regime is the distinction between the executive and judicial authorities, in view of which the government cannot prevent the executions any more than it can order them to be speeded up."

Also:

> The recommendation that the government, in its capacity as an executive organ, should interfere with the judicial authority by suspending or delaying executions or by cancelling decisions of legally instituted courts amounts to a suggestion to the government to assume dictatorial powers. Thus the authors of such suggestions fight Democracy in the name of Democracy.[!]

Perhaps one may close a painful subject by mentioning that I heard one Greek cabinet officer say casually, "When we shot people a few at a time nobody paid attention. Now when there are greater numbers it seems that outsiders make a fuss."

Sophoulis and Tsaldaris

The aged Prime Minister of Greece, Themistocles Sophoulis, is one of the sagest and saltiest old men I ever met. Stories about him are legion in Athens, but they hardly do justice to the immensity of his venerableness and charm. Sophoulis admits to being eighty-eight, but several men who know him well say that he is ninety-two, or possibly even older. He reminded me markedly of Clemenceau, with his old, old eyes almost lost in folds of white flesh, but very dark and luminous. The vitality of the Prime Minister is attested by the fact that, despite his immense age, he recovered nicely from two heart attacks and a bout of pneumonia last year.

Mr. Sophoulis' office is a modest little room, almost like an anteroom, on the ground floor of the old royal palace on Constitution Square; his ministers have quarters much more grandiose. He sits spryly on a little chair, grins, keeps puffing at a pipe, moves across to his desk with the agility of a man forty years younger, chuckles, blinks, and misses nothing.

The Prime Minister began life as an archeologist, and studied at Heidelberg for some years. His German is still fluent, but—something very unusual among educated Greeks—he speaks no French or English. I asked him what his Ph.D. thesis had been about, and he replied with a mildly risqué anecdote saying that it dealt with the domestic life of Greek women in classical days.

Recently a man of seventy-seven was suggested for a cabinet post. "No, no," Sophoulis rejected the idea, "he's too old." Once there came conversation about a nephew of his, aged fifty-five. "He's not very lively any more," Sophoulis remarked. "He behaves as if he were my uncle." One of his predecessors as Prime Minister was named Maximos. Sophoulis nicknamed him "Minimus."

I asked him if the Americans could do anything for Greece

beyond what we were doing. The Prime Minister's reply was a sharp ironical laugh: "We'll be quite satisfied if you don't line up with Markos!" Then he thumbed through some Markos radio reports on his desk, and chuckled; his own government was, as usual, being called "Monarcho-Fascist" in these bulletins. He stuck a thick finger against his chest, and laughed again: "Me—me!—they mean me!" All his life Sophoulis has been an ardent republican and anti-Monarchist.

The Prime Minister was born in Samos, one of the Greek islands, and in his early years was a revolutionist fighting the Turks. He was governor of Macedonia in 1915, a participant in the revolutionary Salonika government during the First World War, and a member of innumerable Venizelist cabinets. He was Prime Minister for a few months in 1924, and reached the job for the second time exactly twenty-one years later, in 1945. He spent most of World War II in a concentration camp.

One item about Sophoulis that amuses Athens is his friendship with a lady who for many years has been his nurse, confidante, and housekeeper. She is supposed to be a Communist!

Constantine Tsaldaris, the head of the Populist party and the strong man of the government, is of totally a different species. His wife, a notably picturesque woman who has had a remarkable career (she was once married to the son of Schliemann, the great German archeologist) is also a substantial power; I even heard it said that she was the country's "real" ruler. Tsaldaris is a lawyer by profession, born in 1885. Most people would say that he is Fascist inclined. He is a thick-set, acquisitive, vigorous, ambitious man, who played little part in public life until 1933 when his elderly cousin, the late Panayotis Tsaldaris, made him a minister. This Tsaldaris died in 1936, and the younger succeeded him as head of the Populist party, which was then in a state of virtual disintegration. Tsaldaris revivified it and his chief political source of power today is that, during the entire war and occupation, when so many people had abandoned the King, he remained faithful to the monarchy and insisted that George must come back. Then, after 1944, his influence grew steeply, because many honest citizens were outraged by Communist excesses and looked to the Monarchist party as their best defense against further bloodshed. Tsaldaris himself denies that he is of the ultra-extreme right; he says that his ambition—and he has great capacity for personal and political maneuver—is to control the center.

Greece: Last Word

The main thing to say in conclusion is that Greece, at the moment, has very little to do with Greece. We, the United States, are not in Greece primarily for the sake of the Greeks, but for the sake of ourselves. Greece has become what has aptly been called a "client" state; it has not lost actual sovereignty, but a situation may easily be foreseen where this small country could become a kind of Haiti or Nicaragua under complete and unmitigated American control. Would that be a good thing for Greece, or, indeed, for the United States? On the other hand, what will happen to Greece if, in the future, the United States should undergo a sudden great depression, or if a change in foreign policy should force a sharp reduction in our Greek expenditures? Greece is utterly at our mercy. At the same time it is a bear we have by a short tail.

I asked one responsible Greek politician what the solution was, if any, and he replied in one word, "War." Indeed many conservative Greeks feel that nothing but outright war between the United States and the Soviet Union can rescue them; they actively want a war, horrible as this may seem, and make no bones about it. I asked my friend, "But do you think there is going to be a war?" He answered, "Europe is in anarchy. One hundred million people are slaves. We *have* to have war. There *must* be a war, or we will all lose everything." But to this other Greeks reply that war would certainly mean the end of Greece itself.

CHAPTER 11
TALKING TURKEY

THE chief difference between Greece and Turkey lies in the realm of morale. That of the Greeks is, by and large, terrible; that of the Turks is quite good. An obvious reason for this is of course that the Greeks are in the midst of an exasperating civil war; the Turks are not. Nor is there any fifth column in Turkey, as we shall see. In the field of world relations the Turks are again a special case. They are dependent on American aid for sustenance, but not survival; nobody in his right mind would call Turkey a puppet or tool of anybody's. These are a tough, resolute, and fibrous people, and they have a tremendous nationalism. They do not want war, and would do nothing to provoke one; but they are not afraid of war, and it is the guess of most observers that, if attacked by Russia or anybody else, they would fight to a man rather than give in.

Turkey is a kind of iron pivot behind the Iron Curtain. Pull the pivot out; the whole structure of defense against possible attack by Russia in this part of the world would collapse. The Turkish control of Anatolia and the Straits is an essential protection to Egypt, Syria, Israel, the Middle East, and much of Africa. I even heard it said: "Let the Turks give way, and the road is open all the way to Dakar."

Another factor contributes to the extreme strategical importance of this people. Not only are the Turks strong; they are the only people hereabouts who are. Greece on the one side is torn by civil strife; Iran on the other is so weak and packed with quislings that, I heard it put, three Soviet divisions could take it in a week. As to the rest of the Middle East, the recent war in Israel has shown how militarily inept the Arab countries are, and Israel itself, the most gallant state in the world, is too small and too preoccupied with its own enormous adventure of rebirth, to play any big international role at present. So, in the whole vital area between, let us say, the Caspian and the Suez Canal, it is the Turks or nothing.

The Turks will certainly resist attack, yes, and they would probably give the Russians plenty of trouble militarily, but they could not possibly stave off the immense impact and mass of Russia alone. In fact, they cannot even begin to maintain their present military establishment without substantial help from outside, which means us. This is how the United States, and every American taxpayer, willy-nilly enters the Turkish picture. We are in Turkey to the tune of several hundred million dollars, with much more to come, and in this expanding era of American foreign policy one of our crucial frontiers has become the Dardanelles.

Istanbul, Once Called Constantinople

But first, a word or two of personal impression. What does Istanbul look like after five years away? It is still one of the most brutally animated and incandescently beautiful cities in the world. You can still stand on Galata Bridge and see the whole panorama of Turkish history symbolized by the domes and minarets of St. Sophia and the Sultan Achmed Mosque. The Bosporus still churns and flashes with brilliant blue water from the Black Sea, and to drive into the Bazaar, inch by thick inch, is like walking backward through a fulminating parade.

Turkey is still a country where you need a license to operate a cigarette lighter, because matches are a zealously maintained government monopoly, and where every taxi must keep the tonneau lit at night, because the modern Turks watch each other's morals. The mosques are still full of the tall wooden clocks that Queen Victoria gave various Sultans as tokens of her esteem (the Turks didn't know what else to do with them), and you still hear stories of the turtles that walked through the Seraglio gardens with lighted candles on their backs. You can still eat ice cream made of roses, and the pigeons are still so tame they nibble filberts off your cocktail dish. Hawkers on the streets still sell trays of birth-control articles fancifully named, and there is nothing changed in the imperiousness of the sunflowers nodding in the grain along the Golden Horn.

Practically from the moment of arrival at the airport you hear the Turks sound their own tough and special note. These are people with brass in their voices—and their pockets. Right away (having gone through the complex ordeal of getting money changed) you get a distinct sensation out of having actual coins in your hand—in acute contrast to Italy and Greece, where all metal currency has long since disappeared, and where even sums as small as a fifth of a cent exist only in the form of dirty paper.

The dour Turks in Istanbul crowd you off the streets; the hotels are jammed, the shops are full. This city has much more vitality, crude as this vitality may be, than Naples say, or even Athens. There are more new American taxis and other cars in a block than in twenty miles in Rome. The whole impression is of a thick bustle and heavy aliveness. You feel that nobody—not even the United States, in case we should ever quarrel—is going to push these people around. Not conceivably would you hear Turks talk as Greeks talk, worrying about whether or not they will have to flee the country. The Turks will stick by Turkey; they believe in Turkey for the Turks.

On the other hand one must not exaggerate. Istanbul itself may seem fairly rich, but the Anatolian hinterland is hopelessly, grindingly poor. Turkey, an American friend told me, suffers from a disease known as "façaditis;" the external façade may look pretty good, but underneath there is a lot of rot. And though the bluster and animation of Turkey are indisputable, there is a certain grimness too. One diplomat, leaving Istanbul after seven years, sighed that it would be good to move to some country where the people sometimes smiled.

The American ambassador to Turkey and chief of the American Mission for Aid to Turkey, Edwin C. Wilson, one of the ablest of our career officers, drove us up the Bosporus in the embassy launch. This, by any count, is as spectacular a trip as the entire world can provide. On one side of the foaming blue channel is Europe, on the other Asia; at one end is Turkey and at the other Russia. Ancient wooden houses, with gray balconies cut as if by jigsaws, alternate with the sumptuous summer embassies of the great powers and the pink and ocher villas of rich

Turks. After forty minutes the launch sharply turns. Ahead is something that looks like a low breakwater, with a narrow passage to one side. This is the entrance to the Black Sea, guarded by a boom. Flung across the Bosporus by the Turks, it symbolizes as well as anything the relationship between Turkey and the USSR, and the ancient tensions of this corner of the world in which America is now so deeply and inextricably involved.

Again the Russian Threat

Several dominating factors exist in Turkey today, and, without assigning priorities, one might list them as follows: (a) fear of Russia; (b) Assistance from the United States; (c) the memory of Kamal Atatürk, the prodigious character who founded the Turkish republic; (d) the person of Ismet Inönü, the present President of Turkey; and (e) the principle of "etatism," or state control. All these factors intermingle into a structure of considerable complexity.

First, fear of Russia. The Turks know the Russians well, and have a healthy respect for their magnitude and power. Long before there was any Soviet Union, the Turks fought war after war—thirteen in three hundred years, Turks say—with czarist Russia. After World War I, in the revolutionary era when both Turkey and the Soviet Union were pariahs, the two countries became good and close friends; people are inclined to forget nowadays that Turkey was the first country in the world to recognize the Soviet Union and sign a treaty of friendship with it. Conversely, Soviet Russia was the first country in the world to recognize the regime of Kamal Atatürk, in the days when he was known as Mustapha Kamal Pasha and during the strenuous period when he tossed the Sultan out of Turkey, drove the Greeks into the sea, thumbed his nose at the British, laicized the Church, had his best friends hung at the drop of a hat, reformed the very alphabet, and set up the present Turkish nation.

Today Turkish relations with the Soviet Union are still, as the diplomats would say, quite "correct." The Russian Consulate General on the main street of Istanbul is conspicuous, and the Russian ambassador to Ankara is, and has to be, an honored guest at official receptions and the like. But since 1939 or thereabouts disturbances and animosity in the relationship of the two countries have developed. The Russians felt that the Turks were pro-German during World War II. Indeed the Turks did, as everybody knows, play a very tight and cagey game during almost the whole of the war period; they stayed neutral, flirted with both sides, and made lucrative profits by so doing until the extreme last moment, when they entered the war as our ally largely to be in on the ground floor of the peace.

The Turks do not say that the Russians intend to attack them, or that the Soviet Union overtly wants war. And, some observers believe, the Turks for their own selfish ends tend to exaggerate the reality and seriousness of the Russian menace. Nevertheless pressure from Russia has been heavy. In 1945 the Soviets began a provocative diplomatic offensive against Turkey. There were public denunciations of Turkey by Russian officials, a campaign of slander and vilification by the Soviet radio, and direct demands on Turkey by the Russian government. The Soviet Union announced that it would not renew the twenty-year-old Soviet-Turkish friendship treaty, it demanded a revision of the agreements covering shipping in the Straits, and it directly asked for the annexation of large areas of eastern Turkey, in the districts known as Kars and Ardahan.[1]

One of the uniquenesses of Turkey is the simple but nevertheless astonishing fact that there is no Russian fifth column. Think of any other country in the world about which this statement may be made, let alone any country on Russia's own borders. None exists. The main reason why there is no fifth column is Kamal and the heritage he left. Even in the days when Russia and Turkey were collaborating closely, the Turkish Communist party was outlawed and forbidden. When Kamal caught a Communist, he had him shot. Even today, when minor secret spurts of Communist activity are discovered, the Turks move

[1] It was a shock visiting the Sultan's palace in Stamboul to discover that the chief royal treasures are still tucked away in hiding in remote caches in Anatolia. Ever since the war, fearing a new one, the Turks have been afraid to bring them back.

hard and fast; Istanbul is full of stories of bodies tied in mail sacks and dumped forthwith into the Bosporus.

The fact that Turkey contains no Communist or even quasi-Communist element means that the Russians, if they should choose to attack, can do so only in a frontal manner, by direct military means. Hence the paramount Turkish problem is that of equally direct military defense. For nearly a decade the Turks have had to maintain an army of some 600,000 men mobilized or semimobilized. In 1939-40 Turkish expenditures for national defense were 95.3 million Turkish pounds, or 36.4 percent of the total budget; by 1944-45 the corresponding sums had soared to 558.2 million pounds and 58.5 per cent. Turkey spends well over half its total national income on defense. These are appalling figures. The drain they would cause to any nation's economy is terrific. But no Turkish government can possibly dare to demobilize. Most Turks consider that they have been spared attack so far only because they *are* mobilized. The crushing weight of the Turkish defense program has other effects. Think of the thousands of young men piped out of civilian pursuits and sterilized into military life every year, of the tremendous wear and tear on the transportation system, of the way the social services, normal industrial pursuits, priorities for industry and so on, have all had to yield place to the voracious military.[2] To keep a whole nation mobilized for almost a decade takes a great deal out of it. But the Turks do not dare relax.

By early 1946 it seemed that Turkey could stand the strain no longer. The United States made one gesture; we sent the great battleship *Missouri* to the Golden Horn, ostensibly to carry home the remains of the Turkish ambassador to Washington, who had died there. The Russians quieted down after this for a brief interval: some people in Istanbul insist that Turkey would have been attacked then and there, had not the Soviets caught the hint implicit in the *Missouri*'s visit. But later Russia resumed the diplomatic and political offensive. Here the story differs from that of Greece. We promulgated the Truman Doc-

[2] And think of the cost to education! In the Turkish army itself illiteracy is at least 80 percent.

trine as regards Greece because of the seeming collapse of authority in the face of civil war. The Russians had not given any direct provocation in the Greek area. But Turkey, we felt, rightly or wrongly, was in imminent danger of forthright attack *by* Russia. In any case, as we know from the foregoing chapter, President Truman announced his doctrine in March 1947, and the program of direct American military aid to Turkey and Greece was inaugurated. This is the step from which all subsequent developments in Turkey derive. Mr. Truman pledged assistance by the United States to "free peoples who are resisting attempted subjugation by armed minorities or by outside pressures." Greece got $300 million from Congress, Turkey only $100 million. Only? It is a lot of money. Why did Greece get so much the bigger share since it was Turkey which was supposed to be more likely to be attacked? For one thing, Greece had been physically devastated by the war, which Turkey was not. For another, it was fighting an actual civil war.

What the Americans Are Doing

First, an exploratory mission of American military, naval and air officers arrived to survey the Turkish ground, and they decided, in collaboration with the Turks, on a tentative breakdown of expenditures as follows: $48,500,000 for the ground forces, $14,500,000 for the navy, $27,000,000 for air, $5,000,000 for arsenal improvement, and, a vital item, $5,000,000 for highway and road development. The first mission was followed by others, until, as of the moment, the United States maintains in Turkey several hundred officers. Civilian experts came in too. Also a considerable number of Turkish officers of various categories are being trained in the United States.

Actually in terms of value the Turks got a good deal more than a hundred million dollars, since the prices of equipment were calculated at bargain rates. For instance an airplane, worth $350,000 new, was classified by us as "obsolete" and delivered to the Turks out of surplus war stock for a tenth of that sum. Americans in Istanbul say that our $100 million really represents a billion, and I heard Turks put it as high as a billion and a half.

The Turks have the reputation of being difficult and obdurate in negotiation, but so far everything has gone quite smoothly. When the survey mission arrived, there was some competition among the American members themselves, representing army, navy, and air force, as to allocations. By and large, the Turks supported their opposite numbers; i.e., the Turk generals would side with the American generals as against the admirals of both, so that any disagreement was on the basis of the rival services, not countries. As a matter of fact such disagreements did not matter much, since both the Turkish navy and air force are completely under the thumb of the army, that is, the general staff.

The American object is, in a nutshell, to give the Turks a modern army, which means to mechanize it and increase its fire power and mobility. By so doing, we will hope to make it possible for the Turks to get along with fewer troops and thus reduce the colossal drain on national expenditure. On the other hand, the Turks themselves say that modernization and mechanization may make the army, even if smaller, more expensive to maintain, and that American financial help will be even more necessary in the future than it is today.

Americans and Turks get on well. Our officers are in Turkey not as employees of the Turkish government but strictly on American assignment, exactly as if they were stationed at Fort Leavenworth. They do not give or take orders; they are advisers pure and simple. We do not try to boss the Turks, or throw weight around. The Americans are, by and large, impressed by Turkish stamina and obedience, and appalled by the backwardness, poverty, and illiteracy they encounter. What do the Russians think of this novel spectacle? One Soviet response is to ask ironically and indignantly what *we* would think if a Russian military mission worked in Cuba.

A hot issue is that of roads and communications. The Turkish railways are catastrophically run down and, even if properly kept up, travel by rail is insanely difficult; for instance three different gauges exist between Istanbul and the Armenian frontier. Even the army is still in the main animal-drawn. As to roads, not a single transcontinental highway crosses Turkey from stem to stern, unbelievable as this fact may seem. The roads are in fact so few and far between and so wretchedly maintained that something like 40 percent of the Turkish wheat crop and 50 percent of the fruit crop is customarily lost, left to rot on the ground or the trees, simply because there is no way to get it to market. So the $5,000,000 allotted to roads is an important item.[3]

The $100 million allotted to Turkey under the first year of the Truman policy was followed by considerably more. The Washington administration asked for $275 million to continue military aid to Greece and Turkey early in 1948, but Congress cut this to $250 million. Also of course the Turks share in the Marshall plan under ERP. For the fiscal year 1949-50 they requested $94,200,000; they have been assigned $30,000,000. Incidentally the Turks are a proud people, and they alone, of the sixteen nations sharing in Marshall aid, objected to the routine phrasing of the ERP agreements, on the ground that the United States was too arbitrary in telling them what they could and could not do.

Politics and Such, Made in Turkey

Not by any stretch of the imagination can Turkey be called a democracy in the Western sense. Let us not fool ourselves about this. We are not spending money to improve or enhance the status of democracy in Turkey (though in the very long run, with luck, our expenditures may well tend toward this end); we are spending money in Turkey as a specific military weapon, to assist the Turks in maintaining their present defense against the possibility of attack by the Soviet Union; moreover, as in the case of Greece, our motive in so doing is not merely to help the Turks, but is part of a much larger strategical conception. The Turks are pawns in a world struggle between the U.S.A. and the USSR, no more, no less. Let this be faced.

[3] The highway program is being directed by the U.S. Public Roads Administration, and some twenty-one American road experts are in Turkey.

But even though Turkey is not a democracy, it is only fair to say that the basis of the Turkish government is broadening steadily. There is a great fermentation here. Power is still, by and large, administered by a series of rotations within a clique,[4] but little by little more and more pressure reaches the top from the people at large. The major issue is *etatism.* This brings us to the interesting point that the Marshall plan is helping Turkey maintain one of the most drastic forms of state socialism, or state capitalism if you prefer, known in the world today.

The President of the republic and its main political stem is General Ismet Inönü. He was born in Izmir (Smyrna) in 1884, and is a professional army officer. For years he was Kamal's right-hand man; he was his chief of staff in the war for Turkish independence, his diplomatic negotiator at the Lausanne settlement, and his Prime Minister for more than ten years. During most of this time he was known as Ismet Pasha; he had to change his name early in the '30's when Atatürk, father of Turks, decreed that all his countrymen had to have last names. Ismet took his, Inönü, from the Anatolian town where he fought his greatest battle and drove the Greeks into the sea. Ismet Inönü is probably the least known and most inaccessible head of state in Europe. A personal peculiarity is that he is very deaf. He is not only President of the republic; he is chairman of the People's Party, which till recently was the only effective political instrument in Turkey. The Turkish constitution is modeled on the French, and in theory Inönü, the chief of state, has a position roughly like that of the President of France, above partisan politics. But he is probably more powerful in his role as head of the People's Party than as President, and so he rules in effect with both hands.

The Prime Minister at the moment this book goes to press is another veteran, Professor Semsettin Gunaltay, born in 1882. He was actually a deputy in the old Ottoman parliament under the Sultans. That Inönü had to choose him, despite his local eminence, shows that the pack cannot be reshuffled much more often. It is also indication—Italy provides another example—

[4] For instance there have been thirteen different Ministers of Commerce in the past ten years.

that very few new and youthful leaders of consequence have been cast up by the turmoil of the last war. Country after country has been forced to go back to men of prewar vintage.

Inönü went so far a few years ago as to permit an opposition party, the Democrats, to arise, and in 1946 the first real elections Turkey ever had took place. The Democrats got 60-odd deputies in a chamber of roughly 468. They are an outspoken minority. Inönü's motive was farseeing; he knew that somehow, some day, the basis of government *must* be broadened, if the state itself was to survive. But the Democrats, thus graciously permitted to exist, held that the elections were unmercifully rigged in the best Balkan manner. A famous joke was, "The People's Party stand for open voting and closed counting; the Democrats for closed voting and open counting." The Democrats claimed, in fact, that they, not Inönü, would have won a clear majority if the polling had been honest, and they remained so untrustful of the electoral procedure that they boycotted important by-elections in August 1948. Still, that a legal opposition exists at all—in Turkey—certainly marks an advance.

There is, moreover, a considerable healthy yeastiness within the ranks of the People's Party itself. Early in 1947 a group of thirty-five deputies revolted in the party caucus—the episode was called the "Rebellion of 35"—urging reforms and liberalization within the party. One of the "rebel" leaders, by name Kasim Gulek, who was educated at Columbia University and is one of the brightest-minded of modern Turks, became Minister of Communications, and three other insurgents were permitted to join the cabinet—another evidence of the way fresh winds are blowing. One of Ismet's own men said recently that the only way to prevent a possible future communization of Turkey is to liberalize the whole structure of the government, now, hard, and fast.

Turkey is unique, because etatism is the program of the right, not the left. The People's Party, under Inönü, which is still the undisputed main force in Turkey, stands for etatism, state control, in its most extreme form. Nothing of any importance in the economic life of Turkey is outside government control, and the government itself is by far the greatest enterprise in the state. Not only does it run the railroads, forests, posts, and telegraphs, and control such monopolies as those on alcohol and cigarettes, in the manner familiar almost everywhere in Europe, but through other monopolies it controls and in fact operates the budding steel industry, coal, other mining enterprises, seaports, oil, textiles, and above all hydroelectric projects. The government owns all subsoil rights, so that if oil or minerals are discovered on private property, these resources go not to the landowner but to the state. Turkey presents, in short, as complete a picture of state controlled enterprise as exists in the world, outside the USSR itself—staggering as this fact may be to most Americans.

The opposition Democrats with their strength focused in the great trading city of Izmir have as their main program the relaxation of these government controls. So, to an extent, do the rebels in the People's Party itself. Thus we have a fascinating paradox: it is the right wing in Turkey which is etatist, the left that wants more encouragement of private enterprise. The liberals in Turkey are those who want less, not more, etatism, and more, not less, initiative to the individual. Etatism is the program of the Turkish right, not of the left; it is the conservatives here who stand for socialism. Americans—observe new vistas!

Finally the greatest and most urgent problem of modern Turkey is something that lies under and over all of this—the education of the masses.

CHAPTER 12
HUNGARIAN NEW WORLD

BUDAPEST is a totally different thing from Belgrade. It still shows severe signs of devastation, whereas Belgrade was hardly touched physically by the war, and it seems much less overtly communized. The people on the streets are better dressed, and the women, who know all about the New Look, are almost as *chic* as in Paris or New York. My wife kept saying that she hardly dared go out, because she felt shabby in comparison to the enormously pretty young Hungarian women. The cafés are animated, and almost everybody makes jokes—typically Hungarian jokes—within the shadow of broken remnants of gutted buildings. Goods of excellent quality are available in the shops, and although everything seemed inordinately expensive on our terms, we saw little evidence of any privation or want though this may well exist. There are no massed red flags, no pictures of Stalin and Lenin, no marching parades of young Communists. "Voluntary" labor is unknown. The good restaurants still maintain their gypsy orchestras, and the night life is almost as picturesque—but with certain differences as we shall see—as before the war.

One theory to account for the comparative well-being of Hungary in general and Budapest in particular under a Communist regime is that the Russians want to make the country a kind of demonstration model or showpiece, purporting to prove to Westerners that life behind the Curtain isn't so bad after all, and that Communism does indeed fulfill its promises of a better living standard. I would take more stock in this theory if there were more foreigners on hand to be impressed. Tourists are still a rare commodity. The true reasons probably reside not in lenience by the authorities, but in the national character (Hungary, be it remembered, is the only important non-Slav state in Europe under Communism) and in the fact that the country has made better use of its natural wealth than its less favored neighbors.

One might also note a negative factor in comparison to Yugoslavia. The Yugoslavs have, as we know, a colossal vitality and capacity to take punishment even when in rags. I am not sure that the easy-going and sophisticated Hungarians have, by and large, anywhere near so much essential stamina—though the handful of Hungarian leaders at the top are certainly tough and adhesive enough, as will soon be pointed out.

Up early the morning after we arrived, we took a stroll. We had not told anybody that we were coming; we were looking forward to a day completely empty. Then in twenty minutes, by pure accident, we ran into two Hungarians whom I knew well before the war, and whom I had not seen since 1939 or earlier. So at once, without choice, we were plunged into this new new world.

Prices were staggering. We dutifully changed some money at the official rate, 11.6 forints to the dollar. The price of our hotel room worked out to $16.00 a day on this basis; a breakfast consisting largely of hot water and rolls was almost $4.00 for two. The hotel was one of those fronting on the Danube that survived the bombardment. The concierge behaved with the elegant proprietariness of all good Swiss-trained concierges; the old man running the elevator bowed with hunched shoulders, murmuring "I kiss your hand" every time we went up or down; the American bar was lively and full of girls; the towels, as big as sheets, were in fact actual sheets; the fifty-year-old boots boy wore a green baize apron and talked all languages—in a word, we felt that we were back in Europe.

What shocked us most was the extent of the destruction. Later we were to see much worse destruction in Berlin, Frankfurt, and above all Warsaw, but this was a preliminary grim taste. We walked down the Corso; every other building is a wreck. We passed the ruins of two celebrated hotels, the Dunapalota (Ritz) and the Hungaria, both of which are gutted; burned bedsprings, lumps of charred furniture, and piles of smashed crockery and other equipment litter the streets. We thought it somewhat strange that such debris should still be out in the open after three years; then we learned that both hotels are being demolished to make way for new structures, and that the old rubbish was simply in process of being cleared out. Our own hotel shook and trembled day and night; two half-wrecked buildings flanking it were being torn down. Showers of bricks kept cascading in the street—traffic was cut off part of the time—and the whole dust-covered area resounded with explosions. Then we looked out over the river at the ruins of the noble bridges. Once seven of these spanned the Danube, including the wonderfully graceful Széchenyi Chain bridge near the Dunapalota. Several are now being rebuilt and are in some sort of service again; traffic on one goes over pontoons, and has to stop in bad weather. Further up on the Pest side we visited the historic Parliament, the oldest in the world; it looks as if a battle had been fought inside. We gazed across to Buda, the old city, where the Royal Palace on Castle Hill is a skeleton. The iron work of the dome survives, but all the interior of this majestic old citadel is gone. Most of the former ministries in this area were destroyed too. Looking down toward the St. Gellért we saw one of the loveliest views in Europe—now defaced by a huge liberation statue erected in honor of the Russians on the brow of the slanting hill. There are smaller Russian monuments in many squares, including one directly in front of the American Legation.

When we told people how savage all this devastation seemed they replied dryly that we should have seen it last year or the year before. Indeed prodigies of reconstruction have taken place. In 1945 Budapest was nothing but a brick jungle. Part of the damage was done by American bombing; more by the fighting when the Russians pushed the Germans out of the city almost literally inch by inch. What Hungarians call the "Siege" lasted from December 23, 1944 to February 12, 1945. Hardly a building on the Buda side is without terrible scars from this encounter. The damage is worse than in Pest because here the Nazis fought not merely street by street, but house by house. Some over-all figures are relevant. Of the 39,643 buildings in the city as a whole 47.1 per cent were damaged, 23.1 per cent badly damaged, and 3.8 per cent completely destroyed. During the Siege alone over 4½ million square yards of window glass were broken; a glass carpet half a mile wide could be made from this amount, stretching clear across the United States. In the zoo—a detail in a different but adjacent field—exactly fourteen animals survived out of three thousand.[1]

But life goes on. We strolled up Vaci Utca, the equivalent of Fifth Avenue, and Andrássy Boulevard, which is the Champs Elysées. The shop windows are full of handsomely designed leather goods, women's shoes and sandals, silk haberdashery, furs, perfumes. Antique shops had Florentine candlesticks and massive Hungarian hand-painted furniture, like the famous *tulipántos láda,* tulip chests. Then at a bookstore I remembered well from before the war we saw a considerable amount of Western periodical literature—*Punch, Harper's Bazaar,* the *Illustrated London News,* the Paris edition of the New York *Herald Tribune,* and the *New Statesman.* The place of honor in the window was held by a translation of a new novel by Ludwig Bemelmans. And in addition to the inevitable Upton Sinclairs and Theodore Dreisers, we saw books by Pearl Buck, Somerset Maugham, Louis Bromfield, Evelyn Waugh. The kiosks told us that a play by J. B. Priestley was a hit, and that you could see both Shaw and Shakespeare.

We turned to sustenance of a different kind. The delicatessens and small groceries, with which Budapest abounds, were stuffed with food; in the cafés nothing was rationed except white bread. At Gerbauld's, one of the most famous confectionery shops in the world, we bought a quarter-pound box of chocolates (price 29 forints or $2.49). These were, alas, stale. We gave the box away to a girl who had become a familiar sight—a pretty teen-ager with one leg, who limped along the Corso day by day. Even Gerbauld's has been nationalized incidentally. Every enterprise in Hungary employing more than one hundred persons has been nationalized.

We walked past the Hangli Kioszk, a café famous as a haunt of journalists, and sat down in the bland sun on what is now called Molotov Square. Around us yawned the dismembered emptiness of buildings half destroyed. But well-dressed people rattled their newspapers on the familiar bamboo frames. It was a little like eating a gay meal in a metal graveyard. We ordered

[1] I am citing here two government pamphlets, *This Is Hungary* and *Reconstruction in Hungary*, Budapest, 1948.

coffee. You ask for a single or a double, and even the latter is not much more than a tablespoonful in a small cup. Price: $1.00. Under the sign MOLOTOV SQUARE is a small placard dutifully telling who Molotov is, and even giving his birth date and various titles and distinctions. It was striking to hear that this square was called Hitler Square only five years ago. Nearby is another square still named Franklin D. Roosevelt Square. We wondered how long it would survive.

One day we went to the St. Gellért, and had tea on the terrace fronting the rococo swimming pool with its famous artificial waves. The old waiters looked very lonely and forlorn. This hotel, once one of the most fashionable in Europe, resembles a warehouse now. Mostly it is used to house visiting party members; the ornate marble lobby is full of wooden partitions, ticket booths, and the like; it is the most proletarian-looking thing I saw in all Hungary. But the artificial waves are still there. Then on another afternoon we drove out to Margitsziget, the beautiful Margaret Island in the Danube; here too the atmosphere was dreary, and the once-gay old hotel almost empty. But the night life still boils and sings. Budapest before the war had, as everybody knows, incontestably the finest night clubs in the world. Think of the fabulous old Arizona, or the Grille Parisienne! These no longer exist, but others have taken their place. They are fascinating to observe, if only because the taxi driver who delivers you to the door walks calmly in and sits at the bar, in cap and sweater, to watch the performance and mingle with the other guests. The texture of the crowd is much like that at a theater in Moscow, with the exception that, in addition to all the shabbily dressed workers present, there still remains a sprinkling of the glittering rich. For instance at a place called the Sanghay the table next to mine was occupied by guests not in black tie, but actually white. But the booth beyond was filled with workmen who, so far as costume was concerned, might have been in overalls. The *Animierdamen*, the ravishingly pretty young "hostesses" who fill the upper booths, dance with all comers, and then retire discreetly to the bar where they seem to favor equally anybody who can still buy a drink, no matter what his dress.

In Hungary, as in Austria, it has always been the convention to tip three different waiters at each meal, the *Herr Ober* to whom you give your order, the *Kellner* who does the work, and the *piccolo* or busboy. Now that Hungary is a Communist state tips are—in theory—forbidden. So a percentage is added to your bill. A percentage? Three different percentages! The total amounts to 26 percent. Atop this there may be a luxury tax, a sales tax, and a music tax. If you go out for a night on the town in Budapest, have your pockets full. But seriously it is important to mention that even staunch adversaries of the regime admit that in several minor directions the town has been cleaned up. Before the war you could tip your way into almost anything; the whole social atmosphere was built on baksheesh. Now most of the petty corruptions have disappeared.

I will mention one meal simply to indicate that for those who can afford it Budapest still has every luxury. A Hungarian friend took us to the celebrated City Park restaurant, in the Városliget, operated by the equally celebrated Mr. Gundel. American and Hungarian flags and white and red carnations decorated our table, and the gypsy musicians purred and crooned. We drank sidecars, beer, a sound red wine, and brandy; we ate—the memory embarrasses me—a chicken consommé of superlative quality, a huge soufflé of *pâté de foie gras,* partridge with wild rice, a purée of apples, fresh green salad, and a spectacular *bombe* of mixed ice cream served with a hot, pale, thick eggnog sauce. I hate to think what the bill must have amounted to.

This prompted us to go to the central market the next morning; we wanted to see what the rank and file of people paid for food. The market was indeed overflowing with produce—again what a contrast to Belgrade or Athens!—but the prices seemed very high. We pushed our way through myriad aisles thick with purchasers, in a great shed clean and well lit. It was almost like California. Bacon was 24 forints a kilo (roughly 95¢ per pound), lard 19 (76¢), and small chickens 15-20 ($1.29-$1.72) a pair. We saw soap, cotton goods, meat, shoes, eggs, oranges, white bread, grapes, peaches, nuts, honey, cheese. Lemons were 1.80 forints (about 15¢) each, and sugar about 32¢ a pound. Everywhere there was corn on the cob, called *kukorica* (the

Hungarians are the only people in Europe who like corn on the cob as we do), paprika, and great heaps of melons and coils of sausage.

How Far Has Communism Infiltrated?

One afternoon we visited a factory, the Manfred Weiss works on Czepel, a Danube island. Once this was owned in part by the Horthy family; during the war and Nazi occupation it was called the Hermann Goering works. This very large plant with 23,000 workers produces heavy machinery, drills and presses, structural steel, bicycles, sewing machines, agricultural tools, and porcelain goods. Our guide was a lady who had once worked at the Boeing plant in Washington. The factory is completely nationalized, and operates under a manager appointed by the Minister of Heavy Industry. The average wage, we were told, was 700 forints a month ($60.00) for unskilled labor, and 800 up for skilled. Also a modified Stakhanoff system is in operation, with bonuses for piecework. If a worker becomes ill, he is on full wages for the first six weeks; then he gets 65 percent of his wages for a year. A forty-eight-hour week is worked, with twenty-five days vacation at full pay, and eight holidays, seven of these religious. The workers get free milk, and pay only a token fee for lunch; they get clothes and so on at sharply reduced prices. The plant has, on the Russian model, a theater, free schools, a nursery, clinics for pregnant women, a college for adult education, various clubs and culture "corners," and a large playground and athletic field. We watched two football teams scrambling together, and some tennis matches. Always, visiting a new city behind the Curtain, we would try to keep one question foremost in mind: "Is this regime really doing something for the *people*?" Visiting this factory anyway we felt that the answer was a fairly clear Yes.

But this is at the cost of much liquefaction of other human values, as in Yugoslavia. There are some crazy mixups. For instance the butler at one of the Western legations is a baron, a landowner whose estates have been broken up—a situation that would be trite in musical comedy, but which is startling when encountered in real life. What is going on is a process of invisible —or not so invisible—dissolution. The Communists are hard. A Communist in a position of power in Budapest today knows what his life has cost. Now he extracts a price from those softer. Very few, if any, people are taken out, put against a wall, and shot. But an employee who has served a bank faithfully for twenty years will suddenly find himself out on the street—with a pension, it is true, but a pension of perhaps 1800 forints a year, $150. And he may find it difficult in the extreme to get another job.

One day the hotel porter gave us a scribbled longhand note:

Dear Mr. Gunther:

do you remember me? Well I am hear and I could help you with some points for the stuff, you are bound to report about, points essential—as I thought to write a book about the happenings of our days—and human to, as I ame a victim of these proceedings. For this, please dont care, because I am not appealing to you in my present state as a beggar. . . . To do this work for the most concerned public: the English speaking nations. So I am awaiting you and would be really disappointed not to shak hands . . . with someone I thought to be a friend.

This man—let us call him Dr. Y—had been well known to me in the 1930's. The fact that he was supposed to have had strong Nazi sympathies at that time did not invalidate the human appeal of this letter. We asked him to come up; I was as shocked as if struck in the face. For I remembered Dr. Y. as a handsome and powerful young man, with a direct military bearing; this person who staggered into our room was a trembling wreck. I would not have recognized him. He told us his story. Apparently while the Germans held Budapest he had a good job. Now of course he is a remnant of a derelict world the Communists hardly bother even to trample on. He had been in jail for four months, on none except the vaguest charges. But of course in many countries—for instance in Germany itself—his political past would have brought him much more grievous punishment. He was treated well enough in jail, and then released as being of no interest to the authorities. But ever since jail he has been unable to find work. No one will hire

John Gunther

This Is Inside Curtained Europe . . . Today

LIKE THOUSANDS of his other readers, I have travelled with John Gunther Inside Europe, Asia, South America and through the U. S. A., and it seems to me that he has been steadily improving and maturing, both as an observer and as a writer. Few, if any, of his contemporaries can touch his trained and disciplined ability to estimate a world situation or to explain it vividly, lucidly, and delightfully to the average reader. Personally, I think that his latest, *Behind the Curtain*, is the best book he has ever written.

¶It is no easy task for any traveller these days to journey behind the Iron Curtain which now separates certain European countries in the Russian orbit from the rest of the world. It is harder still for even the best trained journalist to explain the situations existing in these countries, without becoming didactic, ideological, or egotistic. But there is not a dull page in *Behind the Curtain*, not a paragraph of condescending instruction. Instead, I, at least, was able to stay with him through every turn of his journey. I was able to see and understand places I

(*continued on inside*)

had never seen and to comprehend the language and the poin[t] of the many peculiar and gifted persons John Gunther m[et]... lowed me to do my own thinking, and consequently, it is... analyze or explain his skill, especially since his writing is... and informal that it conceals his careful planning.

¶One reason, I think, for John Gunther's great succes[s]... essentially modest. He would dislike it very much if... an authority on anything. Nevertheless, he has moved... for a long time, and he knows exactly what shoul[d]... omitted in order to convey his impressions to anot[her]... been everywhere before, he knows his Europe back... but he is never an annoying sophisticate. He k... what is for sale in the shops, the number of b... streets, the state of people's clothing, the latest... the bookstalls; and he is glad that the old res... still open and that there is something left... same time, while still dealing with seemin[g]... the fear and desperation, the hope and... around him through all his journey.

¶*Behind the Curtain* is the most comp[l]... anyone has given us of those buffer sta[tes]... of the individual as we know them a[nd]... tic dictatorship. This is a book for eve[ry]... understand it, and anyone who is worried about th[e]... surely be less bewildered after reading it.

JOHN MARQUAND

BELGRADE: *Squalor and luxury*—

"We walked down to the nearest coffee house one morning. She [Mrs. Gunther] was almost blinded by shock. She literally could not believe the squalor that she saw. I had not been too much struck by Belgrade's poverty (Belgrade has always been a city full of poor), nor by Balkan down-to-earthness, greasy tables, or dirty finger nails. But here were crudeness and filth almost beyond belief.

"Then a day or so later an American friend took us out to Avala, a restaurant in the hills nearby, maintained by the state itself as a kind of black market haven for foreign diplomats and the like. I blinked. I gulped. . . . I saw bottles of Scotch whisky at a well-stocked bar; the tables wer[e] cozily set on a terrace with wh[ite] napery and flashing silver; the w[ait]ers were well trained and polite; we... caviar flown in (or so I imagine) the Black Sea and coffee, actual... the bill for five was about $60."

John Gunther: always at the rings[ide of] world events...

ONE OF THE GROUP of famous correspondents, playwrights and novelists who were nurtured by the *Chicago Daily News* in the 1920s, John Gunther was born in that city in 1901. The need to write overcame him even in his high school days and he began setting down his opinions of the Russian Revolution and other weighty matters. At Chicago University he edited the campus daily and contributed essays to magazines like the *Bookman* and *Smart Set.* He left college to take a cattle boat to Europe, where he began his life-long migratory habits.

Back in the U. S., he worked for newspapers long enough to warrant a return to Europe and some free lance journalism. Eventually he insinuated his way back into the *News* in the London office and then began to specialize in the informal background articles and interviews with notable people which became the core of the famous s... which began with *Insid[e]*...

During that period... charge of *Chicago Ne[ws]*... don, Berlin, Vienna,... Paris and he visite[d]... Balkans and Scandi[navia]... hand," he says, "t... panorama of Eur[ope]... I was lucky en[ough]... seat for almost... *Inside Euro[pe]*... and in seven... teen large... Month Cl[ub]... copies as... this har[d]... respon[d]... of all... lousl[y]... dist... the... fo...

BOOK-OF-THE-MO[NTH]...

385 Madison Avenue...

him since he is suspect. Dr. Y. was very fair minded about the regime, which in the long run intends to starve him. He said that there was no "hot" terror, no violent excesses, but instead a relentless steady system of intimidation and discrimination that made it impossible for opponents to earn a living.

Several Hungarians we talked to gave us the same impression. Nonpolitical people go about quite freely without surveillance; there was little thought of a rap on the door at midnight, and the Gestapo bursting in. A professional man told me, "With my own eyes I saw women and children shot by the Germans as they ran down the streets in terror, and their bodies picked up like the bodies of dogs and hurled into the river!" Nothing remotely like this, he went on, goes on today. But day by day, the behavior of non-Communists becomes a little more guarded; day by day, they feel the shadow of eventual liquidation closing in.

The headquarters of the security police, known as the AVD, are at 60 Andrássy Boulevard; occasionally arrests are made which are called "preventive" arrests—the idea being that if you put ten people in jail now, it will save putting one thousand away next year. One recent conspicuous case is that of the journalist Aurel Varranai, formerly the correspondent of Reuters and the *Economist,* who was sentenced to eight months in prison on charges that seem very flimsy. The pretense is made that the press is "free." Folk like the Countess Bethlen, wife of a famous Prime Minister of the *ancien régime,* still write feuilletons. There are no fewer than nineteen Roman Catholic papers still published. But of course in our sense of the term real freedom of the press has long since ceased to exist.

Listen to a statement by Iván Boldizár, the Hungarian Undersecretary of Information, at a recent Geneva conference, which may be taken as a good sample of the official view on these matters in all the satellites:

> The Hungarian Republic insures the widest possible liberty to an honest and progressive press, but refuses to hand over the press, the radio and other means of information to the enemies of popular liberty or to those who seek to strangle peace.

The regime which crumbled in Hungary at the beginning of

1945, by virtue of its antipopular and pro-nazi character, set up a press which, in the hands of the landed gentry and the large trusts, was designed to create a corrupt and pro-fascist public opinion, to build up an effective weapon to bring Hungary into the war and keep it there to the end at the side of the fascist States. This fascist press could have in all good conscience considered itself free. For who could have limited the freedom of the fascist press? The liberal and democratic press, in so far as it existed, was subjected to the most varied limitations and intimidations. This press which struggled most energetically to avoid Hungary's entry into the war, then to liberate the country from Hitler's grip, was reduced to illegality, and gave many martyrs to the cause of Hungarian liberation.

The Hungarian press today is not at the service of individual or particular groups. It is inspired by ideals; and editors, journalists and radio announcers use the liberty granted to them in the service of peace, independence and democracy and carry out their task of education and enlightenment. Since the liberation the Hungarian press has become truly free, for with the old newspapers have disappeared their former proprietors, who saw in their publications commercial and political tools.

Obviously there is no freedom of the press for fascists, for the advocates of the former regime, for the defenders of the large estates which have been confiscated, for the prophets of racial and national hatred. A thug who should cry "Fire!" in a crowded cinema and should then justify himself on the basis of freedom of speech would be severely punished. We do not allow our reactionaries . . . to cry "Fire!"

On our last day in Budapest I took note of the following events among others: (a) A newspaperman came for an interview, and asked blandly if we would furnish him a list of all the "reactionaries" we had seen. This request seemed to us to show a naïveté startling in a Hungarian. (b) A lady called and asked us hysterically if, on serious consideration, we thought "it" (i.e., war) was coming right away, because she had a sudden chance to get out of the country and go to Sweden, and should she take it. (c) A journalist I have known for many years telephoned to ask us not to telephone—this sounds demented but it is true—after meeting us in circumstances of the most exaggerated and frightened secrecy. (d) Another friend told us a wild story of a plot against a cabinet minister and then we had a meeting with the same cabinet minister who was about as worried as a cherub. (e) The porter who put our bags on the train said, "Don't give me a tip. Just tell people what you have seen."

A strange point is that almost all Hungarians maintain their humor. We heard jokes against the government told by members of the government, and even jokes against the Russians. One was that the big Russian liberation monument, known familiarly as the Tomb of the Unknown Plunderer, has its head full of watches—stolen and cached there by the Red army. Another: the net result of the Danube Conference is that the Russians now have the right to navigate up and down the Danube—and the Hungarians across it.

Inch or Two of Background

Most people think of Hungary as predominantly an agricultural state, a green and tawny pool of wheat, nothing more. But also it has important mineral resources and at this very moment it is exporting locomotives to the Argentine and textile machinery to Ethiopia. Hungary is about the size of Kentucky, and has 9,300,000 people. Its area was, as everybody knows, severely truncated by the Treaty of Trianon after World War I; for twenty years thereafter the dominant note in Hungarian foreign policy was a peppery but fruitless nationalism based on the hope that God, or somebody, would give the lost territories back. "*Nem Nem Soha*" (No, No, Never!) was the watchword—meaning that the good Hungarians would never accept permanently the amputations performed on them. Of course the Hungarian chauvinists played down the fact that the areas removed were populated largely by non-Hungarians.

From about 1938 on Hungary followed a strong pro-German course. One Prime Minister, Bela Imredy, was a Jew-baiting sub-Hitler. The Germans rewarded the Hungarians in the early stages of World War II by giving them back parts of Slovakia, Ruthenia, and Transylvania, which properly belonged to Czechoslovakia and Rumania. Hungary—nothing could have been sillier—declared war on the United States on December 13,

1941; we did not declare it back until June 5, 1942. Hungarian troops fought with the Germans on the Russian front, and were duly butchered; but, like the Bulgarians, they had little heart for warfare against the Soviet Union. In fact Hungary got more and more lukewarm about the war; finally on March 19, 1944, the Germans had to march into Hungary themselves and occupy Budapest, to prevent an overt Hungarian defection. The German tenure was brief, if violent. Russian troops fought their way to the outskirts of the city, the great Siege took place, and Budapest was liberated by the Red army in February, 1945.

An item that plays a considerable emotional role in Hungarian affairs today is the terror during the German occupation. Hungarian Nazis and Fascists, known familiarly as members of the Arrow-Cross, behaved even more savagely than the Germans themselves. Many thousands of Hungarian liberals and democrats were tortured, murdered, or deported to a lingering death in German concentration camps. Let one figure alone suffice. The Jewish population of Hungary before the war was about 600,000. Today it is 170,000. Most of these Jews were liquidated by every refinement of bestiality. At least sixty thousand were done to death in a few months in Budapest alone.

Meantime, a provisional Hungarian government had been set up in Debrecen, a town which was already in Russian hands. There was no Hungarian "resistance" comparable to the Greek or Yugoslav resistance. For one thing the flat plains gave no harbor to guerrilla fighters. For another the Germans closely associated with Arrow-Crossists had been in control of the country too firmly. This is an extremely important point to keep in mind. A major reason for the domination of Hungary by the Communists today is that nobody else effective was in the field. Russian Communists and Hungarian Communists trained in Moscow had merely to follow the foaming wake of the Red army—the Second Ukrainian Army to be precise—and seize power. The bulk of the Hungarian people are certainly not Communists but they were carried helplessly into the Communist realm because, among other things, they had no mechanism wherewith to build up something vital of their own. Even so the coalition government set up at Debrecen—it moved to

Budapest in April 1945 immediately the Germans were driven out of the last remnants of Hungarian territory—gave promise of good government, and we must follow its fortunes briefly. One event of considerable interest which came later was the abolition of the monarchy. This had survived uninterruptedly since St. Stephen in the year A.D. 1001.

The first coalition was composed of the Communists, the Social Democrats, the Smallholders, and a minor group known as the National Peasants. In November 1945 the first completely free election, under secret ballot, ever held in the history of Hungary took place; the Smallholders (who are a moderate peasant party) got 57 percent of the vote, the Communists and Social Democrats 17 percent each, and the National Peasants the rest. The leader of the Smallholders, Zoltán Tildy, became President of the new republic in February, 1946, and another Smallholder, Ferenc Nagy, was appointed Prime Minister.

Thus the Communists were a decided minority. But Mátyás Rákosi, the Communist leader, of whom much more later, and Árpád Szakasits, the leader of the Social Democrats, were Vice Prime Ministers, and after a long complex wrangle a Communist became Minister of Interior, which gave the C.P. control of the police and much of the internal administration. Nagy himself has told in great detail how the Communists, though outnumbered, rapidly became the chief power in the country.[2] When they could not get an actual ministry they tried for the undersecretaryship, and then sought to control or by-pass the minister. Also agencies like the Supreme Economic Council, under Communists, were set up with authority outreaching that of the various non-Communist bureaus. Also the Communists were tremendously helped by the fact that the Red army was in occupation of the country, and that Marshal Voroshilov was on the spot as president of the Allied Control Commission. Never forget that it was the prime fact of the war itself that unloosed all these convulsions.

As Nagy puts it: "One could truthfully say that the Com-

[2] See *The Struggle Behind the Iron Curtain*, by Ferenc Nagy, New York, 1948. This contains a wealth of valuable material, but of course it is written from a strongly personal point of view.

munist party conquered the country with the Red army. As the Russians advanced, Communists from Moscow arrived at once in the newly acquired territories; home-grown Communists often slipped through the lines to join leaders fresh from Russia. While the other parties were still in the dark about future events, the Communists went ahead, fully informed and with ready-made plans." Also: "Taught by their failure in 1919, and briefed by Moscow, the Communists now . . . restrained their attacks on the Church and posed as a patriotic organization ready to defend national interests and private property. There was not a word of communism or even socialism." Red troops were, however, at the same time looting the country and performing various types of outrage; Nagy even has a passage describing how Russian *women* of the Red army raped Hungarian males. By election time the Communists had an organization that reached down to the smallest villages, and limitless amounts of money; their propaganda was shrewd and skillful and they had access to big supplies of paper, an important point because this was a very scarce commodity. The official Russians watched these developments with great solicitude. Voroshilov (again I quote Nagy) "asked to be continually informed about our discussions," and when the new government was recognized by Washington—the United States was the first to grant recognition, with Russia following an hour later—the Russians expressed the wish "that the press announcements should state that the Soviet Union had been the first to grant recognition."

Here a point in parentheses. Many Americans in general and Mr. Roosevelt in particular have been blamed for the course of these developments, not merely on the ground of the Yalta agreements but because of the general strategy of the war. To this one might well reply that no strategy could possibly have been devised that would have *prevented* the Soviet troops from advancing through the Balkans and occupying Hungary. If anybody is at fault, it is Hitler. Suppose for the sake of argument that the Anglo-American offensive *had* taken place through southeastern Europe instead of France, as Mr. Churchill wished. The result might easily have been an adhesive and continuous advance of the Red army not only in the Balkan areas, but also in western Europe itself. If we had not fought through France to Germany, the Russians could have fought through Germany to France. And what is going on in Budapest today might well be going on in Paris.

The Nagy coalition held on shakily until December 1946. Then what is called "the Conspiracy" was unearthed and Nagy, who was in Switzerland, lost office. He promised to resign and not to return to Hungary in exchange for the person of his own son, who was delivered to him at the Swiss frontier. The story of the Conspiracy, and how genuine it was or was not, is too elusive and distant to be gone into here. It is something for specialists in occult Balkan melodrama.[3] The Communists took advantage of a witch hunt. Another Smallholder named Lajos Dinnyés became Prime Minister; parliament was dissolved, and a new election held in August 1947. This election was certainly not as free and fair as the one preceding. The total opposition vote was nevertheless about 40 percent. The Communists, running as part of the government coalition, became the largest single party, with 22.2 percent of the vote; the Smallholders dropped to 15.4 percent, and the Social Democrats to 14.8. The net result is that the Communists, under Rákosi and his little group of "Muscovites," have been ruling Hungary ever since.

Meantime several other events and situations demand mention. One is that Hungary was, of course, an enemy state. An armistice was signed in Moscow in January 1945, and the peace treaty in Paris in September 1947. Mostly the frontiers were restored to the pre-Hitler lines. Also Hungary was assessed a severe bill for reparations; for eight years the country is to pay $200 million a year to the Soviet Union, $70 million to Yugoslavia, and $30 million to Czechoslovakia. This added

[3] One word more about this Conspiracy. It consisted apparently of three groups, chiefly disaffected Smallholders. The Communists persuaded Nagy at first that it was directed against himself. For a time it even seemed that the Smallholders were put in a position of allegedly plotting their own destruction. One tragic incident was the arrest of a prominent Smallholder, Bela Kovacs. He was liquidated because it is always a Communist technique to try to get rid of a movement by discrediting the leader. No one knows exactly what has happened to Kovacs. Some Hungarians think that he is still a prisoner of the Red army in Austria.

greatly to the economic difficulties of reconstruction. Then too Hungary was disarmed, and its military strength limited to ninety aircraft, a small river flotilla, and an army of 65,000 men. The Russians, be it noted, were permitted to maintain what are called "communication troops" in Hungary to guard the way to their garrison in Vienna. These troops are, as I have said, carefully kept under cover; at present it is believed that they number about 75,000. The great bulk and mass of the Red army has of course long since been withdrawn. The chief pressure that the Soviet Union exerts on Hungary today, politics aside, is in the realm of trade. Forty-nine percent of Hungarian exports go to Russia, and 45 percent of imports come from Russia.[4] Joint Russo-Hungarian companies, like the "Sovroms" in Rumania, control some industries.

Then too the struggling new government had to combat an inflation which, authorities tell me, was the most fantastic known to history up to that time. Perhaps the Chinese inflation of 1948-49 reached even more staggering proportions. But when the Hungarian currency was stabilized in 1946 the pengö (now replaced by the forint) stood at something like 400,000,000,000,000,000,000,000,000,000 to the dollar. Mr. Vas, the Hungarian Minister of National Economy, gave us as a souvenir a complete set of the inflation banknotes. At the very height, or depth, of the inflation a streetcar fare was 300,000,000,000 pengös. Rich women, to keep alive, cut apart their gold bracelets and sold them half-inch by half-inch. Prices of coffee changed four times a day. A life insurance policy on which somebody had paid all his life might be worth $1.50. A month's wages for a worker was 2¢. Then stabilization was enforced; one can only marvel at the resilience of a people who can go through a crisis like this twice in a generation (because there had been another terrific inflation after World War I) and still survive.

A major event—and accomplishment—of the coalition was the land reform. To tell the story of this properly would take pages. Let us try to squeeze the essentials into an inch. Before the war 980 Hungarians, representatives of the manorial aristoc-

[4] Dean, *Foreign Policy Reports, op. cit.,* and M. W. Fodor, "Along the Danube," *Yale Review,* Spring 1948.

racy, owned one-third of the entire arable land of the nation; some 1,112 magnates of the landed gentry owned a sixth more. So half the productive soil of Hungary was in the hands of around two thousand people. The aristocrats with their bulbous holdings were a lush and fantastic lot. The glamor of names like Esterhazy, Palffy, Szechenyi, and so on, are familiar everywhere. Not so familiar were the uncomfortable crude facts, for instance that before the war some 400,000 Hungarians possessed so little land that they had to sell their labor power as agrarian serfs in order to keep from starvation, and another 400,000 had no land at all. This was proportionately the largest group of landless agricultural proletariat in the world. Such maldistribution was bound in the end to make social revolution inevitable. I was once a guest on a feudal estate in northern Hungary where the owner's income was several hundred thousand dollars a year; he derived straight out of the era when Hungarian noblemen sent sweethearts bottles of precious tokay by special train, or used Titians as linings for their cloaks. On this same estate were six or seven hundred peasants whose whole livelihood depended on the whim of the master. This issue of land has always burned very deep in Hungary. It is one of the vital factors underlying the Mindszenty case, as we shall see.

As a result of the 1945 Land Reform, 34 percent of Hungary's arable land has changed hands, and some 642,000 peasants who were landless before the war or owners of the tiniest parcels now have small holdings of their own. The total amount of land distributed was about three million hectares. No giant latifundia exist at all any more; holdings are limited to the modest average of fifty-seven hectares (100 acres) though some prewar landowners who could prove an exemplary record against the Nazis have been permitted to retain up to 171 hectares each. Before the war 0.2 percent of the population owned 43 percent of the total area of the nation, and 26 percent of the peasantry was landless. Today the state owns 16.5 percent of the total area, none of the very large estates remain at all, and only 6 percent of the peasants are without their own plot of land. The process of reform is not yet complete however. About 100,000 peasants still await allotments. According to UNRRA, "the establishment of a reasonable standard of nutrition in Hungary will depend on the *complete* (italics mine) reshaping" of its agriculture.[5]

After the currency and land reforms the next step was inauguration in August 1947 of a Three Year Plan. The aim of this is, in short, to achieve by 1950 "a living standard exceeding the pre-war level by 14 percent"—an ambitious program. It is very difficult to assess accurately how well it is being fulfilled. Various exercises in nationalization took place before the plan; for instance the coal mines and power plants were declared to be state property early in 1946. Then the five biggest heavy industrial enterprises were taken over, and placed under state control through what is called the N.I.K., Heavy Industry Center. Late in 1947, as the plan itself got under way, banking and insurance were nationalized; finally, on March 26, 1948, all industrial or other plants employing 100 or more workers came under control of the state.[6] Accompanying all this was a very broad educational program, including the establishment of what are known as the "People's Colleges." Forty-three of these have been set up; they are not so much schools in the American sense as centers for adult education.

I was shown a good many diagrams and statistics to indicate that a healthy advance is taking place. Freight traffic, electric power generation, steel production, shoe manufacture, textile production, have already passed 1938 levels. No one may, of course, be sure how long this improvement will continue. But that there has been any improvement at all is remarkable. Consider once again the unbelievably heavy losses Hungary suffered by the war. Twenty-nine percent of the country's agricultural machinery was lost, 44 percent of cattle, 54 percent of horses, 63 percent of pigs. In 1938 Hungary had 1806 locomotives; in 1945, 285. Two thousand three hundred bridges were wrecked. The Germans robbed the country of two hundred

[5] Dean, *op. cit.*

[6] The mechanism by which this was performed has brutal interest. Easter Monday was declared a holiday. People innocently left their businesses, and the government inspectors simply moved into their premises to look over their books and so on while they were out. All manner of property was confiscated. A man went away for the week end—and returned to find his lifework gone.

complete factories, all of its shipping, the entire gold and silver reserve of the national bank, the whole telephone system, and even the pharmaceutical stores and medicines in the hospitals and the fire fighting equipment of the Budapest municipality.[7]

Present Situation

Turn now to the present. In theory Hungary is ruled by a "Democratic" coalition under a regular parliamentary system; actually the real power is held by Rákosi and the "Muscovites." A Muscovite is, in local idiom, one of the clique of Moscow-trained Hungarians who re-entered the country under the wings of the Red army; the term is used in contradistinction to Communists who somehow managed to live out the war in Hungary itself. Most of the leading Muscovites are Jews—Rákosi, Gerö, Vas, Farkas, Verei, Vajda, Revai,[8] and the head of the secret police. László Rajk, the formidably important Foreign Minister, is not Jewish; the joke is that he is a member of the cabinet only because somebody has to be available to sign papers on Saturday. Nor is he a Muscovite. He is a Catholic in fact.

Rákosi is Deputy Prime Minister and has, as it were, two front men. Both are ciphers. Neither is Jewish nor Muscovite. What is more remarkable, neither is a Communist. The President of the Republic, a man named Árpád Szakasits, was a carpenter's apprentice and later a stonemason; he was a trade unionist leader for many years and then the leader of the Social Democrats. When he was named President by the parliament in August 1948, about thirty deputies walked out of the chamber rather than make the vote unanimous—which, whatever it may or may not show about Mr. Szakasits, does show that a good many members of the Hungarian parliament still dare to express open opposition on some issues.

The Prime Minister, by name Istvan Dobi, is a member of

[7] Nagy, *op. cit.*, p. 101.

[8] Again kindly consult Chapter 3 above, before denouncing me as an anti-Semite. But it is undeniable that many citizens of Budapest are fiercely anti-Semitic, partly because they see that the visible executors of Communist policy are mostly Jews. People say, "Those damned Jews-and-Russians!"

the Smallholders, as were both his predecessors; he is about fifty, a farmer by occupation, and a complete nonentity. His chief claim to eminence seems to be that he was a resistance leader during the war, although as we know the Hungarian resistance was not important; also, though not a Communist, he was arrested several times by the prewar dictatorship of Regent Horthy. Mr. Dobi took office late in 1948 after some years as Minister of Agriculture, following a sudden crisis caused by the flight from Hungary of one of his colleagues, the Finance Minister. Dobi, like Szakasits, has no real function except to be a convenient non-Communist façade for Communist manipulation.

A good many other important officials, it should be noted (as in Rumania) are non-Communists. One, Iván Boldizár, is the highly accomplished Undersecretary for Press and Propaganda. And several ministers, even today, are Catholics. Everything is very mixed up. For instance the present Hungarian minister to the United States, Andrew Sík, was not only a Catholic but an actual priest. He was captured during World War I by the Russians, and became converted to Communism. His brother today is still the head of the Benedictine monks in Hungary, and his sister is a nun. One curiosity—in another field—about the Hungarian political structure is its emphasis on sports. There is an "Undersecretary for Sports Affairs." Hungary took fourth place in the 1948 Olympic Games in London, being exceeded only by Sweden, France, and the United States.

We inspect now the parliamentary and party positions, which are curious. The government, consisting of four parties, has 264 deputies; the "opposition," made up of half a dozen groups, has 95. One of these latter, led by a dissident priest named Istvan Balogh, is a "Catholic" party. Of course the "opposition" skates on thin ice and is very discreet indeed most of the time. But there is no *overt* totalitarian suppression of all forms and vestiges of political opposition, as in the other satellites. Such outlawry of the opposition may, however, come at almost any time. Any important person not a Communist is carefully watched. Even the Prime Minister, if he accepts a formal dinner invitation, will be accompanied by a party member. If you call a non-Communist minister on a routine question, he will be likely to consult the C.P. before making reply.

On the government side the tendency—we will see similar tendencies in Czechoslovakia and Poland—is all toward consolidation. In June 1948, the Communist and Socialist parties merged (i.e. the C.P. swallowed up the Social Democrats) and the word "Communist" disappeared so far as official terminology is concerned; today the party is called the Hungarian Working People's Party. Then what had been known as the "Independence Front" comprising the Communists and Socialists became enlarged into—I am following the verbiage carefully—the Hungarian Front of National Independence. On February 1, 1949, this in turn became transmuted into the "Hungarian People's Independence Front," with Rákosi as president of its "Provisionary Council." The Smallholders and National Peasants were sucked into this, and so all loose ends of the old coalition were finally tied together. Hungary formally proclaimed itself to be, not merely the "Republic" of Hungary, but the "People's" Republic.

If the reader is infuriated by this hairsplitting I can infuriate him further. Listen to this from a recent issue of a British Marxist publication, and try to make sense of it:

The Hungarian Working People's Party is based on Marxism-Leninism, adopts the teachings of Marx, Engels, Lenin and Stalin and develops them according to Hungarian conditions. The organization of the Party is on the basis of Democratic Centralism, and it fights for a Socialist society as a stage leading to Communism. It is a revolutionary Party, the vanguard Party of the working class, and is distinct from all other parties.

From the above it will be seen that inside the Independence Front, while leading it and uniting all the progressive elements in Hungarian national life around it, the Hungarian Working People's Party is a separate and distinct revolutionary Party, retaining its identity, with its own program for which it consistently strives. There is thus absolutely no similarity between the Hungarian Front of National Independence and the People's Front in Yugoslavia. The program of the National Independence Front, which is supported by the Party, is a program of common national aims, which, while acknowledging the leading role of the workers, is not the same as the program of the Hungarian Working People's Party. The people of Hungary understand clearly the distinct and separate role of the Party in the Independence Front and also the special leading role of the Party in the whole reconstruction and development of the new democratic Hungarian State in the direction of Socialism.

The Hungarian press is full of interesting nuggets from time to time. After the Kasenkina affair in New York last summer the *Nepszava* accused the political and police leaders of the United States of "international gangsterism" and proceeded:

International gangsterism is also furthered by those State Department heads in America who now have given shelter to the stateless fascist mass murderers. These banditti in American territory will be trained and turned into anti-communist agents. A new kind of Foreign Legion is in the making in the U.S. It was members of this new foreign legion, recruited from fascists, who kidnapped, with the knowledge of the American authorities, the Soviet school teacher Kasenkina, and who are now out to commit acts of sabotage and terrorism as prescribed to them by the new American espionage center in Europe.

Also:

Hungry German imperialism was characterized by cynical nihilism, while American imperialism is characterized by hypocritical nihilism. It is in the name of humanitarianism that the American imperialists exploit the masses, it is under the guise of democracy that they destroy the independence of the nations. The Germans needed a racial theory, but the American imperialists are better off in this respect: all they have to do is to extend their treatment of the Negroes all over the world.

And:

The time has come for Hungarian democracy to solve the problem of amateur sports and to take the road towards a united people's democratic sport without the star-system.

To say nothing of:

Science in the West has come to a deadlock. Lysenko's new biology is based on Marxian principles. These great results will be followed by Marxian physics, chemistry and astronomy.

It happened that the Hungarian minister to Washington early in 1948 was my old friend Dr. Rustem Vambery, who has since died. His death leaves a gap in contemporary culture not easily filled. He took office under the Rákosi regime because he genuinely thought that it would do good to the people. He told me laughingly in Washington how the Communists themselves were merely "children," who could be educated in time; he talked about the free spirit of Budapest, and the naïveté of the government in many respects. That summer Dr. Vambery resigned. His resignation was a protest at the way things were tightening up. He had come to see that Rákosi was not a child, and that the government—which had sent him orders impossible to execute—was not naïve. Dr. Vambery wrote an article which I saw in the London *Daily Mail,* some passages of which are very relevant:

Because of her geographical position and the Teheran and Yalta agreements, Hungary is in the Eastern orbit. This means that Hungarian foreign policy must conform to that of the Soviet Union just as that of Belgium and Holland has had to follow the line of British policy.

Aware of that, I nevertheless hoped that the pre-war economic ties between Hungary and the Allies could be restored and that friendly feelings, such as existed towards Hungary following Kossuth's visit almost a century ago, could be revived. That was not to be.

When I assumed my post last September, I asked Budapest for instruction on the policy I was expected to pursue. I could not obtain an answer. In Washington I found that the Legation was only half-staffed and that it was impossible to handle affairs properly without adequate assistance.

Meanwhile, there was a purge of the Foreign Office which replaced "politically unreliable" members with hastily trained young diplomats more familiar with Marxian dialectics and class struggle than with international law, history, sociology and the practice of diplomacy.

I thus was the head of a phantom Legation. . . I had to get prior permission for even the shortest official trip outside Washington. There was a multiplicity of conflicting instructions which at one time required my presence, all simultaneously, in Washington, New York and Budapest!

It is a phenomenon of this tragic age that the world is divided into two camps and the man who refuses to join either becomes the enemy of both. Neither camp seems prepared to admit the existence of the species of the old-fashioned liberal.

Tightening up is, indeed, the keynote of the past few months in Hungary. Mr. Rákosi began to hint strongly about collectivization, forcible if necessary, of the peasantry, with measures against the "rich" peasants, and the pace of the Three Year Plan was sharply accelerated with a rise in taxes. He announced in January that "the proletarian state is the apparatus for the suppression of the bourgeoisie"; as a result several opposition deputies fled to Vienna or were arrested.[9] The army, courts, and civil service have been purged. Homer Bigart, the correspondent of the *Herald Tribune*, was expelled from the country, as were two Americans representing Standard Oil of New Jersey. A seventy-year-old Hungarian named Papp, head of the local oil company, was accused of sabotage and sentenced to death. Above all, there came the fierce politico-religious crisis of the Mindszenty trial.

The Mindszenty Case

This aroused the most violent passions all over the world. Nothing quite like it has happened, the church historians assure us, since Napoleon Bonaparte arrested and deported Pope Pius VII in 1809, and some authorities even go back as far as Henry VIII to find a precedent; John Cardinal Fisher, Archbishop of Canterbury and Primate of England, was beheaded during Henry's reign. Many other episodes in the conflict of Church and state, though none quite so drastic, may be cited. Bismarck once arrested a Polish cardinal. In England no Catholic was allowed to be a member of the House of Commons from the time of the Tudors till the Catholic Emancipation Act of 1829, incredible as this may seem today.[10]

[9] John MacCormac in the *New York Times*, January 26, 1949.

[10] See a Foreign Policy Bulletin by Blair Bolles, February 18, 1949, and an article by Barrett McGurn in the New York *Herald Tribune*, "Mindszenty Case in Church History."

The bare facts of the Mindszenty case can be outlined as follows. Josef Cardinal Mindszenty, Primate of Hungary, was arrested on December 26, 1948, together with thirteen other defendants, held in jail for thirty-eight days, tried, and on February 8, 1949, sentenced to life imprisonment, for alleged treason, conspiracy to overthrow the Hungarian government, and black marketeering.

The Cardinal was, and is, a personage of very stubborn will and magnificent conviction. It was no secret before the trial that he was an implacable enemy of the regime; we heard his name on every hand in Budapest, as the only important surviving antagonist to Rákosi; several people suggested that we go to see him, because he could tell us the whole opposition story. This is not, of course, to say that he was guilty of treason or anything like it. He was born Joseph Pehm in 1892, of Swabian descent; he took the name Mindszenty from his native village, and was a parish priest for many years. In 1944, during the German occupation, he became Bishop of Vezsprem. The Hungarian Nazis arrested him, and he spent five months in jail. (More than twenty years before he had been briefly imprisoned by the Communists under Bela Kun.) He was a proud man, vain, and a fighter. The Communists make light of the Nazi jail sentence today, saying that Mindszenty would not have been arrested at all except for the fact that he was discovered to be hoarding 1,800 shirts and pieces of underwear in his Bishop's castle. There have been extremely angry polemics about this point. Mindszenty says that this stock of clothing was for distribution to the poor. In any case—it is a strange irony—the Red army eventually released him and he became a national hero. He was named Archbishop of Esztergom and shortly thereafter elevated to be Cardinal. Very few people in the whole history of the church have risen from parish priest to Cardinal in less than five years.

Now back of all such personal details is a basic and inexorable conflict. Hungary is 64.9 percent Catholic; yet slowly, steadily, the Communist grip was tightening. It was inevitable that Mindszenty should become the spearhead of deeply religious and politically minded Catholicism. Not all Catholics, it should be pointed out, necessarily adopted the Mindszenty point of view. For instance several Catholic groups still co-operate with the government under an "opposition" guise, and one very eminent Catholic, Archbishop Gyula Czapik of Eger (who was a Bishop when Mindszenty was still a parish priest) refused to permit Mindszenty's pastoral letters to be read in his diocese. This Archbishop, it was announced in court—by the Communists—went so far as to visit the Cardinal while he was awaiting trial, warning him that the other Hungarian bishops could not promise to support his position.[11] Be this as it may be, Mindszenty and the government came to preliminary fierce clash on two paramount issues. First, the land reform. Second, nationalization of the schools.

The Church was a very important landowner in Hungary; it was the biggest in fact, owning about 900,000 acres. The government set about dividing up the estates of the bishoprics. Naturally this struck at the power of the Church as an economic force, and reduced drastically the income which it used in part for support of the religious schools. But though the very large holdings were broken up, the small plots held by individual parishes were not as a rule touched. The Communists make a considerable point of this. They say in fact that the individual parishes gained in the land distribution, though at the expense of the bishoprics. Mindszenty himself was implacably opposed to the land reform. He is widely quoted now in the Communist press for a statement allegedly defending the old feudal system and its lopsided concentration of economic power. "In the old Hungary," Mindszenty said, "the distribution of arable land between small and large estates could not be considered unhealthy." Whether he actually did make this statement hardly matters. All that Mindszenty stood for was pure anathema to

[11] See *Time*, February 14, 1949, for an admirable sketch of these developments. Two schools of Catholic thought exist not only in Hungary but in Czechoslovakia and particularly Poland. Many ranking dignitaries of the Church, though of course deploring Communism and its excesses, take the line that the only practicable policy at present if anything at all is to be saved is passive resistance rather than active. The Pope himself said on February 20, "She [the Church] does not meddle in problems purely political and economic, nor does she deign to pass judgment upon the usefulness or the harm of one form of government or another." (*New York Times*, February 21, 1948.)

the government. Remember too that the Communists, on their side, represent what might be called a lay "religious" force. The conflict was personal, political, economic, and "theological" all at once. The Communists believed just as fiercely in their own so-called "faith" and mission as Mindszenty did in his. What was at stake was, in the final essence, power.

Almost the same exacerbated situation developed over education. About half the schools in Hungary are operated by the Church, though financially subsidized by the state. The government determined to end what it called this anomaly, and proceeded in the summer of 1948 to nationalize the schools, thus in theory taking them (or most of them—the subject is complicated in the extreme) out of Catholic control. This was naturally an affront that Mindszenty could not tolerate. He fought the government's secularization bill as long as possible, and then took an unprecedented step; when it was finally passed he excommunicated every Catholic member of parliament who had voted for it. The present situation is that priests and nuns still continue to teach in the state schools, partly because no other personnel is available. Next the Hungarian authorities, apparently giving up any hope of ever placating this tremendous Cardinal, offered him safe conduct out of the country. They had to get rid of him somehow. Again, what was at issue was basic power. But Mindszenty refused to go. How could he possibly have gone? This was not a man to desert his flock and life work.

Another point of considerable interest—and one that annoyed the government hotly—was that, strange as it may seem, the high Hungarian clergy is supported financially by the lay state. Mindszenty himself drew a salary as Prince Primate which was twice that of the Prime Minister. The two Hungarian Archbishops get salaries about 50 percent bigger than members of the government, and nine Bishops and the Abbot of Pannonhalma are paid at the same rate as cabinet ministers. So it seemed to the Communists that Mindszenty was biting the hand that fed him. The reply of the Church is that such sums as the Bishops and so on receive are given customarily to a worthy charity. Money is of absolutely no personal interest to a man like Mindszenty.

All this exploded in December with the Cardinal's arrest. A showdown had become inevitable, as his pastoral letters became more frequent. He knew that he was going to be arrested, and in fact he openly invited arrest. It had to be decided once and for all whether the Communists could rule Hungary unopposed. Also he warned his flock that, if arrested and if he "confessed," such confession would be spurious and extracted as a result of duress and his "human frailty."

Events of the trial and his appearance and remarks in court, before his sentence, are widely known and violently puzzling. Mindszenty declared "null and void" the message just mentioned. Yet it is almost inconceivable that a man of such strength of character could have been drugged or tortured to the precise point where the Communists themselves, in open court, would be safe either of the risk that physical or psychological signs of maltreatment would be easily apparent in the Cardinal to all observers, or that he might recant on the recantation. But remember the techniques in interrogation of the Communist police mentioned in Chapter 9 above. Nagy too remarks in his book that a Hungarian technique is to make a man *stand*, without food or water, for five solid days and nights, while being ceaselessly quizzed by relays of interrogators. In any case Mindszenty's behavior was courageous, dignified in the extreme, and honest beyond question. He even went so far as to say that he would like to repay the Hungarian nation for any damage caused by illegal exchange transactions. He denied the accusation "of having participated in a plot to overthrow the democratic regime," but he admitted, "I am guilty in principle and in detail of most of the accusations made," thus confirming the written "confession" he had signed while awaiting trial.

The Catholic line outside Hungary has veered sharply on most of this. At first it was universally stressed that Mindszenty must have been drugged or otherwise maltreated. Perhaps he was. It is more than possible. But the *Osservatore Romano*, the organ of the Vatican, took a different line, that of congratulating Mindszenty and applauding his behavior as exactly what it should have been. Even the Pope, in one of the most beautifully stirring speeches he ever delivered, carefully avoided any allegations of drugging or torture. The *Osservatore*'s statement is, in part, "The Cardinal chose the way of justice and honor; he admitted what was true, and denied what was false. *He never denied any of his work* . . . and he confirmed the supreme principles to which he devoted his life at the cost of life itself."

The procedure of a People's Court, so-called, in Hungary or the other satellites, is totally different from ours. For one thing the person is adjudged guilty *before* he comes to trial, and the purpose of the trial is mainly to set the sentence; for another the judges as a rule are not professional lawyers. In the Mindszenty case four out of the five "judges" were representatives of the trades unions and political parties.[12] Yet, within these circumscriptions, the procedure—though farcical as regards any consideration of abstract justice in the Western sense of the term—is carried out with technical correctness. (Incidentally Mindszenty was tried in the same courtroom where Rákosi had been tried on charges of Communist conspiracy, twenty-four years before to the day, and he began to serve his sentence in the same jail that held Rákosi for many years.) The extremity of viewpoint of several of the defendants was well expressed in a report of the trial by Peter Burchett, reprinted from the London *Daily Express* by the New York *Herald Tribune*. When Prince Paul Esterhazy was asked why he smuggled financial paper abroad (several of the checks involved American dignitaries), he replied, "We did not send them abroad. We sent them to Austria!" The motive for trying Esterhazy certainly included class vengeance, no matter how strenuously the Communists may deny this. Another defendant stated that he momentarily expected a third world war and had made his plans accordingly. "As soon as the Anglo-American forces entered Hungary and overthrew the present government he was ready to create a new one." Mindszenty himself apparently believed that such a war was coming soon, despite the assurances of level-headed Americans in Budapest that he might well be wrong.

Following the storm of protest about the trial in the West, a

[12] Cf. Burchett, quoted below.

group of Hungarian correspondents of American and British newspapers made a protest—in a different direction—of their own. Among them were the representatives of the Associated Press, the *Times* of London, the International News Service, the London *Daily Telegraph,* and Reuters, as well as Mr. Burchett, who wrote, "If there was any trickery by the Hungarian government, it was done long before the prisoners entered the court. Correspondents sat only ten feet away from the prisoners and about thirty feet from the judges. Every word could be heard and every gesture seen."[13] But of course this does not preclude the possibility that the prisoners had had a very bad time before being put on exhibition.

Why, in the last analysis, *did* the Cardinal withdraw his original warning about duress and "confess" his guilt, if indeed he was guilty? Never forget that he was an extremely stubborn, courageous and above all a far-seeing man. Possibly the answer, or part of the answer, may lie in the realm of promises made him by the Hungarian authorities. I do not mean anything so simple as an offer to save his life in exchange for a confession. To die would not have bothered Mindszenty a whit. Far more important than his life or anybody's was the perpetuation of his faith. Perhaps he thought that, by confessing what he did confess, he might lift the *future* burden on his flock, and that, alive in jail, he would at least remain a symbol and be useful. Above all, what he did confess to was not, in his eyes, a crime at all. His behavior was, in fact, quite consistent from the beginning to the end.

[13] The text of the correspondents' statement, as printed in the *New York Times* of February 6, is as follows:

"In view of untrue reports written and broadcast abroad about the journalists' coverage of the Mindszenty trial the undersigned foreign correspondents wish to state that we regard these charges as unfounded attacks upon the integrity of our own reporting and we categorically wish to deny:

"1. That censorship of any kind is being exercised upon our telephonic and telegraphic dispatches.

"2. That the translation of the trial from Hungarian to our various languages is inaccurate; the fact is that the majority of correspondents either speak Hungarian themselves or are accompanied by their personal interpreters, and there have been no complaints, or indications that the official interpreters who are provided in addition are guilty of any kind of sly distortion.

"3. That the only correspondents granted visas or admitted to the courtroom are communist or communist sympathizers."

Following the trial the Hungarian government issued a Yellow Book that, however distorted it may be, fills some interesting gaps. Also a volume of verbatim testimony of the trial was released. Various documents in Mindszenty's own handwriting, which could not easily be forgeries, are reproduced in photostat, as well as several letters from the American Legation, the authenticity of which has never been denied (indeed the letters contain nothing improper) and one long letter from the Archbishop of Salzburg to Cardinal Spellman in New York. This last played a role in Mindszenty's admitted attempt to prevent the Holy Crown of St. Stephen, the symbol of Hungarian monarchy, which is being held by American army authorities in Germany, from being returned to a Hungary under Communist domination. Cardinal Spellman asked the American War Department to intercede in this matter. The Yellow Book goes with much detail into meetings Mindszenty had with Spellman and also with Archduke Otto, the pretender to the Hungarian throne, while on a visit to America. But for one Cardinal to discuss public affairs with another is certainly neither unusual nor a criminal offense. What the Hungarians sought to prove, of course, was that Mindszenty participated in an *active* plot to bring Otto back. The Cardinal wanted to "accomplish a change of regime" in Hungary with American help, he persistently sought to bring about American intervention in Hungarian affairs, and he was in steady touch with Selden Chapin, the American minister—this is what the Yellow Book alleges. Reading between the lines one feels that the Cardinal was not guilty of treason at all by our standards, but was merely indulging in the kind of loose "conspiratorial" talk common to practically all Central Europeans who hate the government—talk quite innocent from a serious point of view. The "confession" goes on to say that he "expected the restoration of the Monarchy after the conclusion of a third world war by an American victory," and that for the transition period until such time as Otto would return, he himself would be head of state. "I acknowledge that from the days of my youth I opposed every democratic policy of the Hungarian people and supported right-wing movements." And, "I wanted to crown Otto myself because it would have secured for me all those privileges that are granted to one who is foremost in the peerage." It is difficult to believe that statements like these last could ever have come from the Cardinal except by extortion, if they are genuine at all.

The following passage from the alleged confession—again I am quoting the text as given *by Communists*—has points of interest. Mindszenty wrote:

> I returned to Hungary from the United States in the middle of July. At home I had secret political talks and I only reported to the monarchist leaders. I convened in secret. . . . I wrote a letter to Mr. Chapin . . . on Sept. 20, 1947, in which I recommended "that the United States should buy up all Russian assets in Hungary, and one of the demands that would be a condition of the purchase would be the complete withdrawal of Soviet troops. In this way the United States, which is anyway interested in oil, would . . . acquire an economic and political basis in Central Europe." After dispatching this, as far as I can remember, I soon got an answer saying that they had sent my letter to Washington. Jusztin Baranyai [another defendant] had exact knowledge of this correspondence but wider Catholic circles also had heard of it and this aroused a hope that the time for a change in the system of government was not far off. It was this that prompted Baranyai to prepare his memorandum on a provisional government and his list of the people who were to be its members.

Another section of the Yellow Book (incidentally I do not think that a reasonably full description of this pamphlet has ever appeared in an American newspaper) goes into Mindszenty's alleged black market dealings. Facts, figures, and names are mentioned, in considerable detail, even to the amount of specific sums involving very eminent people indeed in several countries, including Italy and the United States. The Cardinal's answer to this phase of the indictment was that he "was guilty of black market dealings only in so far as lesser Catholic officials had engaged in them with his knowledge." Of course—let us add promptly—practically every living human being in Hungary has at one time or other dealt in the black market. It was necessary to survival.

Shortly after the trial, to the accompaniment of great excitement, the Hungarian government demanded Chapin's withdrawal as American minister. Duly then he was recalled to Washington "for consultation," and an actual diplomatic break between the two countries was only narrowly avoided. We did not retaliate, however, by ejecting the Hungarian minister to the United States, as might have been expected. Instead the American authorities contented themselves with expulsion of an officer of comparatively minor rank.

The Hungarians—of course—deny firmly today that religion *per se* played any great role in these events. It is their line to think of the whole affair as purely a political conspiracy, but they harp on the fact that the "confession" includes an appeal for an agreement between Church and state.

CHAPTER 13
THE MAN WHO RULES HUNGARY

MÁTYÁS RÁKOSI, the Deputy Prime Minister of Hungary, is in a way the most interesting personality we met all summer. His past is almost as colorful and politically picturesque as his present, which is saying a good deal. Never—this should be a maxim in the rule books—underestimate your adversaries.

So when I say that Mr. Rákosi has a cunning wit and is one of the most efficient and subtle as well as tough-minded men I ever met, do not think I am indulging in an idle puff. If Rákosi and men like him did not offer what they do offer, the movement they represent would not be dangerous. If they were not so able, with such durable roots in a historical process, Communism would be no menace—and we would have nothing to worry about in this emergence of 100 million Europeans in a new Soviet "empire."

Mr. Rákosi (pronounced *Rack-oshy*) is not merely a Hungarian Communist; he is one of the half-dozen most important international Communists in the world today, because of his prestige and influence almost everywhere in the Soviet orbit, from Moscow to Peiping. He rules Hungary, but from a long-range view his importance is probably as great outside Hungary as in. Particularly he is very close to Stalin. Reputedly, like Minc in Poland, he is one of the very few people who can pick up the telephone and call Stalin in the Kremlin without intermediation. Also he is closely intimate with the French and in particular the Italian Communists. One recent report is that he will be the new head of the Cominform.

In Hungary itself he is like the king who can do no wrong. His reputation goes way back; for instance the Hungarian fighters in Spain called themselves the Rákosi Battalion, though Rákosi himself was submerged in jail at the time. He prides himself on his knowledge of the Western world and "understanding" of Anglo-Saxons. In this he is in sharp contrast to his leading subordinate, Ernö Gerö, who is blind with hatred of the Americans and British. It is very shrewd of Rákosi to content himself with the deputy premiership. This relieves him of much ceremonial nuisance and gives him a perfect position as a wire-puller. Also of course he is secretary general of the Hungarian C.P. itself. It is largely Rákosi's decision that Hungary is so "westernized" on the surface. He is clever enough to know that a sprinkling of Western newspapers and so on in the kiosks gives a good impression, while at the same time it can do little damage, since comparatively few of the Hungarian rank and file read Western languages. On the other hand he is prime mover in pushing for the collectivization of the peasants into *kolkhozes,* state farms. This is a man who plays both wings with brilliance.

We called on him one morning. One of his first remarks, in mild irony, was, "As you see, we live peaceably behind the so-called Iron Curtain, besieged only by American and British journalists." Later he pointed at a copy of an American news magazine on his desk. He laughed. "You can buy here all the papers that tell of the horrors of the Iron Curtain."[1]

Rákosi is probably the only human being alive who learned the Italian language in Siberia, of all places, and who was once exchanged (when he was a political prisoner) for a mass of old battle flags. Also he is one of the few men alive, I imagine, who has had confidential talks with both Lenin and Mr. Truman. He has several other distinctions. For instance, he was once sentenced to death twice for the same alleged crime. His enemies adduce a long list of crimes. The major note of his extraordinary career is, indeed, the interminable years spent in jail as a political prisoner.

Mr. Rákosi was born in 1892, in a Hungarian village called Ada; he is of Jewish origin, and the family name was Rosen-

[1] Perhaps I may be forgiven a personal allusion. During our long talk Rákosi quoted some statistics about the United States that seemed to me suspiciously familiar. They could only have come from my own *Inside U.S.A.* I asked Rákosi if he had read it. "Yes," he replied. "It took me six whole weeks, every night. It is a serious task for anybody to read a book so long. But I decided that *somebody* in this country ought to know something about the United States, and that it might as well be me!"

cranz. His father was a schoolteacher and poultry merchant. He went to what was called the Oriental Academy in Budapest as a young man, studying for the imperial Austro-Hungarian Consular Service; he could only be a consul because Hungarians under the old empire were excluded from the actual diplomatic service; here he learned Turkish as well as several Western languages. He speaks eight or nine languages with complete fluency, including almost perfect English.

Then Rákosi went to London, became a Socialist, worked in a bank, and had contacts with the British Labor party. He returned to Hungary when war broke out in 1914, enlisted in the army, was promoted to be an officer, and was taken prisoner in Russia. In the camps he taught other prisoners Marxism. He met Lenin in St. Petersburg, became his close friend, and joined the small group that made the Bolshevik Revolution. He has been a professional Communist revolutionary ever since.

In 1918 he returned to Hungary again, and functioned as a minister (Commissar for Social Production) in the short-lived Communist regime of Bela Kun; he fled to Austria when this regime collapsed. Here he was jailed briefly. From 1920 to 1924, in the words of an official biographical sketch, "he worked as secretary of the Executive Committee of the Comintern, organizing the labor movement in several European countries." Then he risked returning to Hungary secretly in 1924, when the Communist party was illegal, and was promptly caught, arrested and sentenced to death. This caused a world-wide uproar; liberals everywhere, particularly in Great Britain and the United States, protested at the extreme severity of the sentence.

As a result his life was saved. The Horthy regime transferred his case from the special tribunal that had power to inflict the death sentence to the regular courts, and he was given a ten-year term. He should have been released in 1935, when the ten years was up. But the government of the time would not free him, and he was retried and sentenced to death again and the sentence was again commuted, with the result that he remained in jail until 1940.

Then the Russians got him out. This was during the period

of the Nazi-Soviet pact. The Hungarian government released him to let him go to Moscow in exchange for some banners and regimental trophies that the Russians captured from the Hungarians in World War I. Thus, in effect, Rákosi's life was saved in one instance by American and British liberals, in another by the Nazis—because if the Stalin-Hitler pact had not been in force the Hungarians would have had no reason to negotiate with the Soviet Union about anything, let alone the case of Mr. Rákosi.

Rákosi spent fourteen uninterrupted *years* in jail, including three solid years of solitary confinement. "The whole of my youth," he told us, "passed in prison." I mentioned that the experience did not seem to have left him particularly bitter. He replied, "We Communists are not people of emotion. There is no time to spare for bitterness."

He went on to say that for one long period in jail the only reading matter in English he was allowed was the *Saturday Evening Post*. "It taught me patience," he mentioned with a laugh. But he was only permitted to see copies three months late, when any political news would be stale. He learned five other languages besides English while in jail.

No matter what Rákosi's own demeanor is nobody should discount what such an enormous span of time spent in prison can do to a man. It distorts. Also it gives the victim a peculiarly narrow view of such matters as civil liberties. Suppose you went to Rákosi and exclaimed in outrage, "Mr. X was arrested Tuesday night, and it is now Thursday morning, and he is still in jail!" Rákosi's ironical answer might well be, "Dear me! The man has actually passed thirty-six whole hours in confinement! Thirty-six whole *hours*—what horror!"

After 1940 Rákosi lived in Moscow. Here his importance steeply rose. He was chief of the Hungarian section of the Comintern until its dissolution, then a specialist on Hungarian affairs in general and a frequent lively contributor to *Pravda* and *Izvestia*. He returned to Hungary, as we know, with the Red army, as secretary general of the party. He became Deputy Prime Minister the next year, and has in effect run Hungary ever since.

Mr. Rákosi is a short, squat man, bald as an egg, with shining gold teeth. He has shrewd luminous brown eyes, a soft, emphatic voice and a deliberate manner in conversation. He received us at C.P. headquarters, and wore a blue shirt and dark suit. There were no attendants or any sign of surveillance or display; never once were we interrupted. His English, as I say, is almost perfect, and he uses familiar idioms. Halfway through our talk he hospitably poured out a glass of *barack,* local brandy. "Have a drink," he said, "it's easy stuff." When we were talking about Germany he laughed, "But of course your policy there *peps up* German fascism."

As to the substance of Rákosi's conversation, he began by giving us what amounted to a little lecture on Hungary's improved economic situation. He talked to us with a peculiar slow mildness, as if we were children. "Budapest makes even ships, up to 4,000 tons. Never forget we are one-third an industrial nation." He smiled, "The population of Budapest is 1,100,000. . . . The density of population of the country as a whole is greater than that of Denmark or France. . . . We are producing more babies than at any time in nineteen years. . . . In our five biggest factories there are 72,000 workers . . . We have 36 million fruit trees, four per person. . . . There are 400,000 acres of vineyards, and our wine crop last year, brought to market by 70,000 peasants, was 400,000 liters. . . . The present harvest is good, after three years of drought. . . . We have a surplus in wheat, barley, sunflower seeds. . . . The budget is in order, the currency is stable, we have no deficit, purchasing power is up 15 percent. . . . Do not forget also: we won ten first prizes in the London Olympic games."

Then we asked him what had happened to Hungarian nationalism—the famous irredentist spirit the country has long been famous for—and he replied that he had no objection to people being patriots, but that exaggerated nationalism was cultivated by the reactionaries as a stick with which to beat the government. Surprisingly enough he then quoted the Bible. The reference was to sleeping evils. "Twice in our generation we have had the catastrophe of war, caused by nationalism." He mentioned Mindszenty—this was before the Cardinal's arrest of course—and said that he was the archetype of extreme reactionary nationalist, though German by origin. He went on, smiling calmly, "For twenty-five years our youth was fed on nationalism. We cannot change things overnight. We need"—he paused—"a generation."[2]

He turned to the problem of dictatorship *versus* democracy and insisted with great vigor—this was a familiar gambit—that Hungary was a "real" democracy and that his government, far from being a dictatorship, ruled by "virtue of the only real force—the force of the people!" Hungary is a disarmed state, with its army limited. "How can you say we are a dictatorship when we have no weapons!" His eyes clouded. "But let there be trouble, and in ten minutes, half a million workers will be on the streets, to fight for us with their bare hands." At this point oddly enough we heard a loud explosion on the street outside our quiet room. Rákosi leaned back and laughed heartily. "Not a bomb! An automobile has doubtless backfired!"

We talked about Tito. Rákosi was one of the prime forces behind Tito's excommunication. But he pointed out that individual Communist states could have a bright "cultural" life of their own, and that Stalin's own policy, ever since he was Commissar of Nationalities back in 1919 when he invented the concept of Soviet "Union," has always been to encourage the "autonomy" of nationalities. But Tito himself is of course anathema to Rákosi now—as to Stalin—and to keep the Tito "infection" from spreading into Hungary is one of Rákosi's main preoccupations.

As to the possibility of war he was very guarded, but he thought that "probably" a general war was unlikely for twenty years at least. Like all the satellite leaders, he fears attack by the United States. We asked him when he had visited America. "In 1946, for the first—and last!—time." I felt what I have so often felt when talking to Communists, that even when they hear the truth, they cannot bear to believe it; they think they are being deliberately misled. So I am afraid that what I myself

[2] Originally the party insignia in Hungary was a red star. Then a red, green, and white device was added to denote the national colors—an interesting enough concession to nationalist spirit.

said about America fell on deaf ears. I said among much else that I thought the chief danger of war was Russian ignorance. He replied, "Moscow knows even Hungary better than we know it ourselves." He added with a touch of grimness, "The United States will not find it easy to fight, because the American satellites are not ready." By "satellites" in this connection he meant France, Scandinavia, and so on. He said sharply, "It will not be easy to defeat the freedom-loving peoples of Europe. True democracy, you will find, is not so easy to export as motorcars!" Then, "if your capitalist class uses the atomic bomb, it is New York that will suffer most."

Rákosi's belief is that, fundamentally, no sufficient economic reason for war exists. "Russia and the United States lived in friendship for 150 years. You were even confederates. The Russian Czar sold you Alaska. There is great identity between the two countries—a big territory, expansion of the frontier, industrialization, and the like." But Rákosi—of course!—insisted that America had already reached the peak of its development, and is now declining, whereas the USSR is just beginning its steep climb up. The United States is a one-mast schooner, so he put it, and the Soviet Union is a great steamship. (Never mind how silly this sounds: all I am trying to do is reproduce a faithful pattern of our talk.) "Your culture," he affirmed, "the culture of the Anglo-Saxons, is now after four hundred years decadent, and your economy will of course eventually collapse." This last is a point that all Communists stress and reiterate, though events sometimes compel them to modify it in terms of time, namely that capitalism is bound to disintegrate in the end, and that a tremendous depression in America is inevitable. Rákosi went on, "You can be sure that *we*, on our side, will never start a war. The reason is that we know that any winner will be the loser. If the United States makes war, it will end up in the position of France after World War I and England after World War II—exhausted, bloodless, beaten even in victory." He added with a sharp twinkle: "Maybe the chief deterrent to war is that England is not so eager to undergo the strain of a third great victory!"

Rákosi went on: "The principal danger of war is that the

United States has never fought one!" We blinked. He proceeded to "explain." Industrialists get rich by war, and find it profitable; war is a time of easy big incomes, of adventure for the youth. "The United States plays with the idea of war like children with fire!" But the rank and file of the *population,* no matter what our casualties may have been in various wars, has had no experience of real *mass* suffering, he insisted. People in New York did not tear chunks off dead horses for food. They did not see their children shot like rabbits in the streets. And since we in the United States never had to endure invasion and spoliation on a universal mass scale, our people are apt to talk of war in a wholly irresponsible fashion, with no conception whatever of what horrors and sacrifices it may entail. Out of carelessness and ignorance, we have become belligerently war-minded, which, Rákosi concluded, is a mortal danger.

Finally Rákosi said something in a muted intent voice that is a key to much of the strength that fervid Communists have, their conviction that they are part of an inevitable historical process, that the development of mankind itself plays into their hands and is their best ally. "Do not forget—history is on our side."

The Redoubtable Zoltán Vas

This man is interesting too. Big and heavy-set, chockful of rough energy, Zoltán Vas is secretary general of the Supreme Economic Council, author of the Three Year Plan and the Five Year Plan to follow, and one of Rákosi's most intimate associates. He is not, however, as high in the party hierarchy as some others who might be mentioned. Mr. Vas (pronounced Vosh) was born in 1902. He became a Communist at the age of sixteen, and was arrested for party activity and sentenced to death by the Horthy dictatorship while still a boy. Hungarian law forbids the execution of minors, and so his sentence was commuted to life imprisonment. Of this he served sixteen solid years. He and Rákosi were cellmates for a time, and like Rákosi, he was released, exchanged, and sent to Moscow in 1940. The sixteen years in jail do not seem, on the surface, to have left much impression on his blunt and at the same time expressive nature. Mr. Vas is a character of the most formidable vigor.

I asked him a flat question: "Do you feel much pressure in Hungary from the Soviet government?"

His answer was very personal: "I have been a Communist since 1918. I have been sentenced to death twice by Fascists. I spent sixteen uninterrupted years in jail. I fought through the war with the Red army. I have spent my entire life studying Marxism. Here I help try to create a new society. Why should Moscow want to put pressure on *me*?"

During our talk Vas asked us what our next appointment was and then inquired, "Have you a car?"

"A car? Good Lord, no."

"But how do you get around?"

"On our feet."

He turned to an intercommunication device on his desk and with no change of voice murmured a word in Hungarian. The new world prides itself on its efficiency. Within a few seconds he resumed talk with us: "You now have a car."

And indeed when we got downstairs a modest automobile was waiting at the curb, with chauffeur.

Vas is famous for his vivid energy. He was mayor of Budapest at the beginning of the present regime; he got in a horse cart, himself, and tossed potatoes into the streets to the starving, as a symbol of the determination of the government to feed the people. Soon there were trolley cars full of potatoes all over the city, for the people to come to. "There was no gas, no electricity, no water. There were 40,000 dead. The bodies choked the gutters. Nobody had food. It was my responsibility. I went up and down the streets day and night, to give the people food and confidence!"

Today Vas often gets up at four in the morning, and pays unannounced visits to the markets. He summons his coadjutors for conferences at midnight, 5 A.M., or any time. Like so many people who genuinely enjoy hard work, he enjoys hard play too; he has a considerable capacity for food, drink, and human companionship. He likes to be in the thick of things. In Moscow, when it seemed that the city was bound to fall, and when he knew that he would certainly be hanged if the Germans captured him, he risked his life in the front lines time and again—when he might have been working comfortably in the Kremlin library. His outlook is radically different (except in Marxist dialectic) from that of a colleague like Gerö, who is an extreme ascetic. Vas is a realist first and last. He was criticized recently for making a $300 million trade deal with Argentina. "Why not?" was his reply. "Business is business." He was asked not long ago why the Budapest press printed such crazily distorted views of the United States. Reply: "It is necessary to teach our people to hate the United States so long as there is danger of attack from the West."[3]

I asked him how, at the age of sixteen, he had become a Communist. He said it was because of books he read. He added, "I have written a whole book myself telling my story. I give you a copy now!" He fished in a desk for one and wrote a quick inscription. "It is a best seller both here and in the USSR." I said I was afraid that I wouldn't be able to read it, since I don't know Hungarian or Russian. Vas deprecated his own knowledge of English but then said, "In jail I learned seven or eight languages—English, French, German, Russian." He was very bland. I had the feeling he wanted to add that out of jail we should have been able to do the same.

We asked Vas an inevitable question—exactly how far Hungary had gone on the road to becoming a complete socialist state. (This standard question, oddly enough, often embarrassed Communists in various countries; it did not embarrass Mr. Vas.) Nationalized, he said, were big industry and big business; banks and insurance companies; the big estates; foreign trade to an extent, through control of the currency; and the schools. Still private, he said, were agriculture, small commerce, small artisanship, a few special enterprises like publishing, and the professions.

"Do we want to destroy the small shopkeeper? No! We do not want to make life impossible for anybody." He turned to us with a gesture of appeal. "Our chief motive is to raise the living standard. First among all priorities is to raise the standard

[3] Homer Bigart in the New York *Herald Tribune,* December 2 and 12, 1948.

for everybody, by changing the whole economic face of the country. Housing? Ah, but housing cannot get the attention it deserves until reconstruction is complete. Remember we started from zero. Budapest was a shambles. Already we have raised wages and salaries by 17 percent, and we are forcing prices down. All those small people to whom I tossed potatoes, they helped *us* then, and we want to reward them, to draw them into the benefits of our new society. Of course we go *toward* socialization as fast as we can. The question may thus be asked, 'Why *should* we leave any private trade at all?' Because we do not know as yet what the precise rhythm of development should be. We are like an accordion: we can blow air in or let it out. It is quite possible that if state shops and private shops continue to exist side by side (anyway there are too many shops) the private shops will eventually be squeezed out, if we undersell them. That would be logical. But we emphatically do not wish this to happen. The private shops will remain. Anybody can buy in any shop. I assure you there is no punitive assault on a class.[4] In short, frankly, we do not know how fast to go. We are not doctrinaire. We look at each problem on its own practical merits. It is the prime duty of Marxists to explore the historic necessity, to push our development just as strongly as we can afford to push it, without going too far and thus endangering it."

We said good-by after an hour. I had the thought then, and still have, that this was the frankest conversation on economic matters I ever had with a leading Communist.

Other Personalities

Of great importance is Ernö Gerö, who is generally considered to be the No. 2 man in the country, though some would give this place to Jozsef Revai, the outstanding party theoretician and propagandist.[5] As to Gerö, he is a comparatively young man, a veteran Communist, and, in the words of a local document, "the dynamic leader of the Hungarian reconstruc-

[4] Many people would certainly disagree with Mr. Vas on this.
[5] Revai and Rákosi are the two Hungarian members of the Cominform.

tion." His real name is Singer, and his title is the modest one of Minister of Transportation and Communications. In career he follows his colleagues closely. He was arrested after the Bela Kun revolution in 1919 but his sentence was not so severe as those of Rákosi and Vas. From 1936 to 1938 he fought in Spain. Then he found his way to Moscow and returned to Budapest with the other "Muscovites"; he preceded even Rákosi, and was in charge till Rákosi himself arrived. Gerö is called "a machine." He is a fanatic, a man with no interest whatsoever except sixteen or eighteen merciless hours a day of work.

As interesting as these, and quite possibly of more future importance, is László Rajk, for a long period the all-powerful Minister of Interior, and now the Foreign Minister. As I heard it put, "Rajk is so dangerous because he is so appealing." He is inaccessible; but many people, on reaching him, have succumbed to what has been called his "burning charm." Rajk was born a Catholic, the son of a cobbler, in a town with the nice name Székelyudvarhely, in 1909. He did not, like Rákosi and Vas, spend the war years in Russia, and so is not a "Muscovite." This, in a paradoxical way, is a chief source of his potential power, because non-Communists are apt to say, "Rajk is not Jewish and not a Russian puppet; he is really one of ours." In fact, as Minister of the Interior, he went further than any of his colleagues in daring to lay down the law to the Russians; he insisted that looters from the Red army be punished, and even shot. If ever a big change should come in Hungary, Rajk might well emerge as a national leader. At the very least, he stands out to the crowd as someone sharply individual and different.

Rajk worked his way through the University of Budapest, and planned to become a teacher of literature. He was arrested for being a Communist in 1932, but released after a short term. He got a job as a manual laborer, and thus is one of the few Hungarian leaders who has been an actual worker. He joined the International Brigade in Spain, became a political commissar with the Hungarian troops, and was severely wounded in 1937. After the war he found his way to France, where he was arrested and interned. In 1941 he returned illegally to Hungary, and was arrested again; he got out, and became secretary of the

Budapest party organization—clandestinely, of course. He was caught when the Germans invaded the country, and miraculously escaped being shot. Nobody, of course, knew just who he was. He spent some time in a jail at Soprónköhida and then in a concentration camp in Germany. Uniquely among the leading Hungarian Communists, he returned to Budapest not from Moscow, but from imprisonment by the Nazis. Few others who were in Germany had the good luck to survive.

Episode in Manners

We had one experience in Hungary, minor but of a certain interest, that had nothing to do with Hungary. It had to do with Czechoslovakia. We had procured our Czechoslovak visas in New York some months before, and, as a consequence of delays all along the line, they had expired. Normally, once a visa is given, there is little trouble about extending its validity for a week or two. But we were told that we ought to call at the Czechoslovak consulate in Budapest in person and get this done. What followed was the most barbarous couple of hours I ever had in twenty-five years of journalism. It was minor, I repeat, but revolting. Of course it is the kind of thing that can happen in almost any country, Communist or not. In fact it showed a lack of organization and rudeness very rare in the satellite regimes.

We were herded into a thick line in a shabby unkempt building, and there told to wait. Fragments of other folk awaiting visas would break off this line, make a dash for a closed door, and be brutally pushed back. One line then formed into another line, corkscrewing into an inner room. From time to time, a door would open, a churlish head would poke itself out quickly as if to survey the scene, whereupon the door would snap shut again. A woman attendant in another room, where there was no line but a congealed mass of people twisting shapelessly before her, gave me a cardboard ticket numbered 87. This presumably meant that 86 people were still ahead of us. She then darted a quick significant look in my direction, took back the ticket, and gave me one marked 17. When 17 came up and I tried to get through into the next room, a great commotion took place; the lady was accused of having improperly favored me. A cold-eyed official was called and I reverted to another number.

Then—I am foreshortening all this greatly—we were taken by special favor to see the consul general in still another room. He refused to deal with us. Finally we got to the inner room and surrendered our passports. Here we waited at least two hours. A pompous martinet of unbelievable grossness refused (a) to expedite the proceedings; (b) to give us back our passports for another try next day. So we were stuck there. Then the woman who superintended the outer line came up and asked openly how much I was going to pay her for her unsuccessful attempt to slip me forward. I had no small change whereupon she calmly took what I had. Then, amazingly, she asked if I had been a friend of Masaryk's. I said "Yes" whereupon, hardly bothering to whisper, she said to be sure to take food into Czechoslovakia, since everybody there was starving. By this time the corpulent martinet was ready to deal with us. But we were not out of the woods yet.

I tried to explain that we had perfectly good visas which simply needed extension. He replied that this grave situation could only be dealt with by the personal intervention of the Minister of Interior in Prague, which would take two weeks. Finally he gave us transit visas limiting our stay in Czechoslovakia to twenty-four hours. I explained that we planned to go to Warsaw from Budapest, traversing Czech territory briefly on the train; would this, I wanted to know, mean that we would have to go through this whole surly process anew in Warsaw and get other new visas to re-enter Czechoslovakia? Yes, he replied. So we changed our itinerary and went to Prague direct, where a courteous official (who was frightened at first, however, when we told him that we had had visa trouble) fixed everything up for the trip to Poland and back, in two minutes. But to revert—we got out of the Budapest consulate somehow, passports safe in hand. New mobs of applicants were forming, as we pushed our way out. The woman at the desk touched me on the shoulder. "Let me have some more money please.

I did you a big favor." Perhaps I should add that this is the only case of personal corruption (petty as it was) that I ever came across behind the Curtain.

Item in Another Faith

One day I had a lively talk with a young Hungarian Communist, and we happened to mention a mutual friend, a journalist well known for his cynicism and urbane wit. We talked about him, and the Hungarian exclaimed, "But there is something wrong with that man! Do you think he really *believes* in anything? We have no patience here for people without faith!"

CHAPTER 14
THE CZECHOSLOVAK TRAGEDY

ABOUT Czechoslovakia the main thing to say is that Communism was imposed here by *coup d'état*. It did not come in the heat of warfare or by any spontaneous rising of the masses or even through the force of the Red army. A case may be made that Communism came to Bulgaria, say, or Poland, through a kind of process of historical development, assisted by the weakness and corruptions of previous regimes; this was not true in Czechoslovakia. But it is well to point out, on the other hand, that the *coup d'état* of February 1948, blunt and crude as it was, could not have been successful except for a long process of earlier infiltration and the broad mattress of popular support the Communists did indubitably have.

One cannot dismiss the role of the Communists in Czechoslovakia as that of a mere "Fifth Column," if by Fifth Column is meant a handful of individual plotters who gain their ends by stealth. Free and honest elections were held in Czechoslovakia in 1946, and the Communist party got 38 percent of the total vote. More than one-third of a whole electorate cannot legitimately be called a "Fifth Column." (But even in France this term is used to describe the Communist movement, though the Communists are the largest single French party in terms of representation in the National Assembly.) Nevertheless as to Czechoslovakia the basic and root fact of the present situation cannot be gainsaid: *full* control of the government by Communists came by reason of a *coup d'état*, nothing more, nothing less. And the Communists would almost certainly get much less than a 38 percent vote today.

The Czechoslovakia of 1949 has, compared to the other satellites, at least two other uniquenesses. First and most important, it was a true democracy before the war. This means of course that the people, having really known what democracy was, suffer the more acutely now that it has been withdrawn. The shock to the people has been much more grave than to the Yugoslavs, for instance, or Albanians, who never lived under a democracy in our sense of the term.

Second, Czechoslovakia is the only thoroughly industrialized state ever to become Communist. Moreover Czech industry has always been geared to the West, not the East. The Czechs produced floods of textiles, pottery, toys, pencils, munitions, glass, gloves, beer, and luxury goods for Western markets. Now the Russians are attempting to change all of this by transferring the focus of Czech economy to the production of heavy machinery, steel and the like for use in the Soviet Union and other satellites. Also the fact that Czechoslovakia is a tremendously important industrial state makes it doubly important for the Communists to make their regime successful, no matter what hardships have to be imposed on the people.

Orthodox Communist comment on these points is suggestive. The fact that Czechoslovakia was a democracy before is considered a great asset, in that the rank and file of the people were educated. That it was and is an industrial state is likewise considered an advantage, in that it gave the regime (so the argument runs) a disciplined proletariat to work with. The *workers* rule, not just a crowd of ill-trained peasants. Also the Communists say in regard to matters we will touch on presently: (a) the real reason things look so "bad" is that, unfortunately, the opposition was so powerful; (b) the degree of dependence a satellite has on Moscow depends on the status of the opposition. This was strong in Czechoslovakia and hence the country is bound to be very close to Russia.

In another field one more point of difference among the consort states might be mentioned, namely that Czechoslovakia had no devastation problem comparable to those in Hungary or Poland. Prague—in acute contrast to Budapest or Warsaw—was never fought over, and the damage caused by American bombing was almost negligible.

Good-by to a Nation

It happened that we were in Prague on the day of the funeral of Dr. Eduard Benes, one of the founders of the republic and its illustrious President for many years. But this was not merely the funeral of Dr. Benes; it was the funeral of the hopes and dreams of the majority of the Czech people. The massed and tattered thousands who came to watch the parade were not only saying good-by to Dr. Benes; they were saying good-by to themselves. It was not just the body of the former President that was being buried that day, but freedom.

Seldom have I known anything more poignant. With Gaston Coblentz of the New York *Herald Tribune,* and through the courtesy of Ambassador Laurence A. Steinhardt (just about the ablest American diplomat or other official we met in all Europe), who lent us a car, we drove up and down the streets. Czechoslovakia is certainly a police state so far as politics in the large are concerned, but—as of that time at least—there was no interference with the casual movements of the people. So we were able to stop here and there and talk to the peasant women in their lush costumes who had trekked into Prague on foot, to the resplendent Czech legionnaires who fought valiantly for freedom in two world wars, and to members of the patriotic "Sokol" organization, now purged, waiting dourly to find out whether or not they would be allowed to march in the procession.

The Czechs are not emotional people. Famously they are somewhat yeastless. The night before at the Pantheon we saw women who had been standing in line for eleven hours burst into tears and wail and drop broken sprays of flowers as they passed the body of Dr. Benes lying in state. But that might have been the result of exhaustion plus the climactic emotion of the moment.

But the next morning they were still weeping—openly and strenuously. We jumped back into our car after talking to a group of Sokols. Women we had talked to, and who knew we were Americans, stuck their hands through the half-open windows and clutched at us sobbing, trying to keep us with them just another moment. It was as if our mere physical American presence gave them some desperate momentary assurance; once we were gone, they would be gone too, and they knew it.

This was the first time I saw the celebrated Workers Militia.

It is always an odd experience to be challenged by a man wearing overalls or a felt hat and carrying a rifle.

About ten thousand militiamen, who are the armed Communists out of the workshops and factories, stood guard over the parade. Tough babies! As we halted for traffic I would try to catch the eye of one and smile. Nobody ever smiled back. Tough indeed! They stood for mile after mile, sour and stolid, rifles ready, pressing back the crowd of mourners and buttressing the line of the parade itself. Yet, and this we thought remarkable, there was no overt pushing or prodding or even surveillance by the regular police. The night before, among all those tens of thousands of mourners, we hardly saw a single policeman.

One small item fascinated me. The rifles the militiamen carried were a decrepit miscellany—old arms from everywhere—but their shoulder straps were brand new, neat and shiny. So I knew where a lot of leather had gone! Previously we had spent some hours walking down the main streets and looking into the shops. They are as naked as if stripped by buzzards. Not only has virtually all food disappeared; most of the small consumer goods for which Czechoslovakia has always been famous, in particular leather articles, have likewise disappeared.

The reasons for this are various: shortage of foreign exchange (the Czechs, like the British, are forced to export practically everything they produce, including leather in large quantities); a shift in emphasis from light to heavy industry; and, to an extent, the general economic depression which followed last year's bad harvest. But now I became aware of another reason; a great deal of leather must have been used for soldiers' boots and rifle straps instead of portfolios and ladies' handbags.

Background to the Czech Complex

Czechoslovakia is a solid chunk of country, containing some 12 million people wedged in the heart of the continent. Everybody knows its strategic importance; Bismarck once said, "The master of Bohemia is the master of Europe," and one theory—which does not however march with all the facts—is that the motivation of the February *coup* was largely military. In any case Czechoslovakia is a Communist state in *Central,* not just Eastern, Europe, which gives it another interesting uniqueness. It is populated by two closely allied Slav peoples, the Czechs focusing on Prague, and the Slovaks to the south. The population as a whole is 73.54 percent Catholic, which makes it even more Catholic than Hungary; this will be a surprise to many. The Czechs have lived in this region, an indestructible homogeneous unit, for almost 1,400 years. Their ancient kings preceded the Habsburgs by centuries, and their nationalism, though subjected to tremendous strains and subjugations, has always been tenacious. There is a very definite and easily recognized Czechoslovak national character.

The country rose magnificently from Austro-Hungarian domination in 1918, and lived until 1938 when Munich killed it. The Germans after 1939 made Moravia and Bohemia into a "protectorate," gave Subcarpathian Ruthenia to Hungary, let the Poles have part of Silesia, and set up Slovakia as a wretched "autonomous" puppet. Never has a country been dealt with more cruelly; and Neville Chamberlain was as guilty, from one point of view, as Hitler. The Nazi occupation was of course murderous. Everybody remembers—or should remember—Lidice. In the country as a whole a total of 169,000 Czech and Slovak citizens were *executed,* not merely killed in fighting, including 67,000 Jews in Slovakia alone, during the grim frightful years of the Hitler terror.[1]

It is no wonder that almost the first thing the Czechs did in 1945 on regaining their independence—for a pitiably brief interval—was to expel from the country the 2,500,000 Sudeten Germans who lived in its outer fringes. (Now, ironically, the Russian masters of Czechoslovakia are demanding that some of these Germans be brought back, because many are highly trained and industrious skilled workers. A great shortage in all the satellites is first-class personnel.) Another irony is that for strategic reasons Russia appropriated after the war the little stub of territory called Subcarpathian Ruthenia. Having it gives

[1] These are official figures. See *Czechoslovakia: Old Culture and New Life,* Prague, 1947.

the Russians a short common frontier with both Hungary and Czechoslovakia, which they had not had before.

The Czechoslovak liberation is a complex and interwoven story. Dr. Benes formed a government in exile in London. Czech legions were organized both in the West and in Russia. Benes became violently prejudiced against the British, in part because they delayed so long in formally repudiating the Munich pact. He journeyed to Moscow several times, and formed a close connection with Stalin. Meantime the resistance movement grew active and powerful in Czechoslovakia itself, though it was never so big a factor as in Yugoslavia say (for the obvious reason that the country was immediately adjacent to Germany and militarily occupied from top to toe). The government-in-exile and resistance worked closely and harmoniously all through the war; there were no fissures as in Yugoslavia or Greece. The Red army finally reached Czech soil, striking into Ruthenia, on October 18, 1944, and their advance was rapid. But nothing like so overt and intimate a relation developed between Russia and Czech Communists, during the advance, as occurred in the case of Hungary. In fact it was Dr. Benes himself—not any "Muscovite"—who entered with the Russians and set up a provisional government on Czech territory at Košice, in April 1945. Meantime another great Allied army was closing in on Prague—the American army of General Patton. It became a race between Patton and the Red army as to which would liberate Prague first. Then Prague itself revolted against the Germans. Patton was held up on orders from the Supreme Allied Command, and withdrew from his position near Prague, after capturing several nearby cities, and it was the Red army that took the capital. Patton could have captured it himself easily. History might have been different if he had.

The first Czech government was—of course—a coalition. Let us trace subsequent developments briefly; they lead straight into the *coup*. It was not only a coalition; it was a kind of omnibus, since it included *all* parties of any importance, eight in all, four representing the Czechs, four the Slovaks. Its name was "National Front," and it ranged from the Communists on the extreme left to the Catholic People's party on the right.

This government installed itself in Prague, got to work, and on May 26, 1946, held an election beyond doubt free and honest. The Communists became by far the largest single party, with 37.9 percent of the vote and 114 deputies out of a constituent assembly of 300. Again, let it be stressed that this was a fair election. But the fact that the Communists won does not gainsay the fact that they were also a minority, and it certainly does not excuse much of their subsequent behavior.

Now to go back a bit. Dr. Zdeňek Fierlinger was the first Prime Minister of the Košice government, appointed by Benes. It happens that I knew this highly controversial figure well before the war when he was successively Czechoslovak minister to Vienna and ambassador to Moscow. Fierlinger was, and is, an extreme left-wing Social Democrat, not a Communist, but it is he who directly paved the way for Russian power over the country in 1948 and made the *coup* inevitable. He is almost universally despised. When I told people in Prague that I had a talk with him they looked at me as dumbfounded as if I had met Beelzebub. People call him Dr. Quislinger. Be that as it may be, he was certainly a passionate Czech patriot in former years. He wanted to fight at Munich. He showed sympathy for the Russians not necessarily as Communists, but as fellow Slavs and nationalist allies. He could not sleep for weeks, he told me, trying to trace back over and over in his mind exactly *how* the tragedy of Munich had happened, because he literally could not believe that his country had been so wantonly betrayed and destroyed. Like all Czechs, he loathed and detested the Germans. Once I met him in Moscow at the time of the Russo-German pact. He was a man crushed and bewildered. It seemed to him intolerable—then—that the Russians could possibly be playing what appeared to be a German game. As to his present beliefs, all I can say is that he seemed to me in Prague to have lost all contact with reality. If not an actual Laval he had become a dupe.

After the 1946 elections the veteran Communist leader Klement Gottwald became Prime Minister. This was correct inasmuch as the Communists were the biggest party. But Fierlinger, the Social Democrat, held the balance of power in the cabinet. The Communists had no majority unless Fierlinger voted with them, and decisions were usually made on an eleven to ten division. On the other hand, in the usual manner, the Communists had managed to appropriate most of the key cabinet posts—Interior, Finance, National Defense, and Information. But Jan Masaryk was the nonparty Foreign Minister.

It is also worth pointing out—the information should be salutary—that the Communists would never have got their foot in the door in the first place, if the bourgeois parties had not been neglectful, stupid, and at each other's throats. They were overconfident and hardly even bothered to make a campaign in the election. Then the Catholic party and the Benes party, both conservative, quarreled bitterly with each other, of course to Communist gain. In strict contrast, the Communists and a rump of the Social Democrats in time *merged,* largely by act of Fierlinger. They became a united and cohesive block in striking contrast to the disintegration of the opposition. Of course a great number of Social Democrats did not enjoy being swallowed up; Fierlinger himself was expelled by an angry party caucus at Brno in October 1947. But I am not arguing the merits of his position. What should be stressed is the way the Communists and their allies had the nerve and foresight to take advantage of the same situation that the opposition muffed.

The Communist party, called the K.S.C. in Czechoslovakia, is of course superbly organized. Members wear a red and white badge; their motto is *Čest Práci,* "Salute to Work." The party claims a membership of about two million, and is thus the third largest in Europe. Recently, it seems, the ruling bodies have decided that this is too big; a massive purge, called "*Proverka,*" the Russian word for "inspection," got under way, with the object of cutting the roll by 500,000. Later those ejected will be eligible to re-entry, after scrutiny, if they pass "refresher" courses in Marxist doctrine.[2]

The minutiae attending the February *coup* itself hardly matter. The Communists could no longer count on those Social Democrats who refused to follow Fierlinger, and their slim advantage in the cabinet was thus imperiled. As part of a tight-

[2] Dana Adams Schmidt in the *New York Times,* February 17, 1949.

ening-up process the Communist Minister of the Interior discharged eight non-Communist chiefs of police, replacing them with Communists. This seemed to indicate that direct action by the C.P. was impending. The bourgeois parties woke up with a start, and demanded that the eight police chiefs be reinstated; the issue was brought to parliament, and the Communists were beaten. But the Minister of the Interior refused to change his position. The opposition turned indignantly on him to point out that, when the Communists won a majority, they expected the others to abide by a parliamentary decision, and the others had dutifully done so; now that they had lost, they refused to do the same. Anger mounted, and ministers of the two rightist parties lost their heads and resigned. At first Gottwald, who seemingly did not favor violence himself, tried to persuade Dr. Benes to appoint a new cabinet, compromise the issue somehow, and still keep some semblance of representative government. But Gottwald's hand was forced by his own extremists. The town filled up with armed bands. The Prague police were under Communist control. The headquarters of the other parties were seized and taken over, and Gottwald simply announced that a new government had assumed power.

This was all completely extralegal of course. There was no bloodshed, however, and no resistance. The legend that the Red army, which had left Czechoslovakia years before, played any direct role is completely unfounded.[3] In actual fact the *coup* was almost accidental. People scarcely knew what was going on, since the press and radio were controlled. Czechoslovakia lost its freedom, not through a fight, but with a dying squeak. The rightist members of the government bear considerable blame for these proceedings. "The communist coup was, in fact, a spontaneous and quickly organized counterstroke to a legitimate but inept tactical move by the anti-Communist ministers." The preceding sentence is quoted from Sir Robert Bruce Lockhart, an intimately informed expert on Czechoslo-

[3] The Russian troops were maneuvered into withdrawal largely by the astute diplomacy of Ambassador Steinhardt. They were a poor lot—mostly dregs and remnants of Mongolian divisions—but violent. When they came in there were 7,000 cases of rape of Czech women in the city of Brno alone.

vakia, a writer of great note, the director of British psychological warfare during the war, and an inveterate anti-Communist.[4]

The official party press describes the February overturn with a bias so violent that quotations are hardly credible. But it is always useful to see how the Communist mind operates after the event. This is from the journal of the Cominform:

> Reaction sought to violate the main principle of the [Two Year] Plan which, through organizing and further developing industry, aimed at securing closer relations between Czechoslovakia, the Soviet Union and the new democracies, at guaranteeing Czechoslovakia's independence from the capitalist world and at creating conditions for the systematic and speedy development of the country toward socialism.
>
> Reaction . . . spared no efforts in combating the guiding figures of the Plan elaborated by the communist party.
>
> The February events put an end to these machinations of reaction.

Since the *coup* the Communists have, of course, proceeded in their most orthodox and well-tested manner to consolidate power. The cabinet was reorganized, and the party took over all the ministries except a handful. One of the few non-Communists remaining was Jan Masaryk. Another, who still remains, is a Catholic priest, Father Josef Plojhar. Presently Benes, a sick and broken man, resigned the presidency of the republic—in part because he would not sign the new constitution which was being prepared—and Gottwald stepped up to his position as head of state. A trade unionist leader named Zápotocký succeeded him as Prime Minister. Fierlinger, meantime, was Vice Premier; technically the government was still a "coalition." In May 1948, national "elections" were held; these were a complete farce, with only one list presented to the voters. Guess who won. The government "vote" was 89 percent. It should also be noted that 800,000 Czechoslovak citizens still had enough courage to leave their ballots blank.

[4] In an article in *Foreign Affairs*, "The Czechoslovak Revolution," July, 1948.

The Death of Masaryk

On March 10 the robust and unique Jan Masaryk, the Czechoslovak Foreign Minister, son of the statesman who founded the republic and one of the supremely great men of this or any time, jumped, fell, or was pushed from his bathroom window in the Czernin Palace, and was killed. Was this a suicide, as the Czech Communists assert, or murder?

It is too early to elucidate this compelling mystery fully. Much is known to a few people that cannot be printed for fear of getting other people still in Prague in trouble. A lawyer I know of great authority, who has as intimate knowledge of the case as anybody alive, told me after many months of investigation that the affair is unique in his experience—an equally good argument may be made out for either side.

If Masaryk, a profound patriot and also a stupendous lover of life, killed himself as a gesture, why did he leave no message, even to his sister? Or, if he did, what happened to it? If he had been contemplating suicide why did he make hard-and-fast arrangements with a very close friend for events to take place later in the month? That he planned such events is, we know from private sources, incontestable. But if he was *not* planning suicide, why did he take such scrupulous care to put all his financial affairs and the like, which he often neglected for months at a time, in perfect order a few days before his death?

Masaryk was moody, impulsive, turbulent, whimsical, and honest to the bone. His close friends in Prague knew just before the end that he was laboring under frightful tensions. He had come to feel finally that the democratic cause was indeed lost; he knew that the Communists were really closing in. Also, something that he regarded as an indiscretion by a friend, a Czech official in Washington, put increased pressure on him. He spent days and nights burning all his private papers; I have this on the authority of somebody who helped him burn them. But this can be explained either as evidence of an intent to kill himself, *or* of a plan to get out of the country quickly, which would have given the Communists their only good motive for murdering him.

If Masaryk had not planned to flee, there was no point to murder. His name and prestige were still extremely useful to the regime, even if he was a virtual prisoner. And though "defenestration" is a traditional means of death in Prague, it would have been ever so much simpler and easier for the Communists to get rid of him by other means, if they wanted to. But, on the other hand, if he *did* plan to escape from the country, the Communists might well have decided that they had to assassinate him, and might have attempted to disguise this as "suicide," for the obvious reason that his flight to freedom would have so cardinally discredited their regime. To a degree the whole case focuses on whether or not a plane was actually waiting to take Masaryk out secretly that week, as some of his close friends say. If so, he may well have been murdered. If not, he was probably a suicide. The projected flight should be a simple enough matter to get the truth about, yet the facts remain uncertain. Everybody tells a different story, and it is almost impossible, as of this moment, to prove whether or not the plane had really been arranged for.

Also a great deal of mystery devolves on the autopsy. This was performed by government doctors, and it has never, so far as I know, been made fully public.

On the other hand one cannot fairly neglect well-known instabilities and one case of suicide in Masaryk's own family. Nobody knows, nobody can know, exactly what went through his mind in the last five or six hours of his life, which he spent alone. It is a striking irony incidentally that his celebrated father's first published work many decades ago was an essay on suicide.

It happened that I myself last saw Jan Masaryk in New York, at my apartment, in mid-November 1947. A group of friends gathered to meet him, including Dorothy Thompson, and we had several hours of the most vivid, animated, and controversial talk. A day or two later Miss Thompson sent Masaryk one of the most beautiful and moving letters ever written. It was a reiteration of her faith in him and love for what he stood for in the prodigious and ravaging difficulties in which he found himself. Masaryk replied:[5]

[5] I have Miss Thompson's permission to quote this letter in part.

When I walked into John's enclosure the other night I was very glad that you and Maxim were glad to see me. . . . Your letter did much more, much more than that. When I read it and reread it, my feeling was overwhelmingly stronger than just being glad or pleased. You did something, which I could best describe by the words of a war poem (Czech and from the first war)—"You kissed his broken heart"—the "broken" being an exaggeration; in the vernacular I would say not broken but badly bent . . .

It is too true that I am standing (not yet squatting) between two not too static and not too savoury stools, and I fear I have a great many colleagues scattered all over this worrymaking planet.

. . . I am certainly not going down the drain without making a considerable squawk.

For the time being I am persona most grata with my people at home. It is very touching how they hang on to me and expect things from me. How will I fail them the least—that's the question, because *rebus sic stantibus.* I cannot deliver the goods they so vitally need and so deeply deserve. I will think about it and do the best I can.

I must go home as soon as possible to give my fairly passionate support to those who are trying to carry on the lovely Bohemian tradition against cynical and well organized material dialectics. For the time being we can hold our own. How long I know not.

Somewhere, sometime, somehow I am going to stand on my hind legs and shout to the Great Powers. . . . The timing, that's my problem.

Miss Thompson mentioned Hamlet in her magnificent letter. And surely there is much of Hamlet in this reply.

Many of Masaryk's close friends in America, including his doctor (he was suffering from an acutely painful shoulder injury that demanded immediate surgery which he never bothered to have done) repeatedly urged him not to go back to Czechoslovakia at all. But he went, and this brave, honest and immensely candid man died, with the result that we all know. My own deep inner feeling, for what it is worth, is that his death was suicide, though I cannot prove it. But certainly murder cannot be excluded till we know, if we ever will know, more about what happened in Prague just before the final tragic hour. In any case it was the Communists who killed him, for his death was murder—even if a suicide.

Prague: Sidelights and Impressions

The first thing we did on our first walk down and around St. Wenceslas Square was to go into the café of a hotel I remembered and order coffee. No coffee. People around us were drinking a horrible-looking raspberry syrup. But we were obviously foreigners and after a while the waiter came up surreptitiously and slipped us two thimblefuls of coffee in small cups; on the saucers were tiny saccharine tablets carefully cut in half. Price for each serving: 78 crowns, which at the legal rate worked out to $1.56.

I have already mentioned that the food shops are scraped bare. We went into two or three; they were emptier and more desolate even than those in Belgrade. In one automat there was practically nothing to eat except a few preposterously expensive sweets; people looked at them hungrily, fingering their coupons. For Czechoslovakia is the only country we saw, aside from England, where rationing is taken with strict seriousness. One must have food tickets even in the restaurants. A minor point is that, because of shortage of malt and hops, the famous beer tastes as no Pilsner ever ought to taste. As to prices we were used to the expensiveness of the Iron Curtain by this time, but even so Prague shocked us. An American friend took us to dinner in a black market restaurant; the bill for three was about $60. I bought a round of dry martinis for two colleagues in one of the big hotels. Price: $16.[6]

The Communist explanation of the food shortage is the bad harvest, and this is indeed a valid excuse in part. Czechoslovakia always has had to import foodstuffs, but the amount was minor in a normal year, say 70,000 tons. This year between 700,000 and 800,000 tons of grain had to be imported, most of it from Russia. The net visible cost to the state was about 15 billion crowns, or $300 million. As a result, there is a drastic, terrible lack of foreign exchange. I asked several Marxists about this,

[6] Obviously martinis are extreme luxuries. I do not mean that the prices I have just cited represent the general level. In fact, basic necessities in the way of food are cheap. Things may be scarce, but the government has succeeded in keeping the prices down.

wanting to know how they rationalized a bad harvest in terms of the Communist dialectic. Had God stepped in? Exactly how far is the materialist conception of history dependent on weather? The answers I got were various.

While we were in Prague the newspaper *Práce*, noting wistfully that food conditions were better in Poland than at home, performed what I thought was a really masterful verbal twist. It wrote that, though Poland was rich in foodstuffs while Czechoslovakia was all but starving, the reason for this was that the Czechs, unlike the Poles, had a "surplus of purchasing power [!] caused by last year's harvest catastrophe." In other words—the mind reels—the real fault was not lack of food but that the population had too much money with which to buy that which did not exist![7]

We watched people carefully on the main streets, like Prikope and Vaclavske Namesti. Incidentally names like Hoover Street still survive; so does the Wilson railway station. The citizenry walks mostly in shabby clothes with hunched shoulders, as if stupefied by shock and misery. Prague, despite its physical beauty, has nothing of the zip of Belgrade or the flavor and charm of Budapest; the atmosphere is drear, drab, poor, ugly, spiritless. There were pictures of Thomas Masaryk in some shop windows, none of Jan, and some of Benes. There are no massed red flags or overtly Russian posters, and photographs of Lenin and Stalin are not conspicuous.

Charlie Chaplin was playing in *Monsieur Verdoux*, and we saw mention of Greer Garsonová, René Claira, Walterem Pidgeonem, Eugena O'Neilla, Ronalda Colmana, and even Ernsta Lubitsche. Also there were plenty of Russian movies, but they are not patronized nearly as well as those American. The U.S.I.S. library, with its American flag flying conspicuously on a main street, has become risky territory for Czechs, but even so the attendance is almost 10,000 people a month. Our news bulletin has a circulation of about 1,200 copies daily; occasion-

[7] The official *Rudé Pravó* ("Red Truth") wrote savagely at about the same time that "people who ask why there is no prosperity" in comparison to ten or fifteen years ago forget that in those days "the government ordered shooting of workers who wanted work." This is of course a crazy lie.

ally, but not often, an issue is confiscated by the Czech authorities.

We inspected the kiosks, and visited the bookstores; the Moscow papers are on sale, but, so far as I could see, no other foreign dailies. There were, however, a few English weeklies (even the *Tatler* of all things), but no American periodicals at all, except—and this was curious—*back* numbers of *Time*. Some issues dated from 1946. As of the present day *Time* and *Life* are forbidden. The pretext given for the general lack of reading matter, and indeed it may be correct, is shortage of foreign exchange. Some big shops sell *only* for dollars; we saw a tablecloth priced at $140. A small incidental point is that taxis are very scarce; one driver refused a tip, but eagerly took some American cigarettes instead.

Foreign writers in translation included Wells, Maugham, Maurois, Marcia Davenport, and a few others. The Churchill memoirs have been translated, and a biography of him was conspicuous in several stores. Three titles of books in English in one shop were, I swear it, the following:

The Apples of England
The Comet of 1577
Modern Sewage Disposal

One day we called on my Czech publisher; as of the time we were there (I believe this has changed since) there was no overt censorship on foreign books. *Inside U.S.A.* had been translated and the Czechs were interested in the fact that it was also appearing in Hungarian and Bulgarian. We heard that John Steinbeck's work, which is immensely popular throughout all Eastern Europe, had been facing difficulties since the publication of his recent volume on Russia, though to our mind this book should have pleased the Russians. First Steinbeck was denounced in Moscow. Then, so we heard, the Rumanians and Hungarians successively took action against translating or selling his books; the ban works upward and outward slowly. The Czechs thought it would reach them in time. We talked to a prominent literary agent one morning; he had just been plunged into a crisis over Richard Wright, whose play *Black*

Boy was about to open in Prague. But the party authorities heard that Wright, in Paris, had made remarks offensive to the Communists, and it was necessary for the producer to telegraph Wright, get his reply which was straightforward and dignified, and print this in the newspapers, before the play could be put on. A small point that fascinated me was the attention paid in Czechoslovakia, as in several of the other satellites, to the literary merits of the American author Howard Fast. One would have thought that Fast was the only writer in the United States. We were seriously asked for how long a term he had been "imprisoned," and whether the fact that he was embroiled in legal difficulty over Communism meant that American publishers would be forbidden henceforth to issue any of his books!

All Czech writers of consequence—if they want favorable attention—are now organized into a syndicate with 1,700 members; the literary critics are almost all Marxists, most of them young men who are recent members of the party. There is no censorship on foreign telegrams, though these may be delayed, or on telephone calls by foreign correspondents, of whom there are (according to the press bureau of the government) about 140 in Prague. Tass, the official Russian agency, is represented by a small bureau; neither *Izvestia* nor *Pravda* maintains staff correspondents, which is odd. As to the local press and radio, no freedom is left at all. Indeed in this respect Czechoslovakia outdoes the other puppet states. In October 1948, a decree was passed "for the protection of the Democratic People's Republic" which lists even "wrong thinking" as a punishable offense.[8]

Now turn to the other freedoms. The technique of suppression is what we have encountered before. There is no "hot" terror. The Minister of Interior boasted recently that the Czech jails are "the emptiest in the world." There are no concentration camps on the German model or forced labor battalions. But economic pressure, the "cold terror," is merciless and in the long run just as effective. Anybody known to oppose the regime overtly will lose his job, sooner or later, or, what is almost as important, his housing space or ration tickets. This is lethal: after all, one has to eat. One day we met a young and

[8] *New York Times*, November 28, 1948.

very pretty Czech woman; she had just spent several hours being quizzed by the police, politely but intensively, because one of her beaux was a foreigner who had been arrested for espionage. A great deal of espionage and counteractivity has indubitably been going on. As to matters of religion the situation is very mixed. The government is, by its very essence, antireligious, but the churches, even the Roman Catholic churches, are packed full. The Reverend Dr. John S. Bonnell, one of the best-known ministers in New York, visited Czechoslovakia recently and declared, "There is no interference whatsoever up to now with purely religious worship. No obstacles of any kind are being placed in the way of worship in the churches, either Catholic or Protestant, at present."[9]

To attempt to judge what weight of opposition still exists is very difficult; the heart of discontent is in Catholic Slovakia. But anybody who gratuitously asks the Czechs and Slovaks to "revolt" against the duress under which they live, is, of course, talking nonsense. There is no easy way to revolt against absolute police power in a revolutionary regime, and nobody should forget that this *is* a revolutionary regime. Nor should one forget that the Czechs were mercilessly crushed by the Nazis for six long years, and that a resultant combination of fear, apathy, and resignation typifies their personal and political behavior. Benes was their last hope. Then too there is the *élan* of the Communists themselves. I heard one young party zealot exclaim after the Benes funeral, joyously, "Now, the *real* new life of our people's democracy can begin!"

The attitude of one American woman I met in Prague expresses what is likely to be the Western attitude to much of this: "I'd like to go to a country where people don't have stainless steel teeth."

How Socialist is Czechoslovakia?

Czechoslovakia was, under the elder Masaryk and Benes, a progressive and very sensible young country; hence it set about facing the problem of the land at once. The Czechoslovak land

[9] Gaston Coblentz in the New York *Herald Tribune*, August 7, 1948.

reform does not originate with the present regime by any means; it dates back in fact to 1919. All the big estates were then broken up, which was a healthy enough development. This has been carried much farther by the new government so that nobody today is allowed more than fifty hectares, which, many critics say, is too great a fragmentation for efficient agriculture. Moreover, from time to time, parcels of ten or even five hectares are "passed out like rain checks," as I heard it put; the government gains doubly by this process, because in the first place the original owner does not get adequate compensation, and second the authorities extract a healthy price from those to whom the new plots are assigned. About 1,300,000 hectares of land have been distributed to roughly 500,000 families by the new land reform so far.

As of the time I was in Prague there was no talk at all of collectivization. The regime knew when to let well enough alone. Subsequently, however, a strong impetus toward this process (i.e., taking the land, in effect, away from the peasants to whom it was given and operating it through big collectives by the state) has taken place. In Hungary I was assured by almost everybody that the Russians had not interfered in any way whatever with the local agrarian policy. In Czechoslovakia it would be hard to say the same. Certainly the Communist extremists are now demanding action against the "rich" farmers, who are described as "the last frontier of capitalism."

The Czechoslovak Two Year Plan for industrialization and nationalization ran from 1946 to 1948. It is to be followed (here we tread a familiar satellite path) by a Five Year Plan. In the local idiom, the two plans are quite distinct. The earlier shorter plan was supposed to be devoted to recovery, so that the country could rehabilitate itself economically to the prewar level; the second longer plan then proceeds to a full-range program of heavy industrialization and the like. A very substantial nationalization has already taken place. For instance, whereas the relevant figure in the other puppets is generally 100, in Czechoslovakia all industrial enterprises employing more than 50 persons have been nationalized. This legislation, let us point out, predates 1948; it was put into effect by the old coalition which as we know included *rightist* as well as leftist elements, though dominated by the Communists.

In a pamphlet published in early 1947,[10] the extent of nationalization of various industries was given as follows. The figures cover Bohemia, Moravia, and Silesia, but not Slovakia.

Industry	%
Mining	100
Iron and Steel, Engineering	75
Chemical	74
Wood-working	23
Building Materials and Pottery	59
Building	10
Glass	68
Textile and Clothing	46
Leather	60
Paper and Printing	28
Food	39
Electricity, Gas and Water	82
Average	55·3

There are about 900,000 trade unionists in Czechoslovakia; they have a semiautonomous political status, and are a signal influence in the country. An interesting point is that labor may be conscripted by government ukase even to boys and girls of fifteen if "necessary." Strikes are very rare, if they ever occur at all. It is very difficult to estimate wages in terms of a purchasing power understandable to the West; the government itself claims that if 100 is the index for 1939, the present figure is 302.3. Workers work a six-day 48-hour week, as in most of the Eastern European states. Of course, in the long run, if the satellites cannot improve the status of the worker himself, who is supposed to be the key to all, their excuse for existing disappears. The whole pretext for the grisly hardships of nationalization and industrialization is the benefits that are supposed to accrue to the proletariat on some future day.

It is difficult in the extreme to tell how closely the Five Year Plan is proceeding on schedule. Recently a considerable ab-

[10] *Czechoslovakia, Test Case of Nationalization* by Joseph Goldmann. Prague, 1947.

senteeism has developed in factories, with a resultant drop in output. Also, in the words of one observer, "The chief impediment to the Plan has been the shortage of raw materials due to insufficiency of imports from the West. . . . Industrial sloth and 'bourgeois' national characteristics—at least in Bohemia and Moravia—are today the great oppositionist factors."[11] Then too the government has had great difficulty in finding expert managers. In fact these were so scarce that, in many cases, the former bourgeois managers were kept on, though always at the risk of being purged suddenly. Some managers, to hold their jobs, became Communists.

The government itself, in these days of bitter stringency, has a motto which might well be applauded in other circumstances: "We must earn our own prosperity."

Foreign Affairs of the Cat's-Paw State

In a manner of speaking Czechoslovakia has a common frontier with the United States, since it adjoins the American Zone of Germany for one hundred and sixty-five miles, unknown as this fact may be to the immense majority of Americans. It was reported lately that the Czechs are binding this frontier with a hem of barbed wire, because so many of their folk have, despite the most careful precautions, managed to escape across it. In theory any nonpolitical Czech who asks for an exit visa gets it. The actual facts are far otherwise. And since all other frontiers of the country abut on Russian or satellite territory, the American Zone offers the only feasible opportunity for illegal exit. This makes the Czechoslovak authorities angry, and scarcely a day passes without the arrest of somebody in Prague or elsewhere charged with being an American spy furthering the "underground railway" into soil controlled by the U.S.A.

The United States offered Czechoslovakia participation in the Marshall plan in July 1947; the Czech government accepted in principle—largely through the influence of Masaryk—and indeed it would have been delighted to share in ECA benefits. The Russians then intervened, refused to allow the Czechs to

[11] *New Statesman,* December 18, 1948.

join the Paris conference, and forced them to abstain from the plan. Moscow has offered very little as an alternative. To date at least, the flimsy structure set up to offset the Marshall plan and comfort the satellites for being out in the cold, known as the Soviet Council for Economic Mutual Assistance, has had no comparable ameliorative effect.

To read the Czech press about the United States is enlightening. Here is an item that appeared in *Mladá Fronta* on September 1, 1948:

TERROR AGAINST WALLACE

American Reaction Uses Violence as Weapon against Progress

Henry Wallace, Leader of the U. S. Progressive Party, is now touring the Southern States and holding election campaign meetings there. These states are the center of racial discrimination, class-oppression and immense exploitation. . . . To paralyze Wallace's influence on broad masses of working people the planters—these pillars of reaction—organize provocations and terrorist actions at Wallace's meetings. . . . Through this provoked attack the *American reaction joins forces with the Italian, Japanese, and Iranian terrorists.* (Italics mine.)

The *Tvorba* printed at about the same time a fascinating little account of a Communist contretemps. A man named Stanislav Budin wrote a book, *USA—Portrait of a Nation,* about the United States; presently it was reviewed harshly by a well-known local party-line commentator, André Simone. As a result of Simone's attack, Budin was impelled to publish a retraction (this is a familiar enough occurrence in all Communist societies), to deny the essence of what he originally wrote, and to apologize, because he had written (truthfully) what offended or embarrassed the powers that be. Budin's apologia in part:

As a result of renewed consideration of the whole complex American problem a number of questions appear in a different light than when I wrote my book last year. I believe I ought to say where I see its mistakes today. The fact that the American monopolistic capital prefers the other party—the Republicans—does not alter the Democratic Party's bourgeois character. A coalition of classes of the working people can be really democratic only if its leadership belongs to the working class. This was out of the question as far as the Democratic Party was concerned. That is why a third American party is now being formed.

My early erroneous view on the Democratic Party gave rise to another mistake. With reference to the economic crisis of 1929 and its influence on the American society's structure I described it as follows: "*At the moment of the crisis the monopolistic capital lost its head and was unable to enthrone Fascism.* The working class had no capable leadership yet and was not able to seize power. Thus a group of bourgeois intelligentsia, headed by Roosevelt, took over."

This theory conflicts with Lenin's theory of the state and relates incorrectly the role of the intelligentsia which is no independent class. Through Roosevelt's "New Deal" a group of liberal bourgeoisie took power which saved the capitalistic order by introduction of economic and social reforms which had been long overdue. Its seizure of power, however, did not change the American capitalism's imperialistic character.

To conclude that America in pre-war years and in the years of war was not a country of mature capitalism, a country of rotting imperialism, is a great mistake.

These were the main mistakes of my book. . . . I have recognized these mistakes by studying mainly Soviet material. . . .

Turn now to Czech relations with Germany and Russia. One day I met a Catholic dignitary of the highest rank and eminence. I asked him, "Do the Czech people in general hate the Germans most, or the Russians?" He leaned back and laughed. "The Germans, of course!" Pause. "But we hate the Russians *genug* (enough)." By coincidence it happened that, immediately after this meeting, we drove out to Lidice, to see the unbelievable ruin wrought by German murderers for no authentic reason on what had been this peaceable little town. The barrow that was Lidice—with its crown of barbed wire over the memorial crucifix—is the saddest sight in Europe.

Czech relations with Germany pivot, of course, on the fear of German rearmament and the specter of a renascent Naziism in the Reich. Even anti-Communist Czechs are for the most part fiercely anti-German. Once, after some introductory polite fumbling, we had the interesting experience of coming to conversational grips with Vladimir Clementis, the Czech Foreign Minister. I asked, "Do you still fear Germany?" His answer was, "Do you think we are fools? Of course!" Suppose Germany should be permanently split apart, and the Eastern Zone became an official Soviet satellite. Would the Czech Communists accept this segment of a communized Germany, at least, with sympathy and friendship and be sure that it would always be an ally. Answer: No.

As to Russia, its influence on Czechoslovakia—aside from the general inevitable coloration of the political atmosphere—is evident mostly in the army and police, particularly the secret police, called OBZ. The headquarters of one branch of the police is, incidentally, directly across the street from the residence of the American ambassador. The Soviet infiltration into the secret police is so complete and barefaced that interrogations are sometimes conducted by Russians in the Russian language, through interpreters. This does not mean necessarily that Soviet citizens are very numerous. Czechs trained in Moscow, like the Hungarian "Muscovites," do most of the job. And as a matter of fact numbers are not important; a few hundred men scattered in key positions (in the army too) are quite enough.

Also the Russians operate the uranium mines in Bohemia at Jáchymov and Vejprty. This is the district where Madame Curie first got on the trail of radium, because mud in the spas seemed to have peculiar properties. Czech engineers are ostensibly in charge of these highly secret uranium operations, and the labor is mostly German—slave labor in fact—but Russian guards, who do not even make a pretense of speaking Czech, wall off the whole area. Also the Russians occupy at least two of the great hotels at Karlovy Vary (Carlsbad); the pretext, when the Fierlinger government gave them to the Soviets on long lease, was that they were to be used as rest houses for Red army officers. The story now is that they are headquarters for all Russian civilians in the country, in particular the police; also eminent Soviet dignitaries, like Vishinsky, use them for holidays, in fact Vishinsky was vacationing there just before being appointed Foreign Minister.

Plenty of Czechs resent Russian proprietariness. The fact

that the Czechs, when they had to buy 600,000 tons of grain from the Soviet Union, in emergency circumstances, were forced by the Russians to pay $4.00 and up a bushel (when they could have got it from the U.S.A. for $2.50 if they had had hard currency) still rankles among those who know it. The Czech people at large were not, of course, informed. Nor does it particularly please those who know that some Czech food, even in these days of extreme shortage, is being exported to the Soviet Zone in Germany. Nevertheless a $360 million trade agreement was recently signed between Moscow and Prague.

Arnost Heidrich, once secretary general to the Czechoslovak foreign office, and for many years one of the men closest to Dr. Benes, managed to escape from the country recently and duly, after an interval, he arrived in Washington. An authoritative résumé of his views was published recently which throws light on much that has hitherto been mysterious.[12] Stalin is, according to Heidrich, trying to build an "Eastern Ruhr" in Czechoslovakia and Poland. The Soviets "seem to be developing Czechoslovakia primarily as a source of economic reconstruction in Russia, as a source of military supplies, and as a strategic territory that must be denied to the Western Powers" (but not as a base of attack on the West). In particular they need steel rails and rolling stock. In the Crimea last September Stalin met Gottwald, Ana Pauker, Dimitrov, Rákosi, and other supreme Communist leaders, for a secret conference unknown even to the Czechoslovak foreign office. One reason for this meeting was to tighten the screws on their erstwhile consociate, Marshal Tito. The Russians sought among other things to induce the satellites, particularly Czechoslovakia, to stop all shipments of arms to Yugoslavia. This is particularly interesting because the Yugoslav army was, as we know, largely armed and munitioned by Russia, after it sent its own surplus and obsolete stock to Albania and elsewhere. After the Cominform break, it got no more Russian arms of course, which was a grave embarrassment to Tito in that only Russian equipment matched what he already had. He tried apparently to fill the gap by purchases

[12] By James Reston in the *New York Times*, January 16, 1949.

from Skoda, the celebrated Czech munitions works at Pilsen. This the Russians stopped.

Formally Czechoslovak relations with the satellites other than Yugoslavia are correct; in actuality the Czechs and Hungarians, at least, are traditional enemies, and Czechs and Poles do not get along too well. The Czechs are apt to think of the Poles as a romantic gang of shoeless peasants, and in their hearts they will never forgive Poland for having grabbed Teschen (though now they have most of it back) during the Munich tragedy. Of course it is Russian policy to bring the loyal marionettes closer together all the time, largely through interlocking trade.

Finally Personalities

The major actors in the Czechoslovak drama today are virtually unknown, even by name, to most Americans. In general they fall into two camps, those more or less on the moderate side like Gottwald, Clementis, and Nosek, and the extremists, Slánský and Čepička. The Prime Minister, Antonín Zápotocký, whom scarcely anybody has ever heard of outside Czechoslovakia, is in a special category. Of course this stratification into "moderates" and "extremists," or between "Westerners" and "Easterners," is apt to be misleading. The whole group is quite tightly conjoined. And the moderate "Westerners," who stood for maintenance of Czechoslovakia's close economic ties to the West and hence resisted the transfer of emphasis to production for Russia's sake, have been muted lately. Then too American and British observers in Czechoslovakia may, as it was shrewdly pointed out to me in Prague, tend to exaggerate the importance of the "Western" moderates, simply because they are guilty of wishful thinking and like to pretend at least that a "Western" bloc exists.

Klement Gottwald, the President of the Republic, is largely a shadow now. He was kicked upstairs mostly because of his moderation. Masaryk more or less trusted him; he always believed, though a Communist, in the parliamentary process to some extent; he is a good Marxist, but he hates tossing anybody into jail. Gottwald, about fifty-five, is of Austrian origin, and was born a Catholic; his wife, a Sudeten, is also Catholic. It shocked some Catholics that, when he was installed as President, the Archbishop of Prague (the leading Catholic dignitary in the country) officiated at the ceremonies. But the Catholic hierarchy in Czechoslovakia—also in Poland—takes a somewhat different line from that which Mindszenty assumed in Hungary. I went into this briefly in Chapter 12 above.

Gottwald was a carpenter by trade, became a Communist as a very young man, had a lively career as a journalist, and was a deputy in the old parliament. He is a short man, pleasant looking, taciturn, and conventional in exterior, even to the item that he smokes a pipe. He has "a stubborn untrained mind," and so is hard to argue with. He is quite honest, and as a rule foreigners get on with him well; he may try to put something over, but he has the reputation of trying to keep his word.

Prime Minister Zápotocký is of a somewhat different breed. He was born in 1884 near Kladno, the son of a well-known Socialist who was founder, in fact, of the Social Democratic party of Bohemia, and who as a result was interned by the old imperial authorities for twenty years. When Zápotocký told us this his eyes clouded. One could see easily what had been a motivation to his own career. Young Zápotocký began life as a stone mason. He is one of the few present-day Czechoslovak leaders who has spent a good deal of time in jail (not counting imprisonment by the Nazis during the war); the Masaryk-Benes regime, totally unlike that of Hungary, let its Communists pretty well alone; nobody got sentences like those imposed on Rákosi and Vas. But Zápotocký as a young man led some Socialist student demonstrations and was imprisoned. In 1920 he went to Moscow as a representative of the left-wing Social Democratic party, and was promptly converted to Communism; he returned to Prague, and then spent eighteen years as a trade union organizer—his strength derives mostly from his entrenched position as indisputable boss of the unions. As such he is the directive force behind the Workers' Militia, already described in this chapter, and the Action Committees of the party. He was chosen secretary general of the C.P. in 1928; for a time he sat in parliament, but, in the words of an official biographical sketch, he "retired after a time into illegality." This means that he went to jail again—for leading a big miners' strike. When the Nazis came in 1939 he was promptly arrested once more, and spent the whole war in Sachsenhausen, a German concentration camp.

We had a long talk with Zápotocký. He is a very shy man, almost inarticulate, though he has the reputation of being a firebrand public speaker. He has tough, sunburned workman's hands, a nervous manner, very blue eyes, and stainless steel teeth. Like so many of his colleagues, he gives the impression of being almost a Jekyll and Hyde, violent on some days, moderate on others. His office, we noticed, is full of works of art and sculpture, something comparatively rare in this milieu. His hobby is art; he has always loved to carve wood. We asked him if he had been able to do any sculpture while in concentration camp. "Oh yes," he said, "I used bits of bread." Also he has written at least one novel, which I heard described as "tender."

The Foreign Minister, Dr. Vladimír Clementis, is still another type—an intellectual. He was born in 1902 in Slovakia, and became a lawyer; for some years, though a Communist, he had a lucrative practice in Bratislava. Dr. Clementis is a technician in the sense that he handles his country's foreign affairs and diplomacy, and is thus useful to the government though not particularly high in the party hierarchy. "Clementis?—he has no power but to do what he is told," I heard it said in Prague. Maybe this is an exaggeration. During the war he succeeded in escaping from Czechoslovakia to France, where he was interned by the Daladier government. After the fall of France he made his way to England, where he helped organize the Czechoslovak legions fighting on the Allied side. Also he was a broadcaster. It is strange to reflect that, just as Madame Pauker for instance broadcast to the suppressed Rumanians from Moscow during the war, Dr. Clementis helped do the same thing for the Czechoslovaks—from London. He was named a minister in the first government while still absent from Czechoslovakia. He knows English well and is a lively conversationalist. This is a vigorous, forthright, trained, and intelligent man, who enjoys swapping intellectual punches. He told us something that I thought had considerable interest: "There will be no war until a *German* army is ready in Western Germany."

The other leading "moderate" is Václav Nosek, Minister of the Interior. He too spent the war in exile in London. This fact is of course held against him by the "Muscovites," as it is held against Clementis. But Nosek has nevertheless managed so far to retain control of the crucially important Interior ministry; some people think that he is much "worse" than he really is, simply because he has this job. I heard it said, "His wings are bound to be clipped sooner or later, because he is too decent." Nosek was born in 1892 of a worker's family, and spent his youth as a miner and laborer in an iron foundry. He became a Communist in 1920 and the rest of his story follows the familiar avenue.

The most violent member of the government, and one of the most dangerous, is Dr. Alexey Čepička, Minister of Justice—though the ministers of Information (Václav Kopecký) and Agriculture (Julius Ďuriš) run him close as extremists. He was born in 1910; recently he married one of Gottwald's daughters. Čepička was a law student. He joined the party and became an agitator. During the war he was imprisoned by the Germans at Oświęcim, the worst of all concentration camps, and Buchenwald. Somehow, a tough creature, he managed to survive them both. "If there is ever a blood bath in Prague," a friend told me, "you can be sure that Čepička will be at the bottom of it."

Probably the most important man in Czechoslovakia is none of these. First place, in the view of most observers, belongs to Rudolf Slánský, the secretary general of the party. Slánský is a Jew, and—it is important to note—the only really prominent Jew in the Czechoslovak party hierarchy. The situation is very different from that in Hungary or Poland. Slánský was a partisan fighter of renown[13] and is talked of with considerable respect for his personal qualities. He was editor of *Rudé Pravó* for a time; he spent some years in Russia after Munich. His real name is believed to be Salzman; "Slánský" means "salt."

[13] Lockhart, *op. cit.*

We didn't meet him, much to my regret. He is a scholar, retiring, unostentatious, a youngish man with reddish hair—and of course Moscow trained and the absolute boss of the party mechanism. It is he who gives Gottwald orders on any party business, not vice versa. Slánský is the eminence grise, and lives behind the scenes.

But behind him—how the Communists love this kind of setup!—is another eminence grise, a man named Bedrich Geminder, who is supposed to be the chief Cominform "man" in Czechoslovakia. Geminder is of German origin, and has spent most of his life in Moscow. He is the real "button-pusher," and his closest associate, a man named Reicin, is head of the secret police.

Who runs Czechoslovakia aside from (a) Moscow, and (b) men like these? The simplest answer is that it is run by the "Action Committees," which exist in every town, and, moreover, in every professional or workers' group. Every factory, big or small, every village organization of lawyers or businessmen, has its party committee, and these dovetail in an interlocking structure all over the country, and are the indispensable mechanism by which the Prague government rules and functions. The Action Committees have power even to purge an industry of its board of directors—or a tennis club of its coach.[14] Always the most vigorous Communists are members. They build up into what is called the "Central Action Committee of the National Front," and it was this that organized the February *coup*.

Quiz by Believers

By the time we reached Prague we were used to a variety of questions, from Communists and others; we encountered them all during our trip and after. For instance questions like these about American affairs:

Item: If the United States has such faith and trust in democracy, why is it that at least 40 percent of those eligible to vote fail to vote in most elections?

[14] State control was imposed recently on all gymnastic, athletic, and sports organizations in the country.

Item: Every major American university has a *numerus clausus* restricting Jews. Kindly explain in the light of your so-called "democratic" principles.

Item: Is it not correct that in at least seven American states the *majority* of the people have no voice in government, because of the poll tax?

Item: Inasmuch as the United States is 10 percent a black nation, do you consider that Negroes play a proportionate role in the "democratic" life of the country?

Item: Why is it that the United States, if its policy is basically peaceful and "democratic," maintains military and air bases in spots so far separated, remote, and of offensive strategic interest, as Saudi Arabia, Greenland, and Okinawa?

Item: Please explain why citizens of Washington, D. C. the capital, have not the right to vote.

Item: Is it true that only 1.2 percent of the total American national income is spent on education?

Item: Tell us why the "democratic" United States supports Fascism in Greece and flirts with Fascist Spain and Portugal, in view of the language of the Yalta and Potsdam declarations to the effect "that Fascism and all its emanations are to be utterly destroyed," and that the peoples of Europe should be assisted in their effort "to destroy the last vestiges of Fascism on the continent."

Item: Do you honestly think that the governments of Honduras, say, Nicaragua, or even Cuba, are any less dependent on the United States than the governments of Bulgaria or Rumania are on the Soviet Union?

Item: Why, in view of the celebrated American addiction to civil liberties, is it so difficult to pass a civil rights bill in the Senate?

And as to other countries and situations:

Item: Can you fairly call a nation like France "democratic," when the largest single party, the Communist party, is excluded from the government?

Item: Name a single instance of direct or overt territorial aggression by Russia since the war. Is it not true that the Russians have in fact withdrawn from such danger spots as Korea and Iran?

Item: How is it that the Soviet Union, which by treaty has a great number of special rights and privileges with regard to Finland, has to date never sought to exercise them?

Item: Is it not correct that the Berlin crisis would have been settled to mutual satisfaction long ago, except for the fact that the United States has not finally made up its mind what its German policy is to be?

I do not say that any of these statements or questions are particularly embarrassing or difficult to answer. I list them (a few out of many available) merely to show the pattern of the Soviet intellect, and to give the reader a quick opportunity to exercise his wits. Later in this book I hope, if space remains, to list a few items about which Americans, on their side, may well quiz Russians.

CHAPTER 15
WARSAW REDIVIVUS

POLAND was the climax of our whole trip from several points of view. Let me drop politics and personalities, except by implication, in this chapter, and attempt simply to describe the city of Warsaw, the most phenomenal sight in Europe, as we saw it.

First, two blunt and shocking figures. Eighty-four percent of all buildings in this great city, the capital of Poland, were rendered uninhabitable during the war. Not merely "damaged," mind you. But "rendered uninhabitable." And Warsaw, the population of which was 1,300,000 in 1939, lost during the war approximately 700,000 dead. Some appreciation of the enormousness of this figure may be gained from the fact that the total dead of Great Britain and the United States together in World War II was only about 555,000. Warsaw, the city alone, lost 700,000 killed; the entire United States lost roughly 310,000. Warsaw is the most hurt and punished big community in the world, except Stalingrad perhaps.

One Pole we met put it this way with bitter vigor. "You in the West may have the highest standard of living in the world. We Poles have the highest standard of death."

But the point I am hoping to make is not the frightfulness of the destruction we saw in Warsaw, indubitably frightful as that was. The real point is the remarkable success of the Poles in rebuilding their city, the massive energy and zip they have put to the job, and the electric animation and effervescence most citizens seem to show. Warsaw is a ruin. But also it is the liveliest capital in Europe.

Take Berlin by comparison. Berlin has about as much vitality as a mass of putty. The very grass has grown over the streetcar tracks on Kurfürstendamm. People walk slowly, with hunched and sagging shoulders; an almost suffocating dreariness hangs over the community; the food shops are scraped bare; except for the pulsating throb of air lift planes overhead, the city is almost soundless. And we found much the same sort of deadness in Frankfurt and Vienna.

But Warsaw! It bounces, hums and buzzes. Everywhere is the clatter of hammers. Clouds of dust envelop the passer-by; buildings are going down and coming up. The streets are crowded, the hotels and restaurants are full. The people are poor—no one could possibly attempt to deny that—but they are rising out of their own ruins by their own efforts, which helps to give them their spectacular morale.

"Poland has been destroyed four times. Very well! Let us create it all over again, and make it better and make it last!" This, in a phrase, expresses the Warsaw spirit. These people are not cowed like the Czechs. They are alive, tenacious, almost gay in the midst of tragedy, and going places—if history will let them.

There is plenty of discontent and opposition of course. Only an idiot would minimize that. Conversely, very few signs of explicit pressure are manifest. I talked to an American who bitterly hated the regime. He said, "There is no arbitrary use of police power here. The government is detestable, but there are no concentration camps or terrorism. This is the freest of the border states. You can go around pretty much as you please."

We met a Pole whom I have known and trusted for twenty years, and who has held jobs official or unofficial with Polish governments since 1919. "I give you my word," he declared, "there is less suppression under this regime than under Pilsudski or the colonels." But of course no one can know what will happen in the future. Gradually the reins may well be tightened.

First Glimpse of the Town

We flew in from Prague, and the flight scared me. At the Prague airport, isolated from the shining aluminum airliners of half a dozen nations, with their four motors languidly and confidently purring, we saw a small shabby plane silent and alone on a strip of grass. It didn't occur to us till we were marched into it that it could possibly be ours. It was an ancient Russian-built DC-3 carrying cargo as well as passengers. The wings and fuselage were tarnished and rusty. I do not mind planes in war paint, but to fly in one in which the original aluminum looked like an old stovepipe was disconcerting. The seat belts were made of frayed rope, and the cabin door would not close; the pilot, grinning, tried to jam it shut and then half-laced it to the wall with string.

We took off without any warming up of the motors at all, and flew very low. But the pilot, a fat cheerful man, gave me confidence, and so did the stewardess, a fat grinning blonde who spoke a little French. Of course the Poles fly just the way Russians do, with great verve and dash. During the flight something went wrong with the heater and a nervous passenger pointed to the metal ceiling which seemed hot. The pilot came back from the cockpit and just laughed. As a matter of fact these Polish pilots are superb airmen, and Lot, their company, has an enviable safety record. But when we talked to Americans later who asked us how we got to Warsaw and we told them that we had flown Polish and were returning the same way, they exclaimed in horror, "You flew in a *Polish* plane?—good God!"

It was dusk when we arrived, and driving into town we could see little except gaunt shadowy ruins. Our hotel reminded me of Moscow—crowded, not too clean, with people dressed drably but bustling with hard energy, towels made of torn-up old pillow slips, and an ancient wheezing elevator that sucked its way up an oily metal pipe.

We walked around the corner to the Europejski—once one of the supreme hotels of the world—for dinner. Half of this has been destroyed, and it can no longer be used as a hotel, but the restaurant is open. Greeting us was a jazz band—playing American tunes. Along the side of a large open room was a *zakąski* bar. Here we sat on stools, sipped different kinds of vodka, and ate hors d'oeuvres of the richest possible variety—smoked sturgeon, *pâté* of hare, trout in aspic, and cold game with such exotic delicacies as Cumberland sauce. But the atmosphere was that of a proletarian cafeteria. The barman, dressed like a counterman in a New York delicatessen, did not understand any of our languages; a woman superintending the cold buffet rushed to help, and with a maternal conspiratorial air, beaming with delight at our helplessness, took us in hand as if to encourage us to eat, drink, and enjoy Polish hospitality to the full. I noticed that in this people's "democracy" you are told on the bottle exactly how much alcohol the particular kind of vodka contains, and the price per bottle. Once Poland boasted several hundred different types of vodka. We did well on two or three.

We went in to dinner and had a very good, heavy, and comparatively inexpensive meal. We drank some Porter, the superb Polish dark beer, which has an alcohol content of 24 percent. Polish cooking has always been magnificent. Where else could one get ham stuffed with pistachios, black mushrooms as big as saucers, and a miraculous soup made of chicken, beets, cream, shrimps, and fresh cucumbers? I looked around with curiosity. Except that the dress of the people was poorer and there were few pretty women, the atmosphere of the Europejski had changed comparatively little since I last saw it in 1939 a few days before the war. No—the waiters were different. There was an undefinable something about them that showed they had not been waiters under the *ancien régime*. And of course the building itself is a ruin.

We took a walk. The streets were very dark. We circled into the great empty square to the side of the Europejski and stumbled up to a dimly lit open hall, with a colonnade. I had forgotten what it was. Then a patrol of soldiers trod by, and performed with infinite slowness and articulated grace the ceremony of changing the guard. The patrol disappeared, and a very young private came up to us sharply. He peered at us in the gray gloom and said somberly in German, "You are foreigners. Do you speak German?" I thought we were going to be arrested for some kind of trespass. The young soldier went on, "Do you know what this building is? It is the tomb of our unknown soldier. Normally when attending it, a visitor takes off his hat." I took mine off.

We stood chatting then for twenty minutes in the silent darkness. The young unshaven soldier spoke a few words of English as well as German. He had been carted off by the Nazis to a concentration camp when a boy, and had miraculously survived.

There was no nonsense about him. He knew exactly what Poland had suffered and what he himself had suffered. His ignorance of the outside world was, however, considerable. He had never met an American before. He wanted to know if New York had been made "*kaput*" by the war like Warsaw. We covered a good deal of ground and I was getting a considerable insight into things Polish from the point of view of a very youthful army private when the harsh sound of an automobile split the silence, and we saw moving lights across the enormous square. The young soldier instantly clicked his heels, saluted, and in English said a brisk "Good night." Then he was off, as fast as he could walk. Doubtless a patrol was coming up, and he didn't want to be seen with foreigners or neglecting duty.

Facts and Impressions of the Miracle

Next day we began to look around in earnest. I was appalled. I have never seen anything like it. I was stunned. I knew Warsaw fairly well before the war. The destruction was so great that I could not find my way to the simplest objectives. Almost all the landmarks I remembered, like the lovely old Bruehl Palace which housed the Foreign Office, have completely disappeared. The Royal Castle, St. John's Cathedral, the assemblage of graceful buildings near the National Theater, restaurants like Fuggers, the pretty old round Church of Alexander, the Poniatowski monument, have been wiped off all but flat. For acre after acre the city resembles a scene out of H. G. Wells or a gutted moon.

In Berlin, if you stand near Brandenburg Gate, you can at least see the outline of what buildings once were. There, you say to yourself, are the remains of the Hotel Adlon, there is the skeleton of a house I dined in once, there is what was the French Embassy. But in Warsaw it is impossible over large areas to identify any buildings at all, or even to see where street intersections were, because the ruin is total, the devastation is complete. Almost every vista looks like a jumble of enormous broken teeth.

This is the way a spirited Polish document[1] puts it:

Despite the bombs that rained on London, the dome of St. Paul's Cathedral still rises in proud majesty, the houses of Parliament and Nelson's Column are still intact. The spires of the Cathedral of Cologne still stand amid the surrounding ruins. France's Gothic cathedrals still tower toward the sky. . . . The case of Warsaw is different. Gone is every last one of her medieval Gothic landmarks; gone are her baroque churches, her renaissance and rococo palaces. Nothing is left, nothing. The destruction of Warsaw was carried out with truly admirable precision, with calculated and systematic accuracy, according to a prepared and detailed plan. That is what makes the Warsaw tragedy so incredible, that is what distinguishes her fate from that of so many other devastated European capitals.

Rotterdam was destroyed in the course of a few hours. Berlin had excellent anti-aircraft protection. But havoc came to Warsaw not once, but three times in this war and, at no time did she have anti-aircraft protection. . . . There was no protection left at all. . . . The Reichswehr, sole master of deserted Warsaw, unleashed upon the city detachment after detachment of its men, all specially trained in the noble art of arson. . . . House after house, street after street, district after district went up in flames—according to plan. The city in which western European culture had blossomed at a time when in Berlin the Hohenzollerns were erecting barracks instead of museums, the city in which Chopin grew up, where Paderewski spent the years of his youth, the city of Canaletto's paintings, the beloved city of Marie Curie—this was the city that was singled out to be razed from the face of the earth.

How did all this happen? There were three separate and deliberate waves of destruction by the Germans. First, in September 1939, came the Siege of Warsaw, when the Nazis bombed and bombarded the city until it was forced to surrender; roughly 10 percent of the total damage dates from this period. Then after the siege came the first looting; carefully picked details of German professors and other experts went pedantically through the ruins of marvelous seventeenth and eighteenth century structures giving orders as to what should be pillaged, what destroyed.

[1] *Warsaw Accuses*. The front cover of this brochure quotes General Eisenhower's statement after his visit in 1945, "Warsaw is far more tragic than anything I have ever seen."

Second, the destruction that followed the Ghetto uprising. This accounts for perhaps 15 percent more of the total damage. After four years of suffering and misery almost unparalleled in history, the Jews of the Warsaw Ghetto revolted. By that time almost 400,000 had already been seized from their homes, transported to concentration camps, and put to death. The surviving Warsaw Jews, almost 50,000 in number, decided to die fighting rather than perish meekly; the Germans overcame their heroic but pitiably vain resistance in fierce fighting that lasted from April 19 to May 16, 1943. The Germans then butchered all the remaining Jews, blew up the entire area (which is in the center of the city) and scoured out what was left until it was level to the ground like Lidice or Carthage.

Third came the Warsaw insurrection of 1944, when for sixty-three heroic days the underground and populace fought and were finally crushed by powerful divisions of German troops. I will allude later to the controversial political aspects of this heartrending insurrection. After it the Reichswehr proceeded to the job of really finishing Warsaw off. The Nazi commandant boasted to Hitler that never again would a Pole live in Warsaw. The surviving population was carried off to concentration camps, where thousands upon thousands died in the asphyxiation furnaces; the Germans removed everything of the faintest value from the city, and blew up what remained, street by street. Houses were set on fire while still full of people; the victims popped out of the windows to crash to death rather than die trapped by flames. This went on from October 15, 1944, till Christmas. The Nazi looters and destroyers then sank back exhausted. There was virtually no Warsaw left.

Our Polish friends gave us a few figures. Of the city's 1,300,000 people, some 700,000 were killed, as I said above. All archives were wantonly destroyed, all collections of legal documents, and all books and works of art of interest that were not stolen. The Public Library was burned down, the National Museum was blown up, and of course any historic monuments of consequence were demolished. Twenty-five other museums were systematically and deliberately (of course long after fighting had ceased) dynamited into rubble, 24 libraries, 59 churches, 146 hospitals, 335 schools, and 20 theaters. Also the

Germans wrecked anything of use they could find underground—all the sewers, gas lines, telephone and electric cables, and water supply.

This concentrated tornado of pure useless horror turned Warsaw into Pompeii. I heard a serious-minded Pole say, "Perhaps a few cats may have been alive, but certainly not a dog." After liberation early in 1945 the Polish government took the heroic decision to rebuild. This was a herculean step, and Poles nowadays laugh about it with a peculiar rough tenderness, saying that the reason must have been their "romanticism." Even ministers as powerful as Hilary Minc thought that it would be impossible to rebuild, and suggested starting from scratch with a new capital at Lódz. He was outvoted. The decision to rebuild Warsaw, and keep it the capital no matter at what cost, was of course wise—and not romantic at all—in that it gave a patriotic focus and an urgent aggressive faith to the workings of the new regime. The reconstruction has taken place in three stages. First there was the simple imperative matter of cleaning up. The city was totally without transportation, gas, power lines, or sanitation, and no fewer than 40,000 corpses found in the wreckages of streets and buildings had to be buried. It is an extraordinary tribute to Polish zeal that by December 1945 streetcars were running again and the population reached 50,000. (Within six months, it was 375,000; today it has advanced to 600,000. But it will be a long time before the 1939 figure of 1,300,000 is reached again.) Then the public services were restored and a new bridge flung across the Vistula. The second great phase consisted of reconstruction of buildings capable of being reconstructed; those damaged beyond repair were pulled down, if possible. Figures in this realm also give proof of Polish zest and will. For instance something like 105 million cubic feet of buildings have so far been repaired and made habitable, including 40 percent of all the government buildings partially destroyed, 25 percent of dwellings, 15 percent of schools, and 11 percent of hospitals. Finally, the third phase of reconstruction, which overlaps the second and is in progress now, consists of constructing entirely new elements of the city according to strict plan.

Every Pole I met was almost violent with hope. "See that?" A cabinet minister pointed to something that looked like a smashed gully. "In twenty years that will be our Champs Elysées."

The worst area is still the Ghetto, which in literal fact is a heap of rubble, nothing more, nothing less. It looks like a huge empty rocky lot. We prodded through it slowly, scampering up and down hills of crushed debris. A few straggly dandelions and cabbages, bearing pathetically valiant flowers, grow on what was once the busiest section of the city, and a clump of dusty bushes has spurted out over the area where the biggest synagogue in Europe once stood. Grass grows again. Human beings do not. And never let it be forgotten that of the 3,500,000 Polish Jews who lived in this country before the war, more than three solid *million* were murdered by the Germans. The total number of Jews surviving in Poland today is only between 70,000 and 80,000.

In other parts of the city—not the Ghetto, which is beyond any possible hope of restoration—we watched the work of rebuilding. Particularly is this impressive in the Old City, which is almost as complete a ruin as the Ghetto. A patch of ravaged brick is all that remains of the Angelski hotel where Napoleon stayed. The old bricks are used in the new structures, which gives a crazy patchwork effect. Hundreds of houses are only half rebuilt; as soon as a single room is habitable, people move in. I never saw anything more striking than the way a few pieces of timber shore up a shattered heap of stone or brick, so that a kind of perchlike room or nest is made available to a family, high over crumbling ruins. One end of a small building may be a pile of dust; at the other you will see curtains in the windows.

Much of this furious reconstruction is done by voluntary labor; most, moreover, is done by the human hand. Even cabinet ministers go out and work on Sunday. In all Warsaw there are not more than two or three concrete mixers and three or four electric hoists; in all Warsaw, not one bulldozer! A gang of men climb up a wall, fix an iron hook on the end of a rope to the topmost bricks, climb down again, and pull. Presto!—the wall crashes. Then the same distorted bricks go into what is going up. The effect is almost that of double exposure in a film. No time for correct masonry!

So this catastrophically gutted city, probably the most savage ruin ever made by the hand of evil mankind anywhere, is being transformed into a new metropolis boiling and churning with vigor. Brick by brick, minute by minute, hand by hand, Warsaw is being made to live again through the fixed creative energy and imagination of an immensely gifted and devoted people.

Footnotes to the Major Theme

Our guide on several forays through Warsaw was a young American of Polish descent who had been here just after the war and who returned a year later to see again what was going on. He was so impressed by the reconstruction that he decided to stay on; what is more, he became a Communist, surrendered his American citizenship, and is now a discriminating, if devout, minor official in a ministry where his intelligence and knowledge of English are very useful. We asked him if he missed America. "Of course. I like America. But here I feel that I am a pioneer, here I partake of a whole new fresh opening of life!"

We talked at length with this young man. His salary is much less than it would be in America—21,000 zloty a month, or $52.25 at the official rate of exchange. But, he told us, he lives much better than he could in New York on an equivalent sum, despite the obvious Warsaw shortages. His rent is only 1.5 percent of his salary; he is doing useful work, and therefore was assigned a reasonably comfortable place to live, after considerable delay. His biggest expense is coal for heating; the bill is about 8,000 zloty ($20.00) for the winter. A pair of shoes, purchased with coupons to which he is entitled through membership in his white-collar union, costs him about 7,000 zloty ($17.50); if he bought them on the free market they would be twice this sum. He eats lunch (the big meal of the day in Poland) at the office commissary at a cost of 1,040 ($2.60) per month. And food in the shops for breakfast and supper is plentiful and not unreasonably expensive.

Walking through the streets we saw much—women traffic cops; cut flowers on hawkers' stands at almost every corner; the great new bridge over the Vistula; posters advertising an exhibition of paintings by Matisse, and a play by Lorca; untidy files of hapless German prisoners; a few tiny dilapidated green taxis; a considerable number of people (as in Yugoslavia) with bandaged eyes—infection is frequent because of lack of soap; new buses from France and streetcars from Denmark, acquired in exchange for Polish coal; a long queue of women trying to buy cheap textiles. On the outskirts of the city we saw primitive peasant carts, wooden and shaped like troughs—with handsome modern rubber tires. Practically all the carts have tires. Of course these were picked up off abandoned German equipment after the war. Similarly the second-hand shops are full of expensive German cameras and the like. When we asked about more useful consumer goods our guide told us of the new steel factory going up at Gliwice, which will double Poland's steel production; it is built with Soviet machinery throughout, brand new, and is an important item in the Russo-Polish Five Year Economic Agreement of January 1948.[2]

There are, indeed, some strange juxtapositions in this pungent Warsaw of today. This is a Communist-dominated country. But I paused before a well-stocked Catholic bookshop selling only religious works. This is a country supposed to be run by the most severe standards of economic logic. But near our hotel were big posters advertising a national lottery.

One morning we went to a bank, which was housed over a cave in half a broken building. The clerks and tellers, mostly women, were having their second breakfast, and leisurely they dealt with our checks. We chanced to turn around; there behind us on the balcony was a uniformed guard with a tommy gun. He held it ready to use, swinging it slowly to traverse the bare high-ceilinged room from one end to the other. The reason dawned on us sharply. All the vaults, iron meshing, and strong boxes of the Polish banks were of course destroyed, and so today

[2] But Great Britain, following the signature of a $520 million trade treaty early in 1949, has now replaced the USSR as Poland's best customer.

currency is simply piled up on open wooden tables. The guard was ready for instant action. Our checks were cashed with courtesy, deliberation, and only a minor amount of red tape. But it was a far cry from the Guaranty Trust on Rockefeller Plaza!

After this we cut through the crumbling whitish rubble and wandered alone down streets like Marszalkowska and Nowy Swiat. Nobody paid the slightest attention to us. In fact several people assumed that we were Polish; they stopped and asked directions.[3] We ourselves got lost trying to find a short cut back to the hotel; it was only half a mile away but it was confusing to tramp through these broken graveyards of masonry, like shattered quarries, with no tall landmarks at all. The main shopping streets look like those of a wild west town, with one-story stucco or lath-and-plaster shacks. An early rule was, "Get business going, any sort of business, and find a place to sleep later." Now the government insists that any new building have two stories.

The greatest shortages are in clothing (because almost everybody's wardrobe was destroyed) and leather (because almost all the cattle were slaughtered). Most prices were very steep, and perplexingly uneven, but the variety of merchandise available —much of it of indifferent quality, true—was much greater than in Belgrade and Prague, or, in a different category, Frankfurt or Vienna. If you have money, you can get almost anything.

We saw a girl's sweater at 17,800 zloty ($42.50 at the legal rate), a silver tray in an antique shop for $63.75, lipsticks at 525 ($1.32), a cake of coarse soap at 90 (22 cents), a brand of California apricots at 185 a can (46 cents), a muskrat coat at 750,000 ($1,870), a basket of cut roses at 5,700 ($14.25), a cheap pocket knife for $2.75, a can of something called "Tom's Peanuts" for $1.58, a pair of men's shoes at 19,000 ($47.50), an American fountain pen at 2,500 ($6.25), and the shoddiest kind of handbag for $19.60. But it was interesting to note that in things like women's shoes, though the material was terrible, the design was chic. They were impractical—made of suede—but smart. Incidentally, Warsaw was the only Iron Curtain capital we saw

[3] In some shops the clerks thought we were Russian. They would smilingly volunteer, "We speak Russian." A waiter did this too in one restaurant.

where American name-brand cigarettes (at a price), British magazines and French luxury products were available.

As always we looked particularly in the food stores—which were full almost to bursting—and the bookshops. There were translations of Elliott Roosevelt's *As He Saw It* everywhere, also books by Howard Fast and a fair selection of belles-lettres; for instance works by Dr. Cronin, Rosamund Lehmann, and Virginia Woolf. Two prominently displayed books were a recent report by Ilya Ehrenburg on the United States, and something called *Polityka Wall Street,* with a big menacing dollar sign on the cover. The bookshops were not, of course, remotely comparable to those of Warsaw before the war, which were among the best in all Europe.

But to revert to the main theme of this chapter—the rehabilitation of Warsaw after ruin. One of my Polish friends snapped, "War? If we thought war was coming, do you think we'd have bothered to rebuild our capital?"

CHAPTER 16
MORE ABOUT THE POLES

ONE principal thing to say about Poland is that it is the only state in Eastern Europe with the Red army on both sides. Not only does its eastern frontier adjoin the Soviet Union; on the west it abuts the Russian Zone of Germany. Moreover to the north the Baltic is controlled by Russia, and to the south lies satellite Czechoslovakia. Then too, as in Hungary, some Russian troops (though in no great number—"communications troops" they are called) are stationed on Polish soil itself. Poland, it would seem, is both hemmed in and sat upon.

Now it is very striking indeed, in view of all this, that Poland should give the feeling of being much freer of Soviet pressure than any other state we visited. But it does. Never once in Warsaw did we see a red flag, a photograph of Stalin, or the kind of Soviet banner that is common elsewhere in Eastern Europe. These simply do not exist. And the Poles go to much more pains to deny that their country is a satellite than any other in the region. In fact they deny it hotly. It may seem preposterous, but early this year the Polish government even went so far as to demand recall by the United States of an American press attaché in Warsaw, on the ground that an American news bulletin insulted Poland by calling it "a Soviet satellite."[1] Sensitive folk, the communist-nationalists!

A vital point arises here. The Poles stand for Poland. Russia may be a friend and ally, but the Poles did not undertake the terrific adventure of rebuilding Warsaw just for Moscow's sake. They did it for themselves. The British journalist Alexander Werth, a substantial authority on all this part of the world, quotes a Polish Prime Minister as stating, "There is no Russian penetration. What is penetrating Poland is socialism—socialism of our own making." Werth writes, "The Polish Communists give the impression of being Poles first and foremost,

[1] *New York Times,* March 19, 1949.

Communists only next, and pro-Russians last and sometimes not at all."[2]

Even more curious avenues may be explored. Polish propaganda, which is very skilled and agile, differs considerably from that of Moscow or any puppet. For instance a series of brochures has been issued, *Foreigners on Poland*—of course for consumption abroad—in which the preface states, "This is a collection of articles favorable and unfavorable from the foreign press." Naturally nine-tenths of the text *is* favorable. But can one imagine the Kremlin issuing a bulky series of pamphlets including *un*favorable comment on the Soviet regime? One of Mr. Werth's articles begins, "Soviet communism is totally unacceptable to the Polish people, and the Polish Communists know it as well as anybody." That this should be reprinted in an official Polish publication is astounding. The Polish booklets tend to emphasize freely that the regime is by no means fully communized as yet. One pamphlet,[3] designed especially to reach Americans, says, "Poland's economic system is neither capitalistic like America nor communistic like Russia. All big industries—mines, railroads, etc.—are nationalized while land, homes, shops, and small industrial plants . . . are in private hands. Besides these two forms of ownership there is a third one—co-operatives."

Stalin himself once told the former Prime Minister Mikolajczyk, "Communism does not fit the Poles. They are too individualistic, too nationalistic."[4] The claim is customarily made in Polish government circles today that their system undertakes to help, not hinder, small private enterprise, which still employs a large percentage of all Polish workers. The youthful propaganda director himself, General Wiktor Grosz, was quoted recently in a book called *Poland Struggles Forward,* "Nobody will understand Polish democracy if he tries to measure it with a ready yardstick, regardless of whether the yardstick is Amer-

[2] In articles printed recently in *The Nation,* later republished as a pamphlet, *Poland Today.*

[3] *Poland,* published by the Polish Research and Information Service, New York.

[4] *The Rape of Poland,* by Stanislaw Mikolajczyk, New York, 1948. This book contains a mine of fascinating material, but I am not sure that Mr. Mikolajczyk really knows quite how fascinating some of it is.

ican, Russian, French, or British. Our way of democracy is not American, not Russian; it's Polish. It differs from both the Soviet model and the so-called western model. We have a number of political parties, whereas the Soviet Union has only one. We don't have collective farming, as the Soviet Union does. We don't have the big privately owned enterprises and big land holdings that both America and Great Britain have. We call our system a Popular Democracy. Whether right or wrong—that remains to be seen in the future—it is undoubtedly our own Polish system."

Word About the Country

Poland (Rzeczpospolita Polska) has four times gone through the unique and terrible experience of concrete geographical dissolution—partition. Yet when the country disappeared from existence in 1795 there were only eight million Poles; when Woodrow Wilson (amongst others) helped to resurrect it in 1919 this number had risen to 20 million. The country, even when it did not exist, grew. Poland's revival after death gave many of its people what I have heard described as a "crucifixion complex." It rose from the dead and was therefore holy. Of course Poland has a magnificent historical tradition to draw on. The Poles were converted to Christianity as far back as A.D. 966; their first King was crowned in 1025, forty-one years before the Norman Conquest; their first university was founded in the beautiful city of Cracow 250 years before Harvard.

No one should dismiss contemporary Poland from the point of view of potential wealth and bulk. It covers 119,703 square miles, and has about 24 million people. Put one way this means that it is roughly the size of Nevada or New Mexico. (Think how crowded Nevada would be if it had to support a population of 24 million!) Put another way it means that it is the sixth biggest country in Europe, bigger for instance than either Italy or the United Kingdom. It is the fourth country in the world (second in Europe) in coal production, the third in production of both rye and sugar beets, the fifth in zinc, and the third in potatoes. Only five countries in Europe produce more textiles, and it is fifth in cement. It has eleven cities bigger than 100,000—in spite of the tremendous loss in population as a whole caused by the war—and its foreign trade alone runs to something like $545 million in a normal year.

To concentrate the history of Poland since the war into a page or two is not easy. Yet the story is of the utmost challenge and fascination. "Poland," as Vera Micheles Dean writes, "was the first country to be invaded by the Germans, and the last to be liberated."[5] It is impossible to approach understanding of what the present regime, for all its faults, means to the people without awareness of such small items as that prewar Polish landowners sought to keep roads bad, not good. This was not deliberate cruelty; it was partly tradition, partly laziness, partly because anything that served to sterilize the peasantry from the gifts of the modern world, even if by accident, served a purpose. The wife of a former American ambassador to Poland told me how, when her cook became gravely ill and she called her own doctor to treat him, both her aristocratic friends and *her other servants* were scandalized that she had thus gone out of her way to "pamper" a "menial." (P.S. The cook died.)

From 1926 on Poland was governed by a semi-Fascist dictatorship, first under Marshal Pilsudski, then by the so-called clique of "colonels." I do not mean to say that this government was much worse than others in Central and Eastern Europe at the time; I mean merely that it was slipshod, antediluvian, and unwise. Coupled with political immaturity was a chauvinist romanticism. With my own ears I heard Polish officers say, in August 1939, that they would take Berlin in a few weeks "with cavalry." As everybody knows Hitler invaded Poland on September 1, 1939, thus precipitating World War II—and the Poles did not take Berlin by cavalry. The country was totally crushed before the month was out, and the six hideous years of subjugation began. Then on September 17 Soviet troops too invaded Poland from the east and joined forces with the Germans, thus brutally effecting the fourth partition of the country.[6] A year and a half later Hitler attacked the Soviet Union,

[5] *Foreign Policy Reports*, April 1, 1948.

[6] Incidentally, an odd historical point, Russia was the first country to recognize Poland as a new independent state after World War I.

and his troops overran the eastern areas that had been temporarily in Russian hands. So, until liberation, all Poland became a German slave.

Do not think that the Poles did not fight. They did fight. There was never any Polish Quisling. One army of 80,000 men, put together after the most agonizing difficulties, was formed in Russia out of Polish prisoners the Russians themselves had taken during the occupation. Other Polish forces fought in Italy, the Middle East, and elsewhere, side by side with the British and Americans. I quote a small anecdote from the pamphlet *Poland:*

> A German was captured by a Polish detachment in Tobruk, Africa. "These accursed Poles," he complained, "will we never be rid of them? I fought them in Poland in 1939. In 1940 I was sent to Norway—they were there. Then to France—Poles again! They shot down my best friend over London and now they capture me here." If he had not been captured he might have run into Poles at several more places—at Lenino on the Russian front, at Cassino in Italy and on the beaches of Normandy. The fact is that Poles fought on every allied front.

The division of the Polish armed effort into two great wings, one in Russia, one elsewhere, was bound to produce the most stringent difficulties. Envenomed quarrels still rage today—Poles are poles apart—over such episodes as the massacre at Katyn. Here the bodies of 10,000 Polish officers were found. Who murdered them? During the war the Germans said the Russians did, and the Russians said the Germans did. The basic point is all but ignored—that 10,000 splendid young men were killed.

Then consider the insufferable tragedies attending the Warsaw Insurrection of 1944. Between the insurrectionaries of General Bor-Komorowski, fighting from underground, and the advancing Russian armies outside—which included Polish divisions—there was no liaison whatever, and each side now blames the other. There is no doubt so far as impartial evidence can be assembled today that the insurrection was sparked off prematurely, and that the Russian high command had no accurate knowledge of what was going on inside the city. The result was that thousands of brave Poles died in the Warsaw gutters while substantial Russian forces remained squatting for week after week on the other bank of the Vistula, hardly a mile away. Some bitterly antiregime Poles even go so far as to claim that the Russians deliberately encouraged the Nazis to destroy Warsaw. Of course no statement so monstrously extreme should be taken seriously. The Russians had no motive for wanting Warsaw destroyed. Finally the capital was liberated on January 18, 1945. This would seemingly disprove the assertion that the Russians had been lukewarm or inefficient, since it took them three hard months to get into the city after Bor's surrender. The actual liberation was effected by the First Polish Army fighting under Russian command. At least that is the way Polish officials like to describe the operation today. Probably the Russians thought that it was tactically advisable to let the Poles go in first.

Now inevitably during all this time profound and exasperating political difficulties also came up. There emerged two Polish governments, each in a rival foreign sphere, each drawing on substantial numbers of good native Poles, each claiming legitimate authority, and each armed. In London was the Polish government-in-exile, of which the most conspicuous figure was Mikolajczyk. In Lublin (a Polish town already freed by the Red army) was the Polish Committee of National Liberation, which had been formed in Moscow. The London government was anti-Communist; the Lublin government was of course pro-Communist. Finally the two were merged on June 28, 1945, into what was called the Polish Provisional Government of National Unity.

That I have given exactly 112 words in the preceding paragraph to this whole evolution which lasted many anguished months will make any Pole shriek with outraged laughter. Mikolajczyk fought a desperate losing battle. First, Churchill and Roosevelt (to say nothing of Stalin) had been against him, because the Western leaders were still placating Russia. Mikolajczyk himself says that Churchill in particular always played the Lublin side (as he had played the Tito side in Yugoslavia); he even quotes Churchill to the effect that he, Churchill, thought that Mikolajczyk ought to be "in a lunatic asylum." If anybody wants to know how Mr. Churchill stormed and ranted over this, read Mikolajczyk's book.

Second, the tide of military events inexorably favored Lublin. The Londoners were at a hopeless disadvantage because the Lublin Poles were on the ground, in Poland itself, whereas they themselves could not get in. Lublin, in a word, got to Warsaw first. But negotiations for composition of the combined government continued month after angry month. The main point of dispute was over the Curzon line as the new Polish-Russian frontier. Mikolajczyk haggled, fumbled, and sought to stave off the inevitable. Kingsley Martin in *The New Statesman*[7] put it nicely:

> Mikolajczyk was said to have always been one river too late. When the Russians were on the Bug, he could have been Premier with half the Cabinet. He could still have been Premier with three Ministers of his Party when the Russians reached the Vistula. He might still have been Premier when the Red Army was on the Oder, but he only accepted the Vistula terms when the Russians had reached the Elbe, just as before he had been willing to take what he was offered on the Bug when the Russians had arrived at the Vistula.

Meantime the Polish boundaries were approved at Yalta, and soon the United States recognized the new government of National Unity. But the budding Polish regime had to promise to reorganize itself, include democratic leaders "from Poland and from Poles abroad," and to hold "free and unfettered elections" wherein "all democratic and anti-Nazi parties shall have the right to . . . put forward candidates."[8] A temporary period of sporadic disorder intervened, with guerrilla clashes between the two factions of the government. A referendum was held (June 30, 1946) which gave the Communists a strong boost up, followed by elections on January 19, 1947, which they won. There is no doubt that these elections were substantially rigged. The government bloc which the Communists controlled gained a huge majority, with 382 seats out

[7] August 16, 1947. Reprinted in *Foreigners on Poland,* Vol. III.

[8] *The New Poland,* by S. Harrison Thomson, *Foreign Policy Reports,* December 1, 1947.

of a chamber of 444. The British and Americans sent pious protests to Warsaw. Nobody paid attention. The Communists did not run as a "Communist" party incidentally; in Poland the worker's party (predominantly Communist) is known as the PPR. After this election there was very little to do but mop up. Mikolajczyk, who had become the Deputy Premier, fled to London in October 1947. The country quieted down, and a sensible amnesty ended the activity of the anti-Communist "armies" which had been terrorizing the countryside. Ever since, the PPR, in conjunction with its affiliates, has run the country. So once more we see how a Communist minority succeeds in reaching power. Presently we will note what they did with it.

The German Record; Also the New Frontiers

The first job the government faced was to assess what it had lost. In the preceding chapter I gave some details of what happened to Warsaw; let us look briefly now at Poland as a whole. Few countries ever suffered more. A massive sufficient index of this is the fact, almost too gross to be believable, that the country lost *20 percent* of its prewar population; 6,000,000 Poles were killed, some in battle but the great majority in the German concentration camps, including 3,200,000 Jews. If the United States should ever lose 20 percent of its population by warfare or otherwise, the corresponding number of dead would be 28,000,000. Another 3,000,000 Poles were deported to the Reich as slave labor. The total material loss to Poland is calculated at roughly $50 billion; this sum would support the entire American ERP program for more than ten years. It seems almost pointless, however, to mention material loss when one considers the fierce weight of human suffering involved. In one military camp, Lamsdorf, the Germans starved to death more than 100,000 *prisoners of war,* who should, of course, have been protected by terms of the Geneva convention. This is as nothing compared to what happened in the extermination and concentration camps like Oświęcim (Auschwitz), Tremblinka, and Maidanek. In Oświęcim alone two and a half *million* Poles were killed. This is ten times the population of San Antonio or Providence. "We do not admit the right of the Poles to exist in any form," said Hans Frank, the German governor general during the occupation, "Our policy is of biological extermination." But even this does not say enough. For instance 2,647 Polish Catholic priests were murdered. One must talk to surviving Poles. Children were swept alive by Nazis into manholes in the streets, or executed by being burned alive; young women had suppositories soaked in gasoline stuffed up their vaginas and set on fire.

Poland lost roughly 70 percent of all its livestock, 90 percent of its machine tool industry, 70 percent of its textile industry. Fifty percent of the surviving population today is threatened with tuberculosis, as a result of hardship. "The Germans kept all the high schools and universities closed for six years, and so Poland is critically short of doctors, lawyers, craftsmen, mechanics, and teachers."[9] All Polish textbooks were burned, and the loss of scientific equipment in laboratories, hospitals and so on is calculated at 70 percent. Six thousand four hundred schools were burned or otherwise destroyed, 3,350 cultural institutions, 16,000,000 books, and 700,000 maps. Thirty-two percent of all business and trade establishments were destroyed, —think what America would be like if *one-third* of all our business houses had been wrecked!—and 65 percent of all communication and transportation facilities. Not only Warsaw but towns like Poznan and Gdynia were all but obliterated. In the countryside 477,000 farms—one quarter of the total in the country—were sacked, gutted, and despoiled.

But again, what counted most was the acute and irreplaceable human loss. This played to Communist advantage of course. There were few able people left, and it was the Communists who made best use of them. Besides, in the general hopelessness and disintegration, only the Communists were thoroughly trained and efficient. People turned to them out of despair and "idealism" both; people in despair tend generally to seek (a) something that is formulated, and (b) something they think will help. And the Communists had a maxim or ruling ready for any crisis or eventuality; it was usually down in the

[9] *Poland, op. cit.*

books ready to fish out; almost always they knew exactly what to do.

Turn now to the Yalta and Potsdam agreements and the new Polish frontiers. What happened in effect was that Poland was bodily shifted west. To Russia the Poles gave up some 70,000 square miles of territory on the east; in compensation they received about 40,000 square miles of Germany, including Silesia with towns like Breslau (which was indeed Polish in remote origin), a sizable strip of the Baltic coast, and two thirds of East Prussia. It was all very tough on Germany. The vexatious old Danzig Corridor was done away with. Also the Poles got a town as near Berlin as Stettin, which they now call Szczecin. The Russians, on their side, acquired cities as illustrious in Polish history as Lwów (Lemberg) in the Ukraine, and Vilna.

Most nationalist Poles (and what Pole is not a nationalist?) regret that they had to give up so many people to Russia (though these were ethnically more White Russian or Ukrainian than Polish); the subject is discreetly played down. On the whole even though Polish territory and population were severely diminished, the Poles think they got not too bad a bargain. For one thing the country is now an ethnic unit; all the minorities, which were a constant source of embarrassment and irritation before the war, have been eliminated. For another it is now a compact geographical entity with better "natural" frontiers than before. And again, it has acquired the immense coal resources and industry of Pomerania and Silesia. It lost marshes and steppes; it gained a seacoast and a substantial, well-integrated industry.

These changes were attended by one of the most complex and comprehensive—and little known—forced migrations of recent times. About 8,500,000 Germans were expelled from the newly acquired western areas, and so far five million Poles have moved in. Pomerania and Silesia are to Poland today what the country west of the Mississippi was to the United States in the early days of the American frontier, though Germans are not red Indians. Poles talk about the Recovered Territories (the official name) with the greatest zest and atmosphere of adventure, and settling and organizing them is their chief (and most lucrative) contemporary task.[10] That it is hard lines on the Germans does not make them lose much sleep.

Politics and Personalities

The President of the Republic of Poland (not yet "People's" Republic) is Boleslaw Bierut; also he is chairman of the five-man Council of State that ostensibly runs the country. Bierut is an old-time Communist who for a time, on being elevated to the presidency, held a kind of nonparty or supraparty status. He is a man of fifty-eight, born near Lublin. He earned a living as an apprentice printer, fought in the Russian army in the First World War, became a Communist, and was several times arrested by the Pilsudski dictatorship. One of his chief claims to prestige is that he spent most of World War II in the Polish underground in Poland itself; not till the end did he go to Moscow. He became secretary general of the party a good many years ago, and so his hierarchic rank was high. The name he uses today, "Bierut," is taken from two names he assumed in his revolutionary underground days.

The chief intellectual influence on President Bierut is that of a noteworthy comrade named Jakub Berman, of whom more anon. Mr. Berman is usually talked about as the single most important man in Poland, but his force is largely wielded from behind the scenes. His official job is Undersecretary of State at the Presidium of the Council of Ministers. Thus he has no actual portfolio or concrete administrative duties; he is something like the Lord Privy Seal in England—though this analogy will annoy Poles and British both. In any case Berman, at Bierut's shoulder, is at the top.

The Prime Minister, Józef Cyrankiewicz, is not a Communist (PPR), but a Socialist (PPS). Once again we see how these regimes use "fronts." Like practically all Poles, Mr. Cyrankiewicz is a vivid character, with great gusto and personal appeal.

[10] Some statistics if you are interested: Polish "pioneers" have restored 326,000 farms and increased sown acres from 2,000,000 to 9,000,000. Production of coal doubled between 1945 and 1947. By 1949 it is to jump from 9,000,000 tons a year to 25,000,000. Iron ore production is 90 per cent of prewar, and climbing steadily.

He is only thirty-seven. He looks older, because he is bald; he lost his hair at Oświęcim. He was born in Cracow, and thus derives from the cradle of Polish culture; from his earliest years he has been a left-wing Social Democrat. In 1939 he was mobilized as a lieutenant of artillery; he was taken prisoner by the Germans after twenty days, escaped, returned secretly to Cracow, and helped organize the Polish underground. Once he was arrested early in the war; the Nazis did not know who he was, and he got off. Later he spent several years in concentration camps. He is not a Muscovite in the sense that he lived in Russia during the war. Recently he married a well-known Polish actress. His hobbies are mountain climbing near Zakopane, and to drive fast in big cars. Cyrankiewicz has been Prime Minister since the elections of January 1947, and is an extremely able man.

The Foreign Minister, Zygmunt Modzelewski, is not of equal importance, though he is a Communist high in the party. Another minister of great rank is Edward Osóbka-Morawski, in charge of public administration; it was he who led the Polish committee in Moscow and the Lublin "government." More influential than these, both as an intellectual and technician, is the Minister of Industry and Commerce, Hilary Minc. This brilliant administrator (incidentally he bears a strong facial resemblance to Professor Harold Laski) is one of the two or three men who really count, not only in Warsaw but in Communist affairs at large. As I said in a preceding chapter he is supposed to be very close to Stalin himself. Minc is in effect the economic dictator of the country, and the author of both the Three Year and the ensuing Six Year Plan.

But Minc is now in trouble for alleged Titoism and deviationism according to recent reports. If, indeed, the Tito rumpus has reached so high as this, the whole structure of international Communism must be wobbling ideologically. Minc was born in Kazimierz in 1905. He was educated abroad as well as in Poland, and lived for some years in France where (to quote a biographical sketch prepared by American sources) "he established unions among Polish miners." From 1930 to 1939 he worked as a statistician and treasury official for the High Commissariat in Gdynia. When the war came he got out to Moscow, and for some years lectured in economics at, of all places, the University of Samarkand. He was a colonel in the Polish divisions formed in Russia, and editor of *Free Poland,* the Moscow organ of the Poles during the war. Since 1944 he has been Minister of Industry and Trade.

Several stratifications exist in this ruling amalgam. For one thing only a minority of full ministers are actual Communists —six out of twenty-four to be exact as of the time we visited Warsaw. There are, be it remembered, four chief parties in the Polish coalition: the PPR or Polish Workers Party, the PPS or Social Democrats, the SL, a left wing peasant group that split off from Mikolajczyk's peasant party, and the SD, a small group described as being composed of "intellectuals." In a sense these alternative parties were set up so that a Pole wanting to partake of an active political life could take his choice as to which to join, depending on his aptitudes and job. Of course—I hardly need repeat this—the Communist PPR rules the roost. Still, it is important to note that, until the merger, the Polish Socialists had roughly 700,000 members; they were one of the oldest, most entrenched, and most powerful Socialist parties in Europe, and in the 1947 elections they ran neck and neck with the Communists (they got a precisely equal number of seats in the *Sejm,* parliament). But these fissures and ranklings do not matter much. It was interesting to note that, in an official list given me of members of the government, the names of several were marked "party affiliation unknown."

Other stratifications are more suggestive. The Workers Party is today run by two separate groups. One, obviously, is that of the Lubliners who came from Moscow; the other, that of the partisans who operated the Polish underground *inside* the country. The USSR group is of course much less nationalist than the other. Another cleavage is on the line of Jewishness.[11] Poland has always had a strong tradition of anti-Semitism, and it is freely said for instance that Berman would be Prime Minister today except for the fact that he is a Jew. The President of the republic, the Prime Minister, and the recently purged Wlady-

[11] Once more consult Chapter 3 above.

slaw Gomulka, among people at the very top, are not Jewish. One reason for Gomulka's erstwhile popularity among many Poles was that he is not a Jew. Among the prominent Jews who have reached cabinet posts, however, are Minc, Modzelewski, and the powerful Minister of Education, Dr. Stanislaw Skrzeszewski. Most of the Jewish ministers are Muscovites and members of the PPR. Thus, once more, "Jewishness," "Russianness," and "Communism" tend to become one in the common mind, which is unfortunate in the extreme. Of the Politburo of the party today, three out of eight members are Jews. Finally, among those that really count, three military names should be mentioned—Colonel Roman Zambrowski, the vice chairman of the parliament and a member of the Politburo, General Marian Spychaiski, also a Politburo member and Deputy Minister of National Defense, and General Aleksander Zawadski, the governor of Silesia.[12]

Two important political events occurred recently, and they are closely interlocked. One was the attack on Gomulka for alleged deviationism, and the other the merger, in December 1948, of the Communists and Socialists into what is now called the United Party of the Polish Working Classes.

Gomulka was, and is, an old-line Socialist and Communist; at the time we were in Warsaw he was not only Deputy Prime Minister but Minister for the Recovered Territories, and also secretary general of the party. I have not the space to go into the detailed story of the accusations against him, his groveling recantation, and his eventual dismissal. The whole case resembles that of Tito—except that Tito did not recant. Gomulka was accused among other things of "self-idolatry" and of having minimized the role of the Red army in freeing Poland; probably, as in Yugoslavia, a basic reason for the quarrel was not merely "rightist" or "nationalist" deviation, but the simple matter of obedience and discipline; Gomulka, like Tito, resented being handled by the Kremlin as if he were a child. I asked one Polish minister who was "against" Gomulka; the

[12] Arthur Bliss Lane in his *I Saw Poland Betrayed,* who gives a very different interpretation to most of these events, asserts that two of these officers are marionettes for the Red army or the Russian secret police.

laughing answer I got was, "Everybody!" But this is not true; he had a large following in the country. Hence Gomulka was made to recant in the most humiliating and ignominious terms; freely he "confessed" his "false and anti-Marxist" errors, and pleaded with all good party members to learn the lesson of unity from his unfortunate and reprehensible behavior.

If anybody is still curious about Communist technicalities in jargon here is the first paragraph of the text of the Central Committee's communique bringing Gomulka to task:

> The June plenum of the CC-PPR fully exposed the existence of a right-wing ideological deviation which had afflicted a segment of the Party leadership. This deviation was expressed in the report of Comrade Gomulka which contained a false and anti-Leninist appraisal of the Polish workers' movement's past. Contrary to the previous battle of the PPR against opportunism, chauvinism, and social democracy in the Polish Socialist Party (PPS), Comrade Gomulka's report, delivered without coordination with the *Politburo* of the CC, constitutes an actual ideological capitulation to the nationalistic traditions of the PPS.

And Gomulka's reply is mostly in an idiom even worse.

Talks with Two Ministers

Two Poles of stature we met and had long talks with were General Wiktor Grosz, who is in charge of press affairs and information, and Jakub Berman, the eminence grise. We would have met the President, Prime Minister and so on, had we stayed longer. But the Poles have a very touchy pride, and in a quite nice way they felt that they should punish us mildly by not giving us too many interviews because our visit was hurried. This was frankly put to us and I found it very interesting. Far cry from the attitude of some governments which go to almost ridiculous lengths (I hope I don't sound too ungrateful) turning themselves inside out for the benefit of the visitor. The Polish point of view was that by being hard to buy, so to speak, they would gain respect. But personally Grosz and Berman were both hospitable in the extreme.

We telephoned Grosz and he asked us to come over at once—

he happened to have a minute free—and then later he gave us a whole afternoon, three or four hours of solid talk, and took us for a tour of the city too. He is a remarkably interesting character—impassioned, didactic, explosive, ruthless I imagine (his enemies call him the Polish Goebbels) and exuding magnetism and physical charm. I asked him to give us a brief outline of his career, and he exclaimed, "But I am a *professional* revolutionary!" This was the first time in my life I ever heard this said in just this way. Once Grosz made a living as a translator. He knows eight or nine languages well, and one chore many years ago was putting into Polish some Canadian stories about baby animals. Telling this his nose wrinkled in ironic retrospective distaste; then he howled with laughter. Grosz fought all through the war, and was elevated to be a general when the Russian forces were closing in on Berlin. He is only about thirty-five.

This provocative and lively man must, I fear, be assessed ultimate responsibility for much that is silly, stupid, and inflammatory in Polish newspapers about America. See below, under *Posies from the Press*. But as far as other details of his work are concerned he is signally proficient. The Polish propaganda booklets and so on, which I have already alluded to, are by far the most attractive things of their kind I have ever seen put out by any government—from the point of view of typography, format, literary style, wealth of content, and technically superb multicolored maps. Incidentally when I talked to Grosz about our own information services in Washington and said that Americans by and large are very suspicious of any propaganda, even our own, and that the State Department always got its budget severely chopped in these fields, he flatly could not believe it. It was almost inconceivable to him that I could be telling the truth. Once more—the platitude is becoming trite—the chief barrier to decent relations in the world is ignorance.

Items from Grosz's talk: "All commanding posts here are in the hands of the working class. . . . But according to Marx anything that is not fully Communist is still capitalist, and so I suppose we still fall into that category. . . . In time we, this government, will compete with private trade, in order to try to make the private trader sell cheaper. . . . The attitude of the government is to introduce social measures not for the sake of some remote utopia, but to accomplish concrete benefits right now. . . . The Russians built socialism in the midst of capitalism. We build socialism in the midst of socialism. . . . Peasants in Poland will not lose their property. You must read a great speech Minc made yesterday. The land reform has been prodigious, but that is quite a different thing from forcing people into *kolkhozes* (collectives). . . . The membership of the party is about a million now. . . . Censorship? There is none at all on cables or mail, but the local press is certainly censored. I censor it myself. . . .

"What are the chief foci of opposition? Well, let us list them historically. First, the organized legal opposition of Mikolajczyk. Then a strong British-and-American-sponsored underground. Then the right wing Socialists and gentry dispossessed by the land reform. To some extent the petite bourgeoisie. Now all this has been eliminated, but the opposition was not smashed by any formal act of our administration. No! The people themselves came to realize that the government was on their own side, and the speed of our reconstruction helped considerably. The most dangerous oppositionists counted on a war fought by America to liberate them, but war has not come. . . . The Church? That is still a great problem. We do not mix in Church affairs, and we do not want the Church to mix in ours. There is a Catholic political party associated with the government. . . . One thing that contributed to the liquidation of opposition was the return to Russia of Lwów and Vilna, because these two cities had long been centers of separatism and reaction. . . . Also Byrnes' speech at Stuttgart gave the coup de grace to Mikolajczyk.

"War? If war should come, you will have to fight by the aid of German infantry, and if so, every person alive in eastern Europe, even those on the right wing, will struggle to the death rather than submit. . . . Marshall plan? My dear Mr. Gunther, you cannot kill ideas with dollar bills!"[13]

[13] Of course there is some fine wishful thinking in this last remark. It has been a decided unpleasant shock to Communists everywhere that the Marshall plan has in fact been so extremely successful. Also the Poles, like the Czechs, wanted badly to take part in the Plan, but the Russians refused to let them.

Berman is a totally different type of man. Reserved, remote, with an exceptionally sensitive face and a detached slow manner, gentle in speech, unsmiling, poised, he looks the role he plays. He has fine dark brown eyes, and beautifully kept hands. We thought him very guarded at first. He did not erupt like Grosz. He opened up gradually. He is very human, but he hates the limelight. I have little specific to report about what he said, since most of the conversation was in the realm of abstract ideas. If you don't advance, he said, you recede. Always there is an ebb and flow of conflict. What the regime must avoid above all is "petrification." But he added that though it must move forward, it should not do so "adventurously." This (though he was talking in reference to the Gomulka affair, which had just become public) was strikingly reminiscent of Vas in Hungary. All Communists think alike. It is not merely that they are taught to conform; instinctively their minds seek the same fixed channel.

Berman was born in Warsaw of bourgeois Jewish stock, and studied law. He is about forty-six. Almost all the Polish leaders are quite young. He worked in a bank for a time, taught school, and for one brief interval had a job in the Jewish Telegraph Agency. Under Pilsudski he was arrested several times as a Communist, but he did not spend much time in jail. He happened to be in Russian-occupied territory in 1939; he went to Moscow for several years and returned to Poland eventually with the Lublin government. One friend of his told me that he considered Berman to be the "personification of human intelligence," largely because of his ability to smooth difficult things over, but he has very little concrete knowledge of the West or Western patterns of thought and mind.

Berman told us that he had great admiration for much in the United States, politics aside, and he talked with genuine "sorrow" about rifts in the traditional Polish-American friendship. The main Polish anxiety is Germany, and most good Poles, like Berman, feel that the real danger in the Reich is not the Germans themselves, but the Americans. "But we have a deep sentiment for the United States," he went on, not patronizingly, "It is a young country too, with spirit, push, and *joie de vivre*." He proceeded to assert that "Poland would like to have the real truth about the United States" and that he hoped more and more Americans would come into Poland, to carry out a "true picture" of what Poland itself was like. "Our main goal is *social advance*. This is the message we have for the world. We don't want to make millionaires of our people. But we do want to give them a decent standard of living." Then: "There are lots of things about America to be known, and we would like to learn from you!"

As to Polish relations with Russia, Berman said that these were close and friendly, but that there was no pressure. "Poland is represented in the outside world as a puppet. But politically, culturally, economically, we are absolutely free. How *can* we convey to you that we really *are* free?" As to Germany, he considers that the East-West split in the Reich cannot possibly last. As to the possibility of war, he thought it on the whole unlikely.

Posies from the Press

Fierce polemics against the United States are printed in the Warsaw papers, no matter what Mr. Berman says. While we were in Warsaw the campaign was particularly bitter, following a prickly brush between the headstrong Grosz and the U.S.I.S. officials. Also it was exacerbated by the Wroclaw congress which had just been held; American dupes at this affair played right into the hands of the most venomous Polish extremists. Among headlines I saw were, WARSAW WOMEN WILL STRUGGLE AGAINST CRIMINAL SCHEMES OF AMERICAN IMPERIALISM, PROVOCATIVE ACTION BY AMERICAN MILITARY POLICE IN BERLIN, and U. S. SAILORS MURDERING ITALIANS.

Here is one story that shows how Eastern Europeans apply their own standards and idiom to American affairs:

> Dewey, who is positive of his victory, is making concrete plans regarding the composition of his cabinet. Irrespective of changes in the highest positions, a complete and far-reaching purge (*sic!*) is expected in all Federal offices. It is expected that the Democrats will be deprived of at least 150,000 Federal positions.

The following is from an interview in *Robotnik,* the Socialist organ and in former days one of the most respected newspapers in Europe, with two anonymous Americans.

We sat in a small, cozy restaurant in company with an American couple, both writers, whose names I will not mention for reasons easily understandable.

I asked them about the Committee for Investigating anti-American activities. "This is a dreadful thing!" cries the American writer. "Every man may at any moment be called before a tribunal of dunces. . . . This is a kind of parody of a court. It is forbidden to have a counsel, to defend or to explain oneself. You may only say "yes" or "no." There is no appeal from the sentence; it may be imprisonment or at best a civil death. . . . The gentlemen of the inquisition are intoxicated with their power. A man may be crushed into complete slavery. Followers of Roosevelt and of course those of Wallace are being systematically destroyed."

The Americans being interviewed went on to say that anyway they were going back to the United States. *Robotnik*'s reporter proceeds:

This proves that a part of America is now entering a heroic period. They are becoming united and do not fear struggle. They are still in the minority, but all progressive movements were started by minorities and subsequently drew the masses. The attitude of such Americans is dear to us and we understand them very well. They may suffer but the future belongs to them.

This was in a Russian speech at Wroclaw, widely printed in the Polish press:

U. S. reactionary American scientists, writers and artists violently detest the USSR for two reasons. First, as imperialists' obedient dogs, and secondly because science and art in the USSR serve the entire nation and develop freely.

German imperialism needed beasts [like dogs]. They are also necessary for the rulers of American monopolies to realize their plans to dominate the world. The propaganda of crime, demoralization, animal instincts, is needed by the reaction.

The aim of American imperialists is to fetter humanity and turn the entire globe into a huge Police State and its population into capital's slaves.

Under the veil of "Economic Aid" American gendarmes have prepared a plan to create penal expeditions, as in Greece, a plan to take over all military bases, a plan of anti-communist laws, a trade union unity breaking plan and machine guns.

The present U. S. rulers preside over the aggression of ignorance. The short history of the U. S., its racial traditions and moral isolationism, result in the absence of an understanding of another world. Barbarism on the other side of the Atlantic develops daily.

All this sounds like the most blatant Nazis at their most juvenile.

. . . And Still More about the Poles

That Poland has achieved a substantial recovery is incontestable; it is the most prosperous of the Eastern European states by a good margin. One reason for this is the extension of the western frontier at the expense of Germany and the acquisition of the great Silesian iron-*cum*-coal complex. I do not want to burden the reader with too many figures, but it is interesting that the national income in 1948 showed an advance of not less than 33 percent over the last prewar year—to say nothing of the fact that it advanced over 1946 and 1947 by 60 and 72.7 percent respectively. On January 1, 1949, the Poles ended all rationing restrictions, reduced prices on previously rationed goods (for instance bread, sugar, soap, oil, woolens) and lifted wages of some three million workers by 10 percent. Also some prices were raised—for instance of vodka, electricity, and streetcar fares.[14]

How socialist is Poland? Nationalization began early in 1946; the provisions of the law were more flexible than in the adjacent countries. Heavy industry and all German industrial property were taken over in toto; small factories were nationalized only if they employed more than fifty workers in any one shift. Later this figure was raised. Coal, oil, power, most utilities, arms, aircraft, sugar, transportation, breweries, yeast, textiles, and oil and seed factories up to a certain limit, were nationalized outright. But some "newly established" industries

[14] Sydney Gruson in the *New York Times*, January 2, 1949.

were exempt—the motive being to stimulate new enterprise. One effect of this was to do away with ownership of Polish means of production by foreigners. Before the war 87.5 percent of Polish petroleum, 81.3 percent of power, 59.9 percent of the metal industry, and 52.5 percent of chemicals had been owned by foreign capital. Naturally (as in Yugoslavia and elsewhere) this rankled deeply, and the foreign owners and "colonial exploiters" were expropriated.[15]

The situation is difficult to describe today, because it changes so quickly; Poland is a highly fluid state. Probably one quarter of all the productive enterprise of the country is still in the "private" sector. The ratio depends on category. For instance in the field of wholesale merchandising the government controls 59.1 percent of the total, and the cooperatives 36.6. Of the total of *all* people gainfully employed, 14 percent are still private. Minc said in a recent speech, "We have a mixed economy with three separate orders side by side, socialist, capitalist, and co-operative. The socialist elements predominate in industry, transportation, finance, are growing steadily in retail trade, and occupy an important position not fully utilized in agriculture." The transitional nature of the process is always emphasized, and an analogy to England is often made. Another spokesman said: "At any rate the Polish system cannot be called strictly socialistic. It is based . . . on the belief that the roads to socialism may vary from country to country." (In Yugoslavia this was heresy; Poles, look out.) "Obviously this road of 'mild revolution' is easier than that of violent overthrow. But it requires at the same time greater vigilance, lest the ultimate goal be lost sight of."

The Three Year Plan (1947-49 inclusive), with a total investment of $3.4 billions, is said to be going well. The text of the act ("Planned Physical Development of the Country Act") is printed in parallel columns in Polish, English, and Russian in the copy I have. One minor provision, to illustrate how far into detail the plan goes, is that any citizen with $600 a year or more must maintain a savings account.

The Six Year Plan to follow, the favorite brain child of Mr.

[15] Dean, *op. cit.* and Thomson.

Minc, is not for reconstruction but for long-term basic industrialization and permanent development, with considerable attention to consumers goods and agriculture. The ultimate goal is an 85.95 percent increase in industrial production over 1949. Production of cotton goods is to rise 57 percent, of woolens 39 percent, of flax 100, of shoes 250, of sugar 25, of agriculture in general 25-35. One item is that 50-60,000 tractors will be built to put on the farms. In all Poland today there are only 1,085.

We talked to one leading Socialist deputy just before the parties merged. Wages are not high; yet one must always remember in these countries that wages exist in other terms than money. White collar workers have a forty-hour week, manual workers forty-eight; the former get thirty days paid vacation a year, the latter fifteen. The trade unions are very strong, and the social security system covers "sickness, invalidism, old age, maternity, unemployment, occupational disease, death of the bread winner, and family bonuses." One serious bottle neck is housing; nobody without a productive job will have much luck finding a place to live. One striking point, however, is that in spite of the devastation in Warsaw, housing conditions are said to be *better* there than before the war—sufficient indication of the inadequacies, to put it mildly, of the previous regime.

As to agriculture the situation is again mixed. According to conventional theory, any socialist government will be *bound* in the end to collectivize agriculture, if it is too poor to amass purchasing power otherwise through loans, exports, or industrial development. This is the root of the whole question of collectives everywhere. One wing of the party presses for nationalization (this was a factor in the Gomulka case) but it hasn't happened yet. A foreigner told us, "The Poles would not possibly dare collectivize. The peasants would resist by force and there would be bloodshed." The present position is that all properties over fifty hectares have been distributed to peasant holders. No more big estates exist, and the state itself (as in Hungary) now holds about 10 percent of the total arable acreage. A point to remember is that before the war 65 percent of all farms in Poland were not self-subsistent. No wonder there was yearning for reform! Meantime attacks on the so-called "rich" peasant, or kulak, are inevitable; Minc himself has forecast them. In the Communist parlance the "richness" of a peasant has, of course, nothing to do with his wealth, if any; a "rich" peasant is simply one who hires other labor.

The Polish land reform has some markedly interesting special characteristics. For one thing Church property was not touched in the main. For another, state land has been used consistently for scientific agricultural experimentation. For another, the Poles who were dispossessed near Lwów and Vilna were given priority in the new western settlements. Finally, dating back to the first Lublin decrees in September 1944, the principle was established that *no* peasant should be without some land, even if it were a parcel of five acres. So far about 9,300 estates have been broken up, and a total of 75 million acres distributed to 387,000 families.

Another substantial advance, Poles say, has taken place in a different field, that of culture. Indeed Poland has by far the most vigorous and spirited cultural life of any of the border countries. Ten and a half percent of the national budget is allotted to education, and to date, with a start from scratch, seventy-one theaters have been built and six opera companies and seven philharmonic orchestras established. The trade unions alone organized, by the end of 1947, 900 theater troupes, 350 ballet companies, and 650 orchestras—of course most of these small and amateur. Most striking of all is the spectacular advance in book publishing. No fewer than 8,500 different titles were published in Poland in 1947—a good number for any country; the total distribution was fifty *million* volumes. The average number of titles published per year between 1930 and 1939 was four thousand. Technical and scientific books—in fact textbooks of all kinds—lead in the present figures, closely followed by fiction and juveniles. Of the total about forty percent are still published by private firms. One set of literary prizes goes each year to specifically Catholic writers—a revealing point inasmuch as the country is 91 percent Roman Catholic.

Early in 1947 the Polish diet adopted a "Declaration of Rights and Liberties," the first in this area to do so. The clauses read extremely well on paper, with declarations by the government that it affirms and will uphold such fundamental rights as, among others (a) equality before the law regardless of nationality, race, creed, sex, origin, social status, or education, (b) freedom of conscience and worship, (c) freedom of scientific research and the publication of the results thereof, and freedom of creative artistic endeavor, (d) inviolability of the home, (e) secrecy of the mails and other means of communication, (f) the right to work and to periods of rest, (g) the right to education, (h) freedom of press, speech, association, assembly, public meetings, and even "demonstration." But the text of the law includes an obvious joker in that "the abuse" of any of these rights "for the purpose of overthrowing the government of Poland," may be prevented by legal action. As things have worked out the country is still—of course—a complete dictatorship.

CHAPTER 17
VIENNA STILL ALIVE

WE CAME into Austria on a private plane, and landed at Tulln, the American airport near Vienna. It happened to be late on a Saturday afternoon, and not a soul was on duty at the airport. The pilot had received no answer to his request for radio bearings. There was no security control by any officials, either American or Austrian, after we landed, and we thus came into the American Zone of Austria, permission to enter which is so zealously safeguarded by the authorities in Washington, without ever having our passports or special military permits stamped or even inspected. To this day, there is no record that we ever went into Austria.

After some telephoning we got an American army car, and drove the eighteen miles into Vienna. The Tulln airstrip is completely surrounded by the Russian Zone. Not many Americans outside Austria realize this. The only means of communication between the American Zone here and the American Zone in Germany or, for that matter, anywhere in the world, by air, is this small patch of asphalt near the Danube (and a substantial distance from our garrison in Vienna itself), entirely closed in by Russian territory. Big signs in English warn Americans to keep strictly to the main road into Vienna, and at every intersection an arrow points out the only route permitted. Along this specific route Americans go as they please; step a few yards off it, and there may be trouble. We passed one Russian road block, but nobody paid attention. The Russians seldom interfere with military traffic on this road, since our agreement with them gives us complete right of access to the airport. Occasionally a Russian sentry will stop a car for a moment. Our driver told us that these sentries have picked up a few words of English, and are apt to talk in mixed jargon like "Okay—take off!" when an American car goes through.

Vienna itself is full of American, French, and Russian signs, military and other. It was startling to see huge English letters, SLIPPERY WHEN WET on the street where Dr. Freud lived, and to pass large military posters directing traffic to various American and British establishments along the Ring—also to notice familiar streets identified by stenciled signs in Russian characters.

We arrived at the Bristol, the hotel run by the U.S. Army for American personnel and visitors. It is still one of the best hotels in Europe. The servants have lost nothing of their slow efficiency and charm. If you put your shoes out, they will come back—in time—shiny as mirrors. The very first person I met in Vienna was an old friend—Franz, the hall porter. He popped out from behind his desk, greeted me, and in true Viennese fashion kissed my wife's hand.

But if we had thought from our experience at the airport that the Americans in Vienna are not security-minded, we were quickly proved wrong. Two MPs stand at the entrance to the Bristol and check every visitor who enters. Every single time we ever went into the hotel we had to show our papers, and when we called at military headquarters, the MPs or other guards even checked our passports against the local passes, to see if the numbers tallied. We must have had to show papers ten or twelve times a day. This was in acute contrast to what happened in the satellite countries, where we never once had to produce any documents except at frontiers or when registering at a hotel. Then we went out to dinner and got new evidence of how carefully things are watched in Vienna. This was an "American" month when the U.S. is in charge of policing the Inner Stadt. Our MPs were everywhere. They travel in pairs invariably, and are the toughest-looking MPs I have ever encountered. Also they are very smartly uniformed, with brilliant scarlet scarves worn around their collars, and scarlet bands painted on their shining steel helmets. The two who entered the restaurant where we dined had faces made, it seemed, of wood. Slowly, deliberately, they paced through the premises, looking everybody over—coldly. No word was spoken. Nor did anybody pay any attention to them. But, good Americans as they were, they cast a certain chill over the *gemütlich* atmosphere. The Viennese have a little joke, not too affectionate, about our MPs. They call them "Russians with creased pants."

Dinner was a shock. I had known this restaurant on the Rotenturmstrasse well before the war. Both food and atmosphere were terrible. Dreary, hopeless people sat in ancient threadbare clothes, nibbling at dark bread, talking tonelessly, without a spark of animation. Paper tablecloth. No napkins. We had a soup, Wienerschnitzel, and coffee. Price about $8.00. Vienna is, and always has been, full of *Schlamperei* and minor graceful illegality. We noticed the people at the next table surrender their food coupons when they paid the bill. We had none, and wondered what would happen. But the waiter never even asked for them. In all the restaurants we went to, never once were we asked to produce a ration book.

Back in the hotel we paused to read with interest the billboard announcement of theaters and the like, and we saw that the week's fare included a choice of ten or fifteen operas, several magnificent concerts, plays by Shakespeare, Euripides, Hermann Bahr, John Van Druten (both *Voice of the Turtle* and *I Remember Mama* were running), Goethe, and all manner of lighter entertainment. Back in the free world again! Back in a country where art and music, books and theater, were not merely appendages to unitarian politics! Back in the bosom of the West! We felt a considerable warm release and relief. Then upstairs we heard a noisy agitated commotion on the streets, and jumped to the window to peer outside. A torchlight procession was pushing thickly down the Ring, with young people singing lustily and carrying red flags and torches. It was the Communist youth parading. Even here!

Wien, Wien, Nur Du Allein

In the 1930's I lived in Vienna for almost five years and so it was with a good deal of curiosity that I looked around next day. Badly destroyed the city is in part. This was caused partly by American bombing, partly by brief but fierce street fighting when the Red army drove the Germans out of the city. The destruction in Vienna is not so bad as that in Berlin or Frankfurt, and not anywhere near so bad as in Warsaw. Berlin is like a man without arms or legs and Warsaw is a man with no face; Vienna is a face with every other tooth knocked out.

We took a drive among sights once poignantly familiar. First up to Döbling, where I saw for the first time since 1936 the house I had lived in—a big stone house set in a flowery wooded garden. It is still standing, and occupied, but there must have been severe fighting in this neighborhood even though it is in the outskirts, because the walls are scarred and blistered with shellfire and windows are still broken. Then we descended into the town, to inspect another dwelling on Modena Park. It seemed to be quite undamaged, and the shop signs on Neulinggasse were still the same—I remembered vividly the delicatessen on the corner, the *Friseur* (hairdresser), and a vegetable market on the side of the park. No damage. Yet a hundred yards away, on Reisnerstrasse, we saw destruction of the most cruel kind. Whole buildings are gone; the rubble fills entire empty lots. In one tall building, where a colleague of mine lived for years, the outer walls are sliced off as by a cleaver, and you can see, floor by floor, as in a doll's house, the ruined inner contents of each apartment. In one room, clearly visible from the street, two chairs still adjoin a table, as if people had been sitting there ten minutes ago. But that building has been uninhabited since 1945.

We stopped for a moment at the Ballhausplatz, where Austrian foreign policy (such as it was and is) has been made since the days of Metternich. Here, one summer afternoon in 1934, I stood with ten thousand others in the street, while the Nazis ransacked the building and murdered Dollfuss. We drove past the Karl Marx Hof, and, in the Russian Zone, peeked across the Danube to the Goethe Hof. These are two of the most famous of the great *Gemeinde* houses built by the Vienna Socialist municipality before the war, which were attacked and seized by the Austrian Fascists in 1934. Here, during a brief and bloody civil war, I dodged bullets in the worst street fighting I ever saw. These municipal tenements were, and possibly still are, the finest things of their kind in Europe. So far as I could see they are still scarred and pock-marked externally, but not severely damaged, and life apparently goes on in them much as before.

In the center of town, off the half-wrecked Graben, I couldn't resist visiting the building that housed the office where I worked for the Chicago *Daily News*. It seems to be two things now: (a) a night club called the Orientale filled with strip-teasers, and (b) the local headquarters of the Communist party. The Tabak Trafik where I used to buy cigarettes every day (they were called Memphis and came in a green box and have long since ceased to exist) is now the official Russian bookstore.

The Opera (where I once heard Lehmann and Jeritza sing) is being rebuilt; the Burg Theater (where I saw the best *King Lear* I have ever seen) is still a shell; St. Stephen's Cathedral is roofless. But the nave has been patched up and Christmas services were held here this year for the first time since 1944.

The worst destruction seems to be along the Franz-Josefskai and the Danube canal. A huge mound of debris is all that remains of the Hotel Metropole, which will cause little grief to anybody since this was the headquarters of the SS. But for some other hotels—in the center of the city—one can really weep. Where the old building of the Bristol once stood proudly and elegantly is an empty lot. The Meissl und Schadn, my favorite of all Vienna hotels, is a hollow grave of ruins. Here Herr Fruhmann, one of the most celebrated of Viennese headwaiters, used to serve delicacies like *Tafelspitz*—boiled beef on the bone. There is no Meissl und Schadn any more, and very little *Tafelspitz,* but Herr Fruhmann is still alive. He came to see us one morning, still cheerful, still gleaming with Vienna wit, but very old, very poor, and lame.

Gone, gone, almost everything seems gone! The Café Louvre, where the journalists met every evening, was bombed out, and is now a bank. Here I do not know how many hours I spent with colleagues like William L. Shirer, M. W. Fodor, Robert Best (now serving time in an American jail for treason) and Whit Burnett. The Café Central (which before my time was

Trotsky's favorite café) is a barrow of wreckage. The Opern Café, where all the pretty girls—so gracious and pensive and generous—gathered in the twilight in the 1930's, was cut in half by a bomb, and part of it still operates, but I didn't see any pretty girls. The Café Rebhuhn still exists, but I could find no trace of the Vindobona, where I once bought H. G. Wells a drink. The Café Beethoven is intact, but it seemed deserted, and the Mozart is out of bounds.

Among the great restaurants, Schöner's is an army mess, the Three Hussars has disappeared, and Sacher's is the British headquarters, with a sign in front, NO AUSTRIANS PERMITTED. No Austrians allowed in Sacher's! The Russians have both the Grand and the Imperial on the Ringstrasse. It was odd—since I have been in each at least a thousand times—not to be able to enter. Vividly I remembered the old *Stammtisch* of the Balkan spies and agents-provocateurs and shadow conspirators that met at the Imperial every morning, and the wonderful golden glow of Viennese sophistication in the Grand. But now the windows of both are tightly curtained, and sentries with fixed bayonets stand outside the doors.

At night, the Kärntnerstrasse used to be a silken, lacy Broadway. These days, with every other building destroyed, it looks like an empty broken stage set. I walked past the *Würstl* stands late at night, which in the old days sold steaming hot goulash, frankfurters, beer and coffee to the nomads of the Vienna streets, until dawn. Today they have nothing but a peculiarly revolting kind of herring sandwich, and they close at midnight. Two of the finest confectionary shops in Europe still exist in this neighborhood, Gerstner and Demel. But today you have to bring your own sugar in exchange for the sweets you try to buy.

The streets are animated enough by day, but almost deserted at night. The people look drab—there are few bright colors, and clothes are old and shabby; men wearing plus fours and golf socks look like pictures from a tailor's catalogue of forty years ago. There are plenty of taxis—more than in Paris for instance—but most are dilapidated. Except on a few streets like Herrengasse, traffic is negligible; one reason for this is that the Russians control the local gasoline supply, and keep it scant.

Schwartzenbergplatz has been renamed Stalinplatz, but no true Viennese calls it so. (There is a Rooseveltplatz too these days, but it is much smaller and not in so noble a neighborhood.) The Prater, Vienna's famous amusement park, seemed deserted when we visited it, and the great ferris wheel was empty and motionless. Deserted too are the nearby tennis courts. But the Eislaufverein near the Stadtpark (tennis in summer, ice skating in winter) still exists though half of it is cut off, and the loudspeakers no longer sing out with Strauss or other pungent waltzes.

Everywhere the street signs indicate shortages. I saw little shops with notices, BIER HEUTE or EIS HEUTE, indicating that such luxuries as beer and ice were not always to be had. I bought some typewriter paper at a stationery shop; the salesgirl counted it out sheet by sheet. Austrian cigarettes cost about 6¢ (American) each. In fact in the whole realm of consumer goods Vienna seemed very short, though some very expensive luxury products were available. Prices are high in general and wages pegged. It was indeed striking that, from a superficial view, conditions in Warsaw and Budapest under the Russians seemed so much better than here in Vienna under the U.S.A. and the Western allies—this too considering the fact that Austria gets very substantial aid from the Marshall plan.[1]

I tried to locate three friends. One was a doctor. He killed himself, and his wife killed herself, in 1938 when the Nazis came. One was a political journalist. He was murdered in Buchenwald. One was a young sculptress. She has disappeared without trace.[2]

Yet, all this being said, and all this being true, there is much else to say. Vienna may seem gloomy, but every observer I

[1] The ERP allotment for Austria in 1949 is estimated at $197 million. This is on top of previous American contributions of roughly $836 million. About 70 percent of all food Austrians eat comes from the United States.

[2] It happens that these were all Jews. Let us keep in mind (when we happen to be thinking of the Germans) that of the 250,000 Jews in Austria before the war, only about 9,000 survive today.

met agreed that it is in much better shape than last year, or the year before, and that conditions in general are steadily and perceptibly improving, week by week and almost hour by hour. In particular food has become more plentiful.

Two other things are on the positive side. One is that night life is quite lively—neon lights beckon the visitor to innumerable *boîtes de nuit* along streets like Annagasse and Dorotheegasse. To mention night life may seem frivolous, but actually this has always been a very good criterion of the general level of well-being in any Central European town. Then, more important, Vienna's intellectual and artistic life is spirited, though the bookshops did not seem well stocked. We went to the opera once, and saw *Die Walküre*. It was a good sound performance, but what interested me more was the audience and the general atmosphere. Since the big Opera House is not yet reconstructed the company plays at the old Theater an der Wien, a small house; almost a quarter of the orchestra seats had to be ripped out to give room for the immense orchestra of the Wiener Philharmonic. The theater was rather empty; I was told that few Viennese can afford the better tickets, which cost about 30 schillings or $3.00 at the official rate. No one wore evening dress, the theater had a musty reek, and the whole spirit was dreary and plebeian—I felt almost as if I were in Moscow, where, similarly, superb opera is performed to an audience in caps and sweaters.

Face to Face: Stars and Stripes and Red Army

Probably Vienna is the only place in the world where Americans and Russians still work together closely with fairly harmonious relations. This should be an important lesson to everybody—in Washington and Moscow alike—if we are to have peace instead of war, in that it seemingly proves that the barrier to good relations on a local level is neither intrinsic nor insuperable. Given intelligent leadership, even in a touchy situation where each side looks to a different end, the two nations *can* get along. Minor irritations and frictions certainly occur; but they are not allowed to interfere with the basic job being done. In this direction Vienna gives more hope than any city in Europe. This sad, wise, mangled capital, with its easy genius for rationalization and compromise, tells us more of what the future could conceivably turn out to be than any place we visited in our whole trip.

Vienna is a lonely outpost in a Russian ocean. Here, truly, we *are* behind the Curtain. Austria, like Germany, is divided into four zones—American, Russian, French, and British—and Vienna, like Berlin, was internationalized and cut into segments under quadripartite control, *inside* the Russian Zone.

But there is a cardinal difference among the sectors, as they are called in Berlin, and the Vienna zones. Berlin was divided into four, but Vienna into five. In addition to the zones maintained by Americans, Russians, British, and French, a fifth or International Zone exists in Vienna, held by the four powers together with equal authority. A great deal of trouble and nuisance might have been saved in Germany if Berlin had had such a neutral area under similar agreement. But it did not. The International Zone in Vienna is the Inner Stadt, the area enclosed by the celebrated Ring. Each power takes over its administration for a month at a time, by rotation; on the first of each month, the regime changes. For instance if we had arrived a month later, it would have been Russian MPs, not our own, whom we would have seen patrolling the streets and night clubs. Another difference is that in Vienna, unlike Berlin, almost anybody can circulate freely between one zone and another. In Berlin, you risk arrest if you penetrate into the Russian sector. This is not so much true in the Russian Zone in Vienna.

Then finally you see in Vienna something fascinating—and unthinkable in Berlin—the international jeeps and command cars which patrol the whole city from end to end, and which carry one soldier from each nationality. An American, a Russian, a Frenchman, and a Briton make up the four-man teams for each car.[3] To date, there has never been any incident of consequence between members of these teams, which are chosen

[3] Exclusively Russian jeeps also exist and may be identified by their bright red bumpers.

anew each morning and which go out daily. I do not mean that the members kiss each other on the cheek or become friends. I mean merely that they have learned to get along. Coldly, maybe. But they get along.

The Russians, we found, were not much in public evidence, even in their own zone. (Nor were British or French, for that matter.) In the International Zone, near the Imperial, we would occasionally encounter Russian officers, well uniformed with shiny boots, and heavily decorated. Once or twice we saw small detachments of Red army privates lining up to take a bus or streetcar; they were herded to their destinations by groups, like cattle. But, by and large, the Russians prefer to remain unseen. Of course the reason for this is fear of fraternization and the "contamination" of our higher living standard. They even put railings outside their hotels at night, so that passers-by along the Ring have to detour into the street for a few yards.

Vienna is the only place where I ever saw the Soviet equivalent of our U.S.I.S. libraries. Near the Stadtpark we gaped looking at a great display of photographs telling the Viennese of the Russian way of life. I do not know how impressed the sophisticated Viennese are.[4] The emphasis of this propaganda, which was very effectively mounted, was all toward bourgeois ends. Pictures showed the comfortable family man in Moscow listening to the early morning radio news, shiny new streetcars and buses in orderly modern traffic, canoe races on the river outside the Kremlin, workers' houses with flowers blooming idyllically in little gardens, a professor at work in his roomy library, feminine fashions full of New Look (*Schlafrock aus Rosafarben; Crêpe de Chine mit Gestricktem Aufputz*), and scientists experimenting with magnificent new equipment. The only "proletarian" note was a montage of recent gifts to Stalin—a crystal service from the staff of the Roter Gigant factory, a bronze plate from the people of Korea, and silver statuettes of horses and camels from the People's Republic of Mongolia.

[4] The Viennese don't change much. The first newspaper I picked up on arrival carried a feuilleton on—guess what?—Rudolf Habsburg and the Mayerling mystery. It might have been 1932—or 1902.

The chief local issue having to do with the Russians—and an unpleasant one—is that of kidnaping in their zone. Half a dozen times a month, Russian agents will grab and cart off somebody they don't like—if the somebody is unwary enough to be wandering around alone. Some of these kidnapings have taken place in broad daylight. Witnesses—even the Austrian police—are helpless.

Who are the unfortunate victims? For the most part, they are displaced persons whom the Russians consider to be their citizens or citizens of one of the satellites. Occasionally, somebody politically important is grabbed and held. Recently, for instance, an Austrian inspector of police named Anton Marek, who many years ago had been conspicuous in the Dollfuss case, was taken. All efforts to obtain his release are unavailing. Marek had been busy for months organizing espionage against the Russians, so the Soviet officials assert. As a countermeasure, they simply seized him.

Only very rarely are Americans arrested. But we have secret agents in Vienna too, and occasionally one is careless and gets caught. Then we retaliate by catching, or trying to catch, some Russian whom we know to be a spy. Vienna is boiling with espionage and counterespionage. Still, at the moment, such disturbances have not jeopardized basic American-Russian relations.

We had long talks with Lieutenant General Geoffrey Keyes, the American high commissioner and commander, and one of his top-ranking officers, Major General Jesmond D. Balmer. These are first-class men. They are packed with two kinds of sense, common and political. They understand the Russians and know how to deal with them. We wished heartily after seeing them and admiring their calm tenacious discernment that the United States had more officers like them in Europe.

The quadripartite Allied Commission that superintends the Austrian occupation meets once a fortnight in the old Chamber of Commerce building on Schwartzenbergplatz. (Our own headquarters, incidentally, are the former premises of the Austrian National Bank, just off the Ring near Schottentor.) The meetings are very long drawn out, and the Russians as a rule contest every point on the agenda stubbornly. They are extremely legalistic. But once an agreement is reached, and it is *written down,* they stand by it. The Russians in Vienna, we heard, have never violated any promise once it was put in writing and signed; they will go through every kind of maneuver to avoid being pinned down, but once a formal document is agreed upon, they will obey. Actually the Russian tactics at meetings changed abruptly in midsummer. Instead of fighting every point inch by inch as a matter of prestige no matter what the importance of the issue, they began to waive discussion on minor technicalities. The conferences went faster and more smoothly. Sometimes when the Russian member was obstructionist, the Americans felt that he himself deplored this and was sorry to be making a nuisance of himself, but had no choice because of his orders. Once an order is received by any Russian from on high, he has to be absolutely rigid.

For a time occasional brawls took place between American and Russian privates. Bad feeling was inevitable, considering what the Russians had been taught to think about Americans, and vice versa. These incidents have been eliminated now. The Russian commander came to Keyes, on his own initiative, and said, in effect, "Let's do something to stop this pinpricking." Keyes agreed, cautiously, by saying he would be delighted to co-operate in any effort to taper the tension off. The Russian said, "No—not taper off. Let's stop it altogether." Keyes, surprised and pleased, then worked out details whereby the co-operation became really effective, and word was passed down the line that incidents should stop. The Russians did the same, and they stopped.

The chief political problem is that of the so-called German "assets" in Austria, and it is vexing. The difficulty derives mostly from an ill-drafted clause in the Potsdam agreements, which, the Russians contend, gives them the right to take over former *German* property in Austria as a substitute for reparations. So the Russians have confiscated and are exploiting at least three hundred industrial enterprises in their zone, including the Zistersdorf oil fields, and 40,000 hectares of land. The Soviet "justification" for this is that the zonal division of Austria gave the Anglo-Americans the lion's share of industrial property in the country at large particularly in Styria. These Soviet holdings comprise about 12 percent of the nation's total industrial capacity.[5] The Russian-held enterprises are consolidated in a Soviet holding company, the Administration of Soviet Enterprises in Austria, which bears the confusing initials USIA; the unwary are apt to think that this has something to do with the U.S., which it most decidedly has not. USIA is of course a highly convenient device; it is in reality a Russian shadow government, behind the walls of which the Red army does what it likes in the economic field. A recent report of the United States Element, Allied Commission for Austria, puts it this way:

> Many of the difficulties facing the Austrian Government, and the Allied Council as well, arise from the extra-territorial operations of the USIA. The Austrian Government has complained to the Allied Council that the disposal of produce and exports from these factories are outside the control of the government, that the enterprises do not conform to Austrian tax and labor laws, and that the Soviet Element has demanded a privileged status for them within the Austrian economy. The U.S., British and French Elements have repeatedly proposed measures for clarification of the status of this property, but the Soviet Element has in every case refused to discuss the matter on the grounds that it was the sole concern of the Soviet authorities. . . . In other cases, they label their seizures "war booty." It has been practically impossible to reach any agreement on this subject.

Another irritating problem is the censorship. We found this situation almost Alice-in-Wonderlandish, in that censorship of the mails, cables, and telephones, even of Americans, is in effect in Russian hands. If you send a cablegram to New York from the porter's desk at the Bristol by ordinary routes, it will have to pass through censorship, unless you use army channels. Conversely, if you write a letter to the American Legation, say, from New York, it will be liable to interception unless it goes via U.S. Army mail. The censorship was originally set up by the Allied Commission itself; now we wish to abolish or modify it, and return the supervision of communications to

[5] Alexander Kendrick in the *New Republic,* July 26, 1948.

the Austrian government, but the Russians refuse. The censorship is operated, not by the Red army itself, but by Austrian civilians—Communists of course—whom the Russians control. The upshot is that Vienna is the only place in the world where an American citizen, sending a letter by ordinary channels to another American citizen outside Vienna, has to risk that it will be opened and read by a censor under Russian influence.

We did not visit the Russian Zone of Austria outside Vienna. But most of the Americans I talked to—very well-informed Americans—thought that the Russians had, on the whole, behaved tolerably well to the Austrian population under their control, though a few Communist mayors hold office who would never have been elected by free vote. The situation is altogether different from that in the Eastern (Russian) Zone of Germany. Austrian newspapers bitterly anti-Communist are sold freely in the Russian Zone of Austria, and political speakers openly attack the Soviet regime. This must be the only place in the world occupied by the Soviets where agitation against Communism is permitted. The Russians continue to guard their "German" assets zealously, but they have not sought to liquidate the countryside. No estates have been broken up. A farmer in Upper Austria in the Russian Zone is not living under circumstances very different from those of a farmer in the American Zone, we heard it said. The Russians do not seem to intend to take over the territory permanently, and there is no attempt to terrorize or communize the population.

Why does Russian policy in Austria differ so sharply from that in Germany? One reason is that Vienna, to the Russians, is a kind of sideshow, much less important than Berlin. Another is the extremely wise, strong and tactful behavior of the Americans on the spot. But beyond this is the cardinal fact that Germany has no government, whereas Austria has. Thus any radical interference by the Russians in Austrian affairs, beyond the points mentioned above, would immediately provoke a crisis on a national, governmental level.

Why, I heard it asked, did not Russia simply take over all Austria, as it took over Bulgaria in effect, when the Red army first marched in? After all it was the Red army itself that established the first postwar Austrian government. Probably the answer is double: (a) they didn't quite dare; (b) they thought of Austria as part of Germany essentially, and didn't want to.

If the Russians should ever reverse their Austrian policy and blockade Vienna as they blockaded Berlin, the situation would be very serious indeed for our forces. An air lift would be impossible, since no airfields exist in Vienna itself nor in the Russian Zone. Tulln, as we have seen, is completely surrounded by Russian-held areas. But—to repeat—the fact that we hold access to this airport by formal written agreement (no analogous agreement about communications to Berlin was ever prepared or signed, which was a great carelessness on our part) means that the Russians can interfere with our communications only by specific and formal repudiation of their own word, something they are very loath to do.[6]

Finally, Austria is of substantial strategic importance both to the Russians and ourselves, and so nobody wants to upset the applecart. The country is a kind of arrow thrusting into the belly of the satellites, just as Czechoslovakia was once an arrow pointing into Germany. Vienna is our chief periscope behind the Curtain, and an important Russian eye to the world of the West as well.

Affairs Domestic

The Austrian government is a queer sort of mammal. One of the senior governments of Europe, it has held office since 1945. It is a coalition between the People's party, a right-wing group largely Catholic and dominant in the rural areas, and the radical Social Democrats, with their strength concentrated in Vienna and the towns.

The government—and the parties forming it—exists in all four occupation zones, even the Russian. Austria is not like Germany, where (to quote an American information leaflet)

[6] The fact that the United States and British garrisons are so exposed and vulnerable in Vienna has tended to make our own point of view moderate, which is another factor in keeping the peace.

"government is according to the will of the occupying powers in their respective zones." The Austrian regime is on the contrary a *federal government*, (under allied supervision of course), formally recognized as such by the four powers. Also, an important point, the country is not considered an ex-enemy; it is regarded as a "liberated," not a "conquered" nation. It has no treaty as yet, for reasons which we shall see below, though it was promised full independence by an agreement signed by Russia, Great Britain, and the United States in 1943 during the war.

What a political change since I last saw Vienna! No marauding Nazis, no determined monarchists or legitimists, no secret armies! The youthful Foreign Minister, Dr. Karl Gruber of the People's party, one of the most attractive political personalities in the new Europe, told us that all underground political activity had ceased. But only a few years ago the two parties that make up the present coalition were relentless, impassioned enemies. The People's party derives straight from the old Christian Social (not Socialist) party, which for a generation was the hard core of Austrian reaction. It was this party that gave jobs and careers to freebooting insurrectionaries like Prince Starhemberg; it had its own private army, the Heimwehr, and it was supported for years by Mussolini. The Social Democrats—who *are* Socialists—likewise had their private army in the old days, the Schutzbund. The explosion of February 1934, when the Vienna municipal houses were bombarded by Heimwehr artillery, was the bloody climax to a long history of desperate tension between these two opposing forces.

But now, despite this heritage of carnage, the People's party and the Socialists are—if not actually lying down together like lambs—co-operating together effectively. The People's party got 49.8 percent of the vote in the election of November 1945, and the Socialists, 46 percent. So, sensibly, they set up a government together. The chief posts of the state today alternate between the two parties. The President is a Socialist, the Chancellor is a People's party man, the Vice Chancellor a Socialist, the Foreign Minister a People's party man, the Minister of the Interior a Socialist—and so on down the line.

The history behind this needs explanation. The Russians had everything to themselves from April 1945, when they liberated Vienna, until the other armies got there in July. Believing in coalitions then as now, they set up an interim administration under the leadership of the venerable Dr. Karl Renner, a Socialist who is now head of state. The Russians thought, of course, that they would control this government, which had three Communist members.[7] But they got badly fooled. Elections were held in November 1945, and 3,200,000 people (93 percent of the registered electorate) went to the polls. The Austrian Communists, despite their control of the ministries of the Interior and Education, and their usual mass propaganda tactics, and even though Russia occupied part of the country, got only 5.42 percent of the total vote. This was probably the worst purely political defeat Communists have suffered anywhere in Europe since the war.

One of the chieftains of the People's party, Leopold Figl (his nickname is Papa Potatoes) then formed a government including but one Communist. Later, in a reshuffle, even this lone C.P. man (he was Minister of Power and Electrification) was squeezed out. He made the great mistake of resigning office under the assumption that he would be invited back; he wasn't. Ever since the People's party and the Socialists have ruled Austria together. The People's party has eighty-five seats in parliament, the Socialists seventy-six, and the C.P. only four.

We talked to one leading Austrian Communist, Ernst Fischer. He is a literary man, polemicist, a poet, and editor of considerable distinction. For some years he was a Social Democrat (so was Dr. Gruber incidentally); in fact he was editor of the great Vienna Socialist daily, the *Arbeiter Zeitung*. Fischer escaped from Austria in 1934, went to Czechoslovakia, and eventually found himself in Moscow. Here, in regard to Austrian affairs, he held a position analogous to that of Rákosi, Pauker, Berman, and so many others we have mentioned in

[7] The legend is that during this period the Austrian cabinet always had to have two meetings—one with the Communist members present, one secretly with the Communists left out—out of fear that the C.P. members would tip the Russians off as to anything confidential that went on.

this book.[8] Fischer is a lively and persuasive conversationalist, with an exceptionally sensitive erudite mind. When we met him, he had just been translating Baudelaire and Verlaine into German—for fun and relaxation. He has a bright sense of humor—something most Communists don't have. The party line on Austria, as we heard it from Fischer and others, is about what is to be expected. A paramount item is of course disparagement of the Marshall plan. We asked Mr. Fischer (a) what benefits Austria would have under Communism that it doesn't have already (b) if the possibility existed of an Austrian Communism independent of Moscow; (c) what a Communist regime in Vienna would do about civil liberties. His answers were ingenious and also a good deal franker than those we were accustomed to have from most Communists.

Then we got into a somewhat philosophical discussion about freedom. Of course, Mr. Fischer said, he himself believed in freedom. He was the son of an army officer and how could he ever have had the good luck to become a Communist if he hadn't been free to choose! Like all the Austrian Communists, he is fiercely anti-German. When we asked him if a Communist Austria would be willing to join up with Germany under Communism, he exclaimed, "No! No!" One interesting development in Austrian Communism is the effect of the snip-snap between Tito and the Cominform. Many Austrians, even if secretly, have apparently taken the Tito side, though Fischer did not say this. Finally about developments in general he concluded menacingly and cheerfully. "Give us just five years!"

But turn back to the majority parties. The People's party, on the conservative wing, is not very cohesive; it has been described, not as a "party" at all, but as a kind of "roof organization" containing three main elements, the farmers, the Wirtschaftsbund (economic interests), and some white collar workers. The members pay dues to various Bunds, which then run the party. And a very powerful influence on its councils is of course the Roman Catholic Church. The Socialists on their side are more integrated, unified, and disciplined; also

[8] The Viennese do not use the term "Muscovite" to denote Austrian Communists who lived in Moscow. Instead they irreverently say "Turkestaner."

they are strongly anti-Communist. Their support rests basically on the magnificent tradition of Austrian trade unionism; one reason why the Communists are so weak in Vienna is that the Socialists have always stolen their thunder as true representatives of the working class. The Austrian Socialists are by no means mollycoddles; but neither are they fanatic revolutionaries. Their leadership, which is able in the extreme, represents the kind of constructive businesslike socialism that has grown up almost everywhere in Europe since the war; it is the socialism of Attlee, the moderate French, and the Scandinavians. It is interesting, incidentally, that the British in Vienna, by and large, tend to play close to the Socialists, and the Americans with the People's party. Officially of course United States spokesmen say that we are strictly neutral, and try to keep an even balance between the two parties—and so get blamed by both!

What is the chief glue of this remarkable coalition? Fear of Russia! What is the chief source of friction? The past!

The Austrian government composed of such sharply diverse elements has, indeed, many uneasy moments, and plenty of tensions exist beneath the surface. Each party claims patriotically that it gives up the most to keep the coalition alive. Yet obviously it is to the advantage of both to work together, since otherwise the tiny Communist fragment might conceivably hold the balance of power. The People's party claims great virtue by the fact that it *could* rule independently, inasmuch as it has a clear, if slim, majority. Meantime the past rankles to an extent. The clerical stalwarts say, "Don't forget that Dollfuss was killed by the Nazis—and the Socialists were pro-*Anschluss* before Hitler!" The Socialists respond with, "You bombed our houses, and Dollfuss was followed by the semi-Fascist regime of Schushnigg, whom you have never disavowed!"

The Communists, outmaneuvered and discredited, would be an utterly negligible factor were it not for the fact of Russian occupation. People even told us that the great danger in Austria is not that the Communists are too strong, but too weak; they meant that the coalition might well split apart, and Socialists and clericals be at one another's throats as in the

1930's, if the Communists were not a threat. And of course as long as the Red army is in the country, the Austrian Communists, even if their contact with Soviet officials is neither direct nor conspicuous, have something behind them. Usually when the government coalition does get shaky, something that the Russians do pulls it together again. For instance, almost everybody in Austria closed ranks with a snap after the February *coup* in Prague. Also, the coalition would not last twenty minutes without the Marshall plan and the American aid which we have already seen is so substantial.

Does the average Austrian want the occupation to end? This is a difficult question. Day by day various politicians demand that all the occupying forces get out; even Dr. Gruber once called the occupation "capricious, arbitrary, and fanatic." But of course what most politicians mean is that they would like the *Russians* to get out. On the other hand, if the Russians go, the United States and British would presumably go too; and the Austrians like to have us here so long as there is any remote possibility of international danger. After all, it is the U.S.A. and Britain which protect Austria against Soviet designs, if any. The Socialists, however, often criticize the United States sharply—largely with the allegation that we support "everything in Austria that is Catholic and conservative." Sometimes people ask why the clever Austrians do not play one occupying power off against another. They do. But their fear of Russia keeps the maneuver from being effective, since they have to watch out for the interests of their own people in all four zones.

In any event the comparative solidity of the Austrian coalition is a hopeful thing—a really significant example of mature political co-operation. The future of Western Europe probably depends in the last analysis on the merging of democratic Socialist and temperate Catholic groups. The way the Austrians have effected such a merger, no matter how tentatively, holds a lesson for us all. And it is a suggestive irony that the Russians, who hope above all to prevent such mergings, have by their own policy tended to produce them. Vienna is the one place which seems to offer solutions to two enormous questions —how to get along with the Russians to a degree, and how to stop them from going further.

Why No Treaty?

Negotiations for an Austrian treaty have been going on since February 1946 without success; early in 1949 an abortive conference was held in London. The two chief stumbling blocks are the question of German "assets" and a Yugoslav frontier claim for substantial territory in Carinthia. This area, the Yugoslavs say, should rightfully be theirs because the population is largely Slovene in origin; also it has strategic interest. It was noteworthy that the Soviet Union vigorously supported the Yugoslav case in London, despite the Tito disruption.

But behind these specific points are larger elements. Do we, the United States (and also Britain and France), really want a treaty (not a "peace" treaty but just a treaty) and to terminate the occupation? Would we not prefer to keep the loophole of Vienna open a little longer? Is it not advantageous to broader American policy that we should continue to remain in Austria, even if this means that Russia will stay too? The gist of the matter rests on a delicate calculation—whether it will better serve *our* national interest if the *Russians* get out, because obviously the Russians will refuse to go unless we do, and vice versa. This aside, the United States has other motives. For one thing we do not want to approve any treaty that might leave Austria at the economic mercy of Russia after occupation stops. For another we hate to pull out while Austria has no army. And it is indeed a curious thing that this nation in the very core of Europe is one of the few in the world without an army. But nobody is willing to face the problem of how big an army Austria should have, or how it is to be constituted so that it will not degenerate into two—or more—mutually hostile, private, or secret armies.

Russia, too, is hesitant to sign a treaty and withdraw for several reasons. Before the Italian election, which Moscow thought would be won by the Italian Communists, the Russians took up seriously the idea of evacuation, because a Communist Italy would have given them tremendous compensatory advantages. Now, since the fracas with Tito, they are more loath to move; they have a substantial tactical reason for wanting to keep troops close to Yugoslavia, because of the uncertainty of the situation there. Also, quite aside from the 60,000 to 70,000 Red army men in Austria itself, the occupation gives the Soviets the pretext for maintaining the "communications" troops we have mentioned in Hungary and Rumania. Another point is that, if Russia and the United States should both get out, the United States would inherit and presumably maintain a much more substantial role in Austrian affairs than the Russians can acquire themselves, because of the weight of American economic aid. Finally, the Russians always think of Austria in terms of the greater German problem; they want to hold their Vienna position until the fate of Germany is settled.

A more subtle and long-range consideration is that if Russia wants all Europe, whether by war or otherwise, it would be rational for them to try to maneuver the United States garrisons out of Germany and Austria as a prerequisite step. To this end the Russians might well reverse themselves some day and advocate an Austrian treaty. Certainly they will stay as long as we stay. But they might support a treaty in order to get *us* out.

CHAPTER 18
CONFUSIONS AND PERPLEXITIES IN GERMANY

WE FLEW into Berlin along with 19,800 pounds of coal packed carefully into sacks and trussed to the naked inner carcass of an American C-54. Briefly then we were sucked into the phantasmagoric world of contemporary Germany. But this chapter—and the next—are no more than elongated footnotes. To discuss even the basic elements of the German problem and its various interactions would take enough paper to fill an air lift plane.

What struck me most about the air lift itself was the information that if we had been unable to land at Tempelhof on account of bad weather or for some other reason, we would have had to fly all the way back to Frankfurt or Wiesbaden and start over again. The landings are spaced so closely—three minutes apart—that no plane can make a second pass at Berlin without disturbing the entire over-all pattern and complex interlaced procedure.

Aside from its obvious function of bringing calories to beleaguered Berlin in the form of both coal and food, the air lift has served several other striking purposes. I do not know—as of the moment of writing—how long it will continue, inasmuch as an agreement between the powers to raise the blockade may come soon. But the results of the air lift, direct and indirect, will continue to be felt, for good or ill:

1. The Russians know full well now, if they ever had reason to doubt it before, that Americans know how to fly. They know moreover that the American (and British) aircraft shuttling to Berlin with metronome-like precision could easily be carrying calories in still another form—explosives—anywhere in Europe. The Soviet blockade of Berlin challenged us in one field in which we really do excel—the mass application of technology. The Russians never believed we could possibly suc-

ceed in feeding and provisioning Berlin by air; our proficiency has been a stunning shock.

2. The air lift dramatically served to mobilize American public opinion behind the foreign policy of the United States. I even heard bellicose Americans, who want an aggressive foreign policy, assert that they hoped the lift would continue "indefinitely," because it is such a brilliant "window dressing" for the Marshall plan.

3. Because of the air lift powerful units of the U.S. air forces are now openly stationed in England. Our unarmed C-54s actually in Germany would be sitting ducks if war with Russia should break out; hence we have covered them by making much the same kind of military preparation in England that we made in the early days of World War II. Also this weight of American aircraft serves to show Britain—and especially France—that we take our European responsibilities seriously.

4. It has given American pilots intensive and valuable experience in flying semimilitary missions over European areas, and stimulated the training of thousands of others in circumstances resembling combat. For instance an exact replica of the air-lift "course" has been marked out in Montana, where crews train before being sent abroad.

5. It has put a weighty concentration of American power, psychological and political as well as military, right next to Russia's door.

6. The fact that it has operated without incident indicates that the Russians themselves have a considerable will to peace.

No one would want to disparage the unparalleled and unprecedented feats of the air lift, nor minimize the tremendous personal prowess, technical skill and plain dogged endurance of the men who run it. But from one point of view, seen in the abstract as a man from Mars might see it, it is a kind of monstrous *reductio ad absurdum*. That a sleek and shining airplane which cost $800,000 and is operated at the risk of life by the flower of an impeccably skilled manhood, should be used to lug sacks of wheat and coal, is a fitting commentary on the crazily distraught times we are unlucky enough to have to live in.

Physiognomy of Berlin

Berlin itself struck us as the most depressing place we found in all Europe, next to Prague and perhaps Frankfurt. One retreats into an easy cliché: it looks like death warmed over. I have seen horrible and frightening destruction in many cities—for instance Warsaw is much worse destroyed—but nothing I can recall gave me quite the sense of sickening gloom that some things in Berlin did, for instance the Tiergarten.

All the trees are down in this once noble park, and somehow the sight of a green wood amputated and laid waste is almost more cruel than that of damage to man-made structures of brick and metal. Moreover the entire Tiergarten, which once looked like Central Park in New York, has been parceled up into small lots growing cabbages and other provender, each lot demarcated from the others by rusty wire, lines of rocks, and rough timber. Very sensible and proper—but the impression is roughly what the piazza of St. Peter's would give if it were cut up into garbage dumps or cattle pens.

Other items in the prevailing Berlin dreariness: the straggling knots of old men in grimy overcoats worn to the stump peering enviously into cheap jewelry shops; the strange sensation of pressing the bell at a friend's house and hearing no ring, because the electric current is cut off for all but a few hours a day; cigarettes still used for currency, one American cigarette (not a package, but a single cigarette) being worth 40 pfennigs or 12¢ at the legal rate; withered and brutalized old women walking the streets and surreptitiously trying to sell chocolate bars (which they sometimes get in lieu of wages); shops offering the crudest possible brand of flat iron at about $8.00, and a child's pair of shoes at $35.00; building signs still unrepaired, so that they read F RD (Ford), or DRE D R (Dresdner) B NK; virtually complete stultification of intellectual and artistic life; the bleak auction stalls at the street corners, advertising everything from sable wraps to thumbtacks; the charred and desolate wreckage of the Gedächtnis Church; the restaurant, once fashionable, which now has two main dishes, filet of herring and a tunafish-mushroom salad; the statue, still standing and intact, of Friedrich III (*Deutscher Kaiser, König von Preussen*), in the wreckage of the Charlottenburger Chaussee; in a food shop, salted meat from Mexico with no identification except CARNE, sold by the gram out of a dirty open can. It is all like a horrible dawn, after the world has stopped.

I know full well and appreciate that the Germans brought this misery and wretched havoc upon themselves. Mohammed once said, "God is good at accounts." Also I know (a) that Berlin, the city, is a special case and that conditions in western Germany are much better; (b) that the Soviet sector of Berlin is a great deal worse off than the American, French or British; (c) that our sector is improving steadily, and is bound to improve more with time. Yet I could not repel altogether the uncomfortable thought we had already had in Vienna, that from the point of view of average living conditions and the way the streets look, several of the satellite capitals are substantially better off than those in our own American domains.

Behind the Blockade

Each side blames the other for this grim stalemate, and polemics by the bushel have confused and atrophied the issue. Chronologically it is certainly true that the imposition by the Soviets of the blockade followed the provocation of our currency reform, which the Russians considered to be a violation of Potsdam. Walter Lippmann wrote in July 1948, "We now know that the plan [of the western allies] to establish a western government at Frankfurt . . . precipitated the crisis over Berlin." In reply the United States argument is, of course, that Russian maneuvers and infiltrations and obduracies, Russian bad manners and willful lack of co-operation and sabotage, made the decision to create a western government inevitable. In any case the result is the same. As an English commentator put it, "Having thrown over Potsdam and gone into competition with the Russians for the control of Germany, we have got to see it through."

Perhaps a further word—even if primer talk—on background would be useful. The German problem is incomparably the root problem of European peace and recovery, for the simple reason that a viable Europe cannot exist without Germany. The Potsdam Conference (July-August 1945) set up the four zones into which Germany, the crushed and defeated villain, was subdivided. Actually the United States took the lead in the lamentable decision to make zones. The British, French and American zones together have a population of about 45 million, the Russian (eastern) Zone about 17 million. But the western zones, though containing what is by far the richest and most potent agglutination of industrial power in Europe, are not self-sufficient as to food. There is no German peace treaty yet. Roughly in this respect the situation resembles that in Austria which we have just inspected, though it is much thornier and the stakes are Brobdingnagian by comparison.

After Potsdam the situation developed more or less as follows. The Council of Foreign Ministers met intermittently outside Germany to try to negotiate a permanent settlement, while the four-power Allied Control Council functioned in Berlin to supervise and administer the occupation. In December 1947, the Foreign Ministers' conference in London disbanded in utter failure; Mr. Marshall, then our Secretary of State, whose patience and tenacity had been unbounded, had no alternative but to give up. The Russians would not play ball on anything. Yet it was very difficult to determine at that time what their own German policy was. The Americans and British (with the French dragging a lame foot along)[1] then determined, for good or bad, to build some sort of German structure themselves out of the three western zones, prepare for the end of occupation, and set the Reich on the road (they hoped) toward democratic self-government.

Meantime the Russians—it would take a professor of electronics with a lightning calculator to determine who first did which—were proceeding to reconstruct and assimilate their own zone for their own special purposes in the pattern only too

[1] I will pay my respects to the French in this connection in the chapter following.

menacingly familiar, in part as an answer to ERP which earmarked vast sums for the western zones. To compress into a paragraph the multitudinous corollary episodes, tendencies, and influences that contributed to this net result—the splitting up or bisection of Germany into two new entities—is like squeezing a sponge into a thimble. Particularly am I forced to eliminate the inordinately fascinating details attending four-power rule in Berlin itself.

But as to Germany as a whole three events may not be ignored. First, the Anglo-Americans extended Marshall plan aid to western Germany, which became known as "Bizonia" and then "Trizonia"; second, an assembly met at Bonn to write a new German constitution for the west, preparatory to setting up a united western German government; third, we made a currency reform which had markedly beneficial economic results, but only at the cost of infuriating the Russians and thus further exacerbating the political crisis. Finally, in June 1948, came the blockade, the air lift, and what followed.

Now a word on specifically German attitudes. Basically—no matter how they protest—the Germans have to do what we tell them to do, because we feed them. Few citizens of the Reich like the idea of a fragmented nation and a new state in the west. But they say that they will never "get on their feet" at all unless we begin with something, and that the west is the only place to start. On the whole the Germans seem to like the British best among the occupying powers. This is because the shrewd and long-seeing British take the line that, although they certainly do not want Germany ever to be a menace again, it is only sensible to treat enemies so that they will not always remain enemies. Finally, the attitude of German Communists—silly as this sounds—is that all their obstructionism and bad manners is in reply, as I heard it put, to the "undemocraticness" of the Americans.

This whole viscous stalemate, though not insoluble, is not easy to melt down. The Russians cannot easily give up the blockade for two reasons: (1) Probably they will hope against hope that it will work; (2) To withdraw would mean irretrievably damaging loss of prestige. Yet they cannot get rid of the air lift without making war. We on our side, the Americans,[2] cannot give up the air lift because to do so would constitute such a grave confession of political defeat. If we quit Berlin (*before* a new German government is functioning in the west) we are in effect quitting Europe, because the bulk of Europeans would feel that the Americans, for all their big promises, could no longer uphold them in a crisis and they would have no eventual recourse but to make terms with Moscow.

Nevertheless in Paris last fall the Berlin deadlock came within a millimeter of being resolved by agreement. The chief obstacle was the question of currency, that is, whether or not Anglo-American or Russian economic and financial power would be supreme in the future. Mr. Bevin is supposed to have been largely responsible for the final failure in negotiation. But the Americans were lukewarm too. In fact it is sometimes stated that the real reason for failure was that the United States actively *opposed* an agreement. Why? Because we have no policy as to what to do next!

One good reason for hoping, even at this late date, that an agreement can be whittled out somehow goes beyond such obvious items as the strain on our personnel, the fear of a Russian incident, and the like. It is that if a showdown comes and either Americans or Russians are forced to give up Berlin, this will probably eliminate any last lingering possibility of co-operation elsewhere. So long as both sides remain in Berlin, a certain amount of contact still continues to exist, no matter how full of frustration and irritation. This is valuable, because only a maniac can want a war, and so long as any sort of contact at all is maintained, "hot" warfare is unlikely.

A Line about the American Dilemma

Germany is the chief key to the whole world struggle between our way of life and the Soviet system. So here, above anywhere else on earth except possibly China, the United States

[2] And British. Do not forget that the British account for more than one-third of air lift traffic.

should know exactly what it is doing, how, and why. Do we? No. American policy toward Germany has, in fact, been hesitant, torn between two schools, contradictory, and hermaphrodite.

A wisecrack I heard in Frankfurt epitomizes all this nicely: "We do not know what to do about Germany because we have not yet decided whether we want to win the last war or the next one." Or put it another way, "Are we dealing with our former enemies, or our future allies?"

At one extreme in American attitudes is the point of view that a renascent Germany will almost certainly become a ferocious threat to the peace of the world once more, and therefore that it should be kept permanently shattered and weak. But the risk involved in this is that a permanently weak Germany may degenerate into chaos and go Communist. At the other extreme stand those who think that Germany has already been punished enough, and should be permitted to regain substantial strength, because (1) German co-operation is essential to general European economic recovery, and (2) Germany might well be an effective ally in the event of open war between the United States and the Soviet Union.

The great fallacy of this latter point of view is, of course, that, once Germany is rearmed, it might decide to fight on Russia's side, not ours, which would put us in a pretty quandary indeed. To put it a bit differently, a Germany without Anglo-American controls could easily be tempted into a Soviet alliance, or be hijacked by the Russians otherwise. To rearm Germany is to risk throwing it—and the arms too—into the hands of Moscow. No matter which policy we adopt, the danger exists that Germany will go Communist. This is one main reason for our confusion. But I met some belligerently minded Americans who paid little attention to these possibilities. They talked in fact of mobilizing two million Germans as "our" manpower against Russia right away, and to hell with consequences.

Between the two extremes (the keep-Germany-weak school and the make-it-strong) General Clay has hammered out a compromise which satisfies neither. Essentially it boils down to something like this. Eventually the United States must be prepared to quit Germany. The present arrangement cannot possibly be expected to go on forever. But we cannot reasonably pull out, both for our sake and for that of the population of western Berlin, against whom the Russians might take savage reprisals, until we have built up a reasonably strong regime in the west of Germany. Hence our support of the trizonal consolidation.

But the risk of establishing a fragmented Germany at Frankfurt is very considerable, because Frankfurt might become a kind of Vichy. One can imagine easily enough the propaganda the Russians will make urging all Germans to reunite. Moreover nationalist Germans (and practically all Germans are nationalists) will themselves perpetually seek to reacquire the "lost" eastern provinces. So splitting off the west may eventually play straight to Russian advantage. But this risk has to be taken, because the present situation is intolerable. Military government by outside powers, which has already gone on for four years, cannot be allowed to continue indefinitely, or it will impede—instead of fostering—the democratization of Germany it was expected to produce.

Suppose the Russians should volunteer to leave their zone of Germany if we leave ours—would we accept? No. For one thing, the Soviets are next door, whereas if we withdraw we would be three thousand miles away. The Russians could intervene at any future date after our withdrawal, and we would have no effective countermeasure. For another, they would presumably leave behind them (if they withdrew) police, labor battalions, and probably an army, as well as a party organization, under definite Soviet control. And, let it be remembered always, the theoretical root of all American policy is to prevent western Germany (and Western Europe) from being communized.[3]

[3] The above is an attempt to draw the main line. But actually things are even more complicated. A kind of triple struggle for power has gone on within American ranks. One can only say, Gentlemen of the State Department, Pentagon, and White House, kindly get together. Then too there are substantial differences between American and British points of view—to say nothing of the French. As an example the British tend to favor socialization of German heavy industry. We don't.

We had a long talk with Clay. He looked tired and tense. No matter how one may or may not agree with this officer, he is an able, intensely driven, courageous, and honest man. Perhaps like most army engineers he lacks imagination outside the sphere of technique. Most of what he told us he preferred to have off the record, but a few things may be said. No proconsul in history has ever had to take greater risks (largely on his own responsibility too). We mentioned this, and his reply was in the tone of a man stretched to the very limit, "If I wasn't willing to take risks, I wouldn't be worthy of this job." He was not thinking so much of any possible incident on the air lift. The Russians are, by and large, not crazy enough to try anything like shooting down our planes; they will never permit incidents on a "high" level, though of course an accidental fracas might occur. But Clay's risks are in a much bigger realm. What he has to calculate is whether or not the policy of letting the East go hang, at least for the moment, and the resultant fission of Germany into halves, will in the long run be a good thing for America and Europe. Maybe we have no alternative. But what if—as mentioned above—the net eventual result will be to strengthen Communism instead of weakening it? Perhaps—Clay did not say this in so many words—he feels that all risks are worth while on the theory that, if we hold on in Germany long enough, the Russians will lose faith in their own capacity to take the initiative. In any case the United States has got to stick it out. From Clay and several other Americans in Berlin, we got the strong impression that we have a bear by the tail, and that even if we should want to, we cannot let go now. We cannot "let the Germans down." And we cannot leave Berlin because we have no other place to go.

Now a totally different item. No matter what our policy is, no decent excuse exists for some sublimely shocking American favors and concessions to present-day Germans known to have been prominent Nazis. Perhaps it is possible to explain away the recent Ruhr agreement and the path we laid open for resumption of control of the Ruhr properties by their former German owners; perhaps it is even possible—though I do not know how—to explain away the legal process whereby Ilsa

Koch, the Messalina of Buchenwald, had her jail sentence reduced. The American (and British) argument may be that we are indeed helping "to put Germany on its feet." But to what end? *The New Statesmen and Nation* wrote recently:[4]

> The list of Nazis and extreme nationalists in the high posts of industry, administration, politics, law, and education is shockingly long. So flagrant is their presence in the Western Zones that no one bothers any longer to deny it. The real danger of German nationalism lies . . . here where the high hopes of changing Germany and the Germans are brought to nothing; where the plans and efforts made for "re-education" are rendered null and void; where the average German—muddled, anxious, eager above all to justify himself—finds the Western Allies on the same side, and saying the same things, as the leaders of German nationalism; and where the plea of anti-Bolshevism is once more made to serve as mask and covering upon the face of men who have twice killed the peace of Europe and the world."

Perhaps this is putting it a bit strongly. But it is undeniable that our attitude has been "soft" on these matters and apparently is getting softer. The present policy is to play down anything "anti-German." For instance, after considerable prodding, we saw recently the rough cut of the film "Nuremburg," which was made by the Documentary Film Unit of Military Government and which portrays in extremely cogent detail the major Nazi crimes and horrors. So far the film has not been shown publicly in the United States. The army adduces "technical" reasons to excuse this. One young officer told us that it was "too dull." Dull to whom?

Russian Sector

People warned us that even the most cursory inspection of the Soviet sector of Berlin was risky if not impossible for an American visitor; actually, although the expedition was brief, we did manage to make one trip into this forbidden territory. We drove down the Unter Den Linden, where tangles of broken wire still lie twisted on the sidewalks, and round and about the

[4] January 22, 1949.

Wilhelmstrasse district, amid the unbelievably shattered wreckage of the great hotels and embassies and Hitler's public buildings, in an American jeep. We paused for a moment under the red flag above Brandenburger Tor; the Russian sentries paid no attention.

One American officer and one German publicist independently offered to arrange meetings for us with Russian officials, but these never materialized. The implication was that the Russians were afraid to come, not out of fear of us, but of their own superiors. We did talk at some length with several German Communists, and I report their conversation in the last chapter of this book.

What is Russian policy toward Germany? Perhaps it will be a relief to the reader that it is almost as confused as ours. Two or three years ago, the USSR wanted a strong united Germany, pro-Soviet. The Russians have always favored the objective of a *centralized* Germany (the better to control it), whereas we want a federal Germany (to avoid top-heaviness). The basic and ultimate Russian aim—if this can be accomplished without war—is of course complete communization of the Reich. The Russians have, I think, given up all hope of attaining this in the discernible future. So now they seek to content themselves with a lesser objective—a weak disunited Germany which gives them room to move around in, but not one so weak that the Americans control it. Both sides have to try to calculate the area of imponderables with extreme precision. Then too the Russians obviously want Berlin. But if we have made a mess of Germany, so have they. Indeed their prestige, even in their own zone, is probably at its lowest ebb since the war, and their influence and power in the west has diminished heavily. A free vote would probably give the Communists no more than 15 to 20 percent in the three western zones, 10 to 15 percent in Berlin, and as little as 5 in the eastern zone itself. Inference: the Germans closest to the Russians like Communism least. Conditions in the eastern zone differ markedly from those in the analogous Russian Zone in Austria, which as we have noted the Russians have left pretty well alone. But their area in Germany—according to Americans anyway—is completely submerged; it outsatellites the satellites. This is indeed *terra incognita* supposed to be under the absolute control of the Red army and to all intents and purposes indistinguishable from the Soviet Union itself.

Some further Russian attitudes are worth exploring. For instance, Communists seldom forget that Germany was the country of Marx and Engels,[5] that Berlin next to Moscow is traditionally the center of the world, and that before the war the German Communist party was considered by the Kremlin to be by far the most important in Europe outside Russia. So for several reasons Moscow wants to hold on to as much of Germany as possible, no matter what the price. The idea of a free Germany growing up and casting out Communism by its own will is an intolerable thought.

Then there is the factor of nationalism, which is very powerful in Germany. Moreover, it is a fair guess that the longer the Reich continues to be militarily occupied by foreign powers, the stronger will this nationalism become, out of resentment by the German people at the continued occupation. The Russians are prepared to play on this possibility for all it is worth, for clear reasons: (1) A strongly nationalist Germany will put pressure on the occupying western powers to get out; (2) In the event of war, a strongly nationalist Germany might be an opponent of the West.

Derivatively a major Soviet aim is withdrawal of all occupying foreign troops. In fact, the Russians probably want a treaty and a withdrawal more than we do, because in the event of withdrawal, they will remain close, though we will be far away, as pointed out above. Meantime they seek to make an impregnable glacis of what they have. In theory they do not want Germany split up (neither do we—in theory) because their long range objective is a Marxist Germany with the biggest frontiers possible, but if a western government is formed,

[5] It is indeed curious that Communism is so often called "Eastern." People talk loosely of struggle between "East" and "West." But this has no meaning except geographically to an extent. In basic and elemental philosophic root, Communism is mostly Western not Eastern at all. Hegel and Marx were as German as the Nibelungenlied or sauerkraut. See Carr, cited below.

they will try to turn this to their advantage. Soviet policy is not "soft." The Russians know very well how to make use of Germans, both Communists and others.

Addendum on Politics and Personalities

Let us try to simplify. The two chief parties in the three western zones are the CDU (Christian Democratic party) and the SPD (Socialists); probably in a national election each would get roughly 40 percent of the total vote. If a western German government is eventually built up, it will probably be a coalition between these two much like that in Austria; in fact, the present-day provincial governments are almost all coalitions between moderate clericals on one side, and Socialists on the other. In Bavaria incidentally the CDU has a different name, CSU. Then something known as the LDP has arisen, which although called "Liberal" is highly conservative and nationalist. The Communist party, which exists legally in the three western zones, is the KPD, *Kommunistische Partei Deutschland*. But in the eastern zone, following the stereotyped satellite path, the Communists merged recently with the Socialists, and are known now as the Party of Socialist Unity, SED. But (just to make it easy) don't forget that in the three western zones the KPD (Communists) and SPD (Socialists) are violent and remorseless enemies. And (easier still) the SPD Socialists and SED Socialists are, to put it mildly, not on speaking terms.[6]

There has been no national election since the war, which means that the German people have had no chance to express themselves politically in national terms since the last election before Hitler. Sixty-five million people in the heart of Europe without a fair vote since 1932! Let us grant the Reich this final grim uniqueness.

One fantastic thing is the great age of most contemporary German leaders. There are virtually no new personalities. The

[6] In Bavaria and Hesse a small group called the NDP also exists. It contains remnants of the Nazis. The Russians allow it to function in the eastern zone too, strange as this may seem, presumably to draw off and control easily any surviving Nazi sentiment.

delegates to the assembly at Bonn, who for many months have wearily sought to write the western constitution, give the impression of being septuagenarians at least; actually sixty-three out of sixty-five members are over fifty.[7] It is no wonder that German politics seem fretful, lacking in initiative, mossbacked, and very, very tired. Any man over fifty alive in Germany today must have been one of three things in the best years of his manhood: (a) a Nazi; (b) a Nazi prisoner or refugee; (c) a cipher.

Of the CDU leaders the most important is probably Konrad Adenauer. He is seventy-one years old, a former mayor of Cologne, a strong Catholic, a Brüning man in prewar days, and a marked conservative. He lives today in Coblenz in the French Zone. Somewhat younger and more vigorous is Jacob Kaiser, the CDU chief in Berlin. He tried to maintain some sort of *modus vivendi* with the Russians as long as possible (there is a vestigial CDU in the Soviet sector), and then gave up. Though the CDU has a strong Protestant as well as Catholic element, most of its leaders are, I heard it put, "bossed by the Cardinals"; one German Communist told us, "If there ever is a western Germany, count on it that it will be run by the Catholic Church." Also men like Adenauer have close affiliations with the Ruhr and heavy industry.

Of the Communists on an all-German basis the most important is probably Wilhelm Pieck. He too is an old man, born in 1876. He was a cabinetmaker by trade, and a leading Socialist for some years; he became a Communist, and was a Communist member of both the Prussian diet and the Reichstag; his international standing is attested by the fact that he held membership in the executive committee of the Comintern from 1928 until its dissolution. He returned to Western Europe with the Red army after the war (a familiar note) and in 1945 became chairman of the executive committee of the KPD. At present he is co-chairman of the new coalition in the Soviet Zone between Communists and Socialists.

[7] Roger Baldwin in *The Progressive,* January 1949. Mr. Baldwin makes some interesting points. He thinks that "even more dangerous to democracy than . . . tolerance of former Nazis is the hangover of feudalism." One leader favored by the Americans is a Bavarian prince who owns 73,000 acres.

The chief Socialist in this merger (he is called "the Fierlinger") is Otto Grotewohl. It was he who, in February 1949, announced that the eastern zone would soon be transformed outright into "the People's Democracy of Soviet Germany." Like so many converted Socialists, he outcommunists the Communists. Another important Communist, whom a conservative German described to me as "the most dangerous man in Germany," is Walter Ulbricht, a woodworker born in Leipzig in 1893. He, like Pieck, was one of the early Spartacus group, along with legendary figures like Liebknecht and Rosa Luxemburg. Then one should at least mention in passing Albert Buchmann, the chairman of the party in the American Zone, and Max Reimann, the lively boss in the British Zone. Incidentally several Communists are members of the assembly writing the constitution at Bonn.

Finally the Socialists. The titular head of the party on a pan-German level is Kurt Schumacher of Hanover, a very sick old man now; he has lost both a leg and an arm. The "Huey Long" of the party is Franz Neumann; it is he who customarily does the rabble rousing in Berlin. The best brains among the Socialists are supposed to be those of an attractive personality named Carlo Schmid, the heir apparent to party leadership; he is half French, comparatively youthful, and a very able citizen.

More conspicuous than any of these, at the moment, is the new lord mayor of western Berlin, Ernst Reuter. Professor Dr. Reuter is quite a character. It would be interesting to write about him at considerable length, since so much American hope is pinned to him. Reuter is fifty-nine. He was taken prisoner by the Russians in World War I and became a passionate Communist; for a time he held high rank in the party structure. Eventually he became disillusioned, deserted the Moscow fold, and joined the Socialists. The Nazis arrested him, put him in a concentration camp, and then let him go; he left Germany for Turkey, and taught municipal government in a university there. The German ambassador to Turkey, Franz Von Papen, is supposed to have befriended him; as a result the Communists denounce him today as a "Nazi," which he isn't. Reuter is violently anti-Soviet. And the Soviets are certainly violently anti-Reuter. It is indeed remarkable that a man with such a variegated past, who for some years was an avowed and important Communist, and who is still an old-line Marxist, should turn out to be, as was written recently, the "outstanding American ally in the great fight for Berlin."

Coda

We met one estimable Socialist lady—her husband was hanged by the Nazis—who said a word I have been unable to forget: "What a pity it is that the only effective way to fight totalitarianism seems to be war. This is the great tragedy of modern times."

CHAPTER 19

FOOTNOTE ON FRANCE AND ENGLAND

AS OF the time we saw it the struggle for power in France was triple: between the middle-of-the-road government, the Communists, and De Gaulle. The government's position was that of trying to avoid extermination between two extremes almost equally perilous. But it is always risky to write about French politics; they have lost none of their well-known volatility. It takes some months to publish a book, and these words may be obsolete long before they reach print—one can only clutch at fleeting indicators, and try to estimate how the progressive "Marshallization" of France will affect the situation. That ERP has given the country a tremendous boost cannot be doubted. In November 1948, Gaullism[1] won 40 percent of the Council of the Republic, which corresponds to the old Senate. But in cantonal elections in March 1949, the Queuille government beat both Communists and De Gaullists soundly.

Three great questions to ask General De Gaulle are these:

1. Will your movement seek power only by legal means; in other words, do you disclaim any intention of trying to seize office by *coup d'état?*

2. Can you restore order, stability and discipline to France without violation of democratic principles and civil liberties?

3. Will the Communists resort to force, i.e., provoke resistance of such nature that civil war might result, if you do come to power?

The answers given by De Gaullists to these questions are approximately the following:

First, the general absolutely excludes the idea, on his part, of any exercise of force. One reason for this is his conviction, almost messianic in its intensity, that, given time, the application of force will not be necessary. It is not merely that he dis-

[1] Incidentally De Gaulle "fellow travelers" are called "Gaullisants."

likes the idea of a *coup d'état* as untidy and possibly dangerous. It is that he is utterly and sublimely convinced that France will, of her own volition, fall into his rectilinear lap.

The answer the De Gaullists give to the second question is, of course, Yes. The general's program and philosophy are certainly authoritarian in character and his solicitude for legal forms is not particularly tender, but his associates deny with the utmost vehemence that he ever could, or would, become a fascist dictator. Indeed they stake out an argument—somewhat dubious in spots—to the precise contrary, as to wit:

De Gaulle, they say, far from being a forerunner of Fascism, is France's best defense against it. The country is in a condition bordering on anarchy for the simple ethical reason that no one will obey the government. The moral rot has bitten to the bone. Black marketeers sell cheap francs openly on the streets or in the bars, like dirty postcards. Already people (including especially the black marketeers) talk of "cleaning out" Parliament, "marching on Paris" and so on. The real menace is of a real Fascism spurting out of this anarchy. And, say the De Gaullists, their general is the best—indeed the only—alternative to such a catastrophe, since he would be a kind of Clemenceau in office, never a Mussolini or a Hitler.

On the other hand, I heard at least one Frenchman of consequence say that he would enthusiastically welcome De Gaulle because he confidently expected that, immediately on assuming power, the general would outlaw the Communist party (the vote of which, be it remembered, is roughly 30 percent of the entire nation, and which is the No. 1 party in the National Assembly); shoot the leading Communists, declare martial law and abolish strikes. In other words, even if De Gaulle himself foreswears Fascism, a good many of his supporters are close to being fascists.

As to point three, the De Gaullists do not think that the Communists could or would make a revolution if De Gaulle reaches power legally. There might, they concede, be "trouble"; temporary local Soviets might set up in a few towns like Toulouse. But as for the country as a whole—including especially Brittany, the north, Alsace-Lorraine, and even such cities as Marseilles and Toulon—any mass uprising would, they say, be inconceivable.

The official De Gaullists deny that they would outlaw the Communist party. "Nobody," one of them told me, "will deprive the Communists of the right of being a parliamentary minority. But if they make trouble"—again that vague word trouble—"we will deal with them as troublemakers." Yet after the recent Thorez statement that in the event of war French Communists would support Russia, the De Gaullists demanded that "the state be reorganized to wrest from the 'Separatists' [which is what Communists are called in the De Gaulle argot] their power over part of the French people and to save France from Soviet invasion." What De Gaulle would do depends, in a word, on what the Communists will do themselves.

In case anybody is interested in the general's own prose style and will take the trouble to try to make sense of one of his own statements, here is a question-and-answer passage from a recent press conference:

Q.—*Mon General,* if a government were constituted including the Communists, would you be led, in order to save France, to going beyond legality?

A.—Monsieur, you will agree that action which such a case would require, and particularly anticipation of such a case, necessitates a certain discretion concerning the plans which might be formulated. I consider that if the Separatists entered what could still for the sake of convenience be called the government of France, then we would have completely abandoned legality. I will point out to you, moreover, that, already, we are no longer within legality. Following the October elections, I called your attention to the fact that since the country had registered its opinion in the way with which you are familiar, what is still called national representation no longer represented the nation, and that there was no means of returning to real legality other than consulting the French people. You know that the government has been hanging on and has failed to do this. . . . As soon as one begins to violate people's rights and universal suffrage, there is no reason to stop, and I am afraid that in this respect we are heading for the bottom of an abyss. If, in a situation which is already illegitimate and in which the government is on the road toward usurpation, unfortunate persons brought into the country's government men who are not playing on France's side, then who could still believe we would be within legality? I say this in the firmest and clearest manner.[2]

The main things to be said for De Gaulle are roughly the following:

1. He derives from the great tradition of European civilization and stands for it firmly. He can make himself highly unpopular on occasion, but he is no crude upstart or parvenu.

2. The super-extreme right (the corrupt and greedy right that helped cause the downfall of France) detests him—largely because of the nationalization decrees in his first period of power, and because it was he, no less, who first brought Communists into the French government.

3. He is absolutely honest.

Things that might well be said against him:

1. His defects of character—arrogance, rigidity, and an extremity of egoism—may lead him willy-nilly into becoming a totalitarian dictator.

2. His faith in his mission to "save" France has prompted him to develop an incredibly woolly and muddy-minded mysticism. And any Frenchman who goes mystic is a menace.

3. In all the years he has been the leader of a movement, not a single French political leader of real substance has joined him. Around him are adventurers and dilettantes, with a few exceptions.

4. He is anti-American and anti-British, and his German policy makes no sense.

5. If he *should* come to power by *coup d'état,* it might well mean civil war.

The basic sources of De Gaulle's very considerable power might be skeletonized as follows:

1. The distress, restlessness and apathy of France combine to make people want a strong man as deliverer. Folk who are unwilling to make sacrifices themselves ask for a *main fort* to impose them on others. Fascism almost always starts this way.

2. The division of the French left, which is split between Communists and Socialists, plays directly into his hands.

[2] New York *Herald Tribune,* Paris, October 2, 1948.

3. De Gaulle's own capacities, including his superb war record and the fact that, after all, it is he who is mainly responsible for the salvation of the republic.

4. The center-of-the-road government at present ruling France is polarized between the two extremes. Both sides eat its strength away. Hence De Gaulle is seen by many as the only *eventual* alternative to Communism.

Fundamentally the fate of France depends, I think, on a subtle and intermixed combination of economic and moral issues. The root problem at present is the sharp disparity between wages and prices. But no government, as of the moment, can easily put through any drastic measures of amelioration or reform, because it is extremely difficult to impose controls on a nation of forty million anarchic individualists. Controls do work in England. But England has a standard of public and political morality which France has not.

Consider the single but weightily important matter of taxes. It is practically a point of honor for the average Frenchman, like the average Italian, not to pay taxes at all—much less a fair tax—if he can possibly get away with it, and he usually can. You can bribe your way into—or out of—practically anything.

All this being said, France is by no means finished yet. Stalin himself said recently that he thought it would take France thirty years to get back on its feet, but that as things were going now it would take only three or four. Nor should anybody ever forget or minimize what France went through—five grim years of German occupation, and then two in which the chief denominator of power was the black market. At any rate—thanks largely to the Marshall plan—1948 was a spectacularly better year than 1947, and 1949 promises to be better still.

French and Germans

Now a word on French attitudes toward Germany. It will come as a severe shock to most Americans to know that the number of French planes participating in the air lift to Berlin is exactly two.

There are, of course, several reasons for this. One is that the French cannot get very exercised about whether or not Germans starve to death. The more dead Germans, the better it is for France. Another is that the French oppose anything that emphasizes the role of Berlin, the city, in German life. They see Berlin as a symbol of the possible resurgence and unification of Germany, and therefore dislike it heartily. Also they still resent having been excluded from the conference at Potsdam.

What France wants is a Germany permanently weak and, if possible, divided.[3] Hence the continual stubborn obstruction by France to practically every step the Americans and British take to put Germany on its feet, though they would be terrified if we left Germany altogether. General Clay and General Koenig, the French Military Governor, are scarcely on speaking terms. The French provoke and irritate us and hold off agreement on an issue as long as possible, and then do agree only because they fear that if they don't they might lose Marshall aid, which for 1949 will run to the tidy sum of $890 million.

"The French are the weak sisters of Europe, because they want war least." This is a neat way to put it. Nevertheless, they are of colossal importance to United States policy. Also France is the key of all keys to Europe so far as international Communist conspiracy is concerned. Suppose a Communist *coup* should come in France; then France would be neutralized if war broke out, and the Americans (as the Communists love to point out) would have no convenient beachhead for an expeditionary force. Hence, it is Communist policy to keep France vulnerable and unsettled, at all cost (cost to others, that is). The Communist line to the French is, in effect, "Play ball with us, and we won't overrun France when Germany is communized."

But it might not work out that way. I heard American officers say bitterly, "The French try to talk us into their policy of keeping Germany permanently weak. But if war comes, they'll

[3] The French are so eager to emphasize division within Germany that, just as after World War I, they maintain a French minister to Bavaria. Why? Because there is much less reason to fear Prussia, if Bavaria is Separatist and strong.

want us, the Americans, to make it strong, or it will have to be us, the Americans, who will have the job of defending them against *both* the Germans and the Russians."

Unknown Soldier?

Everywhere we went in Western Europe we found as great hatred of war as in Eastern, but much less fear. Perhaps the lack of fear is a result of what might be called ostrichism. The French, the Belgians, the British, the Dutch, may think that war is almost inconceivable chiefly because they hate it so. No one on our side of the water should ever forget the fervent horror and detestation with which almost all Western Europeans still think about war. Nor should we ever forget what the last war cost them.

I remember the shock I felt in Amsterdam when I saw signs in the shop windows notifying the stout Dutch citizenry that they could buy their own precious cigars and chocolate only with foreign currency. This was reminiscent of Prague; it is a minor note of course. But it is illustrative of the appalling toll —in the smallest things—that the last war is still causing people in everyday life. Incidentally, has any Western European country erected a statue to the "Unknown Soldier" of World War II? Maybe they exist, but I never saw or heard of one.

To resume the point and conclude: The unimaginably frightful suffering caused by World War II, which still goes on, makes most Europeans loath even to think about—much less prepare for—the eventuality of World War III. One very prominent Englishman we met went so far as to say that, in his opinion, the entire mass of British labor would strike rather than fight or support a war, unless it came by direct, flagrant, and overt aggression against the British Isles themselves.

A Look at London

First, as to the British themselves, let no one think that they are down and out. It is not merely that most of the relevant statistics prove a degree of economic recovery that most experts would not have dreamed possible a year or two ago. What is more important is the atmosphere of confidence. The British have a doggedness, a cheerfulness, a self-reliance and, above all, an instinct for essential unity and survival that put the people of almost every other nation to shame. The hardships they bear are almost beyond belief. (And they grumble plenty, too.) But they are very far indeed from being down and out. Indeed, in a curious way, the disciplines they have been forced to undergo seem to give them augmented spirit and strength.

Most American opinion about England is strongly influenced by British Tories, by Mr. Churchill in particular. Mr. Churchill hates the Labor government, and what he says about it carries sting. Indeed the Labor government has made terrible and costly mistakes, as for instance over Palestine. And indeed the Labor government may be roundly trounced and turned out of office in 1950. But it would be the depth of folly to discount its present grip on the people or its record of concrete achievement. Simply keep in mind the highly pertinent fact that it has not lost a single by-election since reaching power in 1945, a record unprecedented in British history.

Second, though they are geographically much closer to Russia than the United States is, the British are much less frightened. They were brutally and mercilessly bombed for five long years, which the United States was not, and—even in these days—the English Channel is narrower than the Atlantic Ocean. But the seasoned British show little fear.

There is infinitely less war talk in London than in New York. The London newspapers show little of the overt and degrading hysteria of much of the American press, and Englishmen arriving in New York are all but stupefied at what appears to be the violence of American timidity. An interesting recent point is that the British army is to *reduce,* not augment, its strength by one-third in 1949.

Third, the British are inclined to think that the power of the Communists to penetrate further into Western Europe has been definitely checked, and that the danger of further Communist victories is sharply receding. They point to the severe recent electoral setbacks suffered by Communism in Italy, Germany, and France as the obvious chief evidences of this. The forces of democracy, buttressed by the Marshall plan, have a much more tenacious vitality than most people would have thought possible a year ago.

Fourth, they are fully cognizant of the implications of what they call "the world swing to the left." They are fully cognizant, too, of the peculiar situation implicit in the fact that the United States, the chief anti-Socialist power in the world today, and Britain, the chief Socialist power, are and of necessity have to remain close allies. One of their rationalizations of this paradox is that Americans—when they get to Europe—don't seem to object so much to planned economy. Indeed, the whole apparatus of the ERP structure, its interlockings and calculated priorities in a sixteen-nation pattern, its immense complex effort to stimulate and stabilize economy by a precise control and apportionment of all investment, seems to the canny British one of the most majestic examples of planned economy (and politics) ever known, though the ultimate aim and end in view is the preservation of private enterprise.

Of course the British see this general process—the rehabilitation of the crust that surrounds Europe—as the chief hope for Europe. The best of all auguries for the future, the Laborites think, is the growth and healthy development of governments like their own, or of moderate coalitions including a strong Socialist bloc, as in Belgium, France, Italy, Scandinavia, and the Netherlands.

Fifth, most British feel that the best—perhaps in the long run the only—way to beat Communism is by reform. One cabinet minister said to me frankly, "We will be dished in the long run, and so will you, unless we reform and reform and reform." This attitude finds remarkable expression in British domestic politics, in that almost all Tories I met conceded frankly that they would be at a hopeless disadvantage in the next election if they opposed flatly the whole of the Labor government's nationalization program.

The British people don't want war, and they don't want Communism. What they want is continuing reform as the best security against both, and they will demand a government that gives it to them.

Perhaps I might revert briefly to the question of Anglo-American attitudes and relations. I heard one eminent lady (and she is certainly not a Laborite) say at a fashionable luncheon party, "Frankly we do not know which to fear most, Russian Communism or American capitalism. We don't want invasion from either side!"

The term "Third Force" has two meanings in Europe today. It is the phrase used to describe the present French government, and also it is sometimes used as a term for Great Britain in that the British stand between the two giants, Russia and the United States. The British are of course much closer to us emotionally and politically than to the Russians. Yet a substantial body of British opinion considers that, if the peace is to be held, Great Britain should more and more play the role of mediator between Washington and Moscow. Nor should it be forgotten —even in these days of the North Atlantic Pact—that Britain still maintains a twenty-year treaty of friendship and alliance with the Soviet Union.

A wise Englishman once told me, "The Briton never buys an umbrella till he's wet through. Then he carries it even on a sunny day." (And during the war I once heard a distinguished British editor remark, "We'd like to win the war before the United States saves us and Russia betrays us.")

In a sense it is the United States taxpayer who is the main factor not only in supporting British economy and democracy today but also British Socialism. If it were not for the ERP funds provided for in the last analysis by the American free enterprise system, the British Laborites would probably not be able to proceed with their projected nationalization of steel among other projects. American capitalism is, to repeat, helping not only to socialize much of Europe in general, but Great Britain in particular. Few Americans realize the extent of socialization that has already taken place in England. Two items out of a thousand: (a) The British have, exactly like the satellites we have talked of so much in this book, a "Plan"; it runs to 1952, by which time it is hoped that recovery and rehabilitation will be complete; (b) Only forty-five Englishmen out of the total population have incomes today of more than $24,000 a year after taxes.

American visitors, horrified at the shortages the British take in their stride, ask sometimes about rationing and the queues. But these are simply the price the sensible British pay for having a living standard as good as it is.

Certainly if ERP should stop the British economy would suffer a terrible setback. The United Kingdom is supposed to get $940 million this year. I heard it said by American experts in this connection that the cessation of American aid would mean a choice for the British between mass emigration and starvation, since it would cause an increase of unemployment to two or even three million; I heard it said by British experts that it would probably necessitate the installation in Great Britain of a complete totalitarian economy, which might in turn produce political dictatorship.

To be so dependent on the United States makes the British somewhat sensitive, and several Englishmen we met sought to point out that the Marshall plan is by no means an expression of pure altruism on our part, but that it is almost as necessary to the United States as it is to Europe. The argument is based on the theory that the U.S.A. must perforce have a mechanism for draining off its surplus national income.

Be this as it may, the British also assert with a good deal of emphasis that in any case they give us a substantial *quid pro quo*. One item is the protection provided to American oil in the Middle East by British arms. Another is that the British army would have to bear the first brunt of operations in Germany, if war should come. Another is diplomatic support in the UN. Then too the British are in a position to exercise a good deal of veto power on American foreign policy, and who can say that in the long run this may not turn out to be a good thing.

To conclude, England is probably the healthiest state in Europe. The British work under terrific disciplines and submit to terrific sacrifices, but they remain sane, stable, efficient and united. One feels about most other countries that they are still deep in crisis. In England one feels that it is on the way out, though no one knows exactly what "out" will finally prove to be. One point to be made firmly is something that Americans, from their fortunate vantage point, may not like to hear, namely that old style capitalism is as dead here, as well as in most of the rest of Europe, as the Duke of Burgundy or Nebuchadnezzar's aunt.

CHAPTER 20

CONCLUSION—IRON CURTAIN AND RUSSIAN POLICY

SO NOW to conclude. In Chapter 3 I listed a few preliminary generalizations about the Iron Curtain. Here similarly are a few conclusions tentative in the extreme.

1. A major consideration in the development of the whole area is of course military. It has to be. To what extent the satellites themselves have embarked on ambitious rearmament programs is uncertain. The State Department and the British Foreign Office joined recently to denounce Bulgaria, Rumania, and Hungary at least (which in theory are disarmed states) for flagrant violations of armament provisions in peace treaties.

But what really counts is the attitude of Russia. The Soviets need this whole area as a buffer, a so-called "security belt," a glacis. Communists will argue, of course, that they have no offensive designs whatever, and that considerations of defense determine their whole policy. But for adequate defense they need room, they need a cushion. The Russians are convinced that the Atlantic Pact presages war; they even go so far as to say that it is an act of war, and they have every intention of fighting to the death to defend their system.

A corollary oblique point is their assertion that previous cushions with which they sandbagged themselves turned out in the end to be of substantial value to the West itself in the struggle against Hitler. Russians say that if they had not fought a war with Finland beforehand, Leningrad would have probably fallen; if they had not occupied half of Poland, Moscow and Stalingrad might have been taken by the Nazis. In this case World War II might still be going on, because obviously if Russia had collapsed the Western allies would have had a much harder struggle.

2. It is quite possible that the present satellite regimes, under their contemporary leadership, may not last long. Rákosi five years from now may be as forgotten as Bela Kun.

3. But, and the point is of great urgency, this does not mean that feudalism is going to return. Even if Moscow should be destroyed in a third world war, there will still be Communists in Eastern and Central Europe. Even if Stalin should be murdered, even if the whole Soviet regime should crash, something of what these border regimes represent will remain. Kill off the entire ruling class of Russia and the satellites; there will still be socialism, land reform, and a trained and vocal proletariat in these regions. The permanent transforming force of the contemporary revolution can no more be ignored than that of the industrial revolution a century ago. Nobody in this part of the world is ever going to see 1939 again, if only because no substantial field for old-style capitalist investment survives.

4. Most of the leadership in Eastern Europe is, however, as we have seen, contributed not by workers or peasants but by intellectuals. (In their extreme youth, true, leaders may have been cobblers or stone masons and in almost all cases they came of proletarian families; but their adult lives were spent as intellectuals.) In a curious way this provides a basic strength, not a weakness, to these regimes. Intellectuals became converts to Communism, not merely because of the grudge borne against society by the underprivileged, but out of coldly rational persuasion and conviction. Now they lend themselves to the cultivation of what might be called a "depersonalized" mode of life, but they remain passionate individualists themselves, which greatly increases their effectiveness as leaders.

5. The root question, after the possibility of war, is poverty. The point might well be made that poverty is bound to be a hallmark in this area for a long time to come, not only because it is extremely costly to industrialize an agrarian country, but because the governments concerned cannot, as it were, afford to be well off. Once they are prosperous, they are likely to lose their revolutionary élan.

6. People often ask, "What have these regimes *got*?" Surely in this book we have given plenty of answers—in both directions. The simplest over-all response would be that they promise the people a direct advantageous stake in the future of the nation, political as well as economic. The sacrifices and hardships involved are posited against such immediate

ameliorative factors as the end of the old discriminatory feudalism, and the hope is held out that the practical ultimate benefits of the future society will be shared by all. Whether or not history will ever actually work out this way is, of course, dubious in the extreme.[1] Meantime, discontent (even within the party itself) has to be ruthlessly stamped out, civil liberties asphyxiated, and a regime of authority imposed, all for the sake of the future utopian ideal. Here an important point is often missed by Westerners. Civil liberties are not much of a preoccupation among people who have never had them. The word "freedom" doesn't mean to Eastern Europe what it means to us; it may mean freedom from being a serf. Ask the average Eastern European about freedom of the press, say, and he will hardly know what you are talking about, or care. What he is interested in is freedom to eat and get education and a job.

7. The rank and file of young people become Communists because there is no other choice. No middle ground exists. You become a Communist, or else are excluded from society. This is of vital importance for the next few years. "Give me a generation to train the children," said Lenin, "and the seed I have sown will never be uprooted." And the not-so-blind fervor of youth—a youth barred moreover from all contacts with the West—is a factor never to be minimized. A quotation from Dostoevski, to the point that the Russians "are a God-bearing people," is in a way relevant. It is not God that the surging young Communists bear, but they do bear what they consider to be His equivalent in dialectical materialism.

8. All this brings up once more the exceptionally difficult question of "democracy." It would be unwise to laugh too superciliously at the satellite definition of this term, or ignore too contemptuously the way leaders talk of it, no matter how warmly one may disagree. The basic thing to keep in mind is what I have alluded to before, that whereas we measure democracy in political terms, the Russians measure it in terms of economics. Whereas we in the West "judge everything by the test of political democracy and especially the vote," Sir

[1] Dorothy Thompson once pointed out that "the chief sin of Communism is its exploitation of idealism."

Bernard Pares wrote recently in the *Nation*, "in the East the central test has always been economic security." But also the Soviets do put up a "case" for political democracy too. Let me quote another eminent English authority, Professor E. H. Carr,[2] who has pointed out that orthodox Communists think of the working classes and peasants as the majority of the nation, and that therefore "proletarian democracy," expressing the "will" of the great masses of the people—if it really is their will—is far more truly "representative" than Western democracy. The government (in theory) is for all, and the individual citizen must, if necessary, sacrifice himself (or be sacrificed) for the larger entity.

To quote Carr: "Marx believed, and Soviet practice has been inspired by this belief, that the only effective instrument for the overthrow of the bourgeois regime and the achievement of proletarian democracy would be the dictatorship of the proletariat. There is therefore no essential incompatibility between democracy and dictatorship." Put in another way, "Hegel . . . preached that freedom consisted in the recognition and voluntary acceptance of necessity." And Stalin has said: "Democracy in capitalist countries . . . is in the last analysis democracy for the strong, democracy for the propertied classes. In the USSR, on the contrary, democracy is democracy for the working people, i.e., democracy for all"—since everybody, in a socialist state, is and has to be a worker in some form or other.[3]

Of course some of this is preposterous and hypocritical double talk. But, even if the Communist leaders themselves do not believe in what they say, they are deliberately educating their own people into absolute acceptance of these definitions, and it would be imprudent of us to neglect their force. If we are going to be forced into war, at least it should be useful to know what kind of ideas we are going to war against.

[2] In *The Soviet Impact on the Western World*, London, 1947. This is the most illuminating small book I have ever read on these themes; the paragraph above follows Carr closely. Mr. Carr was an important official in the British Foreign Office during the war and an editor of the *Times*; he is now professor of international politics in the University of Wales.

[3] Parenthetically it is interesting (Carr, p. 2) that the Atlantic Charter never uses the word "democracy," though Stalin did in several speeches delivered at about the same time.

9. The yawning cultural chasm between East and West is probably so deep nowadays as to be unbridgeable. How is it possible to argue with Mr. Vishinsky on a matter of law or human rights when he says publicly in Paris, "Law is merely an instrument of policy"? Or consider such remarks as those of the Soviet writer Alexander Fadeyev at Wroclaw, when he declared that writers like Aldous Huxley and Eugene O'Neill (not to mention such obvious "enemies" as Sartre, Eliot, and Malraux) were "hyenas" and "jackals." This is not merely bad manners; it is willful ignorance. It is, in fact, discomforting to think what superb propaganda the Communists *could* make, considering their talents and the theoretical case they present, if they held to the truth. By crude distortion they lose half their effect. Remember, though, that much Soviet propaganda has a double function; it is for home consumption too. When Fadeyev calls Aldous Huxley a hyena he is simply transmuting class warfare into literary fields. It is to the manifest advantage of the Soviet Union and the satellites that people *should* think that Mr. Huxley and Mr. O'Neill *are* hyenas. Another point: the temptation is merely to laugh at such recent examples of Russian cultural chauvinism as the announcement that penicillin is a Soviet discovery and that Russian astronomers first found out that the planet Venus has an atmosphere. But this kind of nationalist boasting is highly important propaganda-wise, in that it entrenches in the satellite masses the conviction of Soviet superiority in every variety of field.

10. The dilemma for American policy is perplexing. While we were in Warsaw we heard a BBC broadcast about Burma, ten thousand miles away across the world, which said that "the Burmese government will not be able to stem the rising surge of Communism in Burma effectively without outside help." Of course not! In hardly any underprivileged country of the world can Communism be stopped in the long run, without outside help—which means our help. But there are sheer physical limitations to the amount of help the United States can give. We cannot, all at once, save the whole globe. This is easily proved by the fact that, whereas we are openly opposing Communism in Europe, we have completely failed to do so effec-

tively in China. American policy, it seems, is based on the necessity to deal with one continent at a time.

But as to the satellites: the first obvious thing to say is that the United States should try to separate them from Russia, and encourage their growth and development as free independent republics. But this will not be easy. Consider how difficult it has been even to take advantage of the rupture between one satellite, Yugoslavia, and its erstwhile fellows. Larger considerations of American foreign policy are not, after all, the province of this book. But one should at least point out in passing the stupendous difficulties of these new perspectives, in the giant political vacuum to which the United States has succeeded. Help Burma? Detach Poland from the Soviet orbit? But how, exactly how, and what are the risks involved, and to what eventual end? It is no simple thing to talk about American foreign policy in these days when Kansas equals Singapore, and vice versa.

Certainly the United States has a duty to understand the governments of these hundred million eastern Europeans. If war is inevitable, prepare for it. If not, try to get along. Actually these two alternatives merge; preparedness may be the best means of averting war, and if war does come, we shall at least have the advantage of having tried to get along. Meantime the best countermeasures against Communism are not provocative adventures in retaliation or even such structures as the Atlantic Pact, useful as that may turn out to be, but internal health, strength, and harmony. Any satellite ought to be able to look us in the eye and find us decent, moderate, and strong.

11. We have come a long way now since Tito and Yugoslavia, and I do not want to repeat what I have already treated with such length, but the ideological split represented by the Tito-Cominform break, between national and international conceptions of Communist society, may in the long run turn out to be the decisive factor in the future of all these countries.

12. I mentioned ideals and idealism above. The cruel fact is that exploitation in the name of idealism is exploitation just the same. What point is there to being liberated from feudal serfdom, if industrial serfdom under the Soviets is just as bad?

The chief trouble with the Soviet system and the satellites is the simple one that it hasn't worked. This too is the chief reason for satellite fear and hatred of the United States, and why the Iron Curtain itself exists. The Russians have to wall us out, because—to date anyway—we have a better way of life.

Postscript on Russian Attitudes

The Russians do not want war, which would imperil all they got out of the last one, for the most cogent of reasons; all they want, as Clemenceau once said of the Germans, is the rewards of victory. Peace, or what goes for peace nowadays, serves the Soviet objective much better than war, and the Russians, for their own quite selfish reasons, will go to almost any length to avoid an actual outbreak of hostilities. Of course they do not admit the true reason for this, which is that a war with the United States (even though it might wreck the United States too) would destroy them.

John Foster Dulles, certainly no Soviet sympathizer or fellow traveler, said in March 1949, "So far as it is humanly possible to judge, the Soviet government . . . does not contemplate the use of war as an instrument of its national policy. I do not know any responsible high official, military or civilian, in this government or any other government, who believes that the Soviet state now plans conquest by open military aggression."[4]

What are some causes for this? First and above all, fear of losing. Stalin knows full well that the decisive factor in World War III (as in World Wars I and II) would be the American industrial potential, which is something that the Russians cannot touch. Second, the conviction that American capitalist society will in time fall by its own weight, so that attack on the United States is unnecessary. This concept—that the American system is doomed anyway—is paramount in contemporary Soviet thinking. Any Russian economist who breaks away from the party line and dares to doubt it, like Eugene Varga, is pitched to the wolves at once. This explains, too, the general

[4] Speech at Cleveland to the Federal Council of the Churches of Christ in America.

temper of Soviet propaganda about America, that the United States is weak, imperialistic, and corrupt. To Soviet wishful thinkers, we must be called weak to "prove" the point that we will eventually collapse as a result of a profound and shattering depression; imperialistic, because in the Marxist mythology a decaying capitalist power always tries to save itself by external adventures; corrupt, because to the Marxist mind our downfall will be accelerated by decay. The conception that a prodigious economic crisis is inevitable in America, with resultant prostration, is a subsidiary reason—very curious and suggestive—why the Russians hate the Marshall plan so hotly. This, they say, is a mechanism whereby the "inevitable" American deflation and collapse is being artificially fended off; even at the moment (the Soviets assert) we are only able to avoid catastrophic unemployment at home by large forced exports of goods abroad.

Of course the point may be made that, even if the Russians do not want war, the policies they undertake may in the end produce one. Man, Count Keyserling once said, is the most dangerous animal that ever lived.

Certainly American foreign policy is predicated now on the theory that open warfare is unlikely. We would not have inaugurated the revolutionary adventure of the Atlantic Pact unless we were fairly sure the Soviets were in no serious position to retaliate, except by propaganda.

Conundrum in Etiquette

Why, if the Russians do not intend to make war, do they behave so badly? Why, if they could not fight a winning war now, do they persist in irritating the rest of the world to frenzy by their touchiness, aggressive and peremptory tactics, obstructiveness, mendacity, and plain bad manners? There are at least four main reasons:

1. They don't know any better.

2. They're scared. They bluff and bluster out of weakness, not out of strength. This accounts for much of their touchiness too. A point never to be neglected is that the prime and overwhelming Russian motive is, from first to last, to *defend their*

revolution. They consider themselves encircled by "capitalist" enemies, subject to attack at almost any moment; their phobias are almost maniacal; absolutely nothing counts except *defense*. Do not forget what the Germans did to them.

Much incidental Russian bad behavior derives from another factor in this connection, their pathological addiction to secrecy. For instance the reason they have never accepted a compromise on atomic energy is that they cannot bear to be "inspected." Not only pride enters into this, but the driving fear that international inspection will tell the world how weak they really are.

A British cabinet minister told me in London that he soberly considered the Molotov diplomacy to be the most brilliantly successful Europe has known for years. His reasoning was that the Russians, having at all costs to disguise their essential weakness, and thus avoid the attack that they thought might come at any moment from the encircling West if the West knew how weak they actually were, had with consummate skill pulled the wool over the entire world's eyes, by frightening us—irony! —with a campaign of threat, bombast, and harmless bluster.[5]

3. Here we merge into another profound element behind Soviet behavior. The Russians bluff, because they are pretty sure that we, the United States and the Atlantic powers, will not call the bluff.

Perhaps this may seem contradictory to the preceding point. It is true that they are frightened. So would we be frightened, if they had the Bomb and we did not. Nevertheless, contemptuous of what they call democratic slipshodness, lack of consecutive policy, sentimentality, and so on, they count on it that we will probably not commit any deliberate act of aggression that would lead to a preventive war, and they are right, because even the bare idea of war is odious and repulsive to the overwhelming majority of good Americans. They know we have the Bomb; but they are almost certain that we will not use it unless we ourselves are attacked. Hence both their willingness to bluff and their avoidance of any serious military act.

4. Russian bad manners—based in part on an Oriental heritage totally different from ours—are not an accident, but a pre-

[5] Harmless? Not quite! For a contrary view see below, "Russians so Smart?"

meditated and deliberate exercise in policy. This policy is, in a word, to keep the world in ferment. Thus anything the Kremlin can do to provoke or promote irritation with the existing order anywhere is useful. The more friction and tension they can induce the better they like it and the more they profit. I heard this point of view summarized by an Englishman of great prominence who did not mind how he mixed metaphors: "The Russian aim is to cause chaos, so that everything will fall into their lap, like a rotten plum."

In any event Soviet bad manners are a cardinal consideration in the whole story. People—even Foreign Ministers—are human beings; they lose their tempers. The whole Berlin crisis might have been avoided except for the fact that both Americans and British were so violently annoyed at being presented with one more *fait accompli.*

To proceed to another item, and a strange paradox it is: The Russians up to a point—it is important to maintain the qualification "up to a point"—actually *welcome* the American and British rearmament programs. They do not say so publicly, but obviously it serves their purpose if the British, say, should have to spend so much on rearmament that they are forced to starve their social services. The Russians would be delighted—to put it mildly—if their tactics should force the United States to expend so much money on arms as to become bankrupt. The more resources we sterilize into unproductive use, the better it is for the Russian long-range objective—provided, of course, that we do not use our armament in actual warfare. The more we spend wastefully, at the expense of social gain, the better Moscow likes it. From this a further refinement of the point is possible—that the Russians maintain their diplomatic offensive partly in order *to* provoke us deliberately into huge expenditures on armament.

In England I found strong appreciation of this view. It is something that makes British Socialists really angry. A Labor M.P. put it to me this way, "The time will come shortly when we will refuse to endure any longer that our socialist gains should be eaten away by a crazily overextended and exaggerated arms program."

Other Side of the Vistula?

Several American officers we met in Germany, including some of considerable rank, feel so emphatically that the keynote to Soviet policy is Soviet weakness, not strength, that they are convinced that in the event of war, the Russians—far from advancing across Europe to the Atlantic—would promptly and with great prudence withdraw to the Vistula or even further east, leaving the satellites to their fate and entrenching in Russia proper. They will, so to speak, dare us, the United States and the West, to come in and take them—to try intercontinentally what Napoleon and Hitler tried, with results that we know all too well.

Pages might be written about specific Russian weaknesses. Take the single matter of key industrial power as measured in terms of steel. American steel production last year was 84,700,000 tons. Add to this British, French, Benelux, and Ruhr steel production, and you get close to 130,000,000 tons. Russian production last year was roughly 20,000,000 tons. A single American corporation, United States Steel, produced in 1947 twice as much steel as the *entire* USSR! Then too—I mention these matters as if they were postscripts, but their latent importance is tremendous—consider Russian shortages and paucities in petroleum, livestock, transportation, aircraft, machine tools, and all manner of essential subsidiary material. On the other hand the chief Russian strengths—geography, space, and manpower—are not to be ignored. If war should start tomorrow, the Russian armies actually in the field would outnumber us at least ten to one, perhaps twenty to one.

As I have several times said, the chief danger of war is probably Russian ignorance.[6] The Soviets may have a building in Moscow as big as the Pentagon, stuffed with every statistic about the United States ever known; but they know very little about American psychology. I do not think that a major war will ever again be caused by a minor incident. Nobody goes

[6] But also consider American ignorance of Russia. It is a paramount point that Americans and Russians simply do not *think* alike.

to war on account of "insults" nowadays. Yet even in the field of incidents, Russian ignorance plays a certain role, because the Soviet definition of the very word "incident" differs sharply from ours. For instance the Russians called battles against the Japanese in Siberia in which many thousands of men were killed, in the period before World War II, mere "incidents," mere political "episodes" extended into the realm of arms. But the United States once went to war because somebody blew up a battleship in Havana harbor.

Incidents aside, ignorance aside, the principal danger lies in the sphere of Russian internal politics. If there should be a new shakeup in Moscow and the fanatic extremists come out on top—or if the Soviet regime should seem to be in such disintegration that only an external adventure could save it—war might conceivably result, especially if the Russians thought that we in the United States were still too busy making money and having a good time to want to fight. No dictatorship ever dies a natural death.

Against this possibility, however, is the colossal primal fact that we have the Bomb—no matter how the Russians discount its usefulness—while they have not.

Years ago, in 1935 or 1936, I wrote an article about the British rearmament program getting under way at that time, against Hitler; I said that the keynote of all British policy could be summed up in one brief phrase, "Stall and rearm." It may seem odd to compare Britain then with Russia now, but "Stall and rearm" also expresses the Soviet point of view today, if by "rearm" is meant "Get the Bomb." We, the Americans, are to the Russians what the Nazis were to Britain, strange as this may seem. At all costs, the Russians will try to delay a showdown and forestall any general military crisis, until they themselves are better prepared, that is, until they too have made a Bomb.

If the foregoing is kept in mind, all manner of seemingly puzzling contradictions in Russian policy become clear and in fact logical. The Communists play with both hands always. They want "peace"; but their agitation, conspiracy, and propaganda penetrate the spongy frontiers of the entire globe. Early in 1949 the French and Italian Communists announced that they would be loyal to Moscow, rather than to Paris or Rome, in the event of war; at the same time the Kremlin launched a "peace" offensive (e.g., Stalin's invitation to Truman to visit him). In fact the Russian political offensive is essentially a maneuver to cover military weakness. The contour of Soviet policy, to repeat, is double—to be on the defensive militarily, and on the offensive in the realm of politics.

Last Talks with the Brethren

This was the gist of a conversation we had with a well-known Communist intellectual in Berlin:

JG: Do you think there will be a war?

COMMUNIST: Certainly not.

JG: Does this mean that you think that the two systems, Communist and capitalist, can get along together indefinitely and continue to live at peace in the same world?

COMMUNIST: Certainly.

JG: But what about your doctrine of permanent world revolution?

COMMUNIST: The two systems will survive together because both will gradually, inevitably, change.

JG: Which will change most?

COMMUNIST: Yours.

JG: Do you think Poland and the other border states will eventually be absorbed into the Soviet Union?

COMMUNIST: Of course! The whole world will be absorbed.

JG: Suppose we in the United States resist absorption?

COMMUNIST: The great depression you will have probably in the 1950's will produce a different attitude in America.

JG: How long will it take you to reach power in Germany?

COMMUNIST: Three to five years.

JG: But you have only about 20 percent of the German vote, at the extreme maximum. Do you expect that this will rise to 51 percent or more within five years, or will you take over by illegal means?

COMMUNIST: It will not be so simple as that, because long before we reach 51 percent you will try to produce another Hitler to hold us off.

JG: Do you think you will ever have civil liberties under Communism?

COMMUNIST: In about a hundred years.

JG: In other words not till you have conquered the entire world, and it is safe to relax?

COMMUNIST: Correct.

Most Communists are not quite so sure of themselves or so aggressive. Many, especially in Germany, think that the Soviet position is already too far extended; if the Russians could find a graceful method for geographical withdrawal they would take it (the better to make a unified Communist Germany later, of course). There are some Communists who go so far as to insist that the only reason the Russians are in Central Europe at all is that the accident of war brought them there. Politics is like nature, they say, and abhors a vacuum. Europe was full of soft spots, and the Russians were close by and simply filled them. It was like sticking a finger into a dead fish.

One other talk is worth remembering. I asked an important member of the party, "Just for the sake of argument, suppose war comes even if you don't want one, who would win?"

Reply: "We would, of course."

"How?"

"You will drop your atomic bomb and it will cause great distress and destruction and loss of life. But bombing, even atomic bombing, does not win wars. A war is only won in the long run by occupation with infantry. While your bombs are dropping, or even before, we will march across Western Europe and then you will have to bomb Paris and Milan as well as Moscow and Stalingrad, which will not be pleasant. Meantime we will take all Asia—China, India, Indonesia—while integrating our conquest of all Europe. You cannot possibly prevent this. You will then be confronted with the task of mounting invasions on two or perhaps even three immense continents around three-quarters of the world's surface at the same time.

Even Russia alone will not be easy to invade. Ask Hitler. It will take you a good many years we think—years which we know well how to use. Of course you will become bankrupt in the process. Also you will probably lose the democracy you will claim to be fighting for, inasmuch as you will have to become Fascist in order to win. And meantime, you will have destroyed irremediably the Europe that you set out to save. Moreover the more you destroy the better you play into our hands. What will we do? Pick up the ruins, and go forward with the world revolutionary struggle that you can never finally beat down without killing off everybody left in the entire world."

Some Breaches of Soviet Faith

Many times I have alluded to Communist sanctimoniousness about American policy and things Western; nothing is more irritating than the pose of outraged innocence the Soviets commonly adopt. Just for the record, here are a very few examples —out of hundreds available—of violations of pledges by the Russians or satellites, refusals to co-operate, and unilateral obstructionist tactics and behavior. Refusal to participate in the work of UNESCO and most other subsidiary bodies of the UN. Exaggerated use of the veto in the Security Council. Refusal to join the International Civil Aviation body. Withdrawal in 1948 from the Berlin *Kommandatura.* Demand for German reparations in defiance of the Potsdam Declaration. Repeated and flagrant violations of the Yalta pledges that "representative" governments would be set up in the satellites. One could go on almost indefinitely. In fact the State Department issued a document in June 1948 that lists sixty-one different and specific violations by the Russians of the Potsdam agreements alone. These vary from refusal by the USSR to submit any report on "war booty" removals from Germany to indiscriminate use of police power in various of the puppet states.

But never forget, on the other hand, (a) the Russians *do* accept seriously the fact that this is a two-power world, and that the whole of the world not theirs is a mortal enemy, and

(b) much of their bad behavior followed what they interpreted to be even worse behavior by us.

All this is, however, no more than red icing on the cake. The real violation is in spirit, not in detail. After the war when the United Nations organization was born in San Francisco the world might well have achieved a real, decent, and lasting peace. Nobody is altogether blameless for the bitter disillusion that followed, the yawning crash of those high hopes and golden dreams, but the Soviet Union has by far the larger share of responsibility. From the first to the last, it played the role of wrecker, unless, like a child, it got exactly what it asked.

Russians so Smart?

We have talked much in this book of Soviet cleverness, Soviet adroitness in manipulation and sharp political acumen. And indeed it would be a dangerous mistake to underestimate this. But in a good many spheres and circumstances the Russians have not been so smart after all. In fact amazingly gross concrete examples are available of an almost preposterous Soviet ineptitude.[7]

As to wit: (a) Communist ministers were maneuvered into withdrawing from the Italian, French, and Austrian cabinets, thus depriving them of a preciously fertile field of governmental action. (b) Kremlin autocracy, ignorance, and bad manners forced Tito out of the flock. (c) The blockade of Berlin produced the air lift. What brilliant "successes" these were for Soviet foreign policy! Then consider that the Russians, by their own fumbling clumsiness, produced at least four tremendous developments directly contrary to their own major aims and interests. At all costs, they did not want to further American intervention in Europe. They are getting it. At all costs they did not want the creation of Western union, which brings Great Britain much closer to the continent than it has ever been before. They got it. At all costs they did not want the Marshall plan and the artificial insemination given by ERP to

[7] For part of this analysis I am indebted to my friend M. W. Fodor.

the Western European societies. They got it. And at all costs they did not want the North Atlantic Pact, which they got too.

No wonder there came a shakeup in the Politburo!

The Last War and Now

Nevertheless it would be silly for Americans to gloat at Russian discomfiture. This is no occasion for moral or political complacency. For the first time in history, we live in a two-power world, and the fact that both powers *are* world powers, in the literal sense, means that contact between Russia and the United States, whether for good or ill, is bound to continue on a global basis, indefinitely everywhere. Not only is it a two-power world geographically, but ideologically. The crisis—only too obviously—is not merely that of friction in space, but in ideas, which is indeed what makes it by far the most serious that has ever confronted our civilization.

Americans have, it would seem, two prime duties: to try to understand fully and without blinkers every facet of what Russia means and is, and to maintain our own house in good order. The way to deal with internal threats of Communism is to improve ourselves; the way to stop Russia without war is to make America itself better. Why do most Americans hate the Russians so? Because the Russian philosophy cuts directly across ours in relation to three of the most precious shibboleths of the Western world, God, class, and money. Very well. Let us direct our society to take better advantages of the virtues of all three.

If Russia and the United States fight, it will be the greatest *reductio ad absurdum* in history. We talk about competing "power" and "spheres of influence." These terms are almost meaningless unless defined; power, *per se*, is not evil: what can be evil is the wrong use of power. Why was Germany able to rise after 1919 and make war again? There were two main reasons: (1) the United States walked out of the peace; (2) the British and French quarreled over the spoils. Today Russia has virtually walked out of the peace, and it is the Anglo-Americans and Russians who are quarreling. Let us recall that it was always German policy—to the last lurid gasp—to divide the erstwhile allies, and so ruin both. The Nazis failed in this during the war itself. But now when the whole future of mankind is at stake the same phenomenon is manifest. If Russia and the United States fight, it will mean that Hitler, even in death, will have won the war.

Index